Emerging Research on Monetary Policy, Banking, and Financial Markets

Cristi Spulbar
University of Craiova, Romania

Ramona Birau
Constantin Brâncuși University of Targu Jiu, Romania

A volume in the Advances in Finance, Accounting, and Economics (AFAE) Book Series

IGI Global
DISSEMINATOR OF KNOWLEDGE

Published in the United States of America by
IGI Global
Business Science Reference (an imprint of IGI Global)
701 E. Chocolate Avenue
Hershey PA, USA 17033
Tel: 717-533-8845
Fax: 717-533-8661
E-mail: cust@igi-global.com
Web site: http://www.igi-global.com

Library of Congress Cataloging-in-Publication Data

Names: Spulbar, Cristi, 1971- author. | Birau, Ramona, 1986- author.
Title: Emerging research on monetary policy, banking, and financial markets / by Cristi Spulbar and Ramona Birau.
Description: Hershey, PA : Business Science Reference, 2020. | Includes bibliographical references and index.
Identifiers: LCCN 2018060325| ISBN 9781522592693 (hardcover) | ISBN 9781522592716 (ebook) | ISBN 9781522592709 (softcover)
Subjects: LCSH: Monetary policy. | Banks and banking. | Finance.
Classification: LCC HG230.3 .S68 2020 | DDC 332--dc23 LC record available at https://lccn.loc.gov/2018060325

This book is published in the IGI Global book series Advances in Finance, Accounting, and Economics (AFAE) (ISSN: 2327-5677; eISSN: 2327-5685)

British Cataloguing in Publication Data
A Cataloguing in Publication record for this book is available from the British Library.

Advances in Finance, Accounting, and Economics (AFAE) Book Series

ISSN:2327-5677
EISSN:2327-5685

Editor-in-Chief: Ahmed Driouchi, Al Akhawayn University, Morocco

MISSION

In our changing economic and business environment, it is important to consider the financial changes occurring internationally as well as within individual organizations and business environments. Understanding these changes as well as the factors that influence them is crucial in preparing for our financial future and ensuring economic sustainability and growth.

The **Advances in Finance, Accounting, and Economics (AFAE)** book series aims to publish comprehensive and informative titles in all areas of economics and economic theory, finance, and accounting to assist in advancing the available knowledge and providing for further research development in these dynamic fields.

COVERAGE

- Microfinance
- Economics of Risks, Uncertainty, Ambiguity, and Insurance
- Applied Accounting
- Risk Analysis and Management
- Accounting Standards
- Public Finance
- E-finance
- E-Accounting
- Borrowing and Lending
- Economics of Natural and Environmental Resources

IGI Global is currently accepting manuscripts for publication within this series. To submit a proposal for a volume in this series, please contact our Acquisition Editors at Acquisitions@igi-global.com or visit: http://www.igi-global.com/publish/.

The Advances in Finance, Accounting, and Economics (AFAE) Book Series (ISSN 2327-5677) is published by IGI Global, 701 E. Chocolate Avenue, Hershey, PA 17033-1240, USA, www.igi-global.com. This series is composed of titles available for purchase individually; each title is edited to be contextually exclusive from any other title within the series. For pricing and ordering information please visit http://www.igi-global.com/book-series/advances-finance-accounting-economics/73685. Postmaster: Send all address changes to above address.

Titles in this Series

For a list of additional titles in this series, please visit:
https://www.igi-global.com/book-series/advances-finance-accounting-economics/73685

Behavioral Finance and Decision-Making Models
Tripti Tripathi (Jiwaji University, India) Manoj Kumar Dash (Khallikote University, India) and Gaurav Agrawal (Indian Institute of Information Technology and Management Gwalior, India)
Business Science Reference • ©2019 • 333pp • H/C (ISBN: 9781522573999) • US $215.00

Global Challenges in Public Finance and International Relations
Deniz Şahin Duran (Tokat Gaziosmanpaşa University, Turkey) Yusuf Temür (Tokat Gaziosmanpaşa University, Turkey) and Doğan Bozdoğan (Tokat Gaziosmanpaşa University, Turkey)
Business Science Reference • ©2019 • 304pp • H/C (ISBN: 9781522575641) • US $225.00

International Financial Reporting Standards and New Directions in Earnings Management
Jonas da Silva Oliveira (Instituto Universitário de Lisboa (ISCTE-IUL), Portugal) Graça Maria do Carmo Azevedo (University of Aveiro, Portugal) and Augusta da Conceição Santos Ferreira (University of Aveiro, Portugal)
Business Science Reference • ©2019 • 342pp • H/C (ISBN: 9781522578178) • US $225.00

Throughput Accounting in a Hyperconnected World
Ionica Oncioiu (European Academy of the Regions, Belgium)
Business Science Reference • ©2019 • 362pp • H/C (ISBN: 9781522577126) • US $195.00

Organizational Auditing and Assurance in the Digital Age
Rui Pedro Marques (University of Aveiro, Portugal) Carlos Santos (University of Aveiro, Portugal) and Helena Inácio (University of Aveiro, Portugal)
Business Science Reference • ©2019 • 404pp • H/C (ISBN: 9781522573562) • US $225.00

International Firms' Economic Nationalism and Trade Policies in the Globalization Era
Harish C. Chandan (Argosy University, USA) and Bryan Christiansen (Global Research Society, LLC, USA)
Business Science Reference • ©2019 • 299pp • H/C (ISBN: 9781522575610) • US $215.00

For an entire list of titles in this series, please visit:
https://www.igi-global.com/book-series/advances-finance-accounting-economics/73685

IGI Global
DISSEMINATOR OF KNOWLEDGE

701 East Chocolate Avenue, Hershey, PA 17033, USA
Tel: 717-533-8845 x100 • Fax: 717-533-8661
E-Mail: cust@igi-global.com • www.igi-global.com

TESTIMONIAL #1

The book *Emerging Research on Monetary Policy, Banking, and Financial Markets* is a well-researched one. It touches on every aspect of the subject ranging from theoretical references to practical applications with appropriate scientific approach and methodology. The inclusion of the mathematical models and tabular presentations to illustrate the concepts and findings makes the book stands-out among its contemporaries. I therefore recommend it to not only the academics and professionals alike but also to the undergraduate and postgraduate students of economics, finance, management science, political science, public administration, development and strategic studies, as well as allied disciplines, as well as the general readers who wish to upgrade their knowledge in this and similar feeds of life endeavors. I sincerely congratulate the authors for being able to conduct the research to put together this type of book with both theoretical and practical relevance particularly in the contemporary Social and Management Sciences.

Muhammad Omolaja
President/Chancellor, British American University, Florida, USA

Prof. (Sir) Dr. Muhammad Omolaja is the President/Chancellor of the British American University, Florida, USA. Moreover, he is Visiting Professor of Management Science /Corporate Governance at the Saint Thomas University (Universidad Santo Tomas), Nicaragua, Central America, and also Visiting Professor of Public Administration and International Development at the Sastra Angkor University, Cambodia,

South-East Asia. He was a Lecturer in Business Administration of Ogun State Polytechnic (Now Moshood Abiola University of Technology), and he is also a former Lecturer in Business Administration at the Ogun State University, Ago-Iwoye, Nigeria.

TESTIMONIAL #2

Financial intermediation is a sine qua non condition for a modern economy. So much more for post-command economies in central and Eastern Europe, where system wide transformation after the fall of the Belin Wall implied the formation of genuine banking structures and of capital markets. In their studies, Dr. Ramona Birau and Dr. Cristi Spulbar undertake an insightful analysis of financial markets in Romania and in other economies; they use quantitative methods to validate their working assumptions and, nota bene, they do it in a comparative framework. The volume blends microeconomic analysis with macroeconomic policy analysis; it also considers the impact of the global financial crisis on emerging economies in Europe and elsewhere. This volume would be of interest to researchers and policy-makers who focus their attention on European emerging economies, on emerging economies in general.

Daniel Daianu

Titular Member of the Romanian Academy, Member of the Board of the National Bank of Romania and Professor of Economics at the National School of Political and Administrative Studies (SNSPA) in Bucharest

Prof. Dr. Daniel Daianu is also a professor of public finance, at the National School of Political Studies and Public Administration (SNSPA) in Bucharest. Prof. Dr. Daniel Daianu was elected a corresponding member of the Romanian Academy since 2001 and he was upgraded to titular member in 2013. He was the Finance Minister of Romania between December 5, 1997 and September 23, 1998. Prof. Dr. Daianu is Member of the Board of the National Bank of Romania. He is also a member of the European Council for Foreign Relations, since 2012.

TESTIMONIAL #3

The book *Emerging Research on Monetary Policy, Banking, and Financial Markets* is distinguished for the rigorous and integrated approach of the most important current challenges in the field of quantitative finance, the originality of empirical research, and the applied interdisciplinary framework which involves the use of econometric methods, techniques and models. The architecture of financial markets is fascinating, but very complex because it does not respect predictive behavioral patterns. Understanding the behavior of financial markets should rely on solid knowledge of quantitative finance, so this research book can be perceived as a reference point in career development for researchers and financial professionals.

Lucian-Claudiu Anghel
President of the Bucharest Stock Exchange

Dr. Lucian-Claudiu Anghel serves as the President of the Board of Directors at Bucharest Stock Exchange, Romania. He served as President of Management Board and Chief Executive Officer at BCR Pensii from 2012 to 2015 and as the Chief Economist and Executive Director of Strategy and Research, BCR from 2007 to 2012. Dr. Anghel has been the President of the Board of Governors at Bucharest Stock Exchange from 2012 to 2016. He was the Head of Research, Romania and Chief Economist at Erste Bank Group, Research Division. He holds MBA from HEC Montreal Canada; PhD in Economy and Degree in Economic Informatics from ASE Bucharest. Mr. Anghel attended Bank Risk Management course in Georgetown University Washington.

TESTIMONIAL #4

An extensive research work with depth and method, that necessarily complements the available literature dedicated to the banking industry, monetary policy and capital markets, with valuable content for all those interested in the financial field. The book *Emerging Research on Monetary Policy, Banking, and Financial Markets* is characterized by methodological approaches and relevant econometric applications, thus creating a multidimensional overview on understanding financial markets. Financial professionals will be effective beneficiaries after studying this research volume.

Florin Danescu
Executive President of the Romanian Banking Association, Romania

Mr. Florin Dănescu graduated from the Bucharest University of Economic Studies in 1995 and holds an MBA from the University of Vienna. Florin Dănescu boasts a long-standing experience in the commercial banking system. He was a dealer (1996-1997) and Head of the Foreign Exchange and Money Market Department (1997-1999) at the Banca Agricola SA. Over 2000-2011 he worked with the Romanian International Bank as Head of the Treasury Department (2000-2003), Vice-President (2006), First Vice-President (2007), Interim President (2008) and President (2011). At present, Florin Dănescu is the Executive President of the Romanian Banking Association.

TESTIMONIAL #5

As academics, we have more responsibility to guide our future generation on right path through our literature to create a better world. Dr. Cristi Spulbar and Dr. Ramona Birau have written this book *Emerging Research on Monetary Policy, Banking, and Financial Markets* to lead the future world banking system. The financial services sector is emerging from the worst financial crisis for 80 years. Banks in emerging markets are now well capitalized and well-funded and big enough to compete directly against their western counterparts in the global marketplace. They have greater potential for growth because of the relatively immature development of their domestic financial markets and their rapidly growing economies. I am very happy in reading every chapters of the book. This book is very useful to the students, academics and policy makers. This book will lead future banking system reform worldwide.

Riyas Sulaima Lebbe
Regional Director for Sri Lanka at Eurasian Doctoral Summer Academy (EDSA) Bulgaria and Chartered Economist and President at Centre for Peace Studies, Sri Lanka

Prof. Dr. Riyas Sulaima Lebbe is the Vice Chancellor of Yesbud University Zambia and he was also the dean of the School of Business in Yesbud University, Zambia. He is Pro Vice chancellor for the Sri Lanka Campus of the British American University, Florida, USA and Regional Director for Sri Lanka at Eurasian Doctoral Summer Academy (EDSA) Bulgaria. He is a Professor of Human Rights and Peace Studies at BAU in the Department of Human Rights and Peace Studies. Prof (Dr) Riyas Sulaima Lebbe is an Independent Researcher, Management Consultant and Corporate Trainer. He is the Founder and the Executive Director of the Centre for Peace Studies, Sri Lanka and the Universal Management Consultancy service.

Table of Contents

Preface

Based on the most representative scientific papers published in the last 8 years in the field of financial markets, the book *Emerging Research on Monetary Policy, Banking, and Financial Markets* is represents our joint effort to consolidate in a financial corpus over 17 book chapters based on original themes and research directions in our area of expertise. The selected empirical studies have been published in a less elaborate forming internationally renowned research journals or conference proceedings, which gives the book the breadth of a genuine guide of research and analysis of the banking industry, monetary policy and financial markets. This book is dedicated to everyone interested in financial education.

The book entitled Emerging Research on Monetary Policy, Banking, and Financial Markets is organized to be accessible and useful. the book is structured as follows: Section 1, "Measuring Effectiveness and Efficiency of the Banking Systems," which includes four chapters; Section 2, "The Transmission Mechanism of Monetary Policy: Dynamics and Perspectives," which includes three chapters; and Section 3, "Understanding Financial Market Behavior: Empirical Case Studies," which includes 10 chapters. The content of the book *Emerging Research on Monetary Policy, Banking, and Financial Markets* is original. The structure of the book is very complex and unitary, forming a balanced and original content. Moreover, this book examined the existing relationships between Monetary Policy, Banking and Financial Markets.

The selection made by the authors has been focused on achieving a balanced content with complex intrinsic value so we can contribute to the advancement of knowledge through original research, generating innovative solutions that promote creativity and freedom of thought in the context of knowledge-based society. Additionally, we also seek to achieve as much representation of our research ideas as possible in consonance with other relevant publications in this area of study, by covering all three main research directions (i.e., banking, monetary policy, and financial markets), and finally our hope is that the originality of authors contributions and their impact on the financial field will meet the expectations of our readers.

The motivation of the book is related to our goal of creating a solid body of research-based knowledge based on extensive dialogues with literature, on personal contributions establish on the critical analysis of the current state of knowledge compared to the latest achievements quoted in the mainstream publications. The holistic approach to financial market research can provide an alternative and also a complement to the traditional study of financial markets so the book could become a landmark for researchers and professionals.

The literature on banks and banking activities has represented and represent one of the most interesting area of research. As a matter of fact, in the literature there are many descriptive but also quantitative studies about the banking institutions. The intention to bring a contribution to the elucidation of some of the aspects that characterize the credit institutions and the banking systems represents one of the reasons that have been the basis of the analyses which have been carried out and presented here in after. The banks solidity and effective activity present a special importance for the economic growth, the credit allocation, the financial stability, as well as for the firms development and competitiveness. The credit institutions, due to their significant dimension, play an essential role in the economy through the assets transformation, the risk management facilitation, the commerce financing and the technological innovations stimulation.

The monetary policy represents a basic part of the economic policy, the central banks acting through it on the currency demand and offer from the economy. The fundamental objective of the monetary policy is the prices stability, to which the inflation control and the maintenance of the internal and external value of the national currency are added. The prices stability represents at the same time a central objective of the economic policy alongside: the economic growth, the total occupancy of the workforce; the sustainability of the balance of payments etc.

The concept of financial market is very broad and covers different theoretical dimensions. Concretely, the term of financial market has been defined based on a range of different ideas, opinions, judgements and perspectives. However there is no generally accepted definition of financial market despite numerous research studies in the literature. The terminology proposed in the literature highlights a multitude of conceptual approaches that delineate an exhaustive framework. International investors focus on potential correlation between stock returns of different national capital markets in order to diversify portfolio risks by allocating financial asset investments. The multidimensional implications of financial integration generate the possibility of identifying investment strategies in order to optimize the risk management structure.

A financial market is a complex system based on dynamic interactions and correlations. Financial markets have a significant implication in the case of increasing interdependency and interconnectivity between national economies. A financial market provides the structural mechanism that allows trading financial assets which include the following categories: shares, bonds, financial derivatives, currencies, bank deposits, equity stakes, share certificate and other financial securities.

The book *Emerging Research on Monetary Policy, Banking, and Financial Markets* is will add value to the current knowledge base in order to reach a higher level of understanding. The proposed book aims to provide a Scientific Corpus to mostly theoretical available literature in the field of Quantitative Finance. The complex empirical investigations included in this proposed book establish useful input for developing viable strategies in the financial field. The main objective of this proposed book is to provide original insights into Monetary Policy, Banking and Financial Markets thus forming a unitary, exhaustive content.

The target audience of this book will be composed of Academics, Researchers, Students, Advanced-Level Students and PhD Students, Policy Makers, Government Officials, Professionals, Business Analytics and Consultants, working in the field of Quantitative Finance.

At present, there is no book published based on such original structure. The available literature generally includes books with an academic course structure (i.e., definitions, concepts, classifications). The applied methodology used in empirical research studies led to robust results in the field of quantitative finance. Practically, the applied research studies differentiate the proposed book from any other existing book as available literature in the field of quantitative finance. This is just a brief review about what is distinctive about our book *Emerging Research on Monetary Policy, Banking, and Financial Markets.*

We would like to thank our co-authors academic colleagues with whom we have elaborated some of the initial empirical studies underlying this book (i.e., Bogdan Dima Professor Ph.D, Marius Dinca Professor Ph.D, Mihai Nitoi Associate Professor Ph.D, Cristian Stanciu Associate Professor Ph.D, and Jatin Trivedi Associate Professor Ph.D), as well as to all who believed in the idea and necessity of this research project, including our international partners who supported the publication of this volume.

Introduction

The literature on banks and banking activities has represented and represent one of the most interesting area of research. As a matter of fact, in the literature there are many descriptive but also quantitative studies about the banking institutions. The intention to bring a contribution to the elucidation of some of the aspects that characterize the credit institutions and the banking systems represents one of the reasons that have been the basis of the analyses which have been carried out and presented hereinafter.

Blavy (2005) sustains the idea that the monitoring process carried out by banks can determine the characteristics of the banks' lending behavior, especially in the economies where the information about the borrowers are insufficient, and the costs related to giving up a lending-borrowing relation are high. The storage of the non-performing credits in the banks' balance sheet is constituted in a plausible result of the costs high level. Two further characteristics are emphasized in this frame, both being results accepted in the literature referring to the banking credit.

The first comprises the fact that the banks prefer to finance the companies from the formal sector with which they have lasting relations, and the second one refers to the possibility of emphasizing the gap between the active interest rate and the passive interest rate. These characteristics result from the theoretical argumentation, being based on the idea according to which the banks confront themselves with a range of informational problems through the relations on long term with the borrowers and the commitments. Transposed within the asymmetric information between the creditors and the debtors, Blavy (2005) reveals, with plausible conditions, the fact that the debtors' monitoring by the banks grows the credit market efficiency by reducing the interest rate applied to those who contract borrowings and/or growing the profit estimated by the banks and by the weighting growth of the credit level in the economy.

The financial crisis started in 2007 emphasized the importance of the banking sector reliability and efficiency and its role in supplying the credit necessary for the economic activities. Gambacorta and Marques-Ibanez (2011) underline the fact that while the studies before the crisis questioned the banking credit channel reliability, the recent researches show that the specialized banks particularities can have an important impact on lending.

The recent credit crisis reminded us of the crucial role accomplished by the banks in the economy loaning, especially in a situation characterized by serious financial problems. At the same time, this role seems to differ from the description from the traditional models of the banking credit channel. The crisis has especially showed that the entire monetary transmission mechanism has suffered changes, as result of the deregulation, the financial innovation and the institutional investors role growth. This has determined changes in the banks' business models and the intensive use of the financing resources on the market (for example the market of the securitization instruments).

Similarly, the strong interaction between the banks and the financial market exacerbates the impact of the financial market conditions on the bank's decisions. Some authors have argued that the monetary policy effect on the financial stability has grown in the last years, leading to a new monetary policy transmission mechanism: the channel of risk assumption. Gambacorta and Marques-Ibanez (2011) revealed that the changes interfered in the banks' business models and in the market financing conditions have modified the monetary transmission mechanism in Europe and the USA before the crisis burst and prove the existence of some structural modifications during the evolution period of the financial crisis.

The banks with lower rates of capital adequacy, with a higher dependence of financing on the market and of the non-interest income sources limited more the credits offer during the crisis period. After the crisis, the big banks have recorded important assets growths, many of these banks owning assets that overpass the GDP of the countries where they come from. Also, although a basic criterion, the profit is not the only factor which the banks must respect for establishing their policy on different terms. They must assure an active balance between profitability, liquidity, solvability, risk and efficiency.

The banks act in uncertainty conditions, both in the resources domain that don't have a quantifiable stability, unlike the non-banking entities, and in the investment domain, that contains a risk factor through their nature. More profitable an investment is, riskier it is. Also, in the case of the long-term investments the risk is higher.

The monetary policy represents a basic part of the economic policy, the central banks acting through it on the currency demand and offer from the economy. The fundamental objective of the monetary policy is the prices stability, to which the inflation control and the maintenance of the internal and external value of the national currency are added. The prices stability represents at the same time a central objective of the economic policy alongside: the economic growth, the total occupancy of the workforce; the sustainability of the balance of payments etc. If the prices stability is a fundamental but also common objective to the central bank and government, we can also speak of certain objectives specific to the monetary policy that is: i) the monetary mass growth to an optimal level, closely connected to the GDP growth; ii) the interest rate maintenance at an adequate level; iii) the practice of an optimal level of the exchange rate; iv) the logical assignment of the lending resources within the economy.

For accomplishing the monetary policy objectives, the central banks use indirect and direct instruments. The indirect instruments are used by the central bank in relation with the other banks and with the non-financial agents. Traditionally, this category includes the instruments that allow the control on the cost and on the quantity of central currency (the minimum reserves, open market operations etc.). The direct instruments are represented by measures that affect, directly, the users and holders of currency, including the financial institutions (the restriction of credits or of remunerated deposits, the stability of the creditor and debtor interest rate etc.).

The concept of financial market is very broad and covers different theoretical dimensions. Concretely, the term of financial market has been defined based on a range of different ideas, opinions, judgements and perspectives. However, there is no generally accepted definition of financial market despite numerous research studies in the literature. The terminology proposed in the literature highlights a multitude of conceptual approaches that delineate an exhaustive framework. A financial market is a complex system based on dynamic interactions and correlations. Financial markets have a significant implication in the case of increasing interdependency and interconnectivity between national economies.

A financial market provides the structural mechanism that allows trading financial assets which include the following categories: shares, bonds, financial derivatives, currencies, bank deposits, equity stakes, share certificate and other financial securities . The main feature of financial assets is that are intangible or non-physical liquid assets whose value derives from a contractual clause.

The essential role of financial markets is to stimulate economic growth. The globalization of financial markets leads to increasingly complex cross-border financial movements. Moreover, the process of liberalization and integration of financial markets highlights various investment opportunities based on minimizing the cost of capital transactions and inflows of foreign capital. In the context of economic globalization, financial markets are highly integrated thus generating various investment opportunities.

According to the Financial Times Stock Exchange (F.T.S.E) evaluation criteria there are four categories of classification for national markets, ie: developed markets, advanced emerging markets, secondary emerging markets and frontier markets. Standard & Poor's Financial Services suggest that the global classification of markets includes the following subcategories: developed, emerging and frontier. Furthermore, MSCI Country Classification based on the Annual Market Classification Review provides a similar market classification, ie: developed, emerging and frontier.

The degree of financial integration is different in the case of developed markets compared to emerging markets. Financial liberalization generates much higher investment opportunities for developed economies considering the positive effects of economic growth. Contrariwise, global financial liberalization exhibits a much lower influence on emerging economies. Despite global economic interlinkages, the internationalization of financial markets can generate significant investment opportunities based on portfolio diversification. The manifestation of the current trend regarding the global phenomenon of increasing cointegration, correlated movements and financial contagion between developed and emerging stock markets has significantly influenced the behavior of foreign investment.

Prospects for potential investors are also influenced by the fact that financial integration affects the correlated movements in the profitability of the tradable structures forming the financial asset portfolio. Thus, correlated movements of emerging markets with those of developed markets influence the profitability of financial asset portfolio based on international diversification of investment portfolios. Moreover, information asymmetry and liquidity of capital markets generate disruptions in investment behavior.

REFERENCES

Blavy, R. (2005). *Monitoring and Commitment in Bank Lending Behavior*. IMF Working Paper no. 222.

Gambacorta, L., & Marques-Ibanez, D. (2011). The bank lending channel: Lessons from the crisis. *Economic Policy*, *26*(66), 135–182. doi:10.1111/j.1468-0327.2011.00261.x

Section 1
Measuring Effectiveness and Efficiency of Banking Systems

Chapter 1
Determinants of Bank Cost Efficiency in Transition Economies:
Evidence for Latin America, Central and Eastern Europe, and South-East Asia

ABSTRACT

This chapter leads a complex research study on the determinants of bank cost efficiency in transitional economies based on empirical evidence for Latin America, Central, and Eastern Europe, and South-East Asia. The empirical results suggested that banks, which follow a more cautious strategy, characterized by lower risk appetite and average expectations on profitability, have higher cost efficiency. Moreover, the empirical evidence highlighted the fact that a higher gross domestic product growth rate implies an increase in the inefficiency level, indicating an unsustainable bank management behavior, which in periods of economic growth adopts policies that can generate inefficiency in order to gain market share and to obtain higher bonuses. The global financial crisis has had a high negative impact on the banking system in transition economies.

DOI: 10.4018/978-1-5225-9269-3.ch001

INTRODUCTION

The establishment of an efficient and solid banking system is an essential condition for sustainable economic growth. This condition is much more important for the countries in transition towards a market economy. Over the past few decades, banking systems in emerging countries have undergone significant structural reforms. In the early 1990s, most of the countries in our study had implemented financial liberalization policies and had reorganized their banking systems. Thereafter, there were periods when these banking systems passed through financial crises, such as the financial crisis in Asia or the financial crisis in Argentina, but there were also periods of economic growth combined with the expansion of the banking sector. An authentic test for the stability of banking systems in the countries in transition was presented by the financial crisis beginning in 2008 that affected, to a higher or lesser degree, the majority of the economies.

Jeanneau (2007) considered that the banking systems of many countries in Latin America have experienced boom and bust cycles and frequent crises, which have exacerbated economic fluctuations. Figueira et al. (2009) asserted that countries in Latin America adopted reforms, such as the privatization of state-owned banks and the encouragement of foreign capital, in order to increase the efficiency of the banking sector. Also, there was an increase in the share of bank assets owned by foreign investors in these countries.

In the countries of Central and Eastern Europe, the main challenge was represented by the transformation of socialist banking systems into market-oriented ones. Koutsomanoli-Filippaki et al. (2009) showed that most of the countries in Central and Eastern Europe adopted similar measures to ease the transition to a market economy: they introduced a two-tier banking system, restructured and privatized state-owned banks, liberalized interest rates and capital accounts and established a new legal and supervisory banking framework. In Central and Eastern Europe, a significant percentage of banks' assets is owned by foreign capital (Claessens & van Horen, 2012). Klingen (2013) considered that the economies of Central and Eastern Europe suffered more than did those of any other region in the world, due to the global financial crisis that ended various unsustainable domestic booms.

In the countries of South Eastern Asia, financial liberalization programmes were implemented during the early 1990s in order to increase the competitiveness of the national banking sectors (Williams & Nguyen, 2005). The Asian financial crisis, which began in 1997, was a period with negative implications for these banking systems. The last decade witnessed a significant development of the banking systems in this region. Moreover, Montoro and Rojas-Suarez (2012) showed that the real credit growth in Asia was quite resilient to the international crisis, while the real credit growth in the countries of Eastern Europe was drastically affected. Latin America lay in the middle.

The aforementioned aspects fundamentally modified the way in which banks operate, as they were forced to reconsider their strategies. Therefore, bank performance and efficiency acquired an increasingly important role. In this study, we propose to compare the cost efficiency level between the emerging countries from different regions and to emphasize the determinants of the level and variability of cost efficiency over the period 2005 to 2011. Cost efficiency is estimated using a Stochastic Frontier Analysis (SFA). More specifically, we adopted Wang's (2002) heteroscedastic stochastic frontier model, which allowed us to specify both the mean and the variance of the inefficiency turbulence and to investigate the nonmonotonic effects on efficiency. The contribution of our study to the existent literature is significant from many points of view.

Firstly, a considerable number of observations for the banking systems from 16 emerging countries from three different regions - Latin America, Central and Eastern Europe and South Eastern Asia - is included in the model. Secondly, our study provides not only results concerning the inefficiency differences between the analysed countries, but also the factors that influence the level and the variability of the bank efficiency. We consider that this evidence is essential, bearing in mind the effects of the financial crisis on the banking systems. Thirdly, within the inefficiency determinants we included variables that describe the economic and financial development, the banks' risk taking, the bank's performance, the efficiency of financial intermediation and the degree of diversification. Fourthly, taking into account the fact that banks faced higher risks during the analysed period, we included a variable that quantifies the risk of failure for banks within the variables that influence inefficiency.

LITERATURE ON THE EFFICIENCY OF BANKS IN EMERGING COUNTRIES

In the literature, there are multiple cross-country studies that analyse bank efficiency in emerging countries. Hereinafter, we briefly present the studies that emphasize the determinants of bank efficiency in transition countries in Latin America, Central and Eastern Europe and South Eastern Asia.

Most of the studies focus on identifying the impact of various specific measures of transition in these countries, such as financial liberalization, banking reforms, ownership structure, the privatization process, on cost and profit efficiency. In general, the results suggest a positive effect of foreign ownership and reform process on bank efficiency. Hermes and Nhung (2010) investigated the impact of financial liberalization on the efficiency of Latin American and Asian banks over the period 1991 to 2000 using data envelopment analysis (DEA). The results indicated a positive impact of financial liberalization policies on the efficiency of banks. In a study that analysed bank efficiency in Latin America in 2001, Figueira et al. (2009) concluded that there were minor differences between the performance of state-owned and privately-owned banks, as well as between foreign- and domestically-owned banks. With respect to transition countries in Central and Eastern Europe, Brissimis et al. (2008) showed that both banking sector reform and competition have a positive impact on bank efficiency and the effect of reform on productivity growth is significant only towards the end of the reform process, while Fries and Taci (2005) findings indicated that the association between a country's progress in banking reform and cost efficiency is nonlinear.

Koutsomanoli-Filippaki et al. (2009), Staikouras et al. (2008), Havranek and Irsova (2013) found that foreign banks in Central and Eastern European countries are more efficient than domestic banks. Williams and Nguyen (2005) examined the relation between bank governance and bank performance by observing a sample of commercial banks operating in SE Asia over the period 1990 to 2003. The results showed that the state-owned banks underperformed in comparison to the private banks. In addition, bank privatization was associated with superior profit efficiency performance and with strong productivity performance.

Other research studies evaluated the impact of some exogenous factors, such as market concentration, competition, bank size, regulation and endogenous factors, with a focus on risk and performance measures, on bank efficiency.

Kasman and Carvallo (2013) examined the factors that influence bank efficiency for 15 Latin American and Caribbean countries over the period 2001-2008. Their findings indicated that market concentration is related to greater revenue efficiency, while competitive forces and strengthened regulation are positively correlated with cost efficiency. Tabak et al. (2013) studied the relationship between bank size, market concentration and performance for 17 Latin American countries over the period 2001 to 2008. The results indicated that, even in concentrated markets, systemically important financial institutions are more cost and profit efficient than others. Koutsomanoli-Filippaki et al. (2009) used the directional technology distance function to analyse bank efficiency and productivity changes across Central and Eastern Europe. The results showed that a higher competition and more concentrated markets will lead to an increase in banks' cost efficiency.

Pancurova and Lyocsa (2013) analysed the determinants of bank efficiency for 11 Central and Eastern European countries over the period 2005 to 2008. Their results showed that bank size and financial capitalization are positively associated with cost and revenue efficiency, while loans-to-assets ratio was negatively associated with cost efficiency, but positively associated with revenue efficiency. Sun and Chang (2011) investigated the marginal effects of the operational risk, market risk and credit risk on the inefficiency effect in eight emerging countries in Asia. The results showed that the risk measures have a significant effect on both the level and the variability of bank efficiency. Wang et al. (2013) studied bank performance in East Asia. They find that capital adequacy, asset quality, management, earnings, liquidity are manifested more strongly in highly efficient banks. Also, intellectual capital is positively associated with bank efficiency.

In this research book chapter, we propose to analyse the marginal effects of economic and financial development, solvency risk, failure risk, liquidity risk, efficiency of financial intermediation, bank performance and the degree of diversification on both the level and the variability of bank efficiency. Also, cross country differences in banks' efficiency is another objective of our study. The estimation covers 16 transition countries from three regions, namely Latin America, Central and Eastern Europe and South Eastern Asia over the period 2005 to 2011.

METHODOLOGY

In order to measure the cost efficiency level, we used a stochastic frontier model. The main reason behind the choice of the SFA is related to the fact that the DEA does not allow for the presence of a random error term. As a result, any deviation from the efficiency frontier is associated with inefficiency. For instance, DEA considers the influence of factors such as measurement error, luck or extreme observations to indicate inefficiency. SFA, independently proposed by Aigner et al. (1977) and Meeusen and van den Broeck (1977), allows for the specification of an error term with two components: a one-sided error that measures nonnegative inefficiency effects and a classical random error. A detailed review of the non-parametric and the parametric approach can be found in Matoušek and Taci (2004).

In the literature on efficiency, there are numerous models that investigate the manner in which exogenous factors influence the one-sided inefficiency effect (Battese & Coelli, 1995; Kumbhakar et al., 1991; Caudill et al., 1995). Most of the SFA models only show the overall effects of exogenous factors on the level of inefficiency and assume that the determinants have either positive or negative effects on the level of inefficiency.

In Wang's model (2002), Z_{it} can positively (negatively) affect the efficiency when values of Z_{it} are within a certain range, and then turn negative (positive) for values of Z_{it} outside the range. These nonmonotonic effects, which allow us to better understand the relationships between efficiency and its determinants, are measured by the marginal effects. Also, the model that we used is considered by Lai and Huang (2010) to be the best of the most popular eight SFA models.

In this study, we will adopt the model proposed by Wang (2002), in which the relationship of the expectation of u_{it} to Z_{it} could be nonmonotonic. The author assumes that the distribution of u_{it} is $N^{+}\left(\mu_{it}, \sigma_{it}^{2}\right)$, with an observation-specific mean $\left(\mu_{it}\right)$ and variance $\left(\sigma_{it}^{2}\right)$ of its pre-truncated distribution. Moreover, both μ_{it} and σ_{it}^{2} depend on certain determinants $\left(Z_{it}\right)$. The heteroscedastic model can be expressed as follows:

$$TC_{it} = f\left(Y_{it}, P_{it}\right) + v_{it} + u_{it}, v_{it} \sim N\left(0, \sigma_{v}^{2}\right), u_{it} \sim N^{+}\left(\mu_{it}, \sigma_{it}^{2}\right) \quad (1)$$

$$\mu_{it} = \delta_0 + Z_{it}\delta \tag{2}$$

$$\sigma_{it}^2 = \exp\left(\gamma_0 + Z_{it}\gamma\right) \tag{3}$$

where TC_{it} is the total cost of bank *i* in year *t;* Y_{it} and P_{it} are vectors of the output and the price of inputs, respectively, and v_{it} is the stochastic error term with independent and identically distributed normal distribution. In Wang's model, the Z_{it} has two different coefficients: δ is for the mean and γ is for the variance of the pre-truncation normal. As mentioned, the determinant factors $\left(Z_{it}\right)$ can have nonmonotonic effects on the inefficiency $\left(u_{it}\right)$.

The non-monotonic efficiency effects the *k*th element of Z_{it} on $E(u_{it})$ is thus:

$$\frac{\partial E\left(u_{it}\right)}{\partial z\left[k\right]} = \delta\left[k\right]\left[1 - \Lambda\left[\frac{\phi\left(\Lambda\right)}{\Phi\left(\Lambda\right)}\right] - \left[\frac{\phi\left(\Lambda\right)}{\Phi\left(\Lambda\right)}\right]^2\right] + \gamma\left[k\right]\frac{\sigma_{it}}{2}\left[\left(1+\Lambda^2\right)\left[\frac{\phi\left(\Lambda\right)}{\Phi\left(\Lambda\right)}\right] + \Lambda\left[\frac{\phi\left(\Lambda\right)}{\Phi\left(\Lambda\right)}\right]^2\right] \tag{4}$$

where $\delta\left[k\right]$ and $\gamma\left[k\right]$ are the corresponding coefficients in Equations 2 and 3, respectively; $z\left[k\right]$ is the element *k*th of Z_{it}; ϕ and Φ are the probability and cumulative density functions of a standard normal distribution, respectively and $\Lambda = \mu_{it} / \sigma_{it}$.

The marginal effect of Z_{it} on $V\left(u_{it}\right)$ is:

$$\frac{\partial V\left(u_{it}\right)}{\partial z\left[k\right]} = \frac{\delta}{\sigma_{it}}\left[\frac{\phi\left(\Lambda\right)}{\Phi\left(\Lambda\right)}\right]\left(m_1^2 - m_2\right) + \gamma\left[k\right]\sigma_{it}^2\left\{1 - \frac{1}{2}\left[\frac{\phi\left(\Lambda\right)}{\Phi\left(\Lambda\right)}\right]\left[\begin{matrix}\Lambda + \Lambda^3 + \left(2+3\Lambda^2\right)\left[\frac{\phi\left(\Lambda\right)}{\Phi\left(\Lambda\right)}\right] \\ +2\Lambda\left[\frac{\phi\left(\Lambda\right)}{\Phi\left(\Lambda\right)}\right]^2\end{matrix}\right]\right\} \tag{5}$$

where m_1 and m_2 are the first two moments of u_{it} (Wang, 2002).

DATA

In order to build our sample data, we focused on the regions with a significant emerging level. Therefore, we have chosen 16 middle-income countries, from three developing regions. Table 1 presents bank-year observations by country. We consider that these countries represent the characteristics of the regions they belong to and the characteristics of transition economies. In most of these countries, the evolution of the banking system in the last decades has followed similar patterns: reform, liberalization and privatization. Also, the banking system in the countries included in our sample, except Bulgaria, can be found amongst the 24 largest emerging markets that receive cross-country funds from developed countries (Cetorelli & Goldberg, 2010).

Moreover, in the literature there are numerous studies that analyse the characteristics and the performance of the banking system in transition countries across different regions (Hermes & Nhung, 2010 – banking systems in Latin America and Asia; Cull & Martinez Peria, 2012 – banking systems in Latin America and Eastern Europe; Ioannidis et al., 2008 – banking systems in Latin America and Asia; Gelos şi Roldós, 2004 – banking systems in Latin America and Europe).

Our sample covers an unbalanced panel dataset of 2950 observations, corresponding to 481 commercial banks over the period 2005 to 2011. The countries included in the study are Argentina, Brazil, Chile, Mexico, Bulgaria, the Czech Republic, Poland, Romania, Russia, Hungary, China, the Philippines, India, Indonesia, Malaysia and Thailand. Only observations starting in 2008 were available for the banking system of Chile. The data were extracted from the BankScope database. Table 2 provides the descriptive statistics of the exogenous variables used in the analysis.

For the definition of bank inputs and outputs, we used the intermediation approach. This was developed by Sealey and Lindley (1977) and considers banks to be financial intermediaries that buy inputs (labour, physical capital and deposits) in order to generate earning assets. The two output variables are total loans and other earning assets. Loan loss provisions are subtracted from total loans in order to ensure a value that expresses credit quality (Havrylchyk, 2006). The price of funds and the price of capital are the two input prices. Most of the research studies also include the price of labour. However, the data on the number of employees are not available for a significant number of banks in our sample. The price of the funds is calculated by dividing total

Table 1. Number of observations by country and year

	2005	2006	2007	2008	2009	2010	2011	Total
Argentina	29	35	35	39	38	39	35	250
Brazil	24	26	27	28	29	30	26	190
Chile	n.a.	n.a.	n.a.	17	17	17	17	68
Mexico	15	16	20	20	21	21	21	134
Bulgaria	11	13	13	14	16	16	16	99
Czech Republic	11	11	11	11	11	11	10	76
Poland	17	18	19	21	25	25	24	149
Romania	16	16	18	17	19	19	17	122
Russia	35	39	42	42	45	45	43	291
Hungary	11	11	11	13	13	12	11	82
China	43	59	77	90	96	100	98	563
Philippines	15	17	18	18	18	18	18	122
India	43	45	49	51	50	50	48	336
Indonesia	28	32	37	41	43	43	41	265
Malaysia	11	12	12	13	14	14	13	89
Thailand	15	15	17	17	17	17	16	114
Total	324	365	406	452	472	477	454	2950

interests' expenses by total deposits and other purchased funds. The price of capital is measured by the ratio of noninterest expenses to total fixed assets.

The total cost of each bank is the sum of interest expenses and noninterest expenses. In order to ensure price homogeneity, the total cost and the price of funds were normalized by the price of capital. All monetary values were deflated by using the Gross Domestic Product (GDP) deflator provided by the International Monetary Fund, with 2005 as the base year. For all the countries in our sample, we created a dummy variable in order to measure the country's effect. We dropped the first variable in order to avoid multicollinearity. We also included two dummy variables for the years 2008 and 2009 in the model, in order to capture the impact of the financial crisis on cost efficiency. Table 3 presents the summary statistics of the variables used in the cost function.

In order to investigate how exogenous factors influenced the inefficiency level, we included country-specific variables and bank-specific variables in the study. The inclusion of the country-specific variables began with the idea that economic and social conditions affect the way in which banks operate.

Table 2. Descriptive statistics of the dataset (sample means are for bank-year observations and country)

	GDP Growth Rate	Domestic Credit Provided by Banking Sector Over GDP	Equity to Total Assets Ratio	Z Score	Net Loans to Customer and Short Term Funding Ratio	ROA	Noninterest Income to Gross Revenues Ratio
Argentina	7.3158	29.7441	14.9488	19.6514	65.0375	2.2848	57.4978
Brazil	4.0813	91.761	13.6619	19.1137	90.3064	1.9481	26.5896
Chile	3.6773	73.1599	11.2475	34.5313	96.9161	0.8788	38.8477
Mexico	2.1848	39.9367	13.7067	26.2501	79.1963	0.0403	29.2838
Bulgaria	2.7323	60.4666	11.6229	20.1437	83.8770	1.3070	28.3422
Czech Republic	3.2287	54.8790	8.1592	29.7250	60.3907	1.1485	28.9081
Poland	4.3805	55.3262	8.8157	33.2583	67.8177	0.7930	41.4838
Romania	2.5547	42.0539	11.8852	12.5045	80.1303	0.0920	37.6112
Russia	3.9512	29.6392	11.8002	15.7606	91.4440	1.3951	37.7834
Hungary	0.5450	75.5198	10.2198	20.1321	85.1202	0.3265	39.3190
China	10.7055	137.0776	7.1101	32.3324	62.8779	0.9781	14.9546
Philippines	4.7791	48.7643	11.4516	31.1470	52.4220	1.1789	33.9508
India	8.0758	66.8246	8.0235	55.7031	69.0685	1.0429	31.1991
Indonesia	5.8374	39.1441	12.6212	40.8468	76.3580	1.5901	20.7107
Malaysia	4.5969	120.3934	10.5114	54.7045	68.3292	1.2237	31.2642
Thailand	3.2268	133.1404	13.2515	38.4180	89.7631	0.6835	23.9024

Table 3. Descriptive statistics of the variables used in the cost efficiency estimations

	Mean	SD	Min.	Max.
Total cost (in billion US $)	0.9730	3.4722	0.0011	47.8929
Output Quantities (in Billion US $)				
Total loans	12.3810	60.5936	0.0016	985.3659
Other earning assets	9.7204	56.0806	0.0001	974.5864
Input Prices				
Price of funds	0.0467	0.0345	0.0009	0.4059
Price of capital	6.5224	40.8401	0.1384	1553.968

The different strategies adopted by each bank and their impact on costs are quantified through bank-specific variables.

The country-specific variables are GDP real growth rate and the domestic credit provided by banking sector over GDP ratio. The GDP's real growth rate is a measure of the economic development. The impact of this variable on the cost efficiency can be either positive or negative. According to Afanasieff et al. (2002), higher output growth will mean a greater demand for bank loans, leading banks to charge more on their credits. Nevertheless, economic growth is a signal of a more intense competition, implying lower interest margins. The domestic credit provided by the banking sector over GDP ratio is included in the model to control the differences between developments in the financial sector. A higher ratio implies a more developed financial sector, which should lead to lower costs.

Within the bank-specific variables, we included equity to total assets ratio, Z score, net loans to customer and short-term funding ratio, ROA and noninterest income to gross revenues ratio. The equity to total assets ratio is a measure of the solvency risk. Liu and Wilson (2010) considered that banks with a higher capital rate could be extremely careful, ignoring potentially profitable investment opportunities. However, a lower capital asset ratio can signify capital problems, higher risk and higher costs, which imply more expensive barrowed funds.

To conclude, the effect of the equity to total assets ratio on cost efficiency can be either positive or negative. The Z score is a measure of the risk of failure, indicating the probability of bankruptcy for a bank. According to Lepetit et al. (2008), higher values reflect a lower probability of bankruptcy. A lower risk of failure should involve a higher cost efficiency level. The Z score is computed on the basis of the following formula:

$$Z = \frac{ROA + EQ / TA}{SDROA} \tag{6}$$

To capture liquidity and market risk, we used net loans to customer and short-term funding ratio. Also, Fries and Taci (2005) consider this ratio a measure of the efficiency of the financial intermediation process, a very low ratio indicating banks´ inability to transform deposits into loans. Basically, a higher ratio should have a positive impact on efficiency. Nevertheless, net loans to customer and short-term funding ratio of over 100% means that banks are massively more levered, leading to a lower "stickiness" of funds and a higher risk of liquidity.

All these can mean higher costs for the banks. ROA is a proxy for a bank's performance, a higher rate implying higher cost efficiency. The noninterest income to gross revenues ratio is included in the model, in order to capture the business orientation and revenue diversification. Its effect on efficiency can be either positive or negative, according to the ability and expertise of banks in the activities in which they are engaged such as investment banking, asset management, insurance underwriting.

EMPIRICAL RESULTS

Efficiency Estimates

The model estimation was realised using Stata 10.1 software. As mentioned, we used Wang's (2002) heteroscedastic stochastic frontier model. Table 4 provides cost efficiency results.

As we observed, all coefficients for output and input prices are positive and significant. The squared coefficients of output variables are positive and significant. Bearing this in mind, we can draw the conclusion that higher prices and higher output generate higher total costs. The coefficient for the time trend is not significant, but the coefficient of the quadratic term for the time trend is positive and significant, which implies an increase in the level of inefficiency for the analysed period.

The impact of environmental variables on the level and variability of cost efficiency reveals important findings. As we can see, the country's effects play an important role in explaining inefficiency levels. Compared to Argentina, all the countries included in the sample appear to have higher cost efficiency. Also, the inefficiency variability is lower in all the analysed countries, with the exception of Mexico and the Czech Republic, where the coefficients are not significant. The results are in line with expectations, because Argentina suffered severely from the 2000-2001 financial crisis.

The banks in Brazil are 38% more cost efficient than are those in Argentina. What is surprising is the fact that banks in Chile are only 20% more cost efficient than are those in Argentina, but this result can be explained by the fact that, for this country, observations for only the years 2008-2011 are included in the sample. With regard to the banking systems in Central and

Eastern Europe, we noticed that the banks in the Czech Republic had the best performance compared to those in Argentina, being more efficient in managing costs by 32%, while the banks in Romania are only at 18%. In South Eastern Asia, the banks in India are 40% more cost efficient than are those in Argentina, while the banks in Thailand were 12% more efficient.

Regarding the signs of the event dummies, we noticed that the coefficient associated with 2008 is negative but not significant, while 2009 saw an inefficiency growth for the banks included in the analysis. Furthermore, the variability of the inefficiency effect grew significantly in 2009. Taking this into consideration, we can state that the effects of the financial crisis on the banking sectors in the emerging countries were significant in 2009.

The effect of the country-specific variables on the inefficiency level is different. On one hand, a higher output growth pushed bank cost efficiency down. This result can be explained by the high competition and, implicitly, by the higher resources that banks needed in order to maintain and increase their market share. The results from the previous studies regarding the impact of the economic development on the cost efficiency are contradictory. Yildirim and Philippatos (2002) and Grigorian and Manole (2002) found a positive association between real GDP growth and banking costs, while Fries and Taci (2005) did not manage to identify a significant correlation between the two variables.

On the other hand, a higher ratio of domestic credit provided by banking sector over GDP will lead to an increase in the efficiency level. The result is in line with expectations, if we take into consideration that the level of financial intermediation, with a positive impact on the banks expertise, will grow. The result is similar to other empirical research (Lensink et al., 2008).

The influence of the risk factors on inefficiency is mixed. A higher equity to asset ratio, which implies a lower solvency risk, will lead to a growth in inefficiency. It is likely that the high costs associated with equity will not compensate for the benefits obtained from barrowing funds at a lower cost. A lower risk of failure, implying a higher Z score, will improve the banks' cost efficiency level and will reduce the variability of the inefficiency effect. A growth of net loans to customer and short-term funding ratio will reduce the banks' inefficiency levels but will generate an increase in variability of the inefficiency effect. Burki and Niazi (2010) obtained a similar relation between this ratio and inefficiency level.

An increase in the ROA ratio will lead to higher cost efficiency, indicating that banks with higher performance operate more efficiently. The result is similar with the efficiency literature findings, implying that banks with a

Table 4. Estimation results for the cost frontier

Dependent Variable ln(TC/PC)	Coefficient
Independent Variables	
ln(TL)	0.9165*
ln(OEA)	0.0946***
ln(PF/PC)	0.9259*
$\ln(TL)^2$	0.0918*
$\ln(OEA)^2$	0.0953*
$\ln(PF/PC)^2$	0.0035
$\ln(TL)\times\ln(OEA)$	- 0.1877*
$\ln(TL)\times\ln(PF/PC)$	0.0535*
$\ln(OEA)\times\ln(PF/PC)$	-0.0611*
Year	-0.0160
$Year^2$	0.0032*
$\ln(TL)\times year$	0.0033
$\ln(OEA)\times year$	-0.0054***
$\ln(PF/PC)\times year$	-0.0002
Constant	-0.0747
Effects on μ_{it}	
Brazil	-0.3817*
Chile	-0.2021*
Mexico	-0.3162*
Bulgaria	-0.1967*
Czech Republic	-0.3201*
Poland	-0.2845*
Romania	-0.1867*
Russia	-0.2604*
Hungary	-0.2228*
China	-0.2930*

continued on following page

Table 4. Continued

Dependent Variable ln(TC/PC)	Coefficient
Philippines	-0.2006*
India	-0.4055*
Indonesia	-0.3292*
Malaysia	-0.3290*
Thailand	-0.1283*
Year 2008	-0.0013
Year 2009	0.0296*
GDP growth rate	0.0026**
Domestic credit to GDP ratio	-0.0008**
Equity to total assets ratio	0.0048*
Z score	-0.0001*
Net loans to customer and short-term funding ratio	-0.0042*
ROA	-0.0150*
Noninterest income to gross revenues	0.0009*
Constant	0.9009*
Effects on σ^2_{it}	
Brazil	-0.3141
Chile	-1.2855*
Mexico	0.3688
Bulgaria	-2.0163*
Czech Republic	-0.4475
Poland	-0.5944**
Romania	-1.3094*
Russia	-0.5179**
Hungary	-2.0088*
China	-3.2508*
Philippines	-2.2304*
India	-2.8963*
Indonesia	-2.1531*
Malaysia	-2.1922*
Thailand	-2.8039*
Year 2008	0.1014
Year 2009	0.3924**
GDP growth rate	-0.0010

continued on following page

Table 4. Continued

Dependent Variable ln(TC/PC)	Coefficient
Domestic credit to GDP ratio	0.0157*
Equity to total assets ratio	0.0528*
Z score	-0.0097*
Net loans to customer and short term funding ratio	0.0077*
ROA	0.0208
Noninterest income to gross revenues	0.0179*
Constant	-5.5719*
σ_{ν}	-5.6691*
Number of observations	2950
Log-likelihood	2163.4699

Notes: *denotes a test statistic significance at the 1% level; **denotes a test statistic significance at the 5% level; ***denotes a test statistic significance at the 10% level.

higher level of profitability are more efficient (Fries & Taci, 2005; Zajc, 2006; Hermes & Nhung, 2010). A growth of the noninterest income in gross revenues will increase the level of bank inefficiency and will lead to an increase in the variance of the inefficiency effect, reflecting the bank's inability to correlate the costs with the revenue from non-traditional activities, but also the lack of expertise of commercial banks from transition countries in these activities.

Table 4 presents the overall effects of the country-specific variables and bank-specific variables on the level and variability of the inefficiency. The model specifications allow us to calculate the nonmonotonic effects. The marginal effects on the mean and variance of the inefficiency are computed using Equations 4 and 5. Table 5 presents the results.

Our empirical results suggest that a higher GDP growth rate will increase the level of inefficiency. This result may reflect an unsustainable bank management behaviour, who in periods of economic growth adopt policies that can generate inefficiency (i.e. easing credit standards) in order to gain market share and, implicitly, to obtain higher bonuses. The variability of bank inefficiency is lower if the GDP growth rate is higher. We find that the positive effect of domestic credit to GDP ratio on the level and variability of bank efficiency is higher if this rate grows. Hence, we conclude that banks in countries with a more developed financial sector have a higher level of efficiency and lower inefficiency variability.

Regarding the bank-specific variables, the results indicate that equity to total assets ratio and noninterest income to gross revenues show a similar pattern of the marginal effects on $E(u_{it})$ and $V\left(u_{it}\right)$. The higher the level of these ratios, the higher the influence on the level and variation of inefficiency will be. Regarding business orientation and revenue diversification we find that the the focus of the banks towards incomes from activities, such as investment banking, asset management, insurance underwriting, leads to a decrease in the level of efficiency. Z score and ROA have a nonlinear effect on $E(u_{it})$ and $V\left(u_{it}\right)$. The former findings suggest that banks that follow a more cautious strategy, characterized by a lower risk appetite and average expectations on profitability, have a higher efficiency index.

A net loan to customer and short term funding ratio located in the 5th group implies a lower influence on the level of inefficiency, and also a significant growth of the variance of the inefficiency. These findings show the existence of a liquidity risk in the case where such a ratio is very high. As a result, the banks that are efficient in the financial intermediation process, but which do not undertake a high liquidity risk, have a lower level of inefficiency. Also, the variation of inefficiency is lower. Considering this result and also the effect of the noninterest income to gross revenues ratio on the level and variability of inefficiency, we conclude that traditional deposit-taking and loan-making still remain the most efficient activity of the banks, offering a stable level to earnings.

Cost Efficiency Differences Across Countries

Country cost efficiency results show significant differences (see Table 6). In comparison with Latin America and Central and Eastern Europe, the banking systems in transition countries in South Eastern Asia appear to have a higher cost efficiency level. The banking system in Argentina is the most inefficient over the sample period, while the banking system in India has the highest level of efficiency. In Latin America, the banking system in Brazil appears to be the most efficient. In Central and Eastern Europe, the Hungarian banking system has the highest level of efficiency, while the Romanian banking system has the lowest cost efficiency. In South Eastern Asia the banking system in the Philippines appears to have the lowest cost efficiency score. The BRIC countries, especially Brazil, China and India, present higher cost efficiency.

Over the period 2005 to 2009 the efficiency index shows inverse U shape-like patterns. Most of the banking systems in our sample have improved the

Table 5. Marginal effects of cost efficiency determinants

Quintile	Mean of Variables	Average Cost Efficiency	Marginal Effect on $E(u_{it})$	Marginal Effect on $V(u_{it})$
By GDP Growth Rate				
1st	-0.4025	0.6931	0.0022***	0.00005***
3rd	6.2906	0.7173	0.0024***	-0.0001***
5th	10.7410	0.7551	0.0026***	-0.0001***
By Domestic Credit to GDP Ratio				
1st	29.3945	0.6448	-0.0002*	0.0030*
3rd	61.7772	0.7315	-0.0007***	0.0002***
5th	139.6680	0.7380	-0.0008***	0.0001***
By Equity to Total Assets Ratio				
1st	4.8175	0.7458	0.0049***	0.0003***
3rd	9.0344	0.6970	0.0052***	0.0008***
5th	21.1547	0.7004	0.0078***	0.0134*
By Z Score				
1st	6.4828	0.6609	-0.0005***	-0.0007**
3rd	22.5633	0.7170	-0.0003***	-0.0001***
5th	77.0949	0.7471	-0.0004***	-0.0017*
By Net Loans to Customer and Short Term Funding Ratio				
1st	41.3448	0.6163	-0.0041***	0.0001***
3rd	68.6583	0.7416	-0.0041***	0.0001***
5th	122.3961	0.7656	-0.0023***	0.0017*
By ROA				
1st	-0.7750	0.6822	-0.0132***	0.0009*
3rd	1.1529	0.7328	-0.0142***	0.0001***
5th	3.1373	0.6866	-0.0117***	0.0007**
By Noninterest Income to Gross Revenues				
1st	3.9750	0.7599	0.0011***	0.0002***
3rd	28.2818	0.7294	0.0011***	0.0002***
5th	61.0427	0.6201	0.0017***	0.0041*

Notes: *denotes a test statistically significance at the 1% level; **denotes test statistic significance at the 5% level; ***denotes a test statistic significance at the 10% level.

efficiency over the period 2005 to 2008 and presented a downturn in 2009. Afterwards, bank cost efficiency improved. Moreover, the results show that the banking system in South Eastern Asia returned in 2011 to efficiency levels similar to the ones registered in 2008, indicating that the effects of the financial crisis were less significant for the banks in this region.

Hereinafter, we have presented the marginal effects of the exogenous variables on $E(u_{it})$ and $V(u_{it})$ for each country (see Table 7). The objective of this analysis is to see if the marginal effects of the exogenous variables on the level and variability of the inefficiency differ across countries.

The findings suggest that the effect of the GDP growth rate on the level of bank efficiency is similar as impact in most of the countries analysed. In China, the Philippines and India, unlike the rest of the countries included in our study, the growth of the GDP rate leads to a lower variation of the inefficiency. The development of the financial sector has different effects across countries. Somewhat counterintuitive, in Brazil and Mexico, an increase of the domestic credit to GDP ratio will lead to a growth of the level of inefficiency. For the rest of the countries, the results show a decrease in the level of inefficiency as a consequence of the increase of this rate, with a significant impact for the banks in South Eastern Asia.

The equity to total assets ratio has a similar effect on the level and variation of inefficiency across countries. Regarding the magnitude of the impact, the results indicate a higher effect on the level of inefficiency for the banks in Argentina, Brazil and Mexico. Interestingly, Z score effect on the level and variability of the inefficiency is not statistically significant for the banks in Argentina, which also register the lowest level of efficiency. In terms of sign and magnitude, net loans to customer and short-term funding ratio have a similar effect in most of the analysed countries.

The results indicate a significant effect of the noninterest income to gross revenues ratio on the level of inefficiency for the banks in Argentina, Brazil and Mexico. The year 2008 had a different effect on the level of inefficiency across the sample countries. In 2008, the efficiency level of the banks in Argentina, Brazil, Chile, Mexico, the Czech Republic, Poland and Russia dropped, whereas the efficiency of the banks in Bulgaria, Romania, Hungary, China, the Philippines, India and Indonesia has increased. One possible explanation for this is that the scale and the speed of propagation of the effects of the financial crisis in the transition countries were different in 2008. In 2009, the efficiency of the banks across transition countries shows similar patterns, implying a significant decrease on the efficiency level and an increased variation.

Table 6. Mean cost efficiency by country and year

	2005	2006	2007	2008	2009	2010	2011	Total
Argentina	0.4447	0.4791	0.5235	0.5471	0.5240	0.5177	0.5538	0.5152
Brazil	0.7638	0.7693	0.7709	0.8037	0.7388	0.7875	0.8224	0.7795
Chile	n.a.	n.a.	n.a.	0.7885	0.6537	0.6862	0.7617	0.7225
Mexico	0.7946	0.7662	0.7029	0.7194	0.6486	0.6464	0.6590	0.6989
Bulgaria	0.6034	0.6318	0.6837	0.7166	0.7204	0.7105	0.7224	0.6891
Czech Republic	0.6527	0.6860	0.7060	0.7291	0.7097	0.7067	0.7287	0.7024
Poland	0.6329	0.6302	0.6582	0.7325	0.6956	0.6873	0.7298	0.6851
Romania	0.5939	0.5917	0.6637	0.6975	0.6746	0.6184	0.6490	0.6424
Russia	0.7186	0.7241	0.7413	0.6561	0.6330	0.6852	0.7012	0.6926
Hungary	0.7164	0.7233	0.7355	0.7371	0.7243	0.6980	0.7080	0.7206
China	0.7538	0.7558	0.7573	0.7479	0.7261	0.7340	0.7370	0.7424
Philippines	0.5970	0.6028	0.5992	0.6226	0.5982	0.5871	0.5929	0.6000
India	0.7841	0.8003	0.8020	0.8142	0.7893	0.8168	0.8389	0.8069
Indonesia	0.7486	0.7484	0.7529	0.7656	0.7432	0.7579	0.7752	0.7566
Malaysia	0.7975	0.7951	0.7810	0.7997	0.7596	0.7680	0.7840	0.7827
Thailand	0.6842	0.7154	0.7255	0.7211	0.6642	0.6843	0.7519	0.7065
Total	0.6857	0.6946	0.7069	0.7249	0.6877	0.6932	0.7197	0.7027

CONCLUSION

This study studied the cost efficiency of commercial banks in 16 emerging countries over the period 2005 to 2011, using a heteroscedastic SFA model. In our opinion, it is of major importance to identify the way in which the level and variability of cost efficiency in the emerging countries evolved. Another important objective of the study was to investigate the determinants of the level and variability of cost efficiency. In order to study the country's effect on the cost efficiency of banks, we created dummy variables for each country. Also, we included country-specific variables and bank-specific variables in the model. The country-level variables are the real GDP growth and the domestic credit provided by banking sector over GDP. The bank-specific variables included in our model -equity to total assets ratio, Z score, net loans to customer and short-term funding ratio, ROA and noninterest income to gross revenues ratio- are used to measure the marginal effects of solvency risk, failure risk, liquidity risk, efficiency of financial intermediation, bank

Table 7. Marginal effects on $E(u_{it})$ and $V(u_{it})$ by country

		GDP Growth Rate	Domestic Credit to GDP Ratio	Equity to Total Assets Ratio	Z Score	Net Loans to Customer and Short Term Funding Ratio	ROA	Noninterest Income to Gross Revenues	Year 2008	Year 2009
Argentina	Marginal effect on $E(u_{it})$	0.0025***	0.0002	0.0083***	-0.0008	-0.0035***	-0.0130***	0.0021***	0.0057***	0.0553***
	Marginal effect on $V(u_{it})$	-0.0004	0.0076	0.026	-0.0047	0.0036	0.0094	0.0088	0.0494	0.1928
Brazil	Marginal effect on $E(u_{it})$	0.0013***	0.0012***	0.0082***	-0.0011***	-0.0015***	-0.0061***	0.0024***	0.0098***	0.0570***
	Marginal effect on $V(u_{it})$	0.0001***	0.0010***	0.0039***	-0.0007***	0.0002	0.0003***	0.0013***	0.0067**	0.0282***
Chile	Marginal effect on $E(u_{it})$	0.0022***	-0.0002***	0.0059***	-0.0004***	-0.0034***	-0.0122***	0.0014***	0.0021***	0.0380***
	Marginal effect on $V(u_{it})$	0.0001***	0.0003***	0.0014***	-0.0002***	0.0001***	0.0001	0.0005***	0.0024***	0.0102***
Mexico	Marginal effect on $E(u_{it})$	0.0019***	0.0008***	0.0084***	-0.0010***	-0.0025***	-0.0094***	0.0023***	0.0081***	0.0576***
	Marginal effect on $V(u_{it})$	0.0001	0.0026	0.0091	-0.0016	0.0010	0.0024	0.0030	0.0168	0.0674
Bulgaria	Marginal effect on $E(u_{it})$	0.0025***	-0.0008***	0.0049***	-0.0002***	-0.0040***	-0.0144***	0.0009***	-0.0009***	0.0298***
	Marginal effect on $V(u_{it})$	-0.0001	0.0001***	0.0004***	-0.0001***	0.0001***	0.0001***	0.0001***	0.0007***	0.0028***
Czech Republic	Marginal effect on $E(u_{it})$	0.0024***	-0.0005***	0.0054***	-0.0003***	-0.0037***	-0.0133***	0.0012***	0.0007**	0.0341***
	Marginal effect on $V(u_{it})$	0.0001***	0.0002***	0.0009***	-0.0002***	0.0001***	0.0001	0.0003***	0.0016***	0.0069***
Poland	Marginal effect on $E(u_{it})$	0.0023***	-0.0004***	0.0055***	-0.0004***	-0.0036***	-0.0128***	0.0012***	0.0011***	0.0351***
	Marginal effect on $V(u_{it})$	0.0001***	0.0003***	0.0011***	-0.0002***	0.0001***	-0.0001	0.0003***	0.0018***	0.0079***
Romania	Marginal effect on $E(u_{it})$	0.0025***	-0.0007***	0.0050***	-0.0002***	-0.0040***	-0.0143***	0.0010***	-0.0006***	0.0308***
	Marginal effect on $V(u_{it})$	0.0001	0.0002***	0.0007***	-0.0001***	0.0001***	0.0002***	0.0002***	0.0013***	0.0051***
Russia	Marginal effect on $E(u_{it})$	0.0022***	-0.0003***	0.0057***	-0.0004***	-0.0034***	-0.0121***	0.0013***	0.0019***	0.0368***
	Marginal effect on $V(u_{it})$	0.0001***	0.0003***	0.0012***	-0.0002***	0.0001***	0.0001	0.0004***	0.0021***	0.0090***
Hungary	Marginal effect on $E(u_{it})$	0.0026***	-0.0008***	0.0050***	-0.0002***	-0.0041***	-0.0145***	0.0010***	-0.0009***	0.0303***
	Marginal effect on $V(u_{it})$	0.0001*	0.0001***	0.0005***	-0.0001***	0.0001***	0.0001***	0.0002***	0.0010***	0.0040***
China	Marginal effect on $E(u_{it})$	0.0026***	-0.0009***	0.0049***	-0.0002***	-0.0042***	-0.0149***	0.0009***	-0.0012***	0.0296***
	Marginal effect on $V(u_{it})$	-0.0001***	0.0001***	0.0002***	-0.0001***	0.0001***	0.0001***	0.0001***	0.0004***	0.0014***
Philippines	Marginal effect on $E(u_{it})$	0.0027***	-0.0009***	0.0049***	-0.0002***	-0.0042***	-0.0151***	0.0009***	-0.0014***	0.0296***
	Marginal effect on $V(u_{it})$	-0.0001***	0.0001***	0.0002***	-0.0001***	0.0001***	0.0001***	0.0001***	0.0004***	0.0015***

continued on following page

Table 7. Continued

		GDP Growth Rate	Domestic Credit to GDP Ratio	Equity to Total Assets Ratio	Z Score	Net Loans to Customer and Short Term Funding Ratio	ROA	Noninterest Income to Gross Revenues	Year 2008	Year 2009
India	Marginal effect on E(u_{it})	0.0026***	-0.0009***	0.0049***	-0.0002***	-0.0042***	-0.0149***	0.0009***	-0.0013***	0.0296***
	Marginal effect on V(u_{it})	-0.0001*	0.0001***	0.0001***	-0.0001***	0.0001***	0.0001***	0.0001***	0.0002***	0.0008***
Indonesia	Marginal effect on E(u_{it})	0.0025***	-0.0008***	0.0048***	-0.0002***	-0.0041***	-0.0144***	0.0009***	-0.0010***	0.0295***
	Marginal effect on V(u_{it})	0.0001**	0.0001***	0.0002***	-0.0001***	0.0001***	0.0001***	0.0001***	0.0003***	0.0013***
Malaysia	Marginal effect on E(u_{it})	0.0024***	-0.0006***	0.0050***	-0.0003***	-0.0037***	-0.0134***	0.0010***	-0.0001	0.0313***
	Marginal effect on V(u_{it})	0.0001***	0.0001***	0.0005***	-0.0001***	0.0001***	-0.0001	0.0002***	0.0008***	0.0036***
Thailand	Marginal effect on E(u_{it})	0.0026***	-0.0007***	0.0052***	-0.0002***	-0.0041***	-0.0145***	0.0010***	-0.0005	0.0320***
	Marginal effect on V(u_{it})	0.0001*	0.0001***	0.0007***	-0.0001***	0.0001***	0.0002***	0.0002***	0.0013***	0.0053***

Notes: *denotes test statistic significance at the 1% level; **denotes test statistic significance at the 5% level; ***denotes test statistic significance at the 10% level.

performance and degree of diversification on both the level and the variability of bank efficiency.

The results reveal important aspects. Most of the variables included in the model influence the level and variability of inefficiency and are significant, indicating a consistent estimation. The pattern and determinants of cost efficiency reveal some significant findings. Surprisingly, economic development leads to a growth in inefficiency. We interpreted this result as a consequence of the higher concurrence that put pressure on the banks' costs and of unsustainable bank management. Banks in countries with a more developed financial sector have a higher level of efficiency and lower inefficiency variability. We find that banks that follow a more cautious strategy, characterized by a lower risk appetite and average expectations on profitability, have a higher level of efficiency and a lower inefficiency variance. These results indicate that the banks with a higher appetite for risk also reflect a higher degree of inefficiency. We also find that banks that are efficient in the financial intermediation process, but which do not undertake a high liquidity risk, have a lower level of inefficiency. Also, the variation of inefficiency is lower. Income diversification leads to a lower cost efficiency. Therefore, the focus of the banks towards incomes from activities, such as investment banking, asset management, insurance underwriting, leads to a decrease in the level of efficiency.

Our empirical results suggest that the level and variability of the banks' cost efficiency are influenced by the country's effect, as this has a significant contribution to explaining banks' efficiency differences. The banking systems in transition countries in South Eastern Asia have a higher cost efficiency level. Moreover, the effects of the financial crisis were less significant for the banks in this region. The effects of cost efficiency determinants are different across countries. Nevertheless, in the countries from the same region we find some similarities in the results. In China, the Philippines and India, unlike the rest of the countries included in our study, the growth of the GDP rate leads to a lower variation of the inefficiency. In Brazil and Mexico, an increase of the domestic credit to GDP ratio will lead to a growth of the level of inefficiency. The results indicate a significant effect of the noninterest income to gross revenues ratio on the level of inefficiency for the banks in Argentina, Brazil and Mexico. The year 2008 has a different effect on the level of inefficiency across countries, indicating that the scale and the speed of propagation of the effects of the financial crisis in the transition countries were different in 2008. The effects of the financial crisis on banks were noticeable in 2009 across all countries, with cost efficiency decreasing by 2.96%, while the efficiency variability grew by 39%.

Our results have important implications for bank management and policy makers. Firstly, bank management should to pay more attention to cost efficiency, focus more on bank organization and on the structure of the services provided. Secondly, in times of economic growth, bank management should adopt cautious strategies and not manifest a pro-cyclical behaviour. Thirdly, commercial banks in transition countries should focus on the traditional deposit-taking and loan-making, which remains the most efficient activity. Fourthly, policy makers should enhance regional cooperation in order to reduce the effects of the financial crises and should consider adopting some counter-cyclical measures.

Admittedly, it would be interesting to investigate the effect of ownership on cost efficiency in this period, in order to see how foreign-owned banks and domestic banks responded to the financial crisis. We will leave this for future research.

REFERENCES

Afanasieff, T. S., Lhacer, P. M. V., & Nakane, M. I. (2002). The determinants of bank interest spread in Brazil. Central Bank of Brazil, Research Department.

Aigner, D. J., Lovell, C. A. K., & Schmidt, P. (1977). Formulation and estimation of stochastic frontier production function models. *Journal of Econometrics*, *6*(1), 21–37. doi:10.1016/0304-4076(77)90052-5

Battese, G. E., & Coelli, T. J. (1995). A model for technical inefficiency effects in a stochastic frontier production function for panel data. *Empirical Economics*, *20*(2), 325–332. doi:10.1007/BF01205442

Brissimis, S. N., Delis, M. D., & Papanikolaou, N. I. (2008). Exploring the nexus between banking sector reform and performance: Evidence from newly acceded EU countries. *Journal of Banking & Finance*, *32*(12), 2674–2683. doi:10.1016/j.jbankfin.2008.07.002

Burki, A. A., & Niazi, G. S. K. (2010). Impact of financial reforms on efficiency of state-owned, private and foreign banks in Pakistan. *Applied Economics*, *42*(24), 3147–3160. doi:10.1080/00036840802112315

Caudill, S. B., Ford, J. M., & Gropper, D. M. (1995). Frontier estimation and firm-specific inefficiency measures in the presence of heteroscedasticity. *Journal of Business & Economic Statistics*, *13*, 105–111.

Cetorelli, N., & Goldberg, L. S. (2010). Global banks and international shock transmission: Evidence from the crisis. *IMF Economic Review*, *59*(1), 41–76. doi:10.1057/imfer.2010.9

Claessens, S., & van Horen, N. (2012). Foreign banks: Trends, impact and financial stability. IMF.

Cull, R., & Martinez Peria, M. (2012). Bank ownership and lending patterns during the 2008- 2009 financial crisis: evidence from Latin America and Eastern Europe. World Bank.

Figueira, C., Nellis, J., & Parker, D. (2009). The effects of ownership on bank efficiency in Latin America. *Applied Economics*, *41*(18), 2353–2368. doi:10.1080/00036840701222546

Fries, S., & Taci, A. (2005). Cost efficiency of banks in transition: Evidence from 289 banks in 15 post-communist countries. *Journal of Banking & Finance*, *29*(1), 55–81. doi:10.1016/j.jbankfin.2004.06.016

Gelos, R. G., & Roldós, J. (2004). Consolidation and market structure in emerging market banking systems. *Emerging Markets Review*, *5*(1), 39–59. doi:10.1016/j.ememar.2003.12.002

Grigorian, D., & Manole, V. (2002). Determinants of commercial bank performance in transition: An application of data envelopment analysis. IMF.

Havranek, T., & Irsova, Z. (2013). Determinants of Bank Performance in Transition Countries: A Data Envelopment Analysis, *Transition. Studies and Reviews (General Fisheries Commission for the Mediterranean)*, *20*, 1–17.

Havrylchyk, O. (2006). Efficiency of the Polish banking industry: Foreign versus domestic banks. *Journal of Banking & Finance*, *30*(7), 1975–1996. doi:10.1016/j.jbankfin.2005.07.009

Hermes, N., & Nhung, V. T. H. (2010). The impact of financial liberalization on bank efficiency: Evidence from Latin America and Asia. *Applied Economics*, *42*(26), 3351–33. doi:10.1080/00036840802112448

Ioannidis, C., Molyneux, P., & Pasiouras, F. (2008) The relationship between bank efficiency and stock returns: evidence from Asia and Latin America. University of Bath.

Jeanneau, S. (2007). *Banking systems: characteristics and structural changes. Bank for International Settlements.*

Kasman, A., & Carvallo, O. (2013). Efficiency and Risk in Latin American Banking: Explaining Resilience. *Emerging Markets Finance & Trade*, *49*(2), 105–130. doi:10.2753/REE1540-496X490207

Klingen, C. (2013). *Perspectives on Growth Prospects for Central, Eastern and Southeastern Europe, Banking in Central and Eastern Europe and Turkey - Challenges and Opportunities*. Luxembourg: European Investment Bank.

Koutsomanoli-Filippaki, A., Margaritis, D., & Staikouras, C. (2009). Efficiency and productivity growth in the banking industry of Central and Eastern Europe. *Journal of Banking & Finance*, *33*(3), 557–567. doi:10.1016/j.jbankfin.2008.09.009

Kumbhakar, S. C., Ghosh, S., & McGuckin, J. T. (1991). A generalized production frontier approach for estimating determinants of inefficiency in US dairy farms. *Journal of Business & Economic Statistics*, *9*, 279–286.

Lai, H.-P., & Huang, C. J. (2010). Likelihood ratio tests for model selection of stochastic frontier models. *Journal of Productivity Analysis*, *34*(1), 3–13. doi:10.100711123-009-0160-8

Lensink, R., Meesters, A., & Naaborg, I. (2008). Bank efficiency and foreign ownership: Do good institutions matter? *Journal of Banking & Finance*, *32*(5), 834–844. doi:10.1016/j.jbankfin.2007.06.001

Lepetit, L., Nys, E., Rous, P., & Tarazi, A. (2008). Bank income structure and risk: An empirical analysis of European banks. *Journal of Banking & Finance*, *32*(8), 1452–1467. doi:10.1016/j.jbankfin.2007.12.002

Liu, H., & Wilson, J. O. S. (2010). The profitability of banks in Japan. *Applied Financial Economics*, *20*(24), 1851–1866. doi:10.1080/09603107.2010.526577

Matoušek, R., & Taci, A. (2004). Efficiency in banking: Empirical evidence from the Czech Republic. *Economics of Planning*, *37*, 225–244.

Meeusen, W., & van den Broeck, J. (1977). Technical efficiency and dimension of the firm: Some results on the use of frontier production functions. *Empirical Economics*, *2*(2), 109–122. doi:10.1007/BF01767476

Montoro, C., & Rojas-Suarez, L. (2012) Credit at times of stress: Latin American lessons from the global financial crisis. BIS.

Pancurova, D., & Lyocsa, S. (2013). Determinants of Commercial Banks' Efficiency: Evidence from 11 CEE Countries. *Czech Journal of Economics and Finance*, *63*, 152–179.

Sealey, C. Jr, & Lindley, J. T. (1977). Inputs, outputs and a theory of production and cost at depository financial institution. *The Journal of Finance*, *32*(4), 1251–1266. doi:10.1111/j.1540-6261.1977.tb03324.x

Staikouras, C., Mamatzakis, E., & Koutsomanoli-Filippaki, A. (2008). Cost efficiency of the banking industry in the South Eastern European region. *Journal of International Financial Markets, Institutions and Money*, *18*(5), 483–497. doi:10.1016/j.intfin.2007.07.003

Sun, L., & Chang, T.-P. (2011). A comprehensive analysis of the effects of risk measures on bank efficiency: Evidence from emerging Asian countries. *Journal of Banking & Finance*, *35*(7), 1727–1735. doi:10.1016/j.jbankfin.2010.11.017

Tabak, B. M., Fazio, D. M., & Cajueiro, D. O. (2013). Systemically important banks and financial stability: The case of Latin America. *Journal of Banking & Finance*, *37*(10), 3855–3866. doi:10.1016/j.jbankfin.2013.06.003

Wang, H.-J. (2002). Heteroscedasticity and non-monotonic efficiency effects of a stochastic frontier model. *Journal of Productivity Analysis*, *18*(3), 241–253. doi:10.1023/A:1020638827640

Wang, W. K., Lu, W. M., & Wang, Y. H. (2013). The relationship between bank performance and intellectual capital in East Asia. *Quality & Quantity*, *47*(2), 1041–1062. doi:10.100711135-011-9582-2

Williams, J., & Nguyen, N. (2005). Financial liberalisation, crisis, and restructuring: A comparative study of bank performance and bank governance in South East Asia. *Journal of Banking & Finance*, *29*(8-9), 2119–2154. doi:10.1016/j.jbankfin.2005.03.011

Yildirim, H. S., & Philippatos, G. C. (2002) Efficiency of banks: Recent evidence from the transition economies of Europe, 1993–2003. University of Tennessee.

Zajc, P. (2006). A Comparative Study of Bank Efficiency in Central and Eastern Europe: The Role of Foreign Ownership. *International Finance Review*, *6*, 117–156. doi:10.1016/S1569-3767(05)06006-1

Chapter 2
The Relationship Between Bank Efficiency and Risk and Productivity Patterns in the Romanian Banking System

ABSTRACT

This chapter aims to provide additional empirical evidence on the relationship between bank efficiency and risk and productivity patterns in the Romanian banking system. The empirical analysis is based on a data envelopment model and an input slack-based productivity index, in order to examine commercial bank cost efficiency and productivity patterns in the Romanian banking system over the period of 2005 to 2011. The empirical results lead to the conclusion that the contribution of the funds to the increase in productivity is the most significant, while that of labor and capital productivity is lower.

INTRODUCTION

The banking system has a major influence on the economic development of a country. Moreover, within an emerging economy, the efficient functioning of the banking system in allocating resources represents a condition without which the shift to a developed economy cannot be achieved. In Romania, the banking system is the most important part of the financial system, holding more than 90% of its financial assets. Given these conditions, the efficiency

DOI: 10.4018/978-1-5225-9269-3.ch002

and productivity of the Romanian banking system are two elements without which the economy cannot grow in a sustainable and robust manner.

In the last two decades, the banking system in Romania has evolved in a similar manner to the ones in the other Eastern and Central European countries. To be more precise, the shift from a centralized economy to a market economy involved the reorganization of the banking system on two levels and also the reform of the legislative framework, liberalization and privatization. Furthermore, at the end of the century, the banking system in Romania had to face a crisis characterized by bank failures and by severe deterioration of the performance of other banks. Getting rid of non-viable banks and also the end of the privatization process marked, at the beginning of 2000, the entrance of the banking system in a new development period.

This was followed by a period in which the banking system benefited from regained economic growth. Until 2008 the banks in Romania had been extending their loan portfolios in conditions of increased profitability. An important particularity of the banking system in Romania is that more than 90% of the financial assets are owned by foreign banks or banks controlled by foreign shareholders (National Bank of Romania, 2013). Moreover, the Romanian banking system was significantly financed by foreign funds. Thus, the banking system in Romania, as well as other banking systems in Central and Eastern Europe, became vulnerable in the face of sudden slowdown of the external loans that occurred in the autumn of 2008 (Montoro & Rojas-Suarez, 2012; Klingen, 2013). Also, the banking system in Romania was affected after 2008 by a considerable increase of the nonperforming loans. Thus, if in 2008 the percentage of nonperforming loans was 2.75%, in 2013 it had reached 21.75% (National Bank of Romania, 2013). The high percentage of nonperforming loans reflects an unreliable policy adopted by credit institutions in a period of economic growth and also the existence of various unsustainable domestic booms. In our opinion, in Romania, the financial crisis has substantially modified the way banks function and as such the evaluation of efficiency, productivity and risks became the most important component of banks' strategy.

With regard to the organization, the Romanian banking system is a universal one, dominated by commercial banks. Moreover, for the credit institutions in Romania, there is no aspect that particularizes their form of organization, the structure of shareholders or the nature of the ongoing activities. Most of the credit institutions are organized as banks, despite the fact that the law allows the establishment of specialized credit institutions. It is worth mentioning that the banking system in Romania encompasses two building societies, as well as one central credit cooperatives, which include 46 credit cooperatives. Nevertheless, the market percentage of the building societies and credit cooperatives is under 1%.

Having in view the major importance of the banking system within the financial system and that of the commercial banks within the banking system and also the risks the banks have faced in the context of the financial crisis, this study aims at emphasizing the nexus between banks' efficiency and the risks they have undertaken. Moreover, we have also highlighted the relation between banks' efficiency, concentration and performance. Banks' cost efficiency and its determinants will be evaluated in two stages. Firstly, we will obtain the efficiency scores through the data envelopment analysis. Secondly, through a Tobit regression, we will evaluate the determinants of banks' efficiency. A second objective of the study is to emphasize the patterns of banks' productivity and also its sources. To this aim we will use an advanced productivity index that allows the disintegration of productivity in accordance with the contribution of each input (Chang et al., 2012).

The rest of the study is organized as follows: section II reviews the literature on efficiency studies, paying special attention to Romanian commercial banks. Section III presents the methodology framework adopted. Section IV describes the data and variables. Section V displays the empirical results. Finally, section VI presents the conclusions.

LITERATURE REVIEW

In the economic literature there are various studies that use stochastic frontier analysis (SFA) or data envelopment analysis (DEA) to estimate bank efficiency and the Malmquist index or Luenberger index to estimate productivity growth. Hereinafter, we will present those studies that investigated bank efficiency determinants and productivity growth in transition countries and that included the Romanian banking system in the sample.

A significant number of studies focused on cross-country research. Most of these studies aimed at identifying the relationship between efficiency and ownership but was also focused on the factors that influenced efficiency. Koutsomanoli-Filippaki et al. (2009) studied bank efficiency and productivity change in Central and Eastern Europe over the period 1998-2003. The findings revealed strong links of competition and concentration with bank efficiency. Also, productivity declined in the whole region. With respect to the Romanian banking system, the results showed that banks in Romania are among the least efficient and exhibit a clear downward trend in productivity. Fries and Taci (2005) investigated cost efficiency in Eastern European banking systems. They showed that the association between a country's progress in banking reform and cost efficiency is non-linear.

With regard to the Romanian banking system, the findings revealed lower efficiency in comparison with other countries included in the sample. Andrieş and Cocriş (2010) analysed bank efficiency in Romania, the Czech Republic and Hungary over the period 2000-2006. They also found that Romanian banks are among the least efficient. The authors showed that asset quality, bank size, inflation rate, reform, liberalisation and ownership are the main factors that influence the efficiency level in these countries. Spulbar and Niţoi (2014) studied the determinants of bank efficiency in transition economies over the period 2005-2011. The findings revealed that banks with a more cautious strategy, characterized by lower risk appetite and average expectations on profitability, have higher cost efficiency. Also, that traditional deposit-taking and loan-making still remain the most efficient activity of the banks.

Country cost efficiency revealed that the effects of the financial crisis were less significant in South Eastern Asia in comparison with Latin America and Central and Eastern Europe. Also, Romanian banks have the lowest cost efficiency level in Central and Eastern Europe. Pancurova and Lyocsa (2013) analysed the determinants of bank efficiency for 11 Central and Eastern European countries over the period 2005-2008. Their results showed that bank size and financial capitalization are positively associated with cost and revenue efficiency, while loans-to-assets ratio was negatively associated with cost efficiency, but positively associated with revenue efficiency. However, a lot of studies emphasize the ownership effect on bank efficiency in transition economies. In general, most of the results indicated a positive effect of foreign ownership and privatisation on bank efficiency (Koutsomanoli-Filippaki et al., 2009; Bonin et al., 2005; Fries and Taci, 2005; Yildirim & Philippatos, 2007; Fang et al., 2011; Havranek & Irsova, 2013).

In the literature there are also studies that analysed only the Romanian banking system. Asaftei and Kumbhakar (2008) estimated the impact of the regulation implemented by central bank in Romania over the bank cost efficiency in the period 1996-2002. The findings showed that the cost of technical inefficiency decreases in the years following tightening of regulations. Niţoi (2009) examined the efficiency and productivity of Romanian banks over the period 2006-2008. The results indicated low cost efficiency scores and that foreign banks and larger banks had higher efficiency than domestic banks and smaller banks, respectively.

Andrieş et al. (2013) investigated the efficiency and productivity of Romanian banks over the period 2004 to 2008. The results showed that private banks are more efficient and have a higher productivity in comparison with public banks. The study examined the determinants of bank efficiency. The findings revealed that ROA and total assets positively influenced overall efficiency, while net interest margin negatively influenced bank efficiency. Munteanu et al. (2013) analyzed the productivity of Romanian banks over the period 2006-2011. Their findings indicated that scale efficiency and management efficiency influenced the productivity growth and that foreign banks outperform domestic banks.

METHODOLOGY

In order to estimate cost efficiency scores, we will use DEA. Then, we will assess efficiency determinants using a Tobit regression. We used a Tobit regression because it can account for truncated data. As we have mentioned earlier, most of the studies use either SFA, either DEA to estimate bank efficiency. In comparison with a parametric approach, a non-parametric DEA does not require a particular functional form for the frontier. Therefore, in the case of a parametric approach, a misspecification of the production frontier may lead to overstating inefficiency. On the other hand, DEA does not allow for the presence of a random error term. As a result, any deviation from the efficiency frontier is associated with inefficiency. The productivity patterns are computed using an index that disaggregates total factor productivity growth into each input productivity change (Chang et al., 2012).

Charnes et al. (1978) proposed a model based on the allocation of the inputs and outputs for each decision-making unit. The efficiency is measured using linear programming. Coelli (1996) computed the dual solution of DEA using duality as follows:

$$\min \theta_k$$

subject to

$$-y_{ik} + \sum_{n=1}^{N} \lambda_n y_{in} \geq 0,$$

$$\theta x_{jk} - \sum_{n=1}^{N} \lambda_n x_{jn} \geq 0,$$

$$\lambda_n \geq 0$$

where θ represents the technical efficiency of the ith DMU and λ is a constant. In our study, we will use input prices. Therefore, the cost minimization DEA model becomes:

$$\min w'_{jk} x^*_{jk}$$

subject to

$$-y_{ik} + \sum_{n=1}^{N} \lambda_n y_{in} \geq 0,$$

$$x^*_{jk} - \sum_{n=1}^{N} \lambda_n x_{jn} \geq 0,$$

$$\lambda_n \geq 0$$

where w'_{jk} and x^*_{jk} are the input price and cost minimizing input quantities, respectively, for the kth DMU.

To measure productivity, we used the input slack-based productivity index (ISP) proposed by Chang et al. (2012). The productivity index is computed using input-oriented directional distance functions and a Färe–Lovell efficiency measure, as follows:

$$ISP_i = \frac{1}{2}\left[\left(\vec{D}_{i(t)}\left(x^t, y^t\right) - \vec{D}_{i(t)}\left(x^{t+1}, y^{t+1}\right)\right) + \left(\vec{D}_{i(t+1)}\left(x^t, y^t\right) - \vec{D}_{i(t+1)}\left(x^{t+1}, y^{t+1}\right)\right)\right]$$

In order to compute the input-oriented directional distance functions, Chang et al. (2012) used a Färe–Lovell efficiency measure, introduced by Briec (2000). Using linear programming, the distance functions for observation o in time t is calculated as follows:

$$\vec{D}_t\left(x^t, y^t\right) = \max \frac{1}{M}\left(\beta_1 + \ldots + \beta_M\right)$$

$$\text{s.t.} \sum_{j=1}^{N} \lambda_j x_{ij}^t \leq x_{io}^t \left(1 - \beta_i\right),$$

$$\sum_{j=1}^{N} \lambda_j y_{rj}^t \geq y_{ro}^t,$$

$$\lambda_j \geq 0, \beta_i \geq 0,$$

$$j = 1, \ldots, N; i = 1, \ldots, M; r = 1, \ldots, S.$$

where M are the inputs; S the outputs for each N objects in each time period of t; λ_j is an $n \times 1$ vector and β_i is a scalar that indicates indicates the proportional contraction of the ith input in order to catch up the efficient frontier. The ith input and rth output variable of the jth object are represented by x_{ij}^t and y_{rj}^t in time t, respectively. The efficiency measure introduced by Briec (2000) has the advantage of selecting a strong efficient vector onto the frontier, and it is based on the CRS assumption.

Chang et al. (2012) decomposed the total factor productivity change into the productivity change of individual input using the following formula:

$$TFPCH = EFFCH + TECHCH = \frac{1}{M}\left[EFFCH_1 + \ldots + EFFCH_M\right] + \frac{1}{M}\left[TECHCH_1 + \ldots + TECHCH_M\right] = \frac{1}{M}\left[ISP_1 + \ldots + ISP_M\right]$$

where $TFPCH$ is the total factor productivity change, $EFFCH$ is the efficiency change and $TECHCH$ is the technological change. The main advantage of the ISP index is that allows us to calculate how each input factor influences productivity.

DATA

Most of the studies use either the intermediation approach, which considers banks to be financial intermediaries that buy inputs in order to generate earning assets, either the production approach that treats banks as producers of financial services. Having in view the fact that the intermediation approach is closer to the main function of the bank as a financial intermediary (Sealey and Lindley, 1977), in our study we will use the first approach.

The output vector includes total loans and other earning assets. In order to ensure comparable quality, we have subtracted loan loss provisions from total loans (Havrylchyk, 2006). The input vector includes funds (total deposits and short-term funding), physical capital (total fixed assets) and labor (number of employees). The input prices are price of funds, price of capital and price of labor. The price of funds is measured by dividing total interest expenses by total deposits and other short term funding. The price of capital is defined by the ratio of other noninterest expenses to total fixed assets. The price of labor is calculated as personnel expenses divided by number of bank employees. All monetary values were deflated by using the Gross Domestic Product (GDP) deflator provided by the International Monetary Fund, with 2005 as the base year. To estimate productivity, we used the output and the input vector. The input prices were used, alongside output and input vector, to estimate cost efficiency.

Our sample covers a balanced panel dataset of 98 observations corresponding to 14 commercial banks in Romania over the period 2005 to 2011. The data were extracted from the Bankscope database. We should mention that the 14 commercial banks have a market share of over 60% in the banking system. Table 1 presents the summary statistics of the output and input variables.

As we have mentioned earlier, after we have estimated the efficiency scores for each bank, a Tobit regression is run in order to find the main determinants of bank efficiency. We used a Tobit regression because DEA efficiency scores are truncated above at 1, and there are many values of efficiency indices that are equal to 1. The Tobit model can be expressed as follows:

$$y_i = \begin{matrix} x_i\beta + e_i & if\; x_i\beta + e_i < 1 \\ 1 & otherwise \end{matrix}$$

Table 1. Descriptive statistics

	Mean	SD	Min.	Max.
Output Quantities (in Billion US $)				
Total loans	2.1199	3.1390	0.0650	13.6
Other earning assets	0.4622	0.6410	0.0026	3.1845
Input Quantities				
Deposits and short-term funding (in billion US $)	2.8268	4.1353	0.1001	19.2
Fixed Assets (in billion US $)	0.0952	0.1448	0.0028	0.6090
Number of employees	2809.735	3221.213	123	13486
Input Prices				
Price of funds	0.0483	0.0164	0.02	0.1
Price of labour	20.3976	6.1145	9.13	41.97
Price of capital	1.1523	1.2703	0.22	7.67

where y_i is the cost efficiency score, x_i is a vector that includes the explanatory variables, β represents the estimated parameters and e_i is the error term distributed.

Among the explanatory variables we have included bank concentration index, Z score, equity to total assets ratio, liquidity ratio, return on equity (ROE), net interest margin, loans to customer deposits ratio.

Bank concentration index is a proxy of competition in the banking industry. Bank concentration index was extracted from the World Bank Statistics Database. The relation between concentration and efficiency has been widely studied in the bank efficiency literature (Bikker & Haaf, 2002; Kasman & Yildirim, 2006; Yildirim and Philippatos (2007); Koutsomanoli-Filippaki et al., 2009, Hauner, 2005).

On one hand, higher concentration in the banking industry could lead to higher efficiency, if concentration is the result of superior management and greater efficiency in the production process (Demsetz, 1969). Also, Dick and Lehnert (2010) pointed that a more concentrated and competitive market lowers bank credit risk and increases lending efficiency. On the other hand, higher concentration could lead to a decline in bank efficiency, if concentration is associated with market power.

Z score, equity to total assets ratio and liquidity ratio are included in the analysis in order to capture the banks' risk taking. Z score is a measure of failure risk. Lepetit et al. (2008a) used Z score to measure the probability of bankruptcy for a bank. A higher Z score reflects a lower probability of failure. Hence, Z score should have a positive impact on bank cost efficiency. The Z score is computed on the basis of the following formula:

$$Z = \frac{ROA + EQ / TA}{SDROA}$$

where ROA is return on assets ratio; EQ / TA is the equity to total assets ratio and $SDROA$ is the standard deviation of the ROA.

Equity to total assets ratio is a measure of solvency risk. Its effect on efficiency is rather vague. On one hand, banks with higher ratio benefit from lower borrowing costs, which make them be perceived as more reliable, but they can also ignore potentially profitable investment opportunities. On the other hand, a lower ratio can indicate capital adequacy problems (Heffernan and Fu, 2010).

Liquid assets to deposits and short-term funding is a measure of liquidity risk. A higher ratio indicates a lower liquidity risk and reflects a bank´ ability to respond to loan demands. Also, banks with high liquidity can cope easily with possible unexpected deposit withdrawals or liquidity crises occurring on the interbank market. The influence that liquidity risk has on inefficiency should be negative.

ROE, net interest margin and loans to customer deposits ratio are included among the explanatory variables in order to measure banks' performance. ROE and the net interest margin are measures of bank profitability. Basically, banks with a high profitability rate should be more efficient. Moreover, the two rates are commonly used in the literature to describe the performance of banks (De Haas and van Lelyveld, 2006; Otchere, 2005; Xu, 2011). The net interest margin could be also a measure for credit risk. Maudos and de Guevara (2004) and Lepetit et al. (2008b) showed that banks tend to increase the interest margins if credit risk increase.

Fries and Taci (2005) consider that loans to customer deposits ratio is a measure of the efficiency of the financial intermediation process. Thus, a very low ratio could indicate banks´ incapacity to transform deposits into loans. Other authors see this ratio as a measure of the liquidity risk, higher values indicating an increased liquidity risk for banks (Williams and Nguyen, 2005). Basically, a higher ratio should have a positive impact on efficiency.

RESULTS

The cost efficiency score, as well as technical efficiency and allocative efficiency are presented in Table 2. The analysis of cost efficiency discloses important findings. Our results show that the cost efficiency has increased significantly in 2006. Interestingly, in 2007 we find that the banks' cost efficiency decreased. However, 2008 brought a major decrease in efficiency, its level reaching the lowest value for the analyzed period. In our opinion, this result may reflect the effects of the global financial crisis, which has significantly affected the banking system. Interestingly, banks' speed of reaction was quite remarkably. They have managed to rapidly increase the efficiency, and as a consequence the cost efficiency index increased in 2009, 2010 and 2011.

As mentioned earlier, an important objective of the study is emphasizing the determinants of cost efficiency and especially the nexus between efficiency and risks. Also, among efficiency determinants, we introduced, in addition to the risk factors, indicators that characterize concentration in the banking system and banks' performance. The results obtained are presented in Table 3.

Our results suggest that a high level of concentration in the banking system will lead to the lower cost efficiency level. The result supports Hicks's 'quiet life hypothesis' (QLH). Hicks's QLH assumes that in an uncompetitive market, more power market could generate inefficiency. The results in the efficiency literature are mixed. Berger and Hannan (1998), Weill (2004), Hauner (2005) indicated a negative relation between concentration and efficiency, while Kasman and Yildirim (2006), Yildirim and Philippatos (2007), Koutsomanoli-Filippaki et al. (2009) obtained a positive relation.

Table 2. Cost efficiency: Decomposition into technical and allocative efficiency

	Technical Efficiency	Allocative Efficiency	Cost Efficiency
2005	0.911	0.680	0.626
2006	0.914	0.914	0.750
2007	0.848	0.841	0.719
2008	0.782	0.762	0.589
2009	0.883	0.867	0.764
2010	0.906	0.886	0.804
2011	0.883	0.912	0.812

Table 3. Cost efficiency determinants

Dependent Variable	
Cost efficiency	
Independent Variables	
Bank concentration	-0.0110*
Z score	0.0295***
Equity to total assets ratio	-0.0235*
Liquid assets to deposits and short term funding	0.0025***
ROE	0.0009***
Net interest margin	-0.0457*
Loans to customer deposits ratio	0.0022*
Constant	1.5884*
Log-likelihood	7.1810
Sample size	98

Notes: Results are based on a Tobit regression censored above at 1. *denotes a test statistic significance at the 1% level; **denotes a test statistic significance at the 5% level; *** denotes a test statistic significance at the 10% level.

Also, our estimates suggest that the Z score, which measures the risk of failure, has a positive effect on efficiency. As a result, banks with a lower risk appetite and a lower risk of failure are more efficient. Surprisingly, equity to total assets ratio, a measure for solvency risk, has a negative influence on efficiency. Hence, commercial banks with a low solvency risk, namely a higher equity to assets ratio are more inefficient. This result may reflect either the fact that Romanian banks ignore potential investment opportunities, either the fact that they do not manage to borrow at a lower cost.

Our result is similar to that obtained by Sun and Chang (2011); Hermes and Nhung (2010), while Yildirim and Philippatos (2007), Zajc (2006), Berger and DeYoung (1997), Fries and Taci (2005), Hsiao et al. (2010) obtained a positive relation between efficiency and solvency risk. In line with expectations, banks with a higher liquidity ratio are more efficient. One possible explanation for this is that the banks that respond more promptly to the loan demands and to the needs of their customers manage their costs more efficiently.

Banks with a higher ROE are more efficient. The obtained outcome is similar to the efficiency literature findings that indicate the fact that banks with a higher level of profitability are more efficient (Zajc, 2006; Berger & Mester, 1997; Pastor et al., 1997; Yildirim & Philippatos, 2002; Hermes & Nhung, 2010). Surprisingly, the net interest margin has a negative influence on efficiency. The result can be explained through that fact that a higher interest margin is a sign of higher credit risk. Loans to customer deposits ratio have a positive influence on efficiency. Therefore, commercial banks with a higher level of financial intermediation are more cost efficient.

The second objective of the study was to identify the patterns of bank productivity in Romania and the factors which influenced it. The results obtained are presented in Table 4.

The evolution of total factor productivity index (TFP) shows a positive trend over the period 2005 to 2007. The highest productivity growth for the analyzed period was in 2007, when the productivity index increased 20.4%. In 2008 the level of productivity decreased by 3.8%. In our opinion, this result is caused by the negative impact of the global financial crisis on the banks in Romania.

In the period 2009-2011, banks have improved their productivity, significantly in 2009 and subsequently with lower rates of growth. Important aspects can be drawn from the analysis of the influence of funds, labor and capital on productivity. Thus, in 2006 and 2007, fund productivity, labor and capital had a positive influence on productivity. In 2008, the TFP index became negative. The results indicate that the productivity growth in 2009 was due to the significant growth of fund productivity; the labor and capital productivity growth being negative.

Basically, banks have managed to increase fund productivity with 33%. This result may reflect the fact the focus of banks towards increasing the efficiency of resources. On average, the contribution of fund productivity on the increase of productivity is the most significant, while that of the labor productivity is the least important.

Productivity can be decomposed in efficiency change and technological change. Efficiency change means that banks have moved closer to the efficient frontier. Hence, a positive/negative efficiency change indicates a catching up/falling behind effect. Technological change measures the technological progress/regress. Williams et al. (2011) states that a positive technological change, indicating that the efficient frontier has shifted out compared to the previous period, results from innovations and the adoption of new technologies by best-practice banks.

As we can observe from the data presented in Table 4, over the sample period the average growth of TFP has been of 6.09%. Also, efficiency change has a more significant contribution to the average growth of productivity. In fact, in 2006 and 2009, the results indicated an important growth in efficiency change, due to the efforts of inefficient banks to catch up with the best practice

Table 4. Annually productivity change

	TFP Change	Input Contribution to TFP Growth			TFP Decompositions	
		Fund	Labor	Capital	Efficiency Change	Technological Change
2005/2006	0.0547	0.0403	0.0905	0.0333	0.1277	-0.0730
2006/2007	0.2047	0.1603	0.2505	0.2035	-0.0217	0.2264
2007/2008	-0.0384	-0.0766	-0.0775	0.0387	-0.0804	0.0420
2008/2009	0.1095	0.3313	-0.0026	-0.0002	0.1900	-0.0805
2009/2010	0.0262	-0.0163	0.0032	0.0918	-0.0014	0.0276
2010/2011	0.0088	0.0274	-0.0233	0.0224	-0.0071	0.0159
Mean	0.0609	0.0777	0.0401	0.0649	0.0345	0.0264

banks. In addition, having in view the fact that efficiency change grew 19% in 2009, but also that funds productivity was higher with 33% in 2009, we conclude that banks avoided a regress of productivity through an imitation behaviour of fund productivity. To be more precise, the inefficient banks adopted the best practice banks strategies where the management of funds was concerned. With the exception of 2007, the technological growth was relatively modest, which can reflect a lack of innovation among the credit institutions in Romania.

CONCLUSION

In this research study we have analyzed the nexus between cost efficiency, risks and performance and productivity patterns in the Romanian banking system during 2005-2011. In our opinion, it is important to know the way in which the efficiency of the banks has evolved and its determinants. To reach this objective we have included in the model variables that characterize the level of bank concentration, the failure risk, the solvency risk, the liquidity risk and the bank's performance. With regard to the productivity patterns, the model we have used has allowed us to identify the sources of productivity growth.

The results revealed important conclusions. The influence of the banking concentration on the commercial banks´ efficiency support Hicks's 'quiet life hypothesis'. In our opinion, this may result from an uncompetitive banking sector in which the concentration is associated with market power.

The influence of risk factors is mixed. On one hand, the banks characterized by a reduced risk of failure and a higher level of liquidity are more efficient. On the other hand, surprisingly, the equity-to-assets ratio, a proxy for solvency risk, has a negative influence on cost efficiency. The data show that commercial banks in Romania who have a higher rate of financial intermediation and a higher ROE are more efficient. Surprisingly, an increase in the net interest margin will lead to a lower cost efficiency score. In our opinion, this result can indicate a targeting of resources towards riskier assets.

Where productivity is concerned, results indicate a regress in 2008, caused by the effects of the international financial crisis. Moreover, the cost efficiency decreased significantly in 2008. These results can indicate a pro cyclical behaviour. Subsequently, in 2009 banks managed to increase the productivity level due to the increase in the productivity of funds. Another element that contributed in a constructive way to a positive level of productivity in 2009 was the fact that small banks succeeded to get a hold on the catching up effect.

In our opinion, a future direction of analysis could be a comparative study between the cost efficiency and productivity in Central Eastern Europe. Also, it would be interesting to follow the differences in efficiency and productivity in accordance with the size of banks and their ownership type. We will leave this approach this for future research directions.

REFERENCES

Andrieş, A., Mehdian, S., & Stoica, O. (2013). Impact of European integration on efficiency and productivity growth of Romanian banks. *The Engineering Economist*, *24*, 187–197.

Andrieş, A. M., & Cocriş, V. (2010). A comparative analysis of the efficiency of Romanian banks. *Romanian Journal of Economic Forecasting*, *54*, 54–75.

Asaftei, G., & Kumbhakar, S. C. (2008). Regulation and efficiency in transition: The case of Romanian banks. *Journal of Regulatory Economics*, *33*(3), 253–282. doi:10.100711149-007-9041-0

Berger, A. N., & DeYoung, R. (1997). Problem loans and cost efficiency in commercial banks. *Journal of Banking & Finance*, *21*(6), 849–870. doi:10.1016/S0378-4266(97)00003-4

Berger, A. N., & Hannan, T. H. (1998). The efficiency cost of market power in the banking industry: A test of the "quiet life" and related hypotheses. *The Review of Economics and Statistics*, *80*(3), 454–465. doi:10.1162/003465398557555

Berger, A. N., & Mester, L. J. (1997). Inside the black box: What explains differences in the efficiencies of financial institutions? *Journal of Banking & Finance*, *21*(7), 895–947. doi:10.1016/S0378-4266(97)00010-1

Bikker, J. A., & Haaf, K. (2002). Competition, concentration and their relationship: An empirical analysis of the banking industry. *Journal of Banking & Finance*, *26*(11), 2191–2214. doi:10.1016/S0378-4266(02)00205-4

Bonin, J. P., Hasan, I., & Wachtel, P. (2005). Privatization matters: Bank efficiency in transition countries. *Journal of Banking & Finance*, *29*(8-9), 2155–2178. doi:10.1016/j.jbankfin.2005.03.012

Bonin, J. P., & Wachtel, P. (2003). Financial sector development in transition economies: Lessons from the first decade, *Financial Markets. Institutions & Instruments*, *12*(1), 1–66. doi:10.1111/1468-0416.t01-1-00001

Briec, W. (2000). An extended Färe–Lovell technical efficiency measure. *International Journal of Production Economics*, *65*(2), 191–199. doi:10.1016/S0925-5273(99)00019-5

Caporale, G. M., Rault, C., Sova, R., & Sova, A. (2009). Financial development and economic growth: Evidence from ten new EU members. DIW.

Chang, T. P., Hu, J. L., Chou, R. Y., & Sun, L. (2012). The sources of bank productivity growth in China during 2002–2009: A disaggregation view. *Journal of Banking & Finance*, *36*(7), 1997–2006. doi:10.1016/j.jbankfin.2012.03.003

Charnes, A., Cooper, W. W., & Rhodes, E. (1978). Measuring the efficiency of decision making units. *European Journal of Operational Research*, *2*(6), 429–444. doi:10.1016/0377-2217(78)90138-8

Coelli, T. J. (1996). A guide to FRONTIER version 4.1: A computer program for stochastic frontier production and cost function estimation. CEPA.

De Haas, R., & Van Lelyveld, I. (2006). Foreign banks and credit stability in Central and Eastern Europe. A panel data analysis. *Journal of Banking & Finance*, *30*(7), 1927–1952. doi:10.1016/j.jbankfin.2005.07.007

Demsetz, H. (1969). Information and efficiency: Another viewpoint. *The Journal of Law & Economics*, *12*(1), 1–22. doi:10.1086/466657

Dick, A. A., & Lehnert, A. (2010). Personal bankruptcy and credit market competition. *The Journal of Finance*, *65*(2), 655–686. doi:10.1111/j.1540-6261.2009.01547.x

Fang, Y., Hasan, I., & Marton, K. (2011). Bank efficiency in South-Eastern Europe. *Economics of Transition*, *19*(3), 495–520. doi:10.1111/j.1468-0351.2011.00420.x

Fries, S., & Taci, A. (2005). Cost efficiency of banks in transition: Evidence from 289 banks in 15 post-communist countries. *Journal of Banking & Finance*, *29*(1), 55–81. doi:10.1016/j.jbankfin.2004.06.016

Hauner, D. (2005). Explaining efficiency differences among large German and Austrian banks. *Applied Economics*, *37*(9), 969–980. doi:10.1080/00036840500081820

Havranek, T., & Irsova, Z. (2013). Determinants of bank performance in transition countries: A Data Envelopment Analysis, *Transition. Studies and Reviews (General Fisheries Commission for the Mediterranean)*, *20*, 1–17.

Havrylchyk, O. (2006). Efficiency of the Polish banking industry: Foreign versus domestic banks. *Journal of Banking & Finance*, *30*(7), 1975–1996. doi:10.1016/j.jbankfin.2005.07.009

Heffernan, S. A., & Fu, X. (2010). Determinants of financial performance in Chinese banking. *Applied Financial Economics*, *20*(20), 1585–1600. doi:10.1080/09603107.2010.505553

Hermes, N., & Nhung, V. T. H. (2010). The impact of financial liberalization on bank efficiency: Evidence from Latin America and Asia. *Applied Economics*, *42*(26), 3351–3365. doi:10.1080/00036840802112448

Hsiao, H. C., Chang, H., Cianci, A. M., & Huang, L. H. (2010). First financial restructuring and operating efficiency: Evidence from Taiwanese commercial banks. *Journal of Banking & Finance*, *34*(7), 1461–1471. doi:10.1016/j.jbankfin.2010.01.013

Kasman, A., & Yildirim, C. (2006). Cost and profit efficiencies in transition banking: The case of new EU members. *Applied Economics*, *38*(9), 1079–1090. doi:10.1080/00036840600639022

Klingen, C. (2013). *Perspectives on growth prospects for Central, Eastern and Southeastern Europe. Banking in Central and Eastern Europe and Turkey - Challenges and Opportunities*. European Investment Bank.

Koutsomanoli-Filippaki, A., Margaritis, D., & Staikouras, C. (2009). Efficiency and productivity growth in the banking industry of Central and Eastern Europe. *Journal of Banking & Finance*, *33*(3), 557–567. doi:10.1016/j.jbankfin.2008.09.009

Lepetit, L., Nys, E., Rous, P., & Tarazi, A. (2008a). Bank income structure and risk: An empirical analysis of European banks. *Journal of Banking & Finance*, *32*(8), 1452–1467. doi:10.1016/j.jbankfin.2007.12.002

Lepetit, L., Nys, E., Rous, P., & Tarazi, A. (2008b). The expansion of services in European banking: Implications for loan pricing and interest margins. *Journal of Banking & Finance*, *32*(11), 2325–2335. doi:10.1016/j.jbankfin.2007.09.025

Maudos, J., & de Guevara, J. F. (2004). Factors explaining the interest margin in the banking sectors of the European Union. *Journal of Banking & Finance*, *28*(9), 2259–2281. doi:10.1016/j.jbankfin.2003.09.004

McDonald, J. (2009). Using least squares and tobit in second stage DEA efficiency analyses. *European Journal of Operational Research*, *197*(2), 792–798. doi:10.1016/j.ejor.2008.07.039

Montoro, C., & Rojas-Suarez, L. (2012). Credit at times of stress: Latin American lessons from the global financial crisis. BIS.

Munteanu, A., Brezeanu, P., & Badea, L. (2013). Productivity change patterns in the Romanian banking system–the impact of size and ownership on total factor productivity. *Theoretical and Applied Economics*, *20*, 35–52.

National Bank of Romania. (2013). Report on Financial Stability. Retrieved from http://www.bnro.ro/PublicationDocuments.aspx?icid=6711

National Bank of Romania. (2014). Report on Financial Stability. Retrieved from http://www.bnro.ro/PublicationDocuments.aspx?icid=6711

Niţoi, M. (2009). Efficiency in the Romanian banking system: An Application of Data Envelopment Analysis. *Romanian Journal of Economics*, *28*, 159–173.

Otchere, I. (2005). Do privatized banks in middle-and low-income countries perform better than rival banks? An intra-industry analysis of bank privatization. *Journal of Banking & Finance*, *29*(8-9), 2067–2093. doi:10.1016/j.jbankfin.2005.03.001

Pancurova, D., & Lyocsa, S. (2013). Determinants of Commercial Banks' Efficiency: Evidence from 11 CEE Countries. *Czech Journal of Economics and Finance*, *63*, 152–179.

Papke, L. E., & Wooldridge, J. M. (1996). Econometric methods for fractional response variables with an application to 401(k) plan participation rates. *Journal of Applied Econometrics*, *11*(6), 619–632. doi:10.1002/(SICI)1099-1255(199611)11:6<619::AID-JAE418>3.0.CO;2-1

Pastor, J. T., Lozano, A., & Pastor, J. M. (1997). Efficiency of European banking systems: A correction by environment variables. Instituto Valenciano de Investigaciones Económicas.

Sealey, C. Jr, & Lindley, J. T. (1977). Inputs, outputs and a theory of production and cost at depository financial institution. *The Journal of Finance*, *32*(4), 1251–1266. doi:10.1111/j.1540-6261.1977.tb03324.x

Simar, L., & Wilson, P. W. (2007). Estimation and inference in two-stage, semiparametric models of production processes. *Journal of Econometrics*, *136*(1), 31–64. doi:10.1016/j.jeconom.2005.07.009

Spulbar, C., & Niţoi, M. (2014). Determinants of bank cost efficiency in transition economies: Evidence for Latin America, Central and Eastern Europe and South-East Asia. *Applied Economics*, *46*(16), 1940–1952. doi: 10.1080/00036846.2014.889806

Spulbar, C., & Niţoi, M. (2016). The relationship between bank efficiency and risk and productivity patterns in Romanian banking system. *Romanian Journal of Economic Forecasting*, *19*(1), 39–53.

Sun, L., & Chang, T. P. (2011). A comprehensive analysis of the effects of risk measures on bank efficiency: Evidence from emerging Asian countries. *Journal of Banking & Finance*, *35*(7), 1727–1735. doi:10.1016/j.jbankfin.2010.11.017

Weill, L. (2004). On the relationship between competition and efficiency in the EU banking sectors. *Kredit und Kapital*, *3*, 329–352.

Williams, J., & Nguyen, N. (2005). Financial liberalisation, crisis, and restructuring: A comparative study of bank performance and bank governance in South East Asia. *Journal of Banking & Finance*, *29*(8-9), 2119–2154. doi:10.1016/j.jbankfin.2005.03.011

Williams, J., Peypoch, N., & Barros, C. P. (2011). The Luenberger indicator and productivity growth: A note on the European savings banks sector. *Applied Economics*, *43*(6), 747–755. doi:10.1080/00036840802599859

Xu, Y. (2011). Towards a more accurate measure of foreign bank entry and its impact on domestic banking performance: The case of China. *Journal of Banking & Finance*, *35*(4), 886–901. doi:10.1016/j.jbankfin.2010.10.011

Yildirim, H. S., & Philippatos, G. C. (2007). Efficiency of banks: Recent evidence from the transition economies of Europe, 1993–2000. *European Journal of Finance*, *13*(2), 123–143. doi:10.1080/13518470600763687

Zajc, P. (2006). A comparative study of bank efficiency in Central and Eastern Europe: The role of foreign ownership. *International Finance Review*, *6*, 117–156. doi:10.1016/S1569-3767(05)06006-1

Chapter 3
Efficiency in Cooperative Banks and Savings Banks:
A Stochastic Frontier Approach

ABSTRACT

This chapter provides additional empirical evidence on the efficiency in cooperative banks and savings banks by applying a stochastic frontier model to estimate the cost efficiency from nine countries over the period 2005 to 2011. The empirical results suggested that a higher rate of the gross domestic product (GDP) growth implies an increase in the inefficiency level, while smaller cooperative and savings banks are more efficient in managing costs compared to larger banks.

INTRODUCTION

In recent years, the global crisis significantly affected the activity of financial systems and of banking institutions, emphasizing their fragility. In such a context, dominated by intense competition between banks and by significant structural changes in the way they operate, their capacity to increase their efficiency and to reduce costs became essential. Increasing the efficiency in a tumultuous competitive environment ensures stability and can offer a strategic advantage over competitors. Moreover, an efficient banking system is one of the conditions for a wealthy economic environment. Also, given the fact that most of the commercial banks were confronted with higher risks

DOI: 10.4018/978-1-5225-9269-3.ch003

as a consequence of the global financial crisis, the importance of the banks that adopted a traditional model of activity - cooperative banks and savings banks - grew.

Generally, within the banking systems, the institutions embrace different business models, organizational forms and ownership structures. Along with the commercial banks that embrace the universal banking model, a significant number of credit institutions with different organizational forms and ownership structures - cooperative banks and savings banks - play an important role in the banking sector. In addition, Ayadi *et al.* (2010, p. 6) divided banks into two broad categories: Stakeholder Value banks and Shareholder Value banks. The distinction is made according to the banks' bottom line objectives and the extent to which profit maximization is the central focus of their business models. The authors consider that cooperative banks and savings banks represent "dual-bottom line" institutions.

Cooperative banks are not-for-profit organizations, established to sustain the activity of their members. Today, the main clients of the credit cooperatives are individuals and small- and medium-sized enterprises, and their business model approaches the universal bank model. Despite this, there are certain characteristics that cooperative banks retain and that differentiate them from commercial banks. Cooperative banks operate under the regional principle, conferring an important role on them in financing local communities (European Association of Cooperative Banks, Annual Report, 2012). Regardless of the countries in which they operate, most of the cooperative banks have mutual support mechanisms, so that the local cooperatives are supported the moment that difficulties are encountered. Being organizations that do not follow profit maximization, their main aim is to improve the economic welfare of the members, while the members' objective is to use financial services and not to obtain dividends.

Along with cooperative banks, savings banks have an important role in the banking sector, particularly in Europe. Although savings banks were initially created to promote social inclusion, they have evolved into specific, universal banks that are in competition with commercial banks for households and small- and medium-sized enterprises. The main feature that differentiates savings banks from commercial banks is their organizational structure. In Germany, savings banks are public entities and have no owners in the commercial sense, the public authorities being responsible for the activity of these institutions (Clarke, 2010). In Norway, Denmark and Sweden, savings banks are organized as independent foundations. In other words, they do not have stockholders or traditional owners. Their capital consists of profits from previous years (Nordic Banking Structures, 2006; Organisation for Economic Co-operation and Development). On the other hand, the pressure to meet the capital requirements imposed by financial regulations has led to the reorganization of the saving bank sector in some countries. Thus, in Italy, savings banks have been transformed into joint stock companies (Carletti et al., 2005). In Spain, the authorities have decided to change the legal status of savings banks in order to facilitate access to capital markets (Report on Banking Supervision in Spain, 2010). Even so, savings banks remain close to the clients, as they are locally based and are oriented towards long-term lending strategies.

Regardless of the organizational form and the ownership structures, the technological developments and the constraints induced by the financial crisis have intensified the competition in the banking sector. Under these conditions, both efficiency and cost management have become essential in banks' attempts to improve their operational performance and financial reliability. In fact, in recent years, both cooperative banks and savings banks have laid the foundations for intense cooperation within the groups to which they belong, in order to benefit from economies of scale.

In this study, we propose to estimate the cost efficiency of cooperative banks and savings banks in nine countries over the period 2005 to 2011 and to identify how environmental variables and control variables influence the inefficiency effect, using the model proposed by Greene (2005). The contribution provided by our study with respect to the existing literature is manifold. Firstly, the model is based on 12,055 observations of banks within banking systems in which cooperative and savings banks have an important market share. We consider that this gives reliability to the estimations and results.

Secondly, we included variables that describe the risk and performance of cooperative and savings banks among the factors that influence inefficiency. Also, we included environmental variables in the model. Thirdly, we consider that the results are important for understanding the way in which the activity of cooperative and savings banks developed over the period of analysis.

The remainder of the study is organized as follows: section II reviews the literature on efficiency papers, paying special attention to cooperative and savings banks. Section III presents the methodology framework adopted. Section IV describes the data and variables. Section V discusses the empirical results. Finally, section VI presents the conclusions.

COOPERATIVE AND SAVINGS BANKS' EFFICIENCY: LITERATURE REVIEW

In the literature on banking efficiency, we observed numerous studies with different results and aims. Most of them use the stochastic frontier approach (SFA) and data envelopment analysis (DEA) to estimate cost efficiency. Hereinafter, we will review some results of these researches, focusing particularly on those that consider the cooperative bank sector and the savings bank sector.

An important concern within the literature was represented by the attempt to establish whether cooperative banks and savings banks are more efficient than are commercial banks. Kontolaimou and Tsekouras (2010) investigated the productive performance of cooperative banks as compared to commercial banks and savings banks. The authors adopted a methodology based on a metafrontier notion that allows for the identification of technology gaps among different bank types and their decomposition into input- and output-invariant components. The results suggest that the frontier corresponding to cooperative banks lies mainly away from the European metafrontier, while commercial banks practically define this frontier. The authors consider that the cooperatives' technology gap is attributable to output production rather than to input use. The results are in line with Rasmusen's findings (1988), which showed that cooperative banks are less efficient than commercial banks because they are characterized by one person, one vote principle. However, there are studies with different results. Girardone et al. (2009) analysed cost efficiency in EU-15 countries over the period 1998 to 2003, emphasizing the higher performance of cooperative banks. Altunbas et al. (2003) investigated the efficiency of a large number of European and US banks in the period 1999 to 2000. The results indicate higher cost efficiency for cooperative banks compared to commercial banks, but lower profit efficiency.

The determinants of cost efficiency have also been examined in several papers. Battaglia et al. (2010) estimated cost and profit efficiency for cooperative banks in Italy using an SFA model. The authors included environmental variables to account for disparities among Italian regions in their model. The results of the study show that the environmental variables substantially influenced efficiency estimations. Thus, banks in Northern Italy are more cost efficient, benefiting from a favourable environment, while banks in Southern Italy are more profit efficient due to lower competitive pressure.

Assaf et al. (2011) studied the productivity and efficiency of cooperative banks in Japan - Shinkin banks – over the period 2000 to 2006, using the bootstrapped Malmquist index and the Bayesian distance frontier approach. The results do not show a considerable improvement in efficiency and productivity in the analysed period. Also, the efficiency level is homogenous because the variations between banks are low. The authors concluded that the market share on deposit, the number of branches, the return on assets and the concentration ratio of deposits for the five largest banks are important contributors to efficiency and productivity growth. Analysing the credit unions in the USA, Glass and McKillop (2006) found that factors beyond management control could explain much of the variability of the cost efficiency level.

Other studies focused on cross country comparisons of cooperative banks and savings banks regarding cost efficiency. Barros et al. (2010) used the Luenberger productivity index to estimate efficiency and productivity changes in European cooperative banks over the period 1996 to 2003. The results indicate that there has been productivity growth in the cooperative industry with rates that differ across countries, driven by improvements in technological change. The results are similar to those obtained by Molyneux and Williams (2005).

Given that innovation represents the main determinant of the productivity increase in the cooperative sector, Barros et al. (2010) recommended that larger or centralized cooperative banks develop and franchise technology to smaller cooperatives. Williams et al. (2011) used the Luenberger productivity index to estimate productivity growth and its decomposition for savings banks in 10 EU countries in the period 1996 to 2003. The estimations show an annual productivity growth of 2.78%, driven by technological change. The results are similar to those obtained by Williams (2001), who found a growth in productivity of 2.86% for savings banks in six EU countries. Also, Williams et al. (2011) emphasised cross-country differences between savings banks.

Thus, the highest productivity growth is found in Finland, Spain and France, while in Germany the index has a negative value. Carbo et al. (2003) estimated the technological progress of European savings banks over the period 1989 to 1997, using a Fourier flexible form cost function methodology. The results indicate that, on average, technological progress reduced savings banks' total costs by around 3.4% per annum and that this cost reduction was higher for larger savings banks. The savings banks in Sweden, Portugal, Luxembourg, Belgium, Austria and France benefited most from technological progress, while the total cost reduction for banks in Denmark and Germany was below the average.

METHODOLOGY

This section summarizes the theoretical model used to estimate cost efficiency. To measure the efficiency of cooperative banks and savings banks, we used an SFA model. The main reason behind the choice of the SFA is related to the fact that the DEA does not allow for the presence of a random error term. Thus, any deviation from the efficiency frontier is associated with inefficiency. For instance, DEA considers the influence of factors such as measurement error, luck or extreme observations to indicate inefficiency. SFA, independently proposed by Aigner et al. (1977) and Meeusen and van den Broeck (1977), allows for the specification of a composed error that can be decomposed into two parts: a one-sided error that measures the nonnegative inefficiency effects and a classical random error.

Within the literature on efficiency, there are numerous models that model inefficiency within the panel data. A detailed description of these models' specifications can be found in Belotti et al. (2012). Most of the models treat inefficiency as a time-invariant "effect" (Schmidt and Sickles, 1984; Pitt and Lee, 1981). Greene (2005) argued that a preferable approach would be to allow inefficiency to vary freely over time in a panel, to the extent that there is a common time-invariant effect in the model that should be treated as unobserved heterogeneity, not as inefficiency. The SFA model employed in our study adopts the methodology proposed by Greene (2005). The stochastic frontier model specification as proposed by Pitt and Lee (1981) for the cost function can be represented as follows:

$$Y_{it} = f\left(x_{it}, z_i\right) + v_{it} + u_i, i = 1,\ldots,N t = 1,\ldots,T \quad (1)$$

$$= \alpha + \beta' x_{it} + \tau' z_i + v_{it} + u_i \quad (2)$$

$$v_{it} \sim N\left(0, \sigma_v^2\right) \quad (3)$$

$$u_i \sim N^+\left(0, \sigma_u^2\right) \quad (4)$$

where Y_{it} is the total cost of the bank *i* in year *t*; x_{it} is a vector of input prices and z_i is a vector of bank specific characteristics. Greene (2005) considers it would be convenient to include $\tau' z_i$ in $\beta' x_{it}$; thus, Equation 2 becomes:

$$Y_{it} = \alpha + \beta' x_{it} + v_{it} + u_i \tag{5}$$

Schmidt and Sickles (1984) argued that the estimation of a stochastic frontier model with time invariant inefficiency could be done by adapting conventional fixed-effects estimation techniques. Therefore, inefficiency will be correlated with the frontier regressors and distributional assumptions about u_i will be avoided. For estimations based on panel data, the time invariant nature of the inefficiency term has been questioned. Thus, Cornwell et al. (1990) proposed the following stochastic frontier model, where the parameters are estimated by extending the conventional fixed- and random-effects panel data estimators.

$$Y_{it} = \alpha + \beta' x_{it} + v_{it} + u_{it}, i = 1, \ldots, Nt = 4, \ldots, T_i \tag{6}$$

$$u_{it} = \omega_i + \omega_{i1} t + \omega_{i2} t^2 \tag{7}$$

Lee and Schmidt (1993) proposed an alternative specification, in which:

$$u_{it} = g(t) \cdot u_i \tag{8}$$

where $g(t)$ represents a set of dummy variables. Kumbhakar (1990) proposed the ML estimation of a time-varying SF model, in which $g(t)$ is specified as:

$$g(t) = \left[1 + \exp\left(\gamma t + \delta t^2\right)\right]^{-1} \tag{9}$$

A similar model was proposed by Battese and Coelli (1992), as follows:

$$g(t) = \exp\left[-\gamma\left(t - T_i\right)\right] \tag{10}$$

All these models assume that α is the same for all the units included in the analysis. Belotti et al. (2012) considers that this characteristic can generate a misspecification bias in the presence of time-invariant unobservable factors, unrelated to the production process but still affecting the output. As a result, the effect of these factors may be captured by the inefficiency term, producing biased results. In order to avoid this disadvantage, Greene (2005) proposed a model that allows the disentanglement of time-varying inefficiency from unit specific time invariant unobserved heterogeneity:

$$Y_{it} = \alpha_i + {}^{2\prime}x_{it} + v_{it} + u_{it} \tag{11}$$

$$v_{it} \sim N\left(0, \sigma_v^2\right) \tag{12}$$

$$u_{it} \sim N^+\left(0, \sigma^2\right) \tag{13}$$

DATA

Our sample covers an unbalanced panel dataset of 9,352 observations corresponding to 1,059 cooperative banks and 551 savings banks over the period 2005 to 2011. We have chosen to include cooperative banks and savings banks from developed countries and from banking systems in which they play an important role in the sample. Thus, we have included cooperative banks from Austria, Germany, Switzerland, Spain, France and Italy and savings banks from Austria, Germany, Norway, Sweden, Denmark, Spain, France and Italy. The data were extracted from the Bankscope database. Table 1 reports some descriptive statistics for the banks included in the sample.

As we can see, cooperative banks and savings banks have a significant market share in all the countries included in the sample. Consequently, the organization of the activities based on effective principles is essential to ensure the stability of the banking systems of which they are part. Moreover, bearing in mind the fact that cooperative banks and savings banks do not pursue profit maximization, efficiency becomes more important.

Table 1. Descriptive statistics of the dataset and the market share of cooperative banks and savings banks (Sample means are for bank-year observations by bank type and country)

	Equity to Total Assets Ratio	Cost to Income Ratio	ROA	ROE	Net Interest Margin	Liquid Assets to Deposits and Short-Term Funding Ratio	Market Share-2011
Austria							
Cooperative banks	7.58	65.65	0.35	4.06	2.12	28.39	36.9%a
Savings banks	6.71	66.87	0.22	3.09	2.23	18.21	16.5%b
Germany							
Cooperative banks	6.46	69.31	0.31	4.97	2.56	17.03	19.4%a
Savings banks	5.87	67.55	0.17	3.01	2.36	15.28	13.25%c
Switzerland							
Cooperative banks	3.02	64.09	0.17	6.35	1.55	11.89	19.8%a
Spain							
Cooperative banks	10.24	61.58	0.52	5.75	2.39	21.17	6.78%a
Savings banks	7.75	57.36	0.55	5.64	1.90	11.86	30%d
France							
Cooperative banks	11.26	58.89	0.75	6.71	1.83	18.39	38.2%a
Savings banks	9.80	70.85	0.42	5.39	1.83	43.54	N.A.
Italy							
Cooperative banks	10.82	65.69	0.58	5.21	2.87	17.39	33.9%a
Savings banks	8.66	65.58	0.59	6.49	3.07	21.94	N.A.
Norway							
Savings banks	9.61	59.91	0.69	7.39	2.34	9.18	45.2%e
Sweden							
Savings banks	14.27	63.31	0.96	6.85	2.82	13.27	10.0%f
Denmark							
Savings banks	15.18	76.74	0.24	0.28	3.84	15.07	N.A.

[a]Source of data:European Association of Co-operative Banks (2012) Key Statistics Financial Indicators 2011.
[b]Source of data: Oesterreichische Nationalbank (OeNB), Statistics and Reporting - Banks' Business Structure.
[c]Source of data: DeutscheBundesbank (2012) Banking statistics December 2011, Statistical Supplement to the Monthly Report.
[d]Source of data: Bancode España (2010) Report on banking supervision in Spain.
[e]Source of data:Norges Bank (2011) Financial Stability 1/2011, Reports from the Central Bank of Norway No. 2/2011.
[f]Source of data:Swedish Bankers' Association (2011) Banks in Sweden.

For selecting the bank's output vector, we followed the intermediation approach (Sealey & Lindley, 1977). The output vector includes total loans and total other earnings. Loan loss provisions are subtracted from total loans in order to ensure comparable quality (Havrylchyk, 2006). The input prices are the price of labour, the price of funds and the price of capital. The price of labour is calculated as personnel expenses divided by the number of employees. The price of funds is measured by dividing total interest expenses by total deposits and other purchased funds. The capital price is defined by the ratio of other noninterest expenses to total fixed assets. The total cost of each bank is the sum of interest expenses and noninterest expenses. In order to ensure the homogeneity of the cost function, the total cost, the price of labour and the price of funds were normalized by the price of capital.

All the monetary values were deflated using the GDP deflator provided by the International Monetary Fund (IMF), with 2005 as the base year. Table 2 presents the descriptive statistics of the output and input variables used in the model. In order to measure the country's effect, we created a dummy variable for cooperative banks and savings banks. We dropped the first variable to avoid multicollinearity. We included in the model two dummy variables for the years 2008 and 2009, in order to identify the impact of the financial crisis on the level of cost efficiency.

An important aim of our study was to examine how exogenous factors influence inefficiency. Therefore, in order to achieve this objective, we included environmental variables and control variables in the SFA model. The inclusion in the model of some environmental variables is based on the premise that efficiency is influenced by the economic conditions of the countries in which the banks operate. The control variables capture different

Table 2. Descriptive statistics of the variables used in the cost efficiency estimations

	Mean	SD	Min.	Max.
Total cost (in billion US $)	0.2007	1.6610	0.0006	69.9000
Output Quantities (in Billion US $)				
Total loans	2.8341	16.2000	0.0042	492.0000
Other earning assets	2.5535	39.4000	0.0005	1560.0000
Input Prices				
Price of funds	0.0227	0.0080	0.0033	0.0817
Price of labour	75.3291	22.9864	7.7453	792.3094
Price of capital	1.0354	3.6953	0.0803	145.2109

strategies adopted by each institution. Real GDP growth and the Z score are the environmental variables. Real GDP growth was extracted from the IMF International Financial Statistics Database.

Real GDP growth is a proxy for the economic development. An increase in the real GDP should lead to a higher credit demand, a better quality of loan portfolios and, consequently, a lower ratio of nonperforming loans. Therefore, real GDP growth should reduce inefficiency. The Z score is a measure of a bank's risk taking. Lepetit et al. (2008a) posits that the Z score reveals the insolvency risk, indicating the probability of bankruptcy for a bank. The index is estimated by combining the elements that describe profitability, leverage and return volatility:

$$Z = \frac{average\,ROA + average\,EQ\,/\,TA}{VOL(ROA)} \tag{14}$$

Higher Z scores indicate a lower probability of bankruptcy and, therefore, lower costs. In our study, the Z score was calculated for each country and for each banking sector, (the cooperative banking sector and the savings banking sector), based on individual observations of banks.

The bank capital to assets ratio, the loan loss provisions divided by total loans, the Return on Equity (ROE), the net interest margin, the net loans to total assets ratio and the logarithm of total assets are the control variables. Bank capital to assets ratio is associated with lower costs, because banks are perceived of as being less risky. Loan loss provisions divided by total loans is a measure for risk, reflecting the quality of a bank's assets. We included this rate in our model to emphasize the influence of the credit risk on cost efficiency. Furthermore, the loan loss provisions/total loans ratio can also reflect the effects of the financial crisis on the bank's balance sheet. Basically, growth of the loan loss provisions/total loans ratio will lead to a growth in costs and inefficiency. ROE and the net interest margin are proxies for a bank's performance. ROE and the net interest margin are commonly used in the literature to describe a bank's earning ability (de Haas & van Lelyveld, 2006; Xu, 2011; Heffernan & Fu, 2010).

A growth in these two rates should result in better cost efficiency. Net loans to total assets ratio is a measure of loan specialization. Freixas (2005) posits that a high rate provides informational advantages, which reduce intermediation costs and improve profitability. However, Heffeman and Fu (2010) state that very high ratios could also reduce liquidity and increase the number of marginal borrowers that default. Log(assets) is a measurement of the size of banks and may be an important determinant of a bank's efficiency. On one hand, larger banks may be more efficient compared to smaller banks, as a result of the economies of scale. On the other hand, there are also small banks that are efficient.

RESULTS

The determination of cost efficiency by estimating a maximum likelihood function was conducted using Stata 10.1 software. As mentioned, we adopted Greene's (2005) truncated normal model. Table 3 presents the complete results. This indicates consistent and sound results.

Most of the coefficients of output and input prices are positive and significant. Also, the coefficients of the quadratic terms for output are positive. We noticed that the quadratic term PL/PC is negative. However, higher prices and higher output seems to generate higher total costs.

The analysis of cross-country cost efficiency reveals significant findings. Cooperative banks in Switzerland are 14.3% more cost efficient than are cooperative banks in Austria, while cooperative banks in Germany, France, Spain and Italy are less cost efficient than are cooperative banks in Austria. With respect to savings banks, Norway and Sweden's savings banks are more cost efficient than are Austria's cooperative banks. Thus, despite their organizational forms and ownership structures, these institutions are efficient in terms of cost management. The cost efficiency of Germany`s savings banks is 10% lower than that of Austria's cooperative banks. We found similar results for Spain and Italy's savings banks. Thus, cost efficiency for these banks is 3.8% and 7.5% respectively, lower than it is for Austria's cooperative banks.

With respect to the influence of exogenous factors on the inefficiency effect, it is surprising that real GDP growth is positively associated with cost efficiency. Afanasieff et al. (2002) suggested that a higher output growth reflects more intense competition, a lower interest margin and higher costs to resist on the market. Moreover, in periods of economic growth, Rajan (1994) posited that banks concerned with their short-run reputation would reduce credit standards to gain market share. In our opinion, in periods of economic growth, cooperative banks and savings banks have lost market share in favour of commercial banks with more aggressive strategies and which had easier access to cheaper financial resources. However, the result may also suggest a mismatch between wage costs and productivity levels.

Table 3. Stochastic frontier estimates

Dependent Variable ln(TC/PC)	Coefficient Greene (2005)
Independent Variables	
ln(TL)	0.2694*
ln(OEA)	0.6389*
ln(PF/PC)	0.8643*
ln(PL/PC)	0.7241*
$\ln(TL)^2$	0.1658*
$\ln(OEA)^2$	0.1351*
$\ln(PF/PC)^2$	0.0662*
$\ln(PL/PC)^2$	-0.1012*
$\ln(TL) \times \ln(OEA)$	-0.3018*
$\ln(TL) \times \ln(PF/PC)$	-0.0505*
$\ln(TL) \times \ln(PL/PC)$	0.0461*
$\ln(OEA) \times \ln(PF/PC)$	0.0378*
$\ln(OEA) \times \ln(PL/PC)$	-0.0427*
Year	-0.0607*
Year^2	0.0023*
$\ln(TL) \times year$	-0.0043*
$\ln(OEA) \times year$	0.0060*
$\ln(PF/PC) \times year$	-0.0042***
$\ln(PL/PC) \times year$	0.0117*
Germany's cooperative banks	0.0777*
Switzerland's cooperative banks	-0.1431*
Spain's cooperative banks	0.0121**
France's cooperative banks	0.0276*
Italy's cooperative banks	0.0132*
Austria's savings banks	0.0135***
Germany's savings banks	0.1009*

continued on following page

Table 3. Continued

Dependent Variable ln(TC/PC)	Coefficient Greene (2005)
Norway's savings banks	-0.0780*
Sweden's savings banks	-0.0404*
Denmark's savings banks	0.0082***
Spain's savings banks	0.0371*
France's savings banks	0.0332*
Italy's savings banks	0.0758*
Constant	-0.4679*
Effects on μ_{it}	
GDP growth	0.0810*
Equity to total assets ratio	0.0176*
Z Score	-0.0218*
Loan loss provisions/total loans	0.1000*
Net interest margin	0.6345**
ROE	-0.0156***
Net loans to total assets ratio	-0.0393
Log(assets)	0.3336*
Year 2008	-0.3818*
Year 2009	0.3316**
τ_0	-20.3002**
χ_0	-1.1851**
σ_ν	-5.9873*

Notes: *denotes a test statistic significance at the 1% level; **denotes a test statistic significance at the 5% level; ***denotes a test statistic significance at the 10% level.

The results from the literature on efficiency are mixed. For example, Fries and Taci (2005) and Hauner (2005) found that overall economic development is not significantly related to costs. On the other hand, Hermes and Nhung (2010) and Kasman and Yildirim (2006) obtained results that indicated that banks which operate in countries with a higher GDP growth are more cost efficient. The insolvency risk of the cooperative banking sector and of the savings banking sector is negatively associated with cost efficiency. Thus, a higher Z score, which reflects a lower probability of bankruptcy, implies a decrease in the level of bank inefficiency. The result is in line with expectations, taking into consideration the fact that a higher risk increases the banks' operation uncertainty, an inadequate management of risk also implying the poor administration of costs.

The capital ratio has a positive effect on the inefficiency level. Thus, a growth of this rate leads to lower cost efficiency. Banks with a higher credit risk, such as a higher loan loss provisions/loans ratio, will have lower cost efficiency. Havrylchyk (2006) considered that problem loans create additional costs associated with the monitoring and enforcement of loan repayments. Banks with a higher ROE are more cost efficient than are banks with a lower ROE. Somewhat counterintuitive is the positive relation between inefficiency and the net interest margin.

On the other hand, this result can be explained by the fact that a higher net interest margin is a sign of a higher credit risk. Maudos and de Guevara (2004) and Lepetit et al. (2008b) showed that banks charge higher interest margins if their credit risk increases. The loans to assets ratio, a measure of loan specialization, has a negative effect on inefficiency, a growth with 1% of the loans to total assets ratio will lead to a decrease in inefficiency with 0.4%. In these conditions, a higher ratio of the loans in total assets and an increased lending-focused activity of the banks lead to a higher efficiency for the banks.

With regard to the effect of the bank's size on inefficiency, we noticed that smaller banks are more cost efficient than are larger banks. This result is reasonable if we bear in mind the fact that smaller savings banks cooperate with larger banks in technological services and other financial services, benefiting from economies of scale. Also, in the cooperative sector, the central institution provides services to local credit cooperatives.

The coefficient associated with 2008 is negative and significant, implying a decrease in costs for the banks included in the analysis. The coefficient associated with 2009 is positive, indicating an increase in banks' inefficiency, signaling the negative effects of the financial crisis.

CONCLUSION

This study studied the cost efficiency of cooperative banks and savings banks from nine developed countries over the period 2005 to 2011, using an SFA model. In order to measure the country's effect and to identify the impact of the financial crisis on the cost efficiency level, we created dummy variables. Also, the study examined how exogenous variables influenced the level of efficiency. Thus, we included environmental variables and control variables within these variables. Furthermore, control variables captured the performance level and the risk assumed by each bank. We also included risk factors because, over the period of analysis, banks faced higher risks, particularly after 2008.

The results revealed important findings. Firstly, we noticed that the country's effect plays an important role in explaining the differences between the cost efficiency levels. Thus, cooperative banks in Switzerland have a very high level of cost efficiency. Worthy of note is the fact that the savings banks in Norway and Sweden are more cost efficient, despite their organizational form and ownership structures. Secondly, the financial crisis reduced banks' cost efficiency in 2009. Thirdly, the results showed that a higher GDP growth is positively related to inefficiency.

We interpreted this result as a consequence of the fact that commercial banks, compared to cooperative banks and savings banks, had easier access to cheap resources in periods of economic growth. Therefore, commercial banks adopted strategies that are more aggressive in order to obtain a higher market share. This behaviour resulted in a market share reduction for cooperative banks and savings banks and in an increase of inefficiency. Fourthly, banks with a higher credit risk have lower cost efficiency.

Banks with a higher ROE are more cost efficient than are banks with a lower ROE. Cooperative banks and savings banks that focus on the traditional activity of loan granting are more efficient in comparison with the banks that have a lower share of loans to total assets. Finally, the results showed that smaller cooperative and savings banks are more cost efficient than are larger cooperative and savings banks. We considered that this result is a consequence of the advantages from which these institutions benefit within the groups to which they belong.

However, it would be interesting to study the effects of the financial crisis on commercial banks' cost efficiency, as well as how risk and performance factors influence this level compared to that of cooperative banks and savings banks. Future research may consider these factors.

REFERENCES

Afanasieff, T. S., Lhacer, P. M. V., & Nakane, M. I. (2002). The determinants of bank interest spread in Brazil. Central Bank of Brazil.

Aigner, D. J., Lovell, C. A. K., & Schmidt, P. (1977). Formulation and estimation of stochastic frontier production function models. *Journal of Econometrics*, *6*(1), 21–37. doi:10.1016/0304-4076(77)90052-5

Assaf, A. G., Barros, C. P., & Matousek, R. (2011). Productivity and efficiency analysis of Shinkin banks: Evidence from bootstrap and Bayesian approaches. *Journal of Banking & Finance*, *35*(2), 331–342. doi:10.1016/j.jbankfin.2010.08.017

Barros, C.P. Peypoch, N. and Williams, J. (2010). A note on productivity change in European cooperative banks: The Luenberger indicator approach. *International Review of Applied Economics*, *24*, 137–147.

Battaglia, F., Farina, V., Fiordelisi, F., & Ricci, O. (2010). The efficiency of cooperative banks: The impact of environmental economic conditions. *Applied Financial Economics*, *20*(17), 1363–1376. doi:10.1080/09603107.2010.491442

Battese, G. E., & Coelli, T. J. (1992). Frontier production functions, technical efficiency and panel data: With application to paddy farmers in India. *Journal of Productivity Analysis*, *3*(1-2), 153–169. doi:10.1007/BF00158774

Belotti, F., Daidone, S., Ilardi, G., & Atella, V. (2012). *Stochastic frontier analysis using Stata*. Tor Vergata University.

Berger, A. N., Hasan, I., & Zhou, M. (2009). Bank ownership and efficiency in China: What will happen in the world's largest nation? *Journal of Banking & Finance*, *33*(1), 113–130. doi:10.1016/j.jbankfin.2007.05.016

Birchall, J. (2013). *Resilience in a downturn: The power of financial cooperatives*. International Labour Office.

Bonin, J. P., Hasan, I., & Wachtel, P. (2005). Bank performance, efficiency and ownership in a transition countries. *Journal of Banking & Finance*, *29*(1), 31–53. doi:10.1016/j.jbankfin.2004.06.015

Bülbül, D., Schmidt, R. H., & Schüwer, U. (2013). Savings banks and cooperative banks in Europe. White Paper Series no. 5.

Deutsche Bundesbank. (2012). Banking statistics December 2011.

Carbo, S., Gardener, E. P. M., & Williams, J. (2003). A note on technical change in banking: The case of European savings banks. *Applied Economics*, *35*(6), 705–719. doi:10.1080/0003684022000035836

Carletti, E., Hakenes, H., & Schnabel, I. (2005). The Privatization of Italian Savings Banks – A Role Model for Germany? *Vierteljahrshefte zur Wirtschaftsforschung*, *74*(4), 32–50. doi:10.3790/vjh.74.4.32

Clarke, S. L. (2010). German savings banks and Swiss cantonal banks, lessons for the UK. The Institute for the Study of Civil Society.

Cornwell, C., Schmidt, P., & Sickles, R. (1990). Production frontiers with cross sectional and time series variation in efficiency levels. *Journal of Econometrics*, *46*(1-2), 185–200. doi:10.1016/0304-4076(90)90054-W

de España, B. (2010). Report on banking supervision in Spain.

De Haas, R., & Van Lelyveld, I. (2006). Foreign banks and credit stability in Central and Eastern Europe. A panel data analysis. *Journal of Banking & Finance*, *30*(7), 1927–1952. doi:10.1016/j.jbankfin.2005.07.007

Denmark National bank. (2006). Nordic Banking Structures – Report.

European Association of Co-operative Banks. (2012). Key Statistics Financial Indicators 2011. Retrieved from http://www.eacb.coop/en/cooperative_banks/key_figures/last_key_figures.html

European Association of Co-operative Banks, (2013). Annual Report 2012.

Ferreira, C. (2012). Bank efficiency, market concentration and economic growth in the European Union. School of Economics and Management of the Technical University of Lisbon.

Freixas, X. (2005). Deconstructing relationship banking. *Investigaciones económicas*, 29, 3-31.

Fries, S., & Taci, A. (2005). Cost efficiency of banks in transition: Evidence from 289 banks in 15 post-communist countries. *Journal of Banking & Finance*, *29*(1), 55–81. doi:10.1016/j.jbankfin.2004.06.016

Girardone, C., Nankervis, J. C., & Ekaterini-Fotini, V. (2009). Efficiency, ownership and financial structure in European banking: A cross-country comparison. *Managerial Finance*, *35*(3), 227–245. doi:10.1108/03074350910931753

Glass, J. C., & McKillop, D. G. (2006). The impact of differing operating environments on US credit union performance, 1993–2001. *Applied Financial Economics*, *16*(17), 1285–1300. doi:10.1080/09603100500426713

Greene, W. (2005). Reconsidering heterogeneity in panel data estimators of the stochastic frontier model. *Journal of Econometrics*, *126*(2), 269–303. doi:10.1016/j.jeconom.2004.05.003

Hasan, I., Koetter, M., & Wedow, M. (2009). Regional growth and finance in Europe: Is there a quality effect of bank efficiency? *Journal of Banking & Finance*, *33*(8), 1446–1453. doi:10.1016/j.jbankfin.2009.02.018

Hauner, D. (2005). Explaining efficiency differences among large German and Austrian banks. *Applied Economics*, *37*(9), 969–980. doi:10.1080/00036840500081820

Havrylchyk, O. (2006). Efficiency of the Polish banking industry: Foreign versus domestic banks. *Journal of Banking & Finance*, *30*(7), 1975–1996. doi:10.1016/j.jbankfin.2005.07.009

Heffernan, S. A., & Fu, X. (2010). Determinants of financial performance in Chinese banking. *Applied Financial Economics*, *20*(20), 1585–1600. doi :10.1080/09603107.2010.505553

Hermes, N., & Nhung, V. T. H. (2010). The impact of financial liberalization on bank efficiency: Evidence from Latin America and Asia. *Applied Economics*, *42*(26), 3351–3365. doi:10.1080/00036840802112448

Ayadi, R., Llewellyn, D. T., Schmidt, R. H., Arbak, E., & Pieter De Groen, W. (2010). Investigating Diversity in the Banking Sector in Europe – Key Developments, Performance and Role of Cooperative Banks. Centre for European Policy Studies.

Kasman, A., & Yildirim, C. (2006). Cost and profit efficiencies in transition banking: The case of new EU members. *Applied Economics*, *38*(9), 1079–1090. doi:10.1080/00036840600639022

Koetter, M., & Wedow, M. (2010). Finance and growth in a bank-based economy: Is it quantity or quality that matters? *Journal of International Money and Finance*, *29*(8), 1529–1545. doi:10.1016/j.jimonfin.2010.05.015

Kontolaimou, A. (2014). An efficiency analysis of European banks considering hierarchical technologies. *Applied Economics Letters*, *21*(10), 692–696. do i:10.1080/13504851.2014.884693

Kontolaimou, A., & Tsekouras, K. (2010). Are cooperatives the weakest link in European banking? A non-parametric metafrontier approach. *Journal of Banking & Finance*, *34*(8), 1946–1957. doi:10.1016/j.jbankfin.2010.01.003

Kumbhakar, S. C. (1990). Production frontiers, panel data, and time-varying technical inefficiency. *Journal of Econometrics*, *46*(1-2), 201–211. doi:10.1016/0304-4076(90)90055-X

Laeven, L., & Valencia, F. (2013). Systemic banking crises database. *IMF Economic Review*, *61*(2), 225–270. doi:10.1057/imfer.2013.12

Lee, Y. H., & Schmidt, P. (1993). A Production Frontier Model with Flexible Temporal Variation in Technical Inefficiency. In H. Fried, C.A.K. Lovell, and S. Schmidt (Eds.), The Measurement of Productive Efficiency: Techniques and Applications. Oxford University Press.

Lepetit, L., Nys, E., Rous, P., & Tarazi, A. (2008a). Bank income structure and risk: An empirical analysis of European banks. *Journal of Banking & Finance*, *32*(8), 1452–1467. doi:10.1016/j.jbankfin.2007.12.002

Lepetit, L., Nys, E., Rous, P., & Tarazi, A. (2008b). The Expansion of Services in European Banking: Implications for Loan Pricing and Interest Margins. *Journal of Banking & Finance*, *32*(11), 2325–2335. doi:10.1016/j.jbankfin.2007.09.025

Maudos, J., & de Guevara, J. F. (2004). Factors Explaining the Interest Margin in the Banking Sectors of the European Union. *Journal of Banking & Finance*, *28*(9), 2259–2281. doi:10.1016/j.jbankfin.2003.09.004

Maudos, J., Pastor, J. M., Perez, F., & Quesada, J. (2002). Cost and profit efficiency in European banks. *Journal of International Financial Markets, Institutions and Money*, *12*(1), 33–58. doi:10.1016/S1042-4431(01)00051-8

Meeusen, W., & van den Broeck, J. (1977). Technical efficiency and dimension of the firm: Some results on the use of frontier production functions. *Empirical Economics*, *2*(2), 109–122. doi:10.1007/BF01767476

Molyneux, P., & Williams, J. (2005). The productivity of European co-operative banks. *Managerial Finance*, *31*(11), 26–35. doi:10.1108/03074350510769947

Norges Bank. (2011). Financial Stability 1/2011, Reports from the Central Bank of Norway.

Oesterreichische National bank (OeNB). (n.d.). Statistics and Reporting - Banks' Business Structure. Retrieved from http://www.oenb.at/en/stat_melders/datenangebot /finanzinst/kreditinstitute/geschaeftsstruktur/geschaeftsstruktur.jsp

Organisation for Economic Co-operation and Development (OECD). (n.d.). The Norwegian Financial Services Industry. Retrieved from http://www.oecd.org/sti/ieconomy /1939996.pdf

Altunbas, Y., Carbó Valverde, S., & Molyneux, P. (2003). Ownership and performance in European and US banking – a comparison of commercial, cooperative and savings banks. University of Wales.

Pitt, M., & Lee, L. (1981). The measurement and sources of technical inefficiency in Indonesian weaving industry. *Journal of Development Economics*, *9*(1), 43–64. doi:10.1016/0304-3878(81)90004-3

Rajan, R. G. (1994). Why bank credit policies fluctuate: A theory and some evidence. *The Quarterly Journal of Economics*, *59*(2), 399–441. doi:10.2307/2118468

Rasmusen, E. (1988). Mutual banks and stock banks. *The Journal of Law & Economics*, *31*(2), 395–422. doi:10.1086/467162

Schmidt, P., & Sickles, R. C. (1984). Production frontiers and panel data. *Journal of Business & Economic Statistics*, *2*, 367–374.

Sealey, C. Jr, & Lindley, J. T. (1977). Inputs, outputs and a theory of production and cost at depository financial institution. *The Journal of Finance*, *32*(4), 1251–1266. doi:10.1111/j.1540-6261.1977.tb03324.x

Spulbar, C., Niţoi, M., & Anghel, L. (2015). Efficiency in cooperative banks and savings banks: A stochastic frontier approach. *Romanian Journal of Economic Forecasting*, *18*(1), 5–21.

Swedish Bankers' Association. (2011). Banks in Sweden.

Williams, J. (2001). Financial deregulation and productivity change in European banking. *Revue de la Banque*, *8*, 470–477.

Williams, J., Peypoch, N., & Barros, C. P. (2011). The Luenberger indicator and productivity growth: A note on the European savings banks sector. *Applied Economics*, *43*(6), 747–755. doi:10.1080/00036840802599859

Xu, Y. (2011). Towards a more accurate measure of foreign bank entry and its impact on domestic banking performance: The case of China. *Journal of Banking & Finance*, *35*(4), 886–901. doi:10.1016/j.jbankfin.2010.10.011

Chapter 4
Financial Nexus:
Efficiency and Soundness in Banking and Capital Markets

ABSTRACT

This book chapter investigates the financial nexus generated by bank soundness, concentration, and efficiency in the banking sector, as well as the development of the capital markets. The selected databases includes the time period between 1997 and 2010 for a large sample of 63 developed and developing countries. The empirical findings suggested that bank performance has a high impact on the relation between soundness, structural and functional characteristics of the banking sector. The econometric framework is complex and the empirical results appear to be robust for various measures of the selected variables and for distinct estimation techniques.

INTRODUCTION

The current financial turmoil is far from highlighting all its bitter lessons. One conclusion may yet be drawn: the soundness of the banking sector is a key ingredient of the global financial stability. The instability in the banking sector represents a critical transmission channel for various endogenous and exogenous shocks. Among the determinants of the banks' long-run stability, competition seems to be a major driving force. While sometimes this factor is viewed as contributing to a decline in the banks' soundness, the characteristics

DOI: 10.4018/978-1-5225-9269-3.ch004

of the regulatory framework seems to decisively modulate its induced effects. The weaknesses of the regulatory framework are one of the main roots of the financial instability. Of course, this cannot be viewed as an argument against promoting a solid and clear regulatory framework. Rather, as Schaeck and Cihák (2010, p. 2) argue: "it is an argument and motivation to strengthen and further improve upon regulatory frameworks."

LITERATURE REVIEW

The conventional approaches derived from industrial organization theory (Demsetz, 1973) suggest that competition increases the efficiency of banks. The structure–conduct–performance paradigm supposes that competitive large banks are more likely to implement better monitoring mechanisms and hence are less probable to suffer nonperforming loans (Hauswald & Marquez, 2003). Also, these banks are more able to extract monopolistic rents from concentrated markets as these rents are reflected by higher interest rates charged on loans and lower interest rates offered for deposits (see for instance Berger, 1995; Petersen & Rajan, 1995; Berger & De Young, 1997). However, recent research challenges this wisdom arguing that bank competition enhances the performance and stimulates the implementation of prudential mechanisms. Hence, current literature suggests a positive link between bank competition and soundness (Barth et al., 2004; Beck et al., 2006; Schaeck & Cihák, 2007, 2010; Carletti et al., 2007; Hauswald & Marquez, 2006). Schaeck and Čihák (2008, 2010) provide evidences that efficiency plays a key role in the transmission mechanism from competition to soundness. They argue that sound banks are abler to benefit from a competitive environment.

An alternative explanation relates to the efficient-structure hypothesis. According to this hypothesis, larger banks are abler to control their operating costs through better management and operational procedures and to transfer the various categories of risks. Such arguments may provide an explanation for the positive link between the degree of industry concentration and bank soundness (Hay & Liu, 1997; Beck, Demirgüç-Kunt, & Levine, 2006). As Bertay et al. (2011,.3) argue a bank's absolute size thus represents a trade-off between bank risk and return. For an international sample of banks, they found that larger banks tend to be more profitable, while they also display a lower Z-score. The results from Ferreira (2012) point toward a point to a negative causation at the level of European Union running both from the concentration in banking sector to banks' efficiency as well as from efficiency to concentration. Casu and Girardone (2006) found evidences that increased competition forced European Union's banks to become more efficient, even though increased efficiency does not necessarily foster more competitive banking systems.

Our goal is to contribute to this discussion in several ways. Firstly, we employ a modified version of a model used in Corvoisier and Gropp (2002) and de Guevara et al (2005) in order to describe the impact of the banking sector's concentration upon banks' soundness. As a distinctive feature, we consider the choice of the non-financial agents to finance their budget deficits either by borrowing from the banks or by obtaining the financial resources from capital markets. As Antoniou et al (2008) argue, the capital structure decision of a company is not only the product of its own characteristics, but also the result of environmental factors among which capital markets are playing a critical role.

Companies are choosing their capital structure by taking into account the relative costs of various financing sources, with a leverage that tends to decline with the increase in the availability of such resources from the capital markets and with the increases in the shares' prices. In the meantime, the existence of sound capital markets supports the capacity of banks to extend their financial intermediation services. This last argument is in line with the so-called Systemic Scale Economies hypothesis advanced by Bossone and Lee (2004), accordingly to which the production of bank intermediation services features increasing returns in the scale of the financial system. Banks that operate in systems with larger (deeper and more efficient) capital markets are facing relatively lower costs of risk absorption and benefit from reputation bonuses compared to the banks operating in smaller capital markets. Larger capital markets allow banks to access more efficient instruments of risk management, to better screen their borrowers, monitor their investment more efficiently and to signal their risk attitude.

Secondly, we investigate the underlying transmission mechanism for a sample of 63 developed and developing countries. We find evidences that the degree of concentration and the development of the capital market are playing a significant role in the evolution of the banks' soundness during the convergence between the capital market oriented and bank-oriented financing mechanisms. However, this influence is modulated by the banks' efficiency as well as by the overall degree of economic development.

Thirdly, we use two-stage quantile regression techniques to account for the differences in the banks' sizes and general economic development. We find that large and efficient banks are abler to benefit from sector concentration and capital markets' development compared to the weak and inefficient banks. However, the effects exercised by banks' concentration upon their soundness appears to be at a certain degree sensitive to the way in which concentration is measured. As Schaeck and Cihák (2010) argue, such sensitivity may be caused by the endogeneity of the measures of soundness, performance, competition and inferences issues. In the same time, we consider it may be due to the fact that these different measures are not perfectly conceptually and empirically overlapping and in fact these are reflecting various aspects of the mentioned variables. We also find that the development of capital markets supports the sound evolution of banks as substitution effects are linking these two components of the financial sector.

Fourthly, we consider several alternative measures of banks soundness, concentration and efficiency and we highlight that different facets of these variables should be carefully considered before drawing more general conclusions.

The rest of the paper is organized as follows. Section 2 describes the theoretical model. Section 3 provides an overview of the estimation methodology, while Section 4 describes the international data. Section 5 reports on the results of the different models involved as well on the robustness checks, while Section 6 concludes.

METHODOLOGY

Dima, Dincă and Spulbar (2014) estimate initially a baseline static model. Such a model, accounting for cross- and time-specific effects, may be specified as:

$$z_{i,t} = \alpha_0 + \beta x_{i,t} + v_i + \gamma_t + \varepsilon_{i,t}, i = 1,\ldots,N, t = 1,\ldots,T \quad (1)$$

Here $z_{i,t}$ denotes the bank Z-score (or other alternative measures of soundness), $x_{i,t}$ is a vector of Lerner index (or alternative descriptors of banking sector concentration), capital markets development and other control variables for banks efficiency, which are considered endogenous covariates, v_i are the panel-level effects (which may be correlated with the covariates) while γ_t are time effects, and $\varepsilon_{i,t}$ are *i.i.d.* shocks. v_i and $\varepsilon_{i,t}$ are assumed to be independent for each *i* over all *t*.

For the estimation of such model, a critical assumption concerns the possible correlations between the unobserved cross and time-specific effects and the regressors. If there are no evidences of such correlations, then a random effects model, which uses both the within and the between information, may be more parsimonious. However, if correlations between unobserved effects and regressors are present, then a fixed effects model may be preferred.

Here we consider the model developed in Chernozhukov and Hansen (2005, 2006, 2008). Formally, this model is represented by:

$$z = D`\alpha\left(U\right) + x`\beta\left(U\right) U\left|x, Z\, Uniform\left(0,1\right)\right. \tag{2}$$

$$D = \delta\left(x, Z, V\right),, \text{ where } V \text{ is statistically dependent on } U \tag{3}$$

$$\tau \mapsto D`\alpha\left(\tau\right) + x`\beta\left(\tau\right) \text{ strictly increasing in } \tau \tag{4}$$

where: *U* is a scalar random variable that captures all of the unobserved factors which affects the structural outcome equation; *D* is a vector of endogenous variables; *V* is a vector of unobserved disturbances determining *D* and which are correlated with *U*; *Z* is a vector of instrumental variables. These variables are supposed to be independent of the disturbance *U,* but able to impact *D* as described by (3).

The presence of the instrumental variable leads to a set of moment equations that can be used to estimate the parameters involved by (2). From (2) and (4), the event $\left\{z \leq S_z\left(\tau \mid D, x\right)\right\}$ with $S_z\left(\tau \mid D, x\right)$ being the Structural Quantile Function (SQF), is equivalent to the event $\left\{U \leq \tau\right\}$. Thus, from (2) follows that:

$$P\left[z \leq S_z\left(\tau \middle| D, x\right) \middle| Z, x\right] = \tau \tag{5}$$

Relation (5) provides a restriction that can be used to estimate the structural parameters α and β. Further, one may argue that the relationship between bank soundness and sector concentration may also flow in an opposite direction. Large and sound banks may be able to control a greater share of market and to provide diversified services. Hence, since doubts may be raised concerning the exogeneity of Lerner index, we instrument this variable using private-sector bank loans into GDP (%), cost to income ratio (%), and GDP per capita (logarithm) (constant 2000's USD) as instruments. We expect these variables to be uncorrelated with the disturbance *U,* but significantly associated with the Lerner index.

DATA

The dataset covers a time span between 1997 and 2010 for 63 developed and developing countries (Argentina, Australia, Austria, Bangladesh, Belgium, Bolivia, Brazil, Bulgaria, Canada, Chile, China, Costa Rica, Cote d'Ivoire, Croatia, Cyprus, Czech Republic, Denmark, Ecuador, El Salvador, Estonia, Finland, France, Germany, Greece, Hong Kong, China, Hungary, Iceland, India, Indonesia, Ireland, Israel, Italy, Japan, Korea, Latvia, Lithuania, Luxembourg, Malaysia, Malta, Morocco, Netherlands, New Zealand, Nigeria, Norway, Panama, Paraguay, Peru, Philippines, Poland, Portugal, Romania, Russian Federation, Singapore, Slovak Republic, Slovenia, South Africa, Switzerland, Thailand, Tunisia, Turkey, United Kingdom, United States and Venezuela). The data come from World Bank Global Financial Development database.

Dima, Dincă and Spulbar (2014) suggested that the dependent variable reflects the default probability of a country's banking system, calculated as a weighted average of the Z-scores of a country's individual banks. Z-score compares a bank's buffers (capitalization and returns) with the volatility of those returns. The Z-score shows the number of standard deviations that a bank's rate of return on assets can decrease in a single period before it becomes insolvent. Thus, a higher Z-score indicates a lower probability of bank insolvency (Bertay et al., 2013).

In order to facilitate the analysis, the Z-scores are rescaled in order to display a zero mean and unit variance:

$$Z_i^{rescaled} = \frac{Z_i - \overline{Z}}{\sigma^2\left(Z\right)} \tag{6}$$

The main explanatory variables are the Lerner index and the stock market capitalization-to-GDP ratio. The Lerner index seeks to capture market power in the banking market, and it is based on the methodology described in Demirgüç-Kunt and Martínez Pería (2010). It is defined as the difference between output prices and marginal costs (relative to prices). Prices are calculated as total bank revenue over assets, whereas marginal costs are obtained from an estimated translog cost function with respect to output. The general advantage of such a flexible cost function consists in the fact that it does not imply a-priori restrictions on the production technology.

A Lerner index having a value equal to 1 (one) describes a monopolistic banking market, while a value of zero indicates a perfect competition case. Between these two extreme values, higher values of the Lerner index indicate less bank competition. It should be noticed that opposite to other measures of the market power such as the H-statistic, the Lerner index it is not a long-run equilibrium measure of competition and thus may capture short-run adjustments (Demirgüç-Kunt & Martínez Pería, 2010:9).

The stock market variable reflects the total value of all listed shares in a stock market as percentage of GDP. The main statistics for these variables are reported in Table 1. The dataset includes a variety of cases with high market power for the banking sector and lower relative importance of the capital markets in financial intermediation processes, in countries like Costa Rica, Ecuador, Paraguay or Lithuania at one side of the spectrum and, respectively, countries with high concentration in the banking sector and substantial stock markets' capitalization, such as Chile, Malaysia, Hong Kong, Japan or Singapore at the other side of the spectrum.

Between these two groups, there are countries which usually display substantial market power and also an important dominance of capital markets such as Australia, Canada, Finland, United Kingdom or United States (Figure 1).

The values of the skewness and kurtosis parameters highlight important deviations from the normal distribution and fat-tails effects in the data. Hence, the chosen estimation methodologies should account for such data heterogeneity.

Two control variables are also considered: bank loans-to-deposits ratio and, respectively, the weight of non-interest incomes into total incomes. By diversifying its portfolio of operations, an efficient bank is able to better manage its operating expenses and to lower their weight in total revenues. In the meantime, by providing various financial services such a bank is able to better leverage the raised financial resources. Hence, the latter variable may

Table 1. Main statistics of data

	Lerner Index			Stock Market Capitalization (% GDP)			Bank Z-Score	1997-2006	2007-2010
	1997-2010	1997-2006	2007-2010	1997-2010	1997-2006	2007-2010	1997-2010		
Mean	0.21	0.20	0.24	60.86	57.02	70.64	-0.01	-0.01	0.04
Median	0.21	0.20	0.23	37.66	34.62	47.65	-0.15	-0.16	-0.08
Maximum	0.73	0.67	0.73	580.52	417.95	580.52	8.50	8.50	2.58
Minimum	-1.61	-1.61	-0.07	0.03	0.76	1.54	-1.74	-1.61	-1.74
Std. Dev.	0.12	0.13	0.10	67.99	62.73	78.98	1.00	1.06	0.88
Skewness	-3.32	-4.44	1.52	2.81	2.28	3.36	1.70	1.95	0.40
Kurtosis	64.28	74.42	9.10	14.87	9.47	18.38	1.69	11.67	2.52
Jarque-Bera	137899.80	133796.70	473.54	6265.71	1615.68	2875.08	2477.81	2333.87	9.05
Probability	0.00	0.00	0.00	0.00	0.00	0.00	0.00	0.00	0.01
Observations	871	620	245	872	620	245	882	620	245

Figure 1. Z-scores and stock market capitalization, averages, 1997-2010

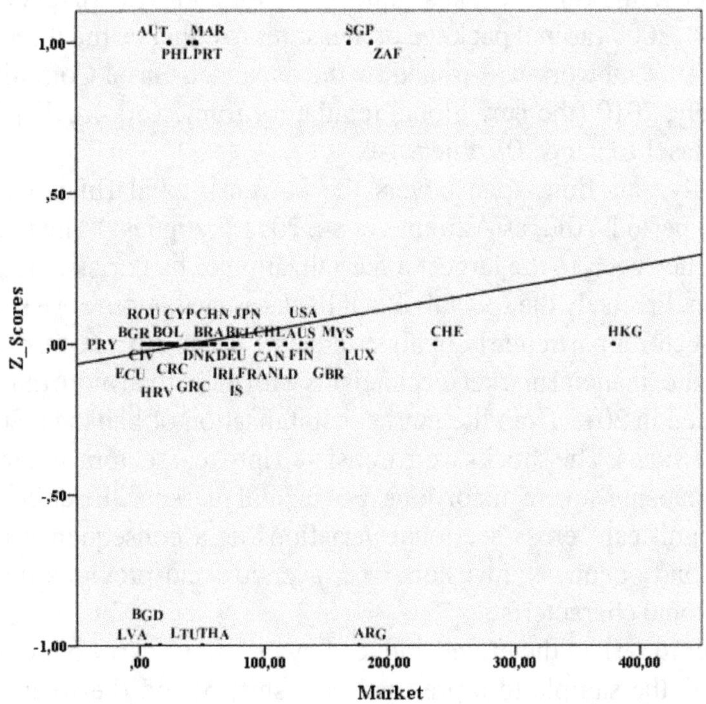

be seen as a proxy for the efficiency in the banking sector, while the first one is a proxy for the diversification of the resources' allocation in banks.

The general statistic properties of the data from Table 1 suggest that there might be some important regime-shifts at the level of data. Several sources of such shifts may be highlighted. Firstly, there are evidences that the soundness of banks is regime dependent. For instance, as Liu et al., 2004: 7, notes for Canadian banks: "The possible regime shifts coincide with regulatory innovations in the financial safety net, which may have helped improve the market's perception of the banks' soundness". Such regulatory innovations might be country-specific but for our analysis period they mainly appear as a consequence of the efforts for implementing Basel II (and Basel 2.5) Capital Agreement. The purpose of Basel II was to reduce provide an answer to the rapid development of the financial markets by reducing the arbitrage opportunities and provide regulatory capital requirements more risk-sensitive in order to promote resilience of the banking sectors.

In order to account for the potential associated effects, we use a dummy variable as explanatory in order to capture three main updates of Basel II. More exactly, this variable takes value of "1" for 2004 (the first version from June 2004), 2009 (a final package of measures to enhance the three pillars of the Basel II framework was issued by the expanded Basel Committee) and, respectively, 2010 (the new global regulatory framework- revisited in June 2011-of Basel III) and "0" otherwise.

Secondly, our time span covers the current global financial and real instability period. And, as Altunbas et al., 2011:5, argues: "The recent crisis gave way, however, to the largest materialization of bank risk since the great depression. Precisely the special role of banks as evaluators of risk makes the banking sector a particularly opaque industry". The current turbulence has disrupted the financial market mechanisms with more than more than 3 trillion euros erased in 2011 from the market capitalisation of banks in Europe and the United States. The shocks were translated into real sectors of international economy causing severe distortions. For capital markets, the effects of crisis display significant cross-sectional variations as a consequence of market deepness and openness, investors' risk aversion and previous institutional and functional characteristics.

In order to reflect the effects induced by crisis, we carry out our analysis by splitting the sample to a pre- and post-shift period (between 1997 and 2006 and, respectively, 2007 and 2010) and we compare the results for all our models. The distribution parameters reported in Table 1 reflect the existence of significant changes in fat tails effects. In details, the Lerner index displays a negative skew for 1997-2006 and a positive skew for the period between 2007 and 2010. Also, substantial differences appear for the corresponding levels of kurtosis parameter associated with a translation from a platykurtic distribution to a leptokurtic distribution in Z-scores. Hence, year 2007 may be seen as a structural breakpoint in our data sample.

Thirdly, there is a convergent literature suggesting that the size of banks may exert a significant influence on market discipline and banks' risk aversion (Demsetz & Stahan, 1997; Demirgüç-Kunt & Huizinga, 2010b; Bertay et al., 2013). Thus, it may be reasonable to expect differences in banks' reactions to various endogenous and exogenous shocks accordingly to their relative size. In order to measure the global size of banking sector, we follow the distinction from Bertay et al, 2013, between banks absolute size and their systemic size, i.e. its size relative to the national economy. We employ the second type of measurement and we measure the size of the commercial banks sector as the deposit money banks' assets-to- GDP ratio.

Assets include claims on domestic real nonfinancial sector which includes central, state and local governments, nonfinancial public enterprises and private sector. This ratio reflects the potential capacity of the banks to cover their liabilities in respect to the size of the economy. We classify the countries with "large commercial banks sector" as being the ones with total assets (scaled to GDP) greater than the average of the whole dataset for the entire time span (with deposit money banks' assets to GDP (%) ratio between 82% and 193%). Correlatively, countries with "small commercial banks sector" are classified as the ones with total assets lower than dataset average (with deposit money banks' assets to GDP (%) ratio between 5% and 73%).

In order to consider all these sources of non-linear evolutions in data, we run our tests by taking into account two sub-samples of data for countries with "large "and, respectively, "small" banking sectors.

RESULTS AND COMMENTS

Static Models

Table 2 reports the results for the +-static frame and different specifications. The first column displays the outcomes for the pooled least-squares estimation with fixed country effects, while the second column shows the results of the generalized least-squares estimation with random country effects.

Regardless the estimation method, for the full data sample and the entire time span (in Panel "A"), the impact exercised by the market power on Z-scores appears to be positive and statistically significant at 1%. The impact of stock market capitalization is also positive and statistically significant at 5% (10%). The effects induced by a change in the Lerner index on rescaled Z-scores lies between 0.98–fold and 1.33-fold, while for the stock market capitalization they are at 0.002-fold, for both fixed and random country effects.

Bank Z-Score and Its Determinants: Fixed and Random Estimations

However, accordingly with the Hausman test, the null hypothesis of no systematic differences in the estimated coefficients between the fixed effects model and the random effects model can be rejected. Supplementary, the likelihood ratio tests for redundant fixed effects highlights that the usage of fixed effects estimations may be seen as appropriate since the null hypothesis of redundant fixed effects can be rejected on a 1% level. In the meantime, based on the values of the Hausman tests, there are no clear evidences that the fixed and random effects models are different enough. Of course, this finding does not necessarily follow that the random effects estimators are free from biases. Thus, the presence of correlations between unobserved effects and regressors should be considered. Moreover, the null of no country specific effects can be rejected both for fixed effects estimation (Chow test) and for random effects estimation (Breusch and Pagan Lagrangian multiplier test). Also, we have got evidences of high serial correlations in the idiosyncratic errors as these are reflected by the Wooldridge (2002) test. Hence, the standard errors may be biased. In order to correct for this, the last columns of Tables 2-4 report the Cochrane-Orcutt estimator based on an iterative approach for the feasible generalized least squares (FGLS) method. This is a generalized least squares (GLS) estimator and assumes that the errors are following a first-order autoregressive process. Z-scores remain significant at 1% and their positive impact is preserved inside this methodology.

If the models are run on the two sub-periods, there appears to be some visible differences in outcomes. For instance, during the crisis the effects induced by market power on Z-scores are two times larger than in the pre-crisis period in the fixed effects estimations. But these effects lost their statistical significance in random effects models. Still, the Hausman tests show that the fixed and random effects are different enough to reject the null hypothesis,

Table 2a. Panel "A": full sample, 63 countries

	Fixed-Effects (Within) Regression With AR(1) Disturbances			Random-Effects GLS Regression With AR(1) Disturbances			Cochrane-Orcutt AR(1) Regression		
	(1)	(2)	(3)	(4)	(5)	(6)	(7)	(8)	(9)
	Full Sample (1997-2010)	1997-2006	2007-2010	Full Sample (1997-2010)	1997-2006	2007-2010	Full Sample (1997-2010)	1997-2006	2007-2010
Lerner index	0.981*** (0.242)	1.004*** (0.281)	2.088*** (0.518)	0.888*** (0.246)	0.879*** (0.279)	0.864 (0.609)	1.326*** (0.264)	1.303*** (0.346)	1.988** (0.778)
Bank credit to bank deposits (%)	-0.002 (0.001)	-0.002 (0.002)	0.000 (0.001)	-0.001 (0.001)	-0.000 (0.001)	-0.002* (0.001)	-0.000 (0.001)	0.000 (0.001)	-0.000 (0.001)
Non-interest income to total income (%)	0.001*** (0.000)	0.001*** (0.000)	-0.000 (0.001)	0.001** (0.000)	0.001* (0.000)	-0.001 (0.001)	0.001*** (0.000)	0.001** (0.000)	-0.001 (0.001)
Stock market capitalization to GDP (%)	0.002* (0.001)	0.003 (0.002)	0.000 (0.001)	0.002** (0.001)	0.001 (0.001)	0.002** (0.001)	0.001 (0.001)	0.001 (0.001)	0.003*** (0.001)
Lerner index*Basel Capital Agreement dummy	0.423** (0.177)	0.392 (0.258)	0.281* (0.154)	0.349* (0.189)	0.362 (0.279)	0.547** (0.223)	0.476*** (0.185)	0.436* (0.239)	0.231 (0.377)
Constant	-0.241*** (0.076)	-0.207* (0.114)	-0.396* (0.224)	-0.210 (0.159)	-0.257 (0.183)	0.110 (0.271)	-0.405*** (0.151)	-0.514*** (0.172)	-0.446 (0.297)
R^2	0.06	0.02	0.12	0.06	0.05	0.17	0.06	0.05	0.18
F(degree of freedom, number of observations)	7.430 (Probability >F=0.000)	5.06 (Probability >F=0.000)	6.50 (Probability >F=0.000)				11.42 (Probability >F=0.000)	5.63 (Probability >F=0.000)	5.54 (Probability >F=0.000)
Wald				30.69 (Probability $>\chi^2$=0.000)	19.36 (Probability $>\chi^2$=0.004)	17.50 (Probability $>\chi^2$=0.008)			
Chow test	4.710 (Probability >F=0.000)	4.24 (Probability >F=0.000)	32.68 (Probability >F=0.000)						

continued on following page

Table 2a. Continued

	Fixed-Effects (Within) Regression With AR(1) Disturbances			Random-Effects GLS Regression With AR(1) Disturbances			Cochrane-Orcutt AR(1) Regression		
	(1)	(2)	(3)	(4)	(5)	(6)	(7)	(8)	(9)
	Full Sample (1997-2010)	**1997-2006**	**2007-2010**	**Full Sample (1997-2010)**	**1997-2006**	**2007-2010**	**Full Sample (1997-2010)**	**1997-2006**	**2007-2010**
Breusch and Pagan Lagrangian multiplier test				864.26 (Probability $>\chi^2$=0.000)	493.54 (Probability $>\chi^2$=0.000)	148.28 (Probability $>\chi^2$=0.000)			
Redundant Fixed Effects Tests(F-statistic)	11.532 (Probability >F=0.000)	10.128 (Probability >F=0.000)	17.223 (Probability >F=0.000)						
Correlated Random Effects - Hausman Test				9.09 (Probability= 0.11)	19.25 (Probability= 0.07)	17.83 (Probability= 0.003)			
Durbin-Watson statistic (transformed)							1.624	1.424	0.430
ρ	0.531	0.459	-0.155	0.529	0.459	0.821	0.697	0.660	0.553

Table 2b.

Hausman Test	**10.23 (Probability $>\chi^2$=0.036)**	**10.93 (Probability $>\chi^2$=0.084)**	**17.07 (Probability $>\chi^2$=0.052)**	**10.23 (Probability $>\chi^2$=0.036)**	**10.93 (Probability $>\chi^2$=0.053**	**17.07 (Probability > χ^2=0.009)**
Baltagi-Wu LBI test	0.937	1.081	2.310	0.937	1.081	2.310
Wooldridge test	53.675 (Probability >F=0.000)	53.033 (Probability >F=0.000)	93.484 (Probability >F=0.000)	53.675 (Probability >F=0.000)	53.033 (Probability >F=0.000)	93.484 (Probability > F=0.000)

Table 3a. Panel "B": Large banks, 28 countries

	Fixed-Effects (Within) Regression With AR(1) Disturbances			Random-Effects GLS Regression With AR(1) Disturbances			Cochrane-Orcutt AR(1) Regression		
	(1)	(2)	(3)	(4)	(5)	(6)	(7)	(8)	(9)
	Full Sample (1997-2010)	1997-2006	2007-2010	Full Sample (1997-2010)	1997-2006	2007-2010	Full Sample (1997-2010)	1997-2006	2007-2010
Lerner index	0.894 (0.819)	0.290 (1.077)	2.979** (1.192)	0.757 (0.820)	0.614 (1.011)	0.867 (1.267)	1.908*** (0.708)	1.863** (0.883)	3.722** (1.597)
Bank credit to bank deposits (%)	-0.001 (0.002)	-0.001 (0.002)	-0.002 (0.003)	-0.001 (0.002)	0.000 (0.002)	-0.002 (0.002)	0.001 (0.001)	0.002 (0.001)	0.003 (0.002)
Non-interest income to total income (%)	0.000 (0.002)	0.000 (0.003)	-0.000 (0.001)	0.000 (0.002)	0.002 (0.003)	-0.000 (0.002)	0.000 (0.002)	0.000 (0.003)	-0.001 (0.003)
Stock market capitalization to GDP (%)	0.003** (0.001)	0.007** (0.002)	0.001 (0.002)	0.001 (0.001)	0.000 (0.002)	0.002 (0.001)	0.001 (0.000)	0.001 (0.001)	0.003** (0.001)
Lerner index*Basel Capital Agreement dummy	0.560* (0.292)	0.493 (0.390)	0.275 (0.349)	0.370 (0.327)	0.454 (0.452)	0.763* (0.463)	0.640** (0.281)	0.523 (0.361)	-0.013 (0.774)
Constant	-0.336** (0.145)	-0.585*** (0.198)	-0.301 (0.386)	-0.084 (0.304)	-0.075 (0.363)	-0.310 (0.448)	-0.708*** (0.254)	-0.769** (0.311)	-1.173** (0.471)
R^2	0.02	0.002	0.21	0.02	0.01	0.17	0.07	0.06	0.24
F(degree of freedom, number of observations)	2.64 (Probability >F=0.023)	2.44 (Probability >F=0.04)	3.36 (Probability >F=0.013)				4.50 (Probability >F=0.001)	2.40 (Probability >F=0.004)	3.51 (Probability >F=0.008)
Wald				4.80 (Probability $>\chi^2$=0.570)	2.10 (Probability $>\chi^2$=0.909)	8.08 (Probability $>\chi^2$=0.232)			
Chow test	3.67 (Probability >F=0.000)	3.54 (Probability >F=0.000)	21.95 (Probability >F=0.000)						

continued on following page

Table 3a. Continued

	Fixed-Effects (Within) Regression With AR(1) Disturbances			Random-Effects GLS Regression With AR(1) Disturbances			Cochrane-Orcutt AR(1) Regression		
	(1)	(2)	(3)	(4)	(5)	(6)	(7)	(8)	(9)
	Full Sample (1997-2010)	**1997-2006**	**2007-2010**	**Full Sample (1997-2010)**	**1997-2006**	**2007-2010**	**Full Sample (1997-2010)**	**1997-2006**	**2007-2010**
Breusch and Pagan Lagrangian multiplier test				196.94 (Probability $>\chi^2$=0.000)	132.99 (Probability $>\chi^2$=0.000)	61.85 (Probability $>\chi^2$=0.000)			
Redundant Fixed Effects Tests(F-statistic)	8.084 (Probability >F=0.000)	12.414 (Probability >F=0.000)	17.223 (Probability >F=0.000)						
Correlated Random Effects - Hausman Test				13.56 (Probability= 0.02)	9.387 (Probability= 0.09)	9.140 (Probability= 0.104)			
Durbin-Watson statistic (transformed)							1.451	1.087	0.421
ρ	0.531	0.479	-0.194	0.531	0.479	0.762	0.634	0.603	0.477

Table 3b.

Hausman test	17.12 (Probability $>\chi^2$=0.004)	9.70 (Probability $>\chi^2$=0.084)	8.85 (Probability $>\chi^2$=0.003)	17.12 (Probability $>\chi^2$=0.004)	9.70 (Probability $>\chi^2$=0.084)	8.85 (Probability $>\chi^2$=0.003)
Baltagi-Wu LBI test	0.938	1.041	2.388	0.938	1.041	2.388
Wooldridge test	14.411 (Probability >F=0.001)	81.229 (Probability >F=0.000)	78.793 (Probability >F=0.000)	14.411 (Probability >F=0.001)	81.229 (Probability >F=0.000)	78.793 (Probability >F=0.000)

Table 4a. Panel "C": Small banks, 35 countries

	Fixed-Effects (Within) Regression With AR(1) Disturbances			Random-Effects GLS Regression With AR(1) Disturbances			Cochrane-Orcutt AR(1) Regression		
	(1)	(2)	(3)	(4)	(5)	(6)	(7)	(8)	(9)
	Full Sample (1997-2010)	1997-2006	2007-2010	Full Sample (1997-2010)	1997-2006	2007-2010	Full Sample (1997-2010)	1997-2006	2007-2010
Lerner index	0.992*** (0.247)	1.030*** (0.288)	1.629*** (0.466)	0.907*** (0.241)	0.927*** (0.278)	0.469 (0.622)	1.176*** (0.301)	1.175*** (0.368)	0.663 (0.779)
Bank credit to bank deposits (%)	-0.002 (0.001)	-0.004* (0.002)	0.002 (0.001)	-0.002* (0.001)	-0.002 (0.002)	-0.002 (0.002)	-0.003* (0.001)	-0.002 (0.002)	-0.003** (0.001)
Non-interest income to total income (%)	0.001*** (0.000)	0.001** (0.000)	-0.001 (0.003)	0.001** (0.000)	0.001* (0.001)	-0.008* (0.005)	0.001** (0.000)	0.001** (0.000)	-0.001** (0.000)
Stock market capitalization to GDP (%)	0.000 (0.002)	-0.004 (0.003)	0.003 (0.003)	0.004*** (0.002)	0.006*** (0.002)	0.006*** (0.001)	0.002 (0.002)	0.002 (0.002)	0.007** (0.003)
Lerner index*Basel Capital Agreement dummy	0.309 (0.235)	0.324 (0.356)	0.148 (0.134)	0.369 (0.244)	0.355 (0.379)	0.398* (0.226)	0.319 (0.230)	0.317 (0.325)	0.245 (0.370)
Constant	-0.150* (0.090)	0.183 (0.157)	-0.461 (0.272)	-0.259 (0.176)	-0.301 (0.212)	0.103 (0.372)	-0.152 (0.213)	-0.255 (0.252)	0.507 (0.428)
R^2	0.03	0.02	0.05	0.18	0.21	0.30	0.07	0.06	0.28
F(degree of freedom, number of observations)	5.46 (Probability >F=0.000)	4.81 (Probability >F=0.000)	4.20 (Probability >F=0.005)				5.50 (Probability >F=0.000)	3.54 (Probability >F=0.004)	4.74 (Probability >F=0.001)
Wald				32.85 (Probability $>\chi^2$=0.000)	25.79 (Probability $>\chi^2$=0.000)	26.41 (Probability $>\chi^2$=0.000)			
Chow test	5.71 (Probability >F=0.000)	5.30 (Probability >F=0.000)	47.66 (Probability >F=0.000)						

continued on following page

Table 4a. Continued

	Fixed-Effects (Within) Regression With AR(1) Disturbances			Random-Effects GLS Regression With AR(1) Disturbances			Cochrane-Orcutt AR(1) Regression		
	(1)	(2)	(3)	(4)	(5)	(6)	(7)	(8)	(9)
	Full Sample (1997-2010)	**1997-2006**	**2007-2010**	**Full Sample (1997-2010)**	**1997-2006**	**2007-2010**	**Full Sample (1997-2010)**	**1997-2006**	**2007-2010**
Breusch and Pagan Lagrangian multiplier test				478.65 (Probability >χ^2=0.000)	215.71 (Probability >χ^2=0.000)	71.42 (Probability >χ^2=0.000)			
Redundant Fixed Effects Tests(F-statistic)	13.295 (Probability >F=0.000)	10.305 (Probability >F=0.000)	36.904 (Probability >F=0.000)						
Correlated Random Effects - Hausman Test				20.778 (Probability= 0.000)	32.133 (Probability= 0.000)	17.288 (Probability= 0.004)			
Durbin-Watson statistic (transformed)							1.177	1.679	0.393
ρ	0.497	0.394	-0.198	0.497	0.394	0.925	0.754	0.712	0.573

Table 4b.

Hausman Test	20.96 (Probability $>\chi^2$=0.000)	71.46 (Probability $>\chi^2$=0.000)	94.48 (Probability $>\chi^2$=0.000)	20.96 (Probability $>\chi^2$=0.000)	71.46 (Probability $>\chi^2$=0.000)	94.48 (Probability $>\chi^2$=0.000)
Baltagi-Wu LBI Test	1.005	1.211	2.396	1.005	1.211	2.396
Wooldridge Test	80.027 (Probability >F=0.000)	102.105 (Probability >F=0.000)	31.704 (Probability >F=0.000)	80.027 (Probability >F=0.000)	102.105 (Probability >F=0.000)	31.704 (Probability >F=0.000)

***/**/* -1%, 5%, 10% significance levels. Notes: Countries with large commercial banks are considered as being the ones with total assets (scaled to GDP) greater than the average of the whole dataset (with deposit money banks' assets to GDP (%) ratio between 82% and 193%). Correlatively, countries with small commercial banks are the ones with total assets lower than dataset average (with deposit money banks' assets to GDP (%) ratio between 5% and 73%). Panel "A" includes all 63 countries. Panel "B" includes 28 countries (Australia, Austria, Belgium, Canada, China, Cyprus, Denmark, France, Germany, Greece, Hong Kong SAR, China, Iceland, Ireland, Israel, Italy, Japan, Korea, Luxembourg, Malaysia, Malta, Netherlands, New Zealand, Panama, Portugal, Singapore, Switzerland, Thailand, and United Kingdom). Panel "C" includes 35 countries (Argentina, Bangladesh, Bolivia, Brazil, Bulgaria, Chile, Costa Rica, Cote d'Ivoire, Croatia, Czech Republic, Ecuador, El Salvador, Estonia, Finland, Hungary, India, Indonesia, Latvia, Lithuania, Morocco, Nigeria, Norway, Paraguay, Peru, Philippines, Poland, Romania, Russian Federation, Slovak Republic, Slovenia, South Africa, Tunisia, Turkey, United States and Venezuela). Basel Capital Agreement dummy takes values of "1" for 2004 (first version of the Capital Agreement in June 2004), 2009 (a final package of measures to enhance the three pillars of the Basel II framework was issued by the newly expanded Basel Committee) and 2010 (the initial Basel III rules) and, respectively, values of "0" for the other years. For the models' quality tests: a) Chow test on the absence of fixed country effects:H0: $v_i = 0$; b) Breusch and Pagan Lagrangian multiplier test on absence of random effects: H0: $\mathrm{var}(v_i) = 0$; c) Hausman test: H0: Differences in coefficients between fixed-effects and random-effects are not systematic; d) ρ is the estimated autocorrelation coefficient from the AR (1) model; e) LBI is the Baltagi-Wu (1999) locally best invariant test statistic for the AR (1) model; f) Wooldridge test for serial correlation from the regression of the first-differences variables- H0: no first-order autocorrelation

and hence to reject the random effects models in the favour of fixed effects models. When the Cochrane-Orcutt estimator is considered, the Lerner index does not any longer appear to be significant for crisis period.

For stock market capitalization, its statistical significance clearly increases during crisis period. This finding may be seen as providing some ground for our hypothesis of the positive association between the soundness of the capital markets and the capacity of banking sector to absorb shocks.

It is interesting to note the fact that for countries with large banks there does not appear a on the full-time span sample a significant impact of Lerner index values on Z-scores nor for fixed nor for random effects models (Panel "B"). However, such impact is clearly present at 1% statistical significance for countries with small banks sectors (Panel "C"). For these countries, the impact is even increasing during the crisis comparing with the pre-crisis period. A different pattern is emerging for the effects associated with market capitalization. While for countries with large banks this variable is positively and significant at 5% impacting in the pre-crisis period the Z-scores (in fixed effects models), there are no evidences of any significant effect for countries with small banking sector for both periods in fixed effects models. Still, such evidences are appearing in random effects specifications. However, the Hausman tests reject the validity of random effects models.

One of the control variables, the non-interest incomes to total incomes ratio, exercise a positive impact on Z-scores, yet its statistical significance is varying over different models. For the crisis period, this statistical significance is vanishing over both large and small banks samples. These results may be correlated with Demirgüç-Kunt and Huizinga (2010a) which find that the non-interest incomes are positively related to bank size.

The bank loans to bank deposits variable display a negative sign, without being statistically significant. The exception appears for small banks sample for which there is a level of 10% significance.

The dummy for Basel Agreement is positively and statistically significant at 1% (for the full sample and the entire time span) associated with Z-scores. However, this association seems to be clear only for the post-2006 sample while there in fact there is no association for the case of the countries with small banking sector. Of course, this outcome is mainly related to the fact that the majority of the countries in our dataset started to implement Basel II and Basel 2.5 from 2007 (for an overview, see Financial Stability Institute, 2012 and Basel Committee on Banking Supervision, 2013).

Dynamic Models

Up to this point the results suggest that there might be some time and space autocorrelations, frequently specific for the errors of pooled time series models. Hence, we involve an Arellano and Bover (1995) dynamic specification of the model. The results are reported in Table 5 and Table 6.

In order to evaluate the quality of the results, firstly we perform an Arellano and Bond (1991) test for serial correlation in the first-differenced errors: the moment conditions are valid only if there is no serial correlation in the idiosyncratic errors. Due to the fact that first difference of the independently and identically distributed idiosyncratic errors will be auto-correlated, the reject of the null hypothesis of no serial correlation at order one in the first-differenced errors does not necessarily imply that the model is misspecified. However, such null should hold for higher orders. Otherwise, the considered moment conditions are not valid.

For our results, the values of the Arellano–Bond test are not presenting evidences for high-order serial correlation in errors in any of the considered models.

Secondly, we consider the Sargan test of over-identifying conditions, as discussed in Arellano and Bond (1991). Accordingly, with this test, the over-identifying conditions are valid for all the specifications.

In the full sample, an increase in the level of Lerner index leads to a 1.15-fold increase in rescaled Z-scores, while an increase in stock market capitalization leads to a 0.03-fold increase in Z-scores with a statistical significance of 1% (see Tables 5 and 6).

The control variables appear to exercise substantially smaller effects. Changes in the bank loans-to-deposits ratio induce only a small reduction of 0.02-fold in Z-scores. The non-interest incomes to total incomes ratio contributes with a positive and statistically significant increase in Z-scores of a 0.01–fold. Still, this last effect is three times larger for the pre-crisis period. While the first effect is more than two times larger during the crisis period, the impact of market capitalization substantially decline, displays a "wrong" sign and lost its statistical significance during the same period. In other words, if an increase in market power may diminish the risk of banks failure even during periods of turbulence, higher levels of instability on capital markets may break their positive influence on banking sector.

Interestingly, for the effects of the Lerner index on Z-scores, there does not appear to be important differences between large and small banking sectors. However, there are striking variances between these two samples in what concerns the impact of market capitalization. If for the overall analysis period, in countries with large banks higher market capitalization positively and significant at 1% support the banks' solvency, for the case of small banks an increased market capitalization appears to exercise a negative effect. Thus, it can be presumed that in countries with small banking sectors, there is a substitution effect in financing the real sector activities between commercial banks and capital markets investors. Still, this effect is significant only during the pre-crisis period while for the crisis sample it lose its significance for both large and small banking sectors.

Bank Z-Score and Its Determinants: GMM Estimations

In order to assess the robustness of the results in respect to how the market power is evaluated for the banking sector, in Columns 4 to 6 of Table 5 we also report the same results, using the bank concentration (i.e. the assets of three largest commercial banks as a share of total commercial banking assets) as an explanatory variable instead of the Lerner index. While the Lerner

Table 5. Panel "A": full sample, 63 countries

	All Countries			All Countries			OECD Countries		Non-OECD Countries	
	(1)	(2)	(3)	(4)	(5)	(6)	(7)	(8)	(9)	(10)
	1997-2010	1997-2006	2007-2010	1997-2010	1997-2006	2007-2010	1997-2010	1997-2010	1997-2010	1997-2010
Lerner index	1.148*** (0.029)	1.207*** (0.026)	2.762*** (0.505)				0.539*** (0.128)		2.216*** (0.156)	
Bank concentration (%)				0.006*** (0.000)	0.004*** (0.001)	-0.009 (0.007)		0.000 (0.002)		0.006*** (0.000)
Bank credit to bank deposits (%)	-0.002*** (0.000)	-0.006*** (0.000)	0.000 (0.001)	-0.002*** (0.000)	-0.005*** (0.001)	-0.001 (0.001)	-0.001 (0.001)	-0.000 (0.001)	-0.001** (0.000)	-0.001*** (0.000)
Non-interest income to total income (%)	0.001*** (0.000)	0.001*** (0.000)	0.000 (0.002)	0.001*** (0.000)	0.001*** (0.000)	0.001 (0.002)	0.001*** (0.000)	0.001*** (0.000)	0.001 (0.001)	-0.000 (0.000)
Stock market capitalization to GDP (%)	0.003*** (0.000)	0.006*** (0.000)	-0.001 (0.001)	0.003*** (0.000)	0.006*** (0.000)	-0.000 (0.001)	-0.000 (0.001)	0.001 (0.001)	0.001*** (0.000)	0.002*** (0.000)
Lerner index*Basel Capital Agreement dummy	0.646*** (0.020)	0.699*** (0.007)	0.153 (0.201)				0.721*** (0.079)		0.403*** (0.070)	
Bank concentration* Basel Capital Agreement				0.004*** (0.000)	0.004*** (0.000)	0.002* (0.001)		0.003*** (0.000)		0.004*** (0.000)
Constant	-0.243*** (0.028)	-0.039 (0.049)	-0.689*** (0.211)	-0.417*** (0.024)	-0.114 (0.081)	0.516 (0.371)	-0.049 (0.112)	-0.105 (0.208)	-0.576*** (0.101)	-0.389*** (0.068)

continued on following page

Table 5. Continued

	All Countries			All Countries			OECD Countries		Non-OECD Countries	
	(1)	(2)	(3)	(4)	(5)	(6)	(7)	(8)	(9)	(10)
	1997-2010	1997-2006	2007-2010	1997-2010	1997-2006	2007-2010	1997-2010	1997-2010	1997-2010	1997-2010
Wald χ^2	130034.11 (Probability > χ^2= 0.000)	20852.86 (Probability > χ^2= 0.000)	97.98 (Probability > χ^2= 0.000)	47344.38 (Probability > χ^2= 0.000)	19912.70 (Probability > χ^2= 0.000)	87.09 (Probability > χ^2= 0.000)	13380.81 (Probability > χ^2= 0.000)	10051.84 (Probability > χ^2= 0.000)	6806.57 (Probability > χ^2= 0.000)	2226.62 (Probability > χ^2= 0.000)
Number of panel observations	714	519	138	718	524	137	325	327	389	391
Arellano-Bond test for zero autocorrelation in first-differenced errors (H0: no autocorrelation) – AR(2)	0.257 (p= 0.797)	-0.832 (p= 0.405)	N.A.	0.261 (p= 0.794)	-0.548 (p= 0.583)	N.A.	0.165 (p= 0.869)	0.385 (p= 0.700)	0.410 (p= 0.682)	0.328 (p= 0.743)
Sargan test of over-identifying restrictions (H0: over-identifying restrictions are valid)	59.150 (Probability > χ^2 = 0.99)	50.079 (Probability > χ^2 = 0.21)	6.764 (Probability > χ^2 = 0.15)	61.361 (Probability > χ^2 = 0.99)	52.956 (Probability > χ^2 = 0.14)	7.769 (Probability > χ^2 = 0.10)	23.130 (Probability > χ^2 = 1.00)	24.709 (Probability > χ^2 = 1.00)	25.759 (Probability > χ^2 = 1.00)	30.985 (Probability > χ^2 = 1.00)

Table 6. Panel "B": Large banks, 28 countries

	All Countries			All Countries			OECD Countries		Non-OECD Countries	
	(1)	(2)	(3)	(4)	(5)	(6)	(7)	(8)	(9)	(10)
	1997-2010	1997-2006	2007-2010	1997-2010	1997-2006	2007-2010	1997-2010	1997-2010	1997-2010	1997-2010
Lerner index	1.597*** (0.197)	1.769*** (0.361)	3.149** (1.258)				0.399 (1.331)		-6.228 (6.264)	
Bank concentration (%)				0.014*** (0.002)	0.014*** (0.002)	-0.023*** (0.006)		0.010*** (0.002)		-0.001 (0.011)
Bank credit to bank deposits (%)	0.002*** (0.000)	0.000 (0.001)	-0.001 (0.001)	0.001 (0.001)	0.000 (0.001)	-0.000 (0.001)	0.001* (0.000)	0.001 (0.001)	-0.000 (0.004)	-0.002 (0.004)
Non-interest income to total income (%)	0.002*** (0.000)	0.002*** (0.000)	-0.001 (0.002)	0.002*** (0.000)	0.001* (0.000)	0.002 (0.002)	0.001** (0.000)	0.001 (0.001)	-0.002 (0.004)	-0.003 (0.005)
Stock market capitalization to GDP (%)	0.002*** (0.000)	0.003*** (0.000)	-0.001 (0.002)	0.001** (0.000)	0.003*** (0.000)	0.000 (0.002)	-0.001 (0.001)	-0.001 (0.001)	0.002** (0.001)	0.002 (0.002)
Lerner index*Basel Capital Agreement dummy	1.139*** (0.181)	0.939*** (0.123)	0.175 (0.428)				0.610*** (0.088)		1.499 (2.698)	
Bank concentration* Basel Capital Agreement				0.004*** (0.000)	0.004*** (0.000)	0.003** (0.002)		0.001*** (0.000)		0.005 (0.004)
Constant	-0.932*** (0.092)	-0.817*** (0.091)	-0.492 (0.312)	-1.174*** (0.207)	-1.215*** (0.093)	1.177*** (0.425)	-0.178 (0.223)	-0.668*** (0.194)	1.523 (1.773)	0.142 (0.999)
Wald χ^2	11316.07 (Probability > χ^2= 0.000)	14108.53 (Probability > χ^2= 0.000)	72.97 (Probability > χ^2= 0.000)	4689.51 (Probability > χ^2= 0.000)	7416.38 (Probability > χ^2= 0.000)	109.17 (Probability > χ^2= 0.000)	886.56 (Probability > χ^2= 0.000)	403.97 (Probability > χ^2= 0.000)	15.28 (Probability > χ^2= 0.002)	6.32 (Probability > χ^2= 0.388)
Number of panel observations	311	216	67	311	216	67	199	199	112	112
Arellano-Bond test for zero autocorrelation in first-differenced errors (H0: no autocorrelation) – AR(2)	0.615 (p=0.539)	0.016 (p=0.988)	N.A.	0.459 (p=0.646)	-0.156 (p=0.876)	N.A.	-0.228 (p=0.819)	-0.598 (p=0.549)	0.229 (p=0.818)	0.150 (p=0.881)
Sargan test of over-identifying restrictions (H0: over-identifying restrictions are valid)	19.974 (Probability > χ^2 = 1.00)	20.952 (Probability > χ^2 = 0.99)	6.559 (Probability > χ^2 = 0.16)	20.248 (Probability > χ^2 = 1.00)	21.798 (Probability > χ^2 = 0.99)	5.980 (Probability > χ^2 = 0.20)	13.236 (Probability > χ^2 = 1.00)	11.110 (Probability > χ^2 = 1.00)	1.807 (Probability > χ^2 = 1.00)	1.991 (Probability > χ^2 = 1.00)

Table 7. Panel "C": Small banks, 35 countries

	All Countries			All Countries			OECD Countries		Non-OECD Countries	
	(1)	(2)	(3)	(4)	(5)	(6)	(7)	(8)	(9)	(10)
	1997-2010	1997-2006	2007-2010	1997-2010	1997-2006	2007-2010	1997-2010	1997-2010	1997-2010	1997-2010
Lerner index	1.085*** (0.049)	1.154*** (0.035)	3.757** (1.654)				0.744* (0.426)		0.991* (0.539)	
Bank concentration (%)				-0.008*** (0.001)	-0.007*** (0.001)	0.007 (0.020)		-0.022*** (0.006)		-0.004* (0.002)
Bank credit to bank deposits (%)	-0.004*** (0.001)	-0.011*** (0.000)	0.003 (0.002)	-0.005*** (0.001)	-0.011*** (0.001)	-0.001 (0.001)	-0.002 (0.002)	-0.002 (0.002)	-0.005*** (0.000)	-0.004*** (0.001)
Non-interest income to total income (%)	0.001*** (0.000)	0.001*** (0.000)	0.005 (0.007)	0.001*** (0.000)	0.002*** (0.000)	-0.009*** (0.003)	0.002*** (0.000)	0.001*** (0.000)	0.000 (0.001)	-0.001 (0.001)
Stock market capitalization to GDP (%)	-0.001*** (0.000)	0.001*** (0.000)	0.002 (0.002)	-0.000 (0.000)	-0.000 (0.000)	-0.004 (0.003)	0.000 (0.007)	0.004 (0.003)	-0.001** (0.000)	-0.001** (0.000)
Lerner index*Basel Capital Agreement dummy	0.346*** (0.057)	0.464*** (0.073)	-0.081 (0.259)				0.805 (0.563)		0.273*** (0.058)	
Bank concentration* Basel Capital Agreement				0.003*** (0.000)	0.005*** (0.000)	-0.000 (0.001)		0.004* (0.002)		0.002*** (0.000)
Constant	0.0128* (0.069)	0.722*** (0.048)	-1.519* (0.885)	0.831*** (0.088)	1.389*** (0.087)	0.199 (1.213)	-0.045 (0.399)	1.429** (0.581)	0.123 (0.153)	0.502*** (0.146)

continued on following page

Table 7. Continued

	All Countries			All Countries			OECD Countries		Non-OECD Countries	
	(1)	(2)	(3)	(4)	(5)	(6)	(7)	(8)	(9)	(10)
	1997-2010	**1997-2006**	**2007-2010**	**1997-2010**	**1997-2006**	**2007-2010**	**1997-2010**	**1997-2010**	**1997-2010**	**1997-2010**
Wald χ^2	174756.12 (Probability > χ^2=0.000)	198644.98 (Probability > χ^2=0.000)	51.80 Probability > χ^2=0.000)	53753.09 (Probability > χ^2=0.000)	109215.91 (Probability > χ^2=0.000)	51.96 (Probability > χ^2=0.000)	238.97 (Probability > χ^2=0.000)	151.23 (Probability > χ^2=0.000)	17097.55 (Probability > χ^2=0.000)	11923.27 (Probability > χ^2=0.000)
Number of panel observations	403	303	69	407	308	68	126	128	277	279
Arellano-Bond test for zero autocorrelation in first-differenced errors (H0: no autocorrelation) – AR(2)	-0.142 (p=0.887)	-0.972 (p=0.331)	N.A.	-0.351 (p=0.726)	-1.056 (p=0.291)	N.A.	0.463 (Probability > χ^2 = 0.64)	0.209 (Probability > χ^2 = 0.83)	-0.232 (Probability > χ^2 = 0.82)	-0.397 (Probability > χ^2 = 0.69)
Sargan test of over-identifying restrictions (H0: over-identifying restrictions are valid)	25.148 (Probability > χ^2 = 1.00)	28.049 (Probability > χ^2 = 0.96)	5.110 (Probability > χ^2 = 0.28)	26.910 (Probability > χ^2 = 1.00)	31.811 (Probability > χ^2 = 0.90)	6.920 (Probability > χ^2 = 0.14)	6.224 (Probability > χ^2 = 1.00)	1.984 (Probability > χ^2 = 1.00)	17.344 (Probability > χ^2 = 1.00)	9.866 (Probability > χ^2 = 1.00)

***/**/* -1%, 5%, 10% significance levels.

Notes: The distinction between countries with large commercial banks and, respectively, countries with small commercial banks, is based on same criteria as in Table 2. Dependent variable: Z-scores; For system dynamic panel-data estimation: Two-step estimators; GMM standard error in (); 3 lags of dependent variable included for full sample and 1 lag for 2007-2010 sample; all available lags of the explanatory variables included as instruments.

index is more related to the functional consequences of concentration, this variable reflects better the structure of banking sector.

The effects of the concentration degree, as measured by such a variable appear to be significant yet substantially smaller compared with the use of the Lerner index. However, the effects of stock market capitalization are pretty much the same as in previous estimations. It can be noticed that higher bank concentration appears to contribute to an increase in the risk of banks insolvency during crisis. This effect is clearer especially for the countries with large and concentrated banking sector. It can be argued that due to their levels of risk exposure and insufficient dispersion of this exposure, such type of banking sectors are facing higher levels of moral hazard and adverse selection issues during the crisis. Also, as Bertay et al., 2013 argues, this may reflect the doubts whether large banks can be bailed out by their public authorities. For countries with small banking sector, an increase in the degree of structural concentration appears to matter only for the pre-crisis period.

For a further assessment of robustness, we also split the dataset accordingly with the scale and general development of the economy as a whole. Hence, in Columns 7 to 10 of Table 5 we report for the entire time span the corresponding results for OECD and, respectively, non-OECD countries.

For the OECD countries sample, the effects associated with the Lerner index are almost two times smaller compared with the full sample: a shock in the level of Lerner index leads to only a 0.54-fold increase in the Z-scores. The stock market capitalization and the non-interest incomes to total incomes ratio play no significant role in the determination of Z-scores, while the influence of bank loans-to-deposits ratio is also smaller comparing with the full sample. The bank concentration variable is not statistically significant, although it displays the correct sign. The dummy for Basel Agreement is preserving its impact and significance in almost all models again for the post-2006 sample.

The Basel Agreement dummy put forth a positive and significant at 1% influence on Z-scores.

In OECD countries with large banking sectors, the effects of an increase in Lerner index on Z-scores are not statistically significant. However, in this case, the structural concentration in banking sector is exerting a positive and significant at 1% role in the dynamic of Z-scores. Still, in OECD countries with small commercial banks the impact of bank concentration is reversed being a negatively one although it preserves a significance of 1%.

For the non-OECD countries, the overall picture reveals a relatively different pattern, since both measures of market power as well as the stock capitalization are statistically significant at 1%. Still, the effects of market power are almost half smaller and both measures lost their significance for the sample of non-OECD countries with large banking sectors.

If the estimation of the static models is also considered, it appears that the effects of stock market upon the banks' efficiency are less clear for the developed countries compared to the developing ones and especially with ones that poses small banking sectors.

From the control variables, the ratio between banks credits and attracted deposits is significant only for non-OECD countries while the share of non-interest income in total income is significant only for OECD countries.

Also, in order to evaluate the explanatory capacity of these models, we consider the average ranks of Z-scores. The largest deviations of the estimated ranks from their observed levels are the ones for fixed and random-effects models.

By countries, the most important under and over-estimations appear for Costa Rica, Denmark, Finland, Hong Kong and Switzerland. With the notable exception of Switzerland, these countries display higher average rescaled Z-scores compared with the average value for our whole data sample. In the meantime, the Lerner index for Denmark, Hong Kong and Switzerland is higher than the average, while for Costa Rica and Finland is substantially lower.

Also, except for Costa Rica, these countries are characterized by high levels of financial intermediation as reflected by the private sector loans, bank deposits and stock market capitalization.

In the same time, the banking sector in these countries is usually efficient, as captured by the bank overhead costs to total assets, net interest margin, return on assets (ROA) and return on equity (ROE) variables.

These cases appear to be outliers in the data sample that may be explained by the stance of the global financial intermediation, as well as by the sector concentration factors.

In the same time, the best in-sample rank predictions are for the countries with lower bank concentration and largely developed stock markets like Australia, Chile, Estonia, Singapore, South Africa and United States.

Overall, the model better describes the cases with an average degree of bank concentration and a stock market capitalization that has reached a certain threshold yet fails to adequately reflect the cases in which the market power in the banking sector is significantly higher or lower.

During the growth and convergence processes between the banks and the capital markets, the economic agents will benefit from an increase in the opportunities to finance their investment and consumption projects through a broader spectrum of sources. In such periods, these agents are choosing accordingly to the costs and general conditions associated to these financing sources. In the same time, banks are starting to use using syndicated loan markets to spread out credit risks. Also, the increase in the credit-linked securities and their taxonomy diversification support the market development as transactions can be made more smoothly. As the banks increase in size, they become large active players on capital markets, both as buyers and sellers of credit protection. After a certain threshold, this evolution leads to the emergence of an integrated bank-capital markets financing system (the cases of Japan and Germany are illustrative for such process; see Vitols, 2001, 2002, Konoe, 2010). In the meantime, the financial globalization mechanisms follow to eliminate the restrictions on banking and securities transactions, the abolition of capital restrictions, as well as with the harmonization of accounting systems for financial reporting. The largest financial institutions from the increasing concentrated banking sector are able to act as international banks able to collect high returns from capital flows. As Konoe (2010, p. 84) notes: „a change in corporate finance toward market-based financing, developments in money markets and financial technological advances have progressed at a global level... A large number of profitable companies started to embark on financing through the issuance of stocks and bonds – a typical case of market-based financing – in overseas capital markets at cheaper costs than those of financing in their domestic markets and through bank borrowing."

Two-Stages Quantile Regression Models

Based on the previous arguments, it seems that for the developed countries the bank soundness is less influenced by the size of capital markets and more so by the supply of credit protection instruments and their characteristics.

In the meantime, the effects of concentration upon soundness may be different for weak and small banks and respectively, for large and strong ones. Hence, a different behaviour of the various sub-groups may be expected in terms of the linkage between concentration and soundness. Such distinctive behaviour may be reflected by the two-stage quantile regression approach. This approach provides several advantages. Among them, it generates robust estimates, particularly for misspecification errors related to heteroskedasticity, non-normality and other error term misspecification. It also allows dealing with measurement error problems. From the seminal paper by Koenker and Basset (1978) and Basset and Koenker (1978), an extensive study of the literature has revealed the asymptotic behaviour of the quantile regression and two-stage least-absolute deviations (2SLAD) (see, for instance, Amemiya, 1982, 1985; Weiss, 1990; Phillips, 1991; Pollard, 1991; Kim & Muller, 2000).

In our specification of models, a problem may arise due to the potential endogeneity of market power measures. Indeed, it may be argued that the causality may run in both directions between banks soundness and market power. The existence of such endogeneity may generate biases in the conventional quantile regression estimates (Koenker & Basset, 1978). This problem can be overcome by the instrumental variable (IV) method (see Chernozhukov & Hansen, 2005). We involve the instrumental variables quantile regression (IVQR) methodology developed in Chernozhukov and Hansen (2005, 2006, 2008). This approach has the advantage of being computationally efficient for a small number of endogenous variables.

As instruments for both measures of market power, we involve the following variables: bank private credit-to-GDP ratio, cost to income ratio and a scale variable for the whole economy (GDP per capita). Drehmann and Juselius (2013) find that the so-called credit-to-GDP gap is a robust long-run indicator of banking crises. Further, the relationship between concentration and cost efficiency is critically depending on the nature of allocation mechanisms for borrowed financial resources as well as on the connections between financial and real sectors. In one hand, there may appear areduction in cost efficiency brought about by the lack of market discipline in concentrated markets. In other hand, banks in less competitive environments may charge higher interest rates to their clients and may benefit from a buffer generated by the differences between current and competitive levels of interest rates (see, for instance, Berger and Hannan, 1989, 1998, Boyd and De Nicoló, 2008). The corresponding results are reported in Table 8.

In the full sample estimations (Panel "A"), the Lerner Index is positive and statistically significant at 5% for the 10^{th}quantile and at 1% for the other quantiles. The F-test that the coefficients of Lerner index are the same across all quantiles is not statistically significant. As for the alternative measure of bank concentration, this is statistically significant at 1% for all the quantiles. The market capitalization is significant at 1% for all the quantiles and displays a high stability of coefficients across all quantiles. For the crisis period, both measures of market power are losing their significance. In the meantime, market capitalization is not significant in the pre-crisis period (with the exception of 50^{th}quantile) but gain statistical significance at 1% during the crisis.

The non-interest incomes to total incomes ratio is statistically significant mainly for the higher quantiles, while bank loans-to-deposits ratio appears to be a less robust explanatory variable.

In the large banks sample (Panel "B"), the Lerner index is not significant for lower quantiles. Still, for medium and upper quantiles the effects induced by shocks at the level of Lerner index are several times larger comparing with the full sample as well as with the small banks sample. For lower and medium quantiles, bank concentration exerts a significant influence only in the pre-crisis period but gain significance for full time span in the case of upper quantiles. The architecture of the effects induced by both market power measures for small banks sample looks more like the one corresponding for the full sample.

The share of non-interest income in total income does not display statistical significance only for the 90thquantile in the crisis period although its sign varies across various estimations. The banks' loan- to- attracted deposits ratio negatively impacts the soundness of banking sector but is not robust over estimations. For the interpretation of these results, we recall an argument advanced in Bertay et al., 2013: banks that are large in an absolute sense are less traditional in focus, with a larger fee income share and a larger non-deposit funding share. Correlatively, systemically large banks have a smaller fee income share and are more focused in their activity in a traditional sense.

In the case of small banking sectors (Panel "C"), the effects associated with both measures of market power are relatively smaller comparing with the case of large banks. While the Lerner index does not appear to impact Z-scores during the crisis period (except the 90thquantile with a significance of 10%), bank concentration variable is significant at 1% inclusively for the period between 2007 and 2010 for the 10thquantile. With the exception of the 90thquantile, in this sample market capitalization induces significant effects not only in the pre-crisis period but also in the post-2006 one. If the structure of income variable is remarkably robust over quantiles, the loan-to-deposit ratio exerts less stable effects. Opposite from the case of large banks, the Basel Agreement dummy virtually plays no role for the dataset of countries with small banking sectors.

For the OECD sample (Panel "D"), the Lerner index is significant only for 50th (during the crisis) and 90thquantile, while the bank concentration is significant only for the 50thquantile. It also can be noticed that for the 90th quantile the Lerner index is significant at 1% during the crisis but displays a negative sign. For this sample it is interesting that the stock market capitalization is not significant for the 90thquantile (with the exception of the crisis period).

For the non-OECD sample (Panel "E"), the Lerner index is positively and significant at 10% associated with Z-scores only for the lower quantiles. One surprising result is that this index is negatively (but significant at 1%)

impacting the Z-scores for upper quantiles during the crisis period. The bank concentration variable is behaving in a distinctive fashion being positively related with Z-scores in all statistically significant estimations (including for upper quantiles the crisis).

Market capitalization is significant for all the quantiles but for lower quantiles exert a negative impact on banks soundness.

Non-Linear Effects of Concentration and Capital Market Development on Z-Scores-Two-Stage Quantile Regressions

This provides at least a limited support for the thesis that the availability of the financial resources supplied through capital markets favours the bank soundness in a distinctive fashion in developed and developing countries and sensitive to a certain threshold.

Bank credit-to-deposits ratio is significant in OECD sample only for the 50th quantile. In non-OECD sample this variable change the sign of the associated impact and its significance vary across quantiles. The non-interest share becomes significant in OECD sample only starting with medium and upper quantiles. For non-OECD countries, this variable is displaying a relatively degree of robustness across estimations.

Overall, it appears that banks at the higher tail of the distribution of the Z-score are abler to benefit from higher concentration than banks operating at the lower tail of the distribution. More accurate, combining the findings for large and small banking sectors and, respectively, OECD and non-OECD countries, it appears that the coefficients obtained from the estimations over different quantiles have a "U-shaped" form. However, the different effects are asymmetrically distributed and are sensitive to the corresponding level of market power.

In the meantime, with the exception of the banks from the highest tail of Z-scores distribution in the developed countries, all types of banks are influenced by the development of capital markets. The relation between concentration and soundness is significantly influenced by the banks' efficiency. In other words, large and efficient banks from countries with developed financial markets are abler to secure high and stable profits.

Since there might be some inference problems due to the small sample size, these results should be considered with caution.

Table 8. Panel "A": full sample, 63 countries

	10th Quantile						50th Quantile						90th Quantile					
	(1)	(2)	(3)	(4)	(5)	(6)	(7)	(8)	(9)	(10)	(11)	(12)	(13)	(14)	(15)	(16)	(17)	(18)
	1997-2010	1997-2006	2007-2010	1997-2010	1997-2006	2007-2010	1997-2010	1997-2006	2007-2010	1997-2010	1997-2006	2007-2010	1997-2010	1997-2006	2007-2010	1997-2010	1997-2006	2007-2010
Lerner index	1.801** (0.728)	1.953* (1.006)	2.128 (1.982)				3.694*** (0.828)	2.556*** (0.778)	7.722*** (2.561)				6.494*** (2.122)	6.113** (3.045)	9.495*** (2.922)			
Bank concentration (%)				0.019*** (0.004)	0.036*** (0.006)	-0.017 (0.023)				0.227*** (0.007)	0.028*** (0.005)	-0.008 (0.029)				0.035*** (0.010)	0.025* (0.015)	0.068*** (0.023)
Stock market capitalization to GDP (%)	0.002*** (0.000)	0.000 (0.001)	0.003*** (0.001)	0.002*** (0.000)	-0.000 (0.001)	0.004*** (0.001)	0.004*** (0.000)	0.004*** (0.001)	0.003*** (0.001)	0.004*** (0.000)	0.004*** (0.000)	0.004** (0.002)	0.004*** (0.000)	0.002* (0.001)	0.004*** (0.001)	0.004*** (0.000)	0.004*** (0.001)	0.003*** (0.001)
Bank credit to bank deposits (%)	-0.001 (0.001)	0.001* (0.001)	-0.001 (0.001)	-0.001** (0.000)	0.001 (0.001)	-0.000 (0.003)	0.002*** (0.001)	0.002** (0.001)	0.002 (0.002)	0.001 (0.000)	0.001 (0.001)	0.000 (0.003)	0.002* (0.001)	0.004** (0.002)	-0.000 (0.002)	0.000 (0.001)	0.004** (0.002)	-0.008*** (0.002)
Non-interest income to total income (%)	0.001* (0.000)	0.001 (0.001)	-0.003 (0.004)	0.001 (0.001)	0.001* (0.000)	-0.002 (0.004)	-0.004*** (0.000)	-0.005*** (0.001)	0.001 (0.004)	-0.010*** (0.001)	-0.010*** (0.001)	-0.007 (0.005)	-0.003*** (0.001)	-0.004*** (0.001)	-0.003 (0.003)	-0.014*** (0.001)	-0.017*** (0.001)	-0.016*** (0.003)
Lerner index*Basel Capital Agreement dummy	-0.036 (0.352)	-0.644 (0.593)	-0.307 (0.322)				-0.794** (0.390)	-0.239 (0.481)	-1.792** (0.853)				-1.581* (0.954)	-1.581 (1.509)	-1.262 (1.224)			
Bank concentration* Basel Capital Agreement				-0.002 (0.001)	-0.005** (0.002)	0.004 (0.005)				-0.003 (0.002)	-0.003** (0.002)	0.000 (0.007)				-0.003 (0.003)	-0.002 (0.005)	-0.008 (0.005)
Constant	-1.513*** (0.184)	-1.629*** (0.229)	-1.360** (0.628)	-2.124*** (0.217)	-3.199*** (0.280)	-0.239 (0.852)	-1.144*** (0.184)	-0.911*** (0.170)	-2.199*** (0.704)	-1.410*** (0.347)	-1.732*** (0.283)	0.335 (1.120)	-0.615 (0.445)	-0.567 (0.624)	-1.094 (0.721)	-0.677 (0.526)	-0.380 (0.780)	-1.117 (0.804)
Observations	762	574	188	767	580	187	762	574	188	767	580	187	762	574	188	767	580	187

Table 9. Panel "B": Large banks, 28 countries

	10th Quantile						50th Quantile						90th Quantile					
	(1)	(2)	(3)	(4)	(5)	(6)	(7)	(8)	(9)	(10)	(11)	(12)	(13)	(14)	(15)	(16)	(17)	(18)
	1997-2010	1997-2006	2007-2010	1997-2010	1997-2006	2007-2010	1997-2010	1997-2006	2007-2010	1997-2010	1997-2006	2007-2010	1997-2010	1997-2006	2007-2010	1997-2010	1997-2006	2007-2010
Lerner index	2.964 (1.964)	2.078 (1.794)	-0.251 (2.599)				5.233*** (1.713)	2.713** (1.287)	10.591*** (3.586)				8.125 (9.893)	11.102** (4.865)	10.172** (4.508)			
Bank concentration (%)				0.019** (0.008)	0.046*** (0.010)	-0.008 (0.018)				0.012 (0.010)	0.047*** (0.018)	-0.035* (0.020)				0.090*** (0.022)	0.157*** (0.055)	0.046*** (0.018)
Stock market capitalization to GDP (%)	-0.000 (0.001)	0.000 (0.001)	0.004*** (0.001)	-0.000 (0.001)	-0.002 (0.001)	0.004*** (0.001)	0.002** (0.001)	-0.000 (0.001)	0.001 (0.002)	0.002** (0.001)	-0.001 (0.002)	0.005*** (0.001)	-0.002 (0.004)	-0.005 (0.005)	0.001 (0.001)	-0.003 (0.002)	-0.010 (0.007)	0.004*** (0.000)
Bank credit to bank deposits (%)	0.003*** (0.001)	0.005*** (0.001)	-0.004* (0.003)	0.003*** (0.001)	0.003*** (0.001)	-0.003 (0.002)	0.001 (0.001)	0.001 (0.001)	0.003 (0.003)	0.001 (0.001)	-0.0000 (0.002)	0.003 (0.003)	-0.001 (0.004)	-0.002 (0.004)	-0.004* (0.002)	-0.005** (0.002)	-0.006 (0.004)	-0.003 (0.002)
Non-interest income to total income (%)	0.004 (0.003)	0.010*** (0.004)	0.002 (0.003)	-0.000 (0.003)	0.013*** (0.003)	0.003 (0.004)	0.002 (0.003)	-0.001 (0.003)	-0.001 (0.003)	-0.005** (0.002)	-0.004 (0.006)	0.001 (0.004)	-0.002 (0.002)	0.014 (0.024)	-0.007*** (0.002)	-0.012* (0.007)	0.026 (0.033)	-0.011*** (0.004)
Lerner index*Basel Capital Agreement dummy	-0.405 (0.853)	-0.673 (0.798)	1.304 (1.167)				-1.143 (0.714)	-0.817 (0.714)	-1.838 (1.375)				-1.593 (3.464)	-0.629 (2.298)	-1.829 (1.779)			
Bank concentration* Basel Capital Agreement				-0.003 (0.002)	-0.006** (0.003)	0.005 (0.004)				-0.003 (0.003)	-0.009* (0.005)	0.010* (0.006)				-0.013** (0.006)	-0.027 (0.019)	-0.004 (0.004)
Constant	-2.056*** (0.421)	-2.479*** (0.360)	-1.015* (0.609)	-2.342*** (0.434)	-4.122*** (0.471)	-0.690 (0.763)	-1.527*** (0.376)	-0.721** (0.322)	-2.788*** (0.708)	-0.823* (0.478)	-2.393** (0.951)	0.679 (0.879)	-0.099 (1.926)	-0.718 (1.612)	-0.440 (0.735)	-2.396** (1.020)	-6.586** (3.125)	-0.870 (0.732)
Observations	333	240	90	333	240	90	333	240	90	333	240	90	333	240	90	333	240	90

Table 10. Panel "C": Small banks, 35 countries

	10th Quantile						50th Quantile						90th Quantile					
	(1)	(2)	(3)	(4)	(5)	(6)	(7)	(8)	(9)	(10)	(11)	(12)	(13)	(14)	(15)	(16)	(17)	(18)
	1997-2010	1997-2006	2007-2010	1997-2010	1997-2006	2007-2010	1997-2010	1997-2006	2007-2010	1997-2010	1997-2006	2007-2010	1997-2010	1997-2006	2007-2010	1997-2010	1997-2006	2007-2010
Lerner index	1.872*** (0.696)	1.813** (0.836)	-2.959 (6.138)				1.893* (1.131)	2.335*** (0.871)	-14.561 (9.357)				3.639** (1.816)	3.641* (1.906)	-20.563* (10.791)			
Bank concentration (%)				0.016*** (0.005)	0.028*** (0.007)	0.017*** (0.006)				0.031*** (0.009)	0.028*** (0.007)	-0.012 (0.032)				0.050*** (0.015)	0.049*** (0.017)	0.036 (0.057)
Stock market capitalization to GDP (%)	0.009*** (0.001)	0.009*** (0.001)	0.008*** (0.001)	0.008*** (0.001)	0.004*** (0.001)	0.007*** (0.001)	0.011*** (0.001)	0.011*** (0.001)	0.008** (0.004)	0.011*** (0.001)	0.012*** (0.001)	0.008* (0.004)	0.009*** (0.001)	0.009*** (0.002)	0.006* (0.003)	0.009*** (0.002)	0.012*** (0.002)	-0.000 (0.003)
Bank credit to bank deposits (%)	-0.001 (0.001)	-0.001 (0.002)	-0.004 (0.003)	-0.002** (0.001)	-0.003 (0.002)	-0.005*** (0.001)	0.001 (0.001)	0.003** (0.001)	-0.014** (0.007)	-0.004** (0.002)	-0.004** (0.002)	-0.003 (0.005)	0.002 (0.002)	0.003 (0.002)	-0.018* (0.009)	-0.008*** (0.002)	-0.005 (0.003)	-0.008 (0.011)
Non-interest income to total income (%)	0.001*** (0.000)	0.001** (0.000)	-0.024 (0.014)	0.001** (0.000)	0.001** (0.000)	-0.013*** (0.004)	-0.007*** (0.001)	-0.004*** (0.001)	-0.052** (0.025)	-0.005*** (0.001)	-0.001*** (0.001)	-0.031* (0.017)	-0.009*** (0.001)	-0.010*** (0.001)	-0.080*** (0.026)	-0.011*** (0.001)	-0.013*** (0.000)	-0.013 (0.011)
Lerner index*Basel Capital Agreement dummy	-0.548 (0.371)	-0.488 (0.506)	1.469 (1.548)				-0.134 (0.619)	-0.107 (0.620)	2.893 (2.513)				-0.890 (0.848)	-0.878 (1.209)	4.619* (2.545)			
Bank concentration* Basel Capital Agreement				-0.001 (0.001)	-0.003 (0.002)	-0.002 (0.003)				-0.002 (0.002)	-0.001 (0.002)	0.002 (0.008)				-0.002 (0.003)	-0.006 (0.005)	-0.003 (0.011)
Constant	-1.620*** (0.220)	-1.606*** (0.283)	0.898 (2.247)	-1.924*** (0.272)	-2.498*** (0.330)	-0.839*** (0.287)	-0.795*** (0.304)	-1.136*** (0.235)	6.356* (3.616)	-1.825*** (0.431)	-1.783*** (0.352)	1.660 (1.563)	-0.036 (0.441)	-0.084 (0.450)	10.204** (4.280)	-1.160 (0.740)	-1.384* (0.831)	0.396 (2.005)
Observations	429	334	95	434	340	94	429	334	95	434	340	94	429	334	95	434	340	94

Table 11. Panel "D": OECD countries, 30 countries

	10th Quantile						50th Quantile						90th Quantile					
	(1)	(2)	(3)	(4)	(5)	(6)	(7)	(8)	(9)	(10)	(11)	(12)	(13)	(14)	(15)	(16)	(17)	(18)
	1997-2010	1997-2006	2007-2010	1997-2010	1997-2006	2007-2010	1997-2010	1997-2006	2007-2010	1997-2010	1997-2006	2007-2010	1997-2010	1997-2006	2007-2010	1997-2010	1997-2006	2007-2010
Lerner index	0.741 (2.861)	-1.319 (1.977)	3.726 (13.158)				2.389 (1.689)	0.033 (1.784)	26.378*** (4.590)				14.172*** (3.703)	13.351*** (5.148)	25.589*** (9.080)			
Bank concentration (%)				-0.004 (0.006)	-0.002 (0.008)	-0.030 (0.028)				0.010*** (0.004)	0.014*** (0.004)	-0.019* (0.011)				-0.017 (0.014)	-0.011 (0.022)	-0.006 (0.024)
Stock market capitalization to GDP (%)	0.006*** (0.001)	0.006*** (0.001)	0.005 (0.005)	0.003** (0.001)	0.004* (0.002)	0.004 (0.005)	0.006*** (0.001)	0.005*** (0.001)	0.012*** (0.001)	0.007*** (0.001)	0.007*** (0.001)	0.005*** (0.002)	0.003 (0.002)	0.003 (0.005)	0.010*** (0.003)	-0.003 (0.004)	-0.003 (0.007)	0.003 (0.004)
Bank credit to bank deposits (%)	-0.001 (0.001)	0.001 (0.001)	-0.001 (0.003)	0.000 (0.001)	0.001 (0.001)	0.005 (0.005)	0.002* (0.001)	0.002* (0.001)	0.003*** (0.001)	0.001* (0.000)	0.001 (0.001)	0.002 (0.002)	-0.002* (0.001)	0.000 (0.002)	0.004 (0.003)	0.004* (0.002)	0.005 (0.004)	-0.001 (0.006)
Non-interest income to total income (%)	0.001 (0.001)	0.000 (0.000)	0.000 (0.005)	0.000 (0.001)	0.001*** (0.000)	0.001 (0.001)	0.001*** (0.000)	0.001*** (0.000)	0.001 (0.001)	0.001*** (0.000)	0.001*** (0.000)	-0.004* (0.002)	0.004*** (0.001)	0.004*** (0.001)	-0.004** (0.002)	-0.007*** (0.001)	0.002*** (0.000)	-0.010*** (0.003)
Lerner index*Basel Capital Agreement dummy	-0.020 (0.821)	0.795 (1.038)	-1.351 (2.642)				-0.561 (0.669)	0.616 (1.003)	-5.479*** (1.068)				-2.809* (1.637)	-2.020 (2.947)	-4.297 (2.624)			
Bank concentration* Basel Capital Agreement				-0.000 (0.002)	-0.001 (0.003)	0.009 (0.007)				-0.002 (0.001)	-0.002 (0.002)	0.002 (0.003)				0.001 (0.006)	0.007 (0.009)	0.007 (0.008)
Constant	-1.243** (0.496)	-1.068*** (0.383)	-1.653 (3.213)	-0.845** (0.374)	-1.057** (0.521)	-0.090 (1.563)	-1.159*** (0.292)	-0.817*** (0.304)	-6.005*** (1.003)	-1.311*** (0.224)	-1.562*** (0.305)	0.510 (0.479)	-1.498** (0.613)	-1.454** (0.736)	-4.551** (1.790)	2.115** (0.841)	1.448 (1.483)	1.506*** (0.569)
Observations	345	256	89	347	258	89	345	256	89	347	258	89	345	256	89	347	258	89

Table 12. Panel "E": Non-OECD countries, 33 countries

	10th Quantile						50th Quantile						90th Quantile					
	(1)	(2)	(3)	(4)	(5)	(6)	(7)	(8)	(9)	(10)	(11)	(12)	(13)	(14)	(15)	(16)	(17)	(18)
	1997-2010	1997-2006	2007-2010	1997-2010	1997-2006	2007-2010	1997-2010	1997-2006	2007-2010	1997-2010	1997-2006	2007-2010	1997-2010	1997-2006	2007-2010	1997-2010	1997-2006	2007-2010
Lerner index	1.380* (0.718)	1.230 (1.140)	-0.816 (4.611)				-0.175 (1.241)	0.493 (1.127)	-3.249 (7.983)				2.652 (2.037)	1.205 (1.930)	-30.220*** (5.063)			
Bank concentration (%)				0.007 (0.006)	0.030*** (0.005)	0.000 (0.030)				0.031*** (0.009)	0.033*** (0.009)	-0.030 (0.024)				0.046*** (0.011)	0.035** (0.014)	0.051** (0.025)
Stock market capitalization to GDP (%)	-0.000 (0.000)	-0.001 (0.001)	0.003** (0.002)	-0.001* (0.000)	-0.002*** (0.000)	0.003** (0.001)	0.004*** (0.000)	0.002** (0.001)	0.005** (0.002)	0.003*** (0.001)	0.001 (0.001)	0.006*** (0.002)	0.007*** (0.001)	0.006*** (0.001)	0.014*** (0.001)	0.004*** (0.001)	0.005*** (0.001)	0.003* (0.002)
Bank credit to bank deposits (%)	-0.001** (0.000)	-0.001 (0.001)	-0.003 (0.004)	-0.001* (0.000)	-0.001** (0.000)	-0.003 (0.004)	0.002* (0.001)	0.003*** (0.001)	0.001 (0.004)	0.001 (0.001)	0.002 (0.001)	0.002 (0.003)	0.003 (0.002)	0.005*** (0.002)	-0.019*** (0.004)	0.001 (0.001)	0.003 (0.002)	-0.006 (0.004)
Non-interest income to total income (%)	-0.004* (0.002)	-0.008*** (0.003)	-0.009 (0.014)	-0.007*** (0.001)	-0.009*** (0.001)	-0.006 (0.017)	-0.018*** (0.003)	-0.016*** (0.003)	-0.029 (0.022)	-0.020*** (0.003)	-0.021*** (0.003)	-0.021** (0.009)	-0.010 (0.009)	-0.015* (0.009)	-0.102*** (0.014)	-0.023*** (0.004)	-0.020*** (0.005)	-0.026*** (0.010)
Lerner index*Basel Capital Agreement dummy	-0.083 (0.302)	-0.442 (0.575)	0.513 (1.759)				1.203** (0.579)	0.852 (0.690)	1.512 (2.187)				-0.821 (1.111)	-0.424 (1.110)	8.506*** (1.509)			
Bank concentration* Basel Capital Agreement				-0.000 (0.001)	-0.001 (0.001)	0.001 (0.009)				0.001 (0.002)	0.002 (0.003)	0.008 (0.006)				-0.000 (0.003)	-0.002 (0.005)	-0.001 (0.008)
Constant	-1.182*** (0.245)	-0.933** (0.364)	-0.287 (1.633)	-1.134*** (0.269)	-2.202*** (0.246)	-0.699 (1.974)	0.034 (0.404)	-0.249 (0.346)	1.307 (3.075)	-1.455*** (0.459)	-1.577*** (0.488)	1.611 (1.241)	0.170 (0.782)	0.401 (0.734)	13.741*** (2.029)	-0.983 (0.611)	-0.760 (0.792)	-0.232 (1.116)
Observations	417	318	99	420	322	98	417	318	99	420	322	98	417	318	99	420	322	98

***/**/* -1%, 5%, 10% significance levels.

Notes: The distinction between countries with large commercial banks and, respectively, countries with small commercial banks, is based on same criteria as in Table 2. Dependent variable: Z-scores; Instruments used both for Lerner Index and bank concentration: bank private credit to GDP (%), cost to income ratio (%), and GDP per capita (logarithm) (constant 2000's USD).

A complementary analysis that might be carried out in the frame of quantile regression concerns the differences in the impact of the explanatory variable for market measure of banks' soundness (Z-scores) versus a non-market measure (such as the weight of non-performing loans in total loans). Hence we involve further as dependent variable the bank non-performing loans to gross loans (%) computed as ratio of defaulting loans (payments of interest and principal past due by 90 days or more) to total gross loans (total value of loan portfolio). The results for the full sample and the whole-time span are shown in Table 13.

An increase in the Lerner index leads to a significant decrease in the levels of non-performing loans. This effect is substantially increasing with the shift from lower to upper quantiles. However, such influence is not observable during the crisis period. In the meantime, the bank concentration variable does not appear to be related to the evolution of non-performing loans.

A higher stock market capitalization also supports a reduction in the banks' inefficiency. Except the upper quantiles, this influence is manifested for both pre and crisis periods. This last outcome is in the line with Beck et al. (2013). They find that a decline of stock prices can negatively affect bank asset quality, in particular in countries with large stock markets relative to GDP. They identify as a potential transmission channel the correlation between share prices and house prices. A drop in the value of collateral for housing loans could negatively affect the loan quality of consumer loans. For corporate loans, the prices of financial assets may reflect general financial conditions which appear to affect the ability of borrowers to repay loans. To these potential channels, we add the possibility of securitization of distressed consumer and other type of loans supported by markets with higher degree of liquidity.

As expected, an increase in both non-interest income and credit-to-deposits ratio is contributing to a reduction of non-performing loans but this influence is diminished for upper quantiles.

Since the values of non-performing loans are not previously rescaled, the amplitude of such effects is not directly comparable with the one exercised for the Z-scores. Still, the overall emerging picture is a relatively consistent one: a consolidation of market power of banks is leading to an improvement in their soundness. Nevertheless, the weak significance of bank concentration variable highlights a possible caveat in considering these results since they seem to display certain sensitivity to the various used proxies. Hence, we turn further to robustness assessment by involving different measures of soundness, concentration and efficiency.

Table 13. Non-linear effects of concentration and capital market development on non-performing loans-Two-stage quantile regressions

	10th Quantile						50th Quantile						90th Quantile					
	(1)	(2)	(3)	(4)	(5)	(6)	(7)	(8)	(9)	(10)	(11)	(12)	(13)	(14)	(15)	(16)	(17)	(18)
	1997-2010	1997-2006	2007-2010	1997-2010	1997-2006	2007-2010	1997-2010	1997-2006	2007-2010	1997-2010	1997-2006	2007-2010	1997-2010	1997-2006	2007-2010	1997-2010	1997-2006	2007-2010
Lerner index	-5.475*** (1.268)	-3.470** (1.623)	-6.908* (4.149)				-26.221*** (5.635)	-28.503*** (5.457)	0.795 (5.869)				-90.574*** (26.748)	-64.604*** (22.448)	24.270 (15.243)			
Bank concentration (%)				-0.004 (0.009)	-0.006 (0.008)	0.002 (0.003)				-0.021 (0.035)	-0.028 (0.039)	-0.033 (0.041)				0.236* (0.136)	-0.013 (0.129)	-0.067 (0.150)
Stock market capitalization to GDP (%)	-0.009*** (0.000)	-0.012*** (0.001)	-0.007*** (0.001)	-0.011*** (0.000)	-0.013*** (0.001)	-0.008*** (0.002)	-0.010*** (0.003)	-0.013*** (0.004)	-0.009*** (0.002)	-0.014*** (0.003)	-0.015*** (0.004)	-0.007** (0.002)	-0.017 (0.018)	-0.036** (0.017)	-0.017* (0.010)	-0.042** (0.018)	0.048*** (0.018)	-0.004 (0.008)
Bank credit to bank deposits (%)	-0.009*** (0.001)	-0.012*** (0.002)	-0.006** (0.003)	-0.010*** (0.001)	-0.012*** (0.001)	-0.006* (0.003)	-0.020*** (0.005)	-0.034*** (0.006)	0.000 (0.004)	-0.016*** (0.005)	-0.029*** (0.007)	0.003 (0.004)	0.018 (0.020)	0.015 (0.021)	0.017* (0.009)	-0.0162 (0.025)	0.003 (0.030)	0.018 (0.015)
Non-interest income to total income (%)	-0.016*** (0.001)	-0.018*** (0.001)	-0.006 (0.006)	-0.010*** (0.000)	-0.015*** (0.000)	-0.007 (0.004)	-0.027*** (0.002)	-0.025*** (0.002)	-0.004 (0.008)	-0.008* (0.005)	-0.006 (0.005)	-0.002 (0.007)	-0.028** (0.011)	-0.022** (0.009)	0.040 (0.034)	-0.003 (0.010)	-0.009 (0.010)	0.021 (0.027)
Lerner index*Basel Capital Agreement dummy	2.052*** (0.629)	0.578 (0.913)	4.119*** (1.585)				8.875*** (2.274)	6.605* (3.462)	3.699* (2.178)				17.092 (12.671)	20.921** (10.219)	-3.670 (6.764)			
Bank concentration* Basel Capital Agreement				0.000 (0.002)	0.000 (0.003)	0.004 (0.009)				-0.002 (0.010)	-0.010 (0.015)	0.024** (0.010)				-0.127*** (0.035)	-0.078* (0.045)	0.047 (0.031)
Constant	4.457*** (0.281)	4.702*** (0.321)	3.919*** (1.221)	3.712*** (0.447)	4.317*** (0.437)	2.500* (1.466)	12.969*** (1.253)	15.693*** (1.224)	3.222** (1.593)	8.220*** (1.727)	10.683*** (1.999)	4.417*** (1.625)	34.810*** (5.914)	31.845*** (5.065)	-0.910 (4.233)	8.950 (6.823)	22.227*** (6.233)	6.616 (6.378)
Observations	630	459	171	634	463	171	630	459	171	634	463	171	630	459	171	634	463	171

***/**/* -1%, 5%, 10% significance levels.

Notes: Dependent variable: Bank nonperforming loans to gross loans (%) ;Ratio of defaulting loans (payments of interest and principal past due by 90 days or more) to total gross loans (total value of loan portfolio). The loan amount recorded as nonperforming includes the gross value of the loan as recorded on the balance sheet, not just the amount that is overdue; Instruments used both for Lerner Index and bank concentration: bank private credit to GDP (%), cost to income ratio (%), and GDP per capita (logarithm) (constant 2000's USD).

Robustness Check

In order to assess the robustness of our results, we involve GMM-System estimations for three other measures of the banks' soundness (regulatory capital to risk-weighted assets ratio, bank non-performing loans to gross loans ratio and, respectively, bank capital to total assets ratio), for a measure of banking sector concentration (Boone indicator), as well as for three other measures of banks efficiency (return on equity ratio, lending-deposit spread and net interest margin). We also consider the stock market turnover ratio as a proxy for the stock markets' performances. To account for the various types of non-linearity, we also include in the models the squared values of the concentration and turnover variables.

When Z-scores are considered as a measure for soundness in Panel "A" (full sample and whole time span), the concentration, as reflected by the Lerner index, still appears to support a stable evolutionary path of the banks, as does the development of the capital markets. If the sign of the Boone indicator squared values is considered, the same conclusion emerges for this indicator. Still, when considering the variable represented by the squared levels of the assets of the three largest commercial banks as share into total commercial banks' assets, we obtain an ambiguous negative effect upon soundness.

The capital market turnover plays a small yet positive and significant role at 1% in such an evolution. The banks' efficiency as measured by ROE clearly enhances the banks soundness: an increase in this variable contributes to a 0.003–fold increase in the Z-scores. However, it is interesting to note that higher lending-deposit spread, and net interest margin actually negatively impact the soundness. One possible explanation for this outcome may be related to the fact that such increases can be driven by the existence of inflationary tensions or other factors disturbing the financial stability. The effects of lending-deposit spread are almost three times larger than the effect of net interest margin, perhaps due to the fact that at least some of the bank portfolio diversification effects that may be captured by the interest margin are actually shadowed by the influence of capital markets' variables.

Further, we consider the fact that banks may use their capital as a buffer to absorb shocks and we replace Z-scores with two variables, reflecting the capital-to-assets ratio. The Lerner index and the Boone indicator appear once again to exercise a positive. Still, the statistical significance of the Boone indicator is weak and there is no such significance for the specification in which the net interest margin is used as a proxy for banks' efficiency.

Various Measures of Soundness, Concentration and Efficiency (GMM-System Estimations)

Panel "A": Full Sample, 63 Countries, 1997-2010

See Tables 14-17.

Panel "B": Full Sample, 63 Countries, 1997-2006

See Tables 18-21.

Panel "C": Full Sample, 63 Countries, 2007-2010

See Tables 22-25.

The share of the three largest commercial banks is positively related to the regulatory capital to risk-weighted assets ratio, but negatively impact the bank capital to total assets ratio. In other words, highly concentrated banks may implement better mechanisms of risks' transfer, with lower incentives to hold capital above the levels imposed by the regulatory framework. As Allen et al. (2011) argue, in perfectly competitive markets, banks may consider it optimal to use excess buffers of capital instead of interest rate, in order to monitor the borrowers. T he main rationale for this is that greater credit market competition increases capital holdings, since this competition may stimulate the market discipline from the asset side. When such reasons are less stringent then the buffer role and operational objectives become more important. Also, the market discipline act differently on small and large banks, with the first group of banks being more sensitive to the pressure of moral hazard factors. The risks-taking behaviour of banks is not a uniform process, depending on the banks' characteristics. Among these characteristics, the capital size may play a critical role.

The relations between market concentration and capital holds are significant influenced by the banks' efficiency. On the one hand, higher capital returns contribute to the diminishing of the risks; on the other hand, such returns facilitate an increase in the capacity of banks to raise capital and better allocate their own financial resources. However, the net interest margin negatively affects the capacity of banks to manage various types of risks and decreases their propensity to hold higher levels of capital.

Table 14. Dependent: Z-scores

	(1)	(2)	(3)	(4)	(5)	(6)	(7)	(8)	(9)
Lerner index	1.622*** (0.074)			1.974*** (0.068)			1.706*** (0.048)		
Lerner index (squared)	0.417*** (0.037)			0.441*** (0.074)					
Bank concentration (%)		0.023*** (0.003)			0.017*** (0.002)			0.020*** (0.002)	
Bank concentration (%) (squared)		-0.000*** (0.000)			-0.000*** (0.000)			0.000*** (0.000)	
Boone indicator			-0.041* (0.025)			-0.015*** (0.006)			-0.043*** (0.008)
Boone indicator (squared)			0.003 (0.004)			0.008*** (0.001)			0.003 (0.003)
Stock market capitalization to GDP (%)	0.003*** (0.000)	0.004*** (0.000)	0.004*** (0.000)	0.002*** (0.000)	0.003*** (0.000)	0.003*** (0.000)	0.003*** (0.000)	0.004*** (0.000)	0.004*** (0.000)
Stock market turnover ratio	-0.004*** (0.000)	-0.004*** (0.000)	-0.004*** (0.000)	-0.002*** (0.000)	-0.003*** (0.000)	-0.002*** (0.000)	-0.004*** (0.000)	-0.004*** (0.000)	-0.004*** (0.000)
Stock market turnover ratio (squared)	0.000*** (0.000)	0.000*** (0.000)	0.000*** (0.000)	0.000 (0.000)	0.000*** (0.000)	0.000** (0.000)	0.000** (0.000)	0.000*** (0.000)	0.000*** (0.000)
Bank credit to bank deposits (%)	-0.001*** (0.000)	-0.001*** (0.000)	-0.001*** (0.000)	-0.001*** (0.000)	-0.000 (0.000)	-0.000*** (0.000)	-0.001*** (0.000)	-0.001*** (0.000)	-0.001*** (0.000)
Return on equity (%)	0.003*** (0.000)	0.004*** (0.000)	0.004*** (0.000)						
Lending-deposit spread (%)				-0.021*** (0.006)	-0.034*** (0.004)	-0.032*** (0.003)			
Net interest margin (%)							-0.011*** (0.004)	-0.014*** (0.003)	-0.014*** (0.005)
Constant	-0.316*** (0.020)	-0.022 (0.016)	-0.022 (0.016)	-0.273*** (0.038)	-0.306*** (0.080)	0.109*** (0.030)	-0.279*** (0.019)	-0.612*** (0.062)	0.070*** (0.027)
Number of panel observations	708	708	711	526	526	529	718	718	721
Arellano-Bond test for zero autocorrelation in first-differenced errors (H0: no autocorrelation) – AR(2)	0.472 (p=0.637)	0.490 (p=0.624)	0.357 (p=0.720)	0.557 (p=0.577)	0.736 (p=0.461)	0.527 (p=0.597)	0.607 (p=0.544)	0.579 (p=0.562)	0.443 (p=0.657)
Sargan test of over-identifying restrictions(H0: over-identifying restrictions are valid)	52.394 (Probability > χ^2 = 0.99)	55.316 (Probability > χ^2 = 0.99)	50.842 (Probability > χ^2 = 0.99)	41.844 (Probability > χ^2 = 1.00)	42.825 (Probability > χ^2 = 1.00)	42.030 (Probability > χ^2 = 1.00)	53.746 (Probability > χ^2 = 0.99)	53.161 (Probability > χ^2 = 0.99)	55.132 (Probability > χ^2 = 0.99)

Table 15. Dependent: Regulatory capital to risk-weighted assets (%)

	(1)	(2)	(3)	(4)	(5)	(6)	(7)	(8)	(9)
Lerner index	-1.858*** (0.188)			-0.427 (0.486)			-2.275*** (0.290)		
Lerner index (squared)	1.733*** (0.604)			2.662*** (0.638)			1.843*** (0.672)		
Bank concentration (%)		-0.059*** (0.008)			-0.014* (0.008)			-0.069*** (0.010)	
Bank concentration (%) (squared)		0.001*** (0.000)			0.000*** (0.000)			0.001*** (0.000)	
Boone indicator			0.287* (0.159)			0.609** (0.269)			0.204 (0.244)
Boone indicator (squared)			-0.003 (0.303)			0.043 (0.034)			-0.010 (0.032)
Stock market capitalization to GDP (%)	-0.007*** (0.001)	-0.010*** (0.001)	-0.009*** (0.001)	0.001 (0.001)	-0.001 (0.001)	0.000 (0.001)	-0.009*** (0.000)	-0.010*** (0.001)	-0.010*** (0.000)
Stock market turnover ratio	0.008*** (0.002)	0.005*** (0.002)	0.004** (0.002)	0.012*** (0.001)	0.006*** (0.001)	0.005** (0.002)	0.010*** (0.002)	0.004* (0.002)	0.008** (0.003)
Stock market turnover ratio (squared)	-0.000 (0.000)	0.000 (0.000)	0.000 (0.000)	-0.000*** (0.000)	-0.000 (0.000)	0.000 (0.000)	-0.000 (0.000)	0.000 (0.000)	0.000 (0.000)
Bank credit to bank deposits (%)	-0.000 (0.001)	0.000 (0.001)	0.004** (0.001)	0.019*** (0.001)	0.021*** (0.002)	0.017*** (0.001)	0.002** (0.001)	0.001 (0.001)	0.000 (0.000)
Return on equity (%)	-0.008*** (0.002)	-0.002*** (0.001)	-0.007*** (0.001)						
Lending-deposit spread (%)				0.216*** (0.011)	0.219*** (0.018)	0.230*** (0.014)			
Net interest margin (%)							-0.125*** (0.013)	-0.072*** (0.018)	-0.127*** (0.013)
Constant	3.536*** (0.276)	4.895*** (0.430)	2.681*** (0.289)	-1.404*** (0.330)	-0.764*** (0.180)	-0.234 (0.253)	3.447*** (0.197)	5.484*** (0.281)	3.422*** (0.243)
Number of panel observations	573	574	575	418	418	420	582	583	584
Arellano-Bond test for zero autocorrelation in first-differenced errors (H0: no autocorrelation) – AR(2)	-0.935 (p=0.350)	-0.982 (p=0.323)	-0.649 (p=0.516)	-0.689 (p=0.491)	-0.523 (p=0.597)	-0.328 (p=0.742)	-1.224 (p=0.221)	-1.094 (p=0.274)	-0.939 (p=0.348)
Sargan test of over-identifying restrictions(H0: over-identifying restrictions are valid)	50.371 (Probability > χ^2 = 0.98)	50.392 (Probability > χ^2 = 0.98)	50.593 (Probability > χ^2 = 0.98)	42.204 (Probability > χ^2 = 0.99)	40.590 (Probability > χ^2 = 0.99)	41.989 (Probability > χ^2 = 0.99)	51.170 (Probability > χ^2 = 0.98)	52.623 (Probability > χ^2 = 0.98)	51.741 (Probability > χ^2 = 0.98)

Table 16. Dependent: Bank non-performing loans to gross loans (%)

	(1)	(2)	(3)	(4)	(5)	(6)	(7)	(8)	(9)
Lerner index	-4.796*** (0.447)			-11.723*** (0.229)			-4.826*** (0.427)		
Lerner index (squared)	-3.085*** (0.507)			-7.591*** (0.194)			-2.620*** (0.350)		
Bank concentration (%)		0.119*** (0.006)			0.038*** (0.010)			0.135*** (0.005)	
Bank concentration (%) (squared)		-0.001*** (0.000)			-0.000** (0.000)			-0.001*** (0.000)	
Boone indicator			0.920*** (0.089)			0.176* (0.089)			0.969*** (0.078)
Boone indicator (squared)			0.202*** (0.017)			0.165*** (0.011)			0.235*** (0.012)
Stock market capitalization to GDP (%)	-0.006*** (0.000)	-0.006*** (0.000)	-0.006*** (0.000)	-0.007*** (0.000)	-0.011*** (0.001)	-0.013*** (0.000)	-0.013*** (0.000)	-0.013*** (0.001)	-0.014*** (0.000)
Stock market turnover ratio	-0.002** (0.001)	0.002** (0.001)	-0.005*** (0.000)	0.012*** (0.000)	0.009*** (0.003)	0.013*** (0.002)	0.003*** (0.000)	0.009*** (0.001)	0.003*** (0.001)
Stock market turnover ratio (squared)	-0.000 (0.000)	-0.000 (0.000)	0.000*** (0.000)	0.000 (0.000)	0.000 (0.000)	0.000 (0.000)	-0.000*** (0.000)	-0.000*** (0.000)	-0.000*** (0.000)
Bank credit to bank deposits (%)	0.050*** (0.002)	0.050*** (0.002)	0.047*** (0.001)	0.083*** (0.001)	0.084*** (0.000)	0.084*** (0.000)	0.072*** (0.001)	0.075*** (0.001)	0.071*** (0.000)
Return on equity (%)	-0.050*** (0.001)	-0.050*** (0.001)	-0.048*** (0.001)						
Lending-deposit spread (%)				-0.009*** (0.003)	-0.027*** (0.006)	-0.017* (0.010)			
Net interest margin (%)							0.202*** (0.006)	0.248*** (0.011)	0.217*** (0.006)
Constant	-2.077*** (0.111)	-6.890*** (0.191)	-3.013*** (0.133)	-4.710*** (0.130)	-9.249*** (0.400)	-7.907*** (0.155)	-5.589*** (0.208)	-11.630*** (0.262)	-6.716*** (0.084)
Number of panel observations	566	566	567	416	415	417	575	575	576
Arellano-Bond test for zero autocorrelation in first-differenced errors (H0: no autocorrelation) – AR(2)	-0.146 (p=0.884)	-0.037 (p=0.970)	-0.029 (p=0.973)	-1.913 (p=0.006)	-1.879 (p=0.006)	-1.711 (p=0.087)	-0.162 (p=0.871)	-0.045 (p=0.964)	-0.031 (p=0.975)
Sargan test of over-identifying restrictions(H0: over-identifying restrictions are valid)	54.404 (Probability > χ^2 = 0.97)	55.098 (Probability > χ^2 = 0.96)	52.985 (Probability > χ^2 = 0.98)	45.620 (Probability > χ^2 = 0.99)	37.607 (Probability > χ^2 = 0.99)	43.873 (Probability > χ^2 = 0.99)	53.962 (Probability > χ^2 = 0.97)	51.923 (Probability > χ^2 = 0.98)	53.042 (Probability > χ^2 = 0.98)

Table 17. Dependent: Bank capital to total assets (%)

	(1)	(2)	(3)	(4)	(5)	(6)	(7)	(8)	(9)
Lerner index	1.381*** (0.284)			1.449*** (0.326)			1.481*** (0.285)		
Lerner index (squared)	2.836*** (0.407)			3.035*** (0.411)			2.653*** (0.449)		
Bank concentration (%)		0.013*** (0.003)			0.034*** (0.003)			0.019*** (0.006)	
Bank concentration (%) (squared)		-0.000*** (0.000)			-0.000*** (0.000)			-0.000*** (0.000)	
Boone indicator			0.362*** (0.122)			0.089 (0.102)			0.194*** (0.078)
Boone indicator (squared)			0.057** (0.027)			0.009 (0.017)			0.021 (0.017)
Stock market capitalization to GDP (%)	-0.006*** (0.000)	-0.005*** (0.000)	-0.005*** (0.000)	-0.006*** (0.000)	-0.004*** (0.000)	-0.004*** (0.000)	-0.006*** (0.000)	-0.004*** (0.000)	-0.005*** (0.000)
Stock market turnover ratio	0.005*** (0.001)	0.006*** (0.001)	0.007*** (0.001)	0.003** (0.001)	0.003** (0.001)	0.002** (0.001)	0.007*** (0.001)	0.006*** (0.001)	0.007*** (0.000)
Stock market turnover ratio (squared)	-0.000* (0.000)	-0.000*** (0.000)	-0.000*** (0.000)	-0.000*** (0.000)	-0.000*** (0.000)	-0.000*** (0.000)	-0.000* (0.000)	-0.000* (0.000)	-0.000* (0.000)
Bank credit to bank deposits (%)	-0.001*** (0.000)	-0.001*** (0.000)	-0.001*** (0.000)	-0.008*** (0.001)	-0.009*** (0.001)	-0.007*** (0.001)	-0.003*** (0.000)	-0.004*** (0.000)	-0.004*** (0.000)
Return on equity (%)	0.011*** (0.000)	0.011*** (0.000)	0.012*** (0.000)						
Lending-deposit spread (%)				0.022*** (0.002)	0.039*** (0.003)	0.040*** (0.004)			
Net interest margin (%)							-0.003 (0.008)	-0.015 (0.009)	-0.001 (0.010)
Constant	1.536*** (0.148)	1.549*** (0.173)	1.974*** (0.134)	2.525*** (0.135)	1.899*** (0.170)	2.481*** (0.239)	2.237*** (0.158)	2.073*** (0.239)	2.072*** (0.142)
Number of panel observations	565	566	567	410	410	412	571	571	573
Arellano-Bond test for zero autocorrelation in first-differenced errors (H0: no autocorrelation) – AR(2)	0.429 (p=0.668)	0.407 (p=0.684)	0.447 (p=0.654)	0.680 (p=0.496)	0.633 (p=0.507)	0.727 (p=0.467)	0.479 (p=0.631)	0.432 (p=0.665)	0.497 (p=0.612)
Sargan test of over-identifying restrictions (H0: over-identifying restrictions are valid)	52.463 (Probability > χ^2 = 0.98)	54.336 (Probability > χ^2 = 0.97)	53.210 (Probability > χ^2 = 0.98)	42.820 (Probability > χ^2 = 0.99)	43.544 (Probability > χ^2 = 0.99)	41.039 (Probability > χ^2 = 0.99)	53.702 (Probability > χ^2 = 0.97)	54.055 (Probability > χ^2 = 0.97)	55.265 (Probability > χ^2 = 0.96)

Table 18. Dependent: Z-scores

	(1)	(2)	(3)	(4)	(5)	(6)	(7)	(8)	(9)
Lerner index	1.463*** (0.067)			1.810*** (0.041)			1.491*** (0.057)		
Lerner index (squared)	0.246*** (0.038)			0.356*** (0.064)			0.277*** (0.043)		
Bank concentration (%)		0.022*** (0.002)			0.013*** (0.002)			0.021*** (0.003)	
Bank concentration (%) (squared)		-0.000 (0.000)			-0.000*** (0.000)			-0.000*** (0.000)	
Boone indicator			-0.013 (0.035)			-0.038*** (0.008)			-0.052*** (0.013)
Boone indicator (squared)			0.010 (0.008)			0.004*** (0.000)			0.007* (0.003)
Stock market capitalization to GDP (%)	0.005*** (0.000)	0.006*** (0.000)	0.007*** (0.000)	0.005*** (0.000)	0.005*** (0.000)	0.006*** (0.000)	0.006*** (0.000)	0.006*** (0.000)	0.007*** (0.000)
Stock market turnover ratio	-0.005*** (0.000)	-0.004*** (0.000)	-0.005*** (0.000)	-0.002*** (0.000)	-0.003*** (0.000)	-0.002*** (0.000)	-0.004*** (0.000)	-0.003*** (0.000)	-0.004*** (0.000)
Stock market turnover ratio (squared)	0.000*** (0.000)	0.000*** (0.000)	0.000*** (0.000)	0.000*** (0.000)	0.000*** (0.000)	0.000*** (0.000)	0.000*** (0.000)	0.000*** (0.000)	0.000*** (0.000)
Bank credit to bank deposits (%)	-0.003*** (0.000)	-0.003*** (0.000)	-0.003*** (0.000)	-0.005*** (0.000)	-0.004*** (0.000)	-0.004*** (0.000)	-0.004*** (0.000)	-0.003*** (0.000)	-0.003*** (0.000)
Return on equity (%)	0.003*** (0.000)	0.004*** (0.000)	0.004*** (0.000)						
Lending-deposit spread (%)				-0.016*** (0.004)	-0.030*** (0.003)	-0.027*** (0.004)			
Net interest margin (%)							-0.014*** (0.003)	-0.016*** (0.002)	-0.013*** (0.001)
Constant	-0.102* (0.058)	-0.578*** (0.101)	0.090* (0.053)	-0.015 (0.055)	0.111 (0.078)	0.315*** (0.068)	-0.047 (0.063)	-0.420*** (0.123)	0.156*** (0.040)
Number of panel observations	517	518	520	415	415	523	524	524	526
Arellano-Bond test for zero autocorrelation in first-differenced errors (H0: no autocorrelation) – AR(2)	-0.152 (p=0.879)	0.095 (p=0.924)	-0.087 (p=0.931)	-0.390 (p=0.697)	0.064 (p=0.949)	-0.218 (p=0.827)	0.232 (p=0.817)	0.232 (p=0.817)	0.031 (p=0.975)
Sargan test of over-identifying restrictions (H0: over-identifying restrictions are valid)	44.238 (Probability > χ^2 = 0.42)	45.331 (Probability > χ^2 = 0.38)	47.479 (Probability > χ^2 = 0.29)	42.931 (Probability > χ^2 = 0.47)	42.533 (Probability > χ^2 = 0.49)	42.451 (Probability > χ^2 = 0.50)	49.267 (Probability > χ^2 = 0.24)	49.267 (Probability > χ^2 = 0.24)	46.781 (Probability > χ^2 = 0.32)

Table 19. Dependent: Regulatory capital to risk-weighted assets (%)

	(1)	(2)	(3)	(4)	(5)	(6)	(7)	(8)	(9)
Lerner index	-5.624*** (0.954)			-0.835 (0.555)			-4.646*** (0.931)		
Lerner index (squared)	-1.515** (0.645)			1.271*** (0.371)			-1.020 (0.634)		
Bank concentration (%)		-0.049** (0.024)			-0.006 (0.012)			-0.056** (0.028)	
Bank concentration (%) (squared)		0.001*** (0.0000			0.000* (0.000)			0.001*** (0.000)	
Boone indicator			1.000*** (0.220)			0.397*** (0.133)			0.652*** (0.177)
Boone indicator (squared)			0.120*** (0.033)			0.028 (0.018)			0.104*** (0.031)
Stock market capitalization to GDP (%)	-0.007*** (0.003)	-0.009*** (0.002)	-0.007*** (0.002)	-0.004 (0.003)	-0.005*** (0.002)	-0.005** (0.002)	-0.003 (0.003)	-0.009*** (0.003)	-0.008*** (0.002)
Stock market turnover ratio	0.010* (0.006)	0.005 (0.005)	-0.001 (0.007)	0.013*** (0.002)	0.009*** (0.001)	0.008*** (0.002)	0.012*** (0.004)	0.009** (0.004)	0.000 (0.000)
Stock market turnover ratio (squared)	0.000 (0.000)	0.000 (0.000)	0.000 (0.000)	-0.000*** (0.000)	-0.000** (0.000)	-0.000 (0.000)	-0.000 (0.000)	0.000 (0.000)	0.004 (0.004)
Bank credit to bank deposits (%)	-0.000 (0.003)	0.002 (0.003)	-0.008** (0.003)	-0.004* (0.002)	-0.000 (0.002)	-0.008*** (0.003)	-0.011*** (0.003)	-0.005 (0.004)	-0.016*** (0.003)
Return on equity (%)	0.001 (0.005)	0.001 (0.007)	-0.003 (0.006)						
Lending-deposit spread (%)				0.201*** (0.017)	0.261*** (0.013)	0.265*** (0.017)			
Net interest margin (%)							-0.125*** (0.025)	-0.089*** (0.030)	-0.108*** (0.020)
Constant	5.054*** (0.667)	3.572*** (1.323)	4.468*** (0.522)	2.828*** (0.487)	2.240*** (0.590)	3.470*** (0.507)	6.462*** (0.569)	5.531*** (1.376)	5.808*** (0.530)
Number of panel observations	401	402	403	317	317	319	406	407	408
Arellano-Bond test for zero autocorrelation in first-differenced errors (H0: no autocorrelation) – AR(2)	-0.801 (p=0.423)	-0.698 (p=0.485)	-0.411 (p=0.681)	-0.122 (p=0.902)	0.042 (p=0.967)	0.289 (p=0.772)	-1.075 (p=0.282)	-0.866 (p=0.387)	-0.676 (p=0.499)
Sargan test of over-identifying restrictions(H0: over-identifying restrictions are valid)	39.172 (Probability > χ^2 = 0.25)	39.686 (Probability > χ^2 = 0.23)	36.116 (Probability > χ^2 = 0.37)	35.140 (Probability > χ^2 = 0.41)	40.441 (Probability > χ^2 = 0.21)	34.629 (Probability > χ^2 = 0.44)	34.355 (Probability > χ^2 = 0.32)	37.302 (Probability > χ^2 = 0.32)	36.746 (Probability > χ^2 = 0.34)

Table 20. Dependent: Bank non-performing loans to gross loans (%)

	(1)	(2)	(3)	(4)	(5)	(6)	(7)	(8)	(9)
Lerner index	-9.176*** (0.905)			-14.646*** (0.497)			-7.562*** (0.570)		
Lerner index (squared)	-6.168*** (0.652)			-9.573*** (0.392)			-4.905*** (0.442)		
Bank concentration (%)		0.105*** (0.013)			-0.005 (0.159)			0.095*** (0.014)	
Bank concentration (%) (squared)		-0.001*** (0.000)			0.000* (0.000)			-0.001*** (0.000)	
Boone indicator			0.844*** (0.291)			0.454*** (0.065)			0.778*** (0.230)
Boone indicator (squared)			0.183*** (0.055)			0.188*** (0.013)			0.198*** (0.050)
Stock market capitalization to GDP (%)	-0.014*** (0.003)	-0.010*** (0.002)	-0.011*** (0.002)	-0.009*** (0.002)	-0.009*** (0.001)	-0.012*** (0.002)	-0.013*** (0.002)	-0.011*** (0.002)	-0.014*** (0.002)
Stock market turnover ratio	-0.003 (0.003)	0.003 (0.003)	-0.009** (0.004)	0.016*** (0.002)	0.018*** (0.003)	0.016*** (0.002)	0.002 (0.004)	0.013*** (0.003)	0.004 (0.003)
Stock market turnover ratio (squared)	-0.000 (0.000)	-0.000 (0.000)	0.000 (0.000)	-0.000 (0.000)	-0.000 (0.000)	0.000 (0.000)	-0.000** (0.000)	-0.000*** (0.000)	-0.000** (0.000)
Bank credit to bank deposits (%)	0.061*** (0.005)	0.042*** (0.002)	0.038*** (0.003)	0.087*** (0.004)	0.074*** (0.002)	0.075*** (0.002)	0.070*** (0.003)	0.059*** (0.003)	0.054*** (0.003)
Return on equity (%)	-0.032*** (0.003)	-0.032*** (0.002)	-0.026*** (0.002)						
Lending-deposit spread (%)				-0.066*** (0.009)	-0.085*** (0.013)	-0.094*** (0.013)			
Net interest margin (%)							0.143*** (0.019)	0.171*** (0.024)	0.146*** (0.017)
Constant	-1.530*** (0.330)	-5.594*** (0.518)	-1.825*** (0.309)	-4.037*** (0.286)	-6.862*** (0.720)	-6.484*** (0.013)	-4.309*** (0.330)	-8.675*** (0.572)	-4.725*** (0.339)
Number of panel observations	397	397	398	316	315	317	402	402	403
Arellano-Bond test for zero autocorrelation in first-differenced errors (H0: no autocorrelation) – AR(2)	0.092 (p=0.927)	-0.014 (p=0.998)	-0.036 (p=0.971)	-1.667 (p=0.096)	-1.720 (p=0.086)	-1.608 (p=0.108)	-0.012 (p=0.990)	-0.007 (p=0.995)	-0.008 (p=0.996)
Sargan test of over-identifying restrictions(H0: over-identifying restrictions are valid)	38.042 (Probability > $\chi^2 = 0.29$)	39.489 (Probability > $\chi^2 = 0.24$)	36.183 (Probability > $\chi^2 = 0.37$)	39.543 (Probability > $\chi^2 = 0.24$)	38.445 (Probability > $\chi^2 = 0.27$)	38.603 (Probability > $\chi^2 = 0.27$)	37.567 (Probability > $\chi^2 = 0.31$)	41.038 (Probability > $\chi^2 = 0.19$)	38.808 (Probability > $\chi^2 = 0.26$)

Table 21. Dependent: Bank capital to total assets (%)

	(1)	(2)	(3)	(4)	(5)	(6)	(7)	(8)	(9)
Lerner index	1.980*** (0.494)			2.479*** (0.281)			1.979*** (0.506)		
Lerner index (squared)	3.501*** (0.413)			3.400*** (0.211)			3.448*** (0.370)		
Bank concentration (%)		0.041*** (0.013)			0.057*** (0.008)			0.050*** (0.013)	
Bank concentration (%) (squared)		-0.000*** (0.000)			-0.000*** (0.000)			-0.000 (0.000)	
Boone indicator			0.655** (0.290)			0.251** (0.123)			0.475** (0.189)
Boone indicator (squared)			0.130** (0.051)			0.052*** (0.018)			0.096*** (0.031)
Stock market capitalization to GDP (%)	-0.009*** (0.002)	-0.004*** (0.001)	-0.003 (0.002)	-0.006*** (0.002)	-0.003*** (0.001)	-0.002 (0.001)	-0.008*** (0.002)	-0.003* (0.002)	-0.002 (0.001)
Stock market turnover ratio	0.008* (0.004)	-0.001 (0.003)	-0.005 (0.004)	0.008*** (0.003)	0.002 (0.002)	0.000 (0.000)	0.004 (0.004)	-0.002 (0.004)	-0.006 (0.004)
Stock market turnover ratio (squared)	-0.000 (0.000)	0.000 (0.000)	0.000** (0.000)	-0.000*** (0.000)	-0.000** (0.000)	-0.000 (0.000)	-0.000 (0.000)	0.000 (0.000)	0.000** (0.000)
Bank credit to bank deposits (%)	-0.009*** (0.003)	-0.007*** (0.002)	-0.008*** (0.002)	-0.014*** (0.002)	-0.012*** (0.001)	-0.015*** (0.002)	-0.013*** (0.003)	-0.014*** (0.002)	-0.013*** (0.002)
Return on equity (%)	0.010*** (0.002)	0.010*** (0.002)	0.011*** (0.002)						
Lending-deposit spread (%)				0.049*** (0.007)	0.063*** (0.009)	0.062*** (0.009)			
Net interest margin (%)							-0.036* (0.022)	-0.058*** (0.020)	-0.054** (0.027)
Constant	1.060*** (0.597)	0.813 (0.545)	2.218*** (0.370)	1.508*** (0.216)	0.804** (0.407)	2.704*** (0.315)	2.073*** (0.443)	1.514** (0.725)	3.159*** (0.303)
Number of panel observations	392	393	394	311	311	313	396	397	398
Arellano-Bond test for zero autocorrelation in first-differenced errors (H0: no autocorrelation) – AR(2)	0.774 (p=0.439)	0.700 (p=0.484)	0.797 (p=0.425)	0.929 (p=0.353)	0.899 (p=0.368)	1.026 (p=0.304)	0.844 (p=0.398)	0.748 (p=0.454)	0.949 (p=0.342)
Sargan test of over-identifying restrictions(H0: over-identifying restrictions are valid)	29.336 (Probability $> \chi^2 = 0.70$)	37.913 (Probability $> \chi^2 = 0.29$)	40.761 (Probability $> \chi^2 = 0.20$)	27.938 (Probability $> \chi^2 = 0.76$)	36.162 (Probability $> \chi^2 = 0.37$)	35.550 (Probability $> \chi^2 = 0.39$)	31.844 (Probability $> \chi^2 = 0.57$)	38.258 (Probability $> \chi^2 = 0.28$)	39.894 (Probability $> \chi^2 = 0.22$)

Table 22. Dependent: Z-scores

	(1)	(2)	(3)	(4)	(5)	(6)	(7)	(8)	(9)
Lerner index	2.898** (1.212)			3.892*** (1.009)			3.230*** (1.254)		
Lerner index (squared)	-0.862 (2.889)			-1.985 (2.032)			-1.085 (2.986)		
Bank concentration (%)		0.027 (0.027)			0.114*** (0.038)			0.049* (0.023)	
Bank concentration (%) (squared)		-0.000 (0.000)			-0.001*** (0.000)			-0.000 (0.000)	
Boone indicator			0.296 (0.629)			0.074 (1.036)			0.708*** (0.265)
Boone indicator (squared)			-0.175 (0.221)			0.454 (0.281)			0.315*** (0.079)
Stock market capitalization to GDP (%)	-0.001 (0.001)	-0.001 (0.001)	-0.001 (0.001)	-0.000 (0.001)	0.001 (0.001)	-0.000 (0.002)	-0.001 (0.001)	-0.000 (0.001)	0.000 (0.002)
Stock market turnover ratio	0.005** (0.002)	0.005 (0.003)	0.006 (0.004)	0.010** (0.004)	0.006 (0.004)	0.010*** (0.004)	0.005** (0.002)	0.003 (0.003)	0.005 (0.003)
Stock market turnover ratio (squared)	-0.000*** (0.000)	-0.000*** (0.000)	-0.000*** (0.000)	-0.000*** (0.000)	-0.000** (0.000)	-0.000*** (0.000)	-0.000*** (0.000)	-0.000*** (0.000)	-0.000*** (0.000)
Bank credit to bank deposits (%)	0.004** (0.002)	0.003** (0.001)	0.004** (0.002)	0.002 (0.001)	0.001 (0.002)	0.002 (0.001)	0.001 (0.001)	-0.001 (0.002)	-0.000 (0.001)
Return on equity (%)	0.002 (0.001)	0.003*** (0.001)	0.004** (0.002)						
Lending-deposit spread (%)				-0.047** (0.022)	-0.050* (0.027)	-0.065* (0.038)			
Net interest margin (%)							0.084** (0.042)	0.129** (0.064)	0.142** (0.006)
Constant	-1.014*** (0.302)	-0.740 (0.836)	-0.389 (0.334)	-1.059*** (0.303)	-3.078*** (1.184)	-0.057 (0.346)	-1.099*** (0.273)	-1.744* (0.999)	-0.396 (0.376)
Number of panel observations	137	136	137	77	77	77	140	139	140
Arellano-Bond test for zero autocorrelation in first-differenced errors (H0: no autocorrelation) – AR(2)	N.A.	N.A.	N.A.	N.A.	N.A.	N.A.	N.A.	N.A.	N.A.
Sargan test of over-identifying restrictions(H0: over-identifying restrictions are valid)	9.855 (Probability $> \chi^2 = 0.04$)	7.364 (Probability $> \chi^2 = 0.12$)	5.851 (Probability $> \chi^2 = 0.21$)	4.692 (Probability $> \chi^2 = 0.32$)	5.421 (Probability $> \chi^2 = 0.25$)	4.700 (Probability $> \chi^2 = 0.32$)	9.123 (Probability $> \chi^2 = 0.06$)	9.394 (Probability $> \chi^2 = 0.05$)	6.751 (Probability $> \chi^2 = 0.15$)

Table 23. Dependent: Regulatory capital to risk-weighted assets (%)

	(1)	(2)	(3)	(4)	(5)	(6)	(7)	(8)	(9)
Lerner index	-10.878 (12.217)			-24.068* (12.620)			-5.132 (11.812)		
Lerner index (squared)	27.498 (22.919)			68.560** (27.538)			24.882 (23.984)		
Bank concentration (%)		0.106 (0.199)			0.288 (0.344)			0.086 (0.189)	
Bank concentration (%) (squared)		-0.000 (0.001)			-0.002 (0.003)			0.000 (0.001)	
Boone indicator			1.177 (4.070)			2.119 (4.713)			2.333** (1.110)
Boone indicator (squared)			-0.678 (1.473)			2.194 (1.462)			0.995*** (0.314)
Stock market capitalization to GDP (%)	-0.021** (0.010)	-0.044*** (0.011)	-0.025** (0.010)	-0.004 (0.012)	-0.030** (0.014)	-0.015 (0.012)	-0.019** (0.009)	-0.046*** (0.010)	-0.021** (0.009)
Stock market turnover ratio	0.018 (0.018)	0.011 (0.017)	0.017 (0.019)	0.034 (0.039)	0.057* (0.034)	0.120*** (0.036)	0.014 (0.016)	0.006 (0.015)	0.013 (0.017)
Stock market turnover ratio (squared)	-0.000* (0.000)	-0.000 (0.000)	-0.000* (0.000)	-0.000 (0.000)	-0.000* (0.000)	-0.000*** (0.000)	-0.000 (0.000)	-0.000 (0.000)	-0.000* (0.000)
Bank credit to bank deposits (%)	0.029*** (0.010)	0.020** (0.010)	0.029*** (0.009)	0.024** (0.011)	0.002 (0.001)	0.022 (0.017)	-0.073 (0.241)	0.007 (0.012)	0.019 (0.013)
Return on equity (%)	0.008 (0.008)	0.009 (0.008)	0.017 (0.009)						
Lending-deposit spread (%)				-0.019 (0.103)	-0.128 (0.122)	-0.373*** (0.117)	-0.073 (0.241)		
Net interest margin (%)								0.243 (0.245)	0.256 (0.241)
Constant	-0.225 (2.900)	0.732 (6.253)	0.412 (3.383)	4.545 (3.458)	-4.380 (11.459)	2.309 (4.829)	2.727 (3.510)	2.234 (7.055)	0.989 (3.579)
Number of panel observations	126	126	126	72	72	72	129	129	129
Arellano-Bond test for zero autocorrelation in first-differenced errors (H0: no autocorrelation) – AR(2)	N.A.	N.A.	N.A.	N.A.	N.A.	N.A.	N.A.	N.A.	N.A.
Sargan test of over-identifying restrictions (H0: over-identifying restrictions are valid)	12.210 (Probability > χ^2 = 0.02)	39.686 (Probability > χ^2 = 0.05)	13.274 (Probability > χ^2 = 0.01)	13.675 (Probability > χ^2 = 0.01)	12.042 (Probability > χ^2 = 0.02)	11.875 (Probability > χ^2 = 0.02)	14.078 (Probability > χ^2 = 0.01)	9.912 (Probability > χ^2 = 0.04)	12.026 (Probability > χ^2 = 0.02)

Table 24. Dependent: Bank non-performing loans to gross loans (%)

	(1)	(2)	(3)	(4)	(5)	(6)	(7)	(8)	(9)
Lerner index	11.274 (13.522)			-51.637** (24.676)			-14.605 (16.849)		
Lerner index (squared)	-7.398 (23.882)			92.824* (54.395)			52.744 (36.065)		
Bank concentration (%)		0.376* (0.195)			-0.325 (0.386)			-0.269 (0.213)	
Bank concentration (%) (squared)		-0.004*** (0.001)			0.001 (0.003)			0.001 (0.002)	
Boone indicator			7.891 (5.977)			27.882 (17.056)			1.947 (4.999)
Boone indicator (squared)			9.284*** (2.302)			-7.135* (4.013)			0.093 (0.871)
Stock market capitalization to GDP (%)	-0.007 (0.012)	-0.015 (0.010)	-0.011 (0.010)	0.006 (0.020)	-0.013 (0.021)	-0.007 (0.018)	-0.022 (0.019)	-0.027 (0.016)	-0.021 (0.017)
Stock market turnover ratio	0.009 (0.021)	0.014 (0.021)	0.031* (0.018)	-0.027 (0.052)	-0.096 (0.096)	0.048 (0.067)	0.039*** (0.011)	0.053*** (0.016)	0.051** (0.020)
Stock market turnover ratio (squared)	-0.000 (0.000)	-0.000 (0.000)	-0.000*** (0.000)	0.000 (0.000)	0.000 (0.000)	-0.000 (0.000)	-0.000*** (0.000)	-0.000*** (0.000)	-0.000** (0.000)
Bank credit to bank deposits (%)	0.038* (0.022)	0.041** (0.021)	0.032** (0.016)	0.085** (0.034)	0.090** (0.044)	0.071* (0.043)	0.103** (0.040)	0.098** (0.047)	0.076* (0.045)
Return on equity (%)	-0.133*** (0.016)	-0.129*** (0.014)	-0.119*** (0.013)						
Lending-deposit spread (%)				1.335** (0.553)	1.823** (0.777)	0.828 (0.658)			
Net interest margin (%)							-0.136 (0.599)	-0.578 (0.657)	-0.156 (0.661)
Constant	-1.752 (3.255)	-7.090 (5.878)	0.386 (2.469)	-8.353 (6.727)	2.386 (15.067)	-11.376 (7.216)	-9.278 (5.982)	3.706 (8.730)	-6.589 (6.200)
Number of panel observations	124	124	124	70	70	70	127	127	127
Arellano-Bond test for zero autocorrelation in first-differenced errors (H0: no autocorrelation) – AR(2)	N.A.	N.A.	N.A.	N.A.	N.A.	N.A.	N.A.	N.A.	N.A.
Sargan test of over-identifying restrictions(H0: over-identifying restrictions are valid)	9.926 (Probability $> \chi^2 = 0.04$)	39.489 (Probability $> \chi^2 = 0.03$)	13.055 (Probability $> \chi^2 = 0.01$)	5.000 (Probability $> \chi^2 = 0.29$)	4.922 (Probability $> \chi^2 = 0.29$)	4.527 (Probability $> \chi^2 = 0.34$)	11.051 (Probability $> \chi^2 = 0.03$)	8.265 (Probability $> \chi^2 = 0.08$)	8.221 (Probability $> \chi^2 = 0.08$)

Table 25. Dependent: Bank capital to total assets (%)

	(1)	(2)	(3)	(4)	(5)	(6)	(7)	(8)	(9)
Lerner index	-7.016 (7.495)			1.387 (9.425)			-3.859 (7.327)		
Lerner index (squared)	24.829 (15.704)			8.953 (19.775)			17.874 (14.785)		
Bank concentration (%)		0.088 (0.115)			0.604*** (0.204)			0.121 (0.109)	
Bank concentration (%) (squared)		-0.001 (0.001)			-0.005*** (0.002)			-0.001 (0.001)	
Boone indicator			-0.556 (1.776)			0.227 (3.623)			0.102 (1.143)
Boone indicator (squared)			-1.153 (0.776)			1.167 (0.954)			0.536 (0.348)
Stock market capitalization to GDP (%)	-0.022*** (0.008)	-0.017*** (0.006)	-0.025*** (0.007)	-0.015** (0.007)	-0.003 (0.004)	-0.018*** (0.005)	-0.022*** (0.007)	-0.021*** (0.006)	-0.020*** (0.006)
Stock market turnover ratio	0.016* (0.009)	0.021** (0.010)	0.019** (0.008)	0.043* (0.023)	0.040*** (0.012)	0.060*** (0.017)	0.014* (0.008)	0.017* (0.009)	0.014* (0.008)
Stock market turnover ratio (squared)	-0.000*** (0.000)	-0.000*** (0.000)	-0.000*** (0.000)	-0.000* (0.000)	-0.000*** (0.000)	-0.000*** (0.000)	-0.000** (0.000)	-0.000** (0.000)	-0.000*** (0.000)
Bank credit to bank deposits (%)	0.007 (0.006)	-0.005 (0.009)	0.004 (0.009)	-0.002 (0.009)	-0.000 (0.011)	-0.010 (0.011)	-0.005 (0.009)	-0.017 (0.011)	-0.013 (0.011)
Return on equity (%)	0.014*** (0.005)	0.012** (0.006)	0.016** (0.007)						
Lending-deposit spread (%)				-0.243* (0.143)	-0.187 (0.141)	-0.314* (0.169)			
Net interest margin (%)							0.145 (0.170)	0.142 (0.178)	0.355** (0.154)
Constant	4.947** (2.379)	3.810 (3.773)	4.189* (2.437)	5.503* (3.256)	-11.302* (6.837)	5.691** (2.851)	6.317*** (2.460)	4.502 (4.462)	6.893*** (2.212)
Number of panel observations	125	125	125	70	70	70	127	127	127
Arellano-Bond test for zero autocorrelation in first-differenced errors (H0: no autocorrelation) – AR(2)	N.A.	N.A.	N.A.	N.A.	N.A.	N.A.	N.A.	N.A.	N.A.
Sargan test of over-identifying restrictions (H0: over-identifying restrictions are valid)	7.278 (Probability $> \chi^2 = 0.12$)	10.864 (Probability $> \chi^2 = 0.03$)	9.480 (Probability $> \chi^2 = 0.05$)	7.122 (Probability $> \chi^2 = 0.13$)	6.780 (Probability $> \chi^2 = 0.15$)	4.721 (Probability $> \chi^2 = 0.32$)	5.152 (Probability $> \chi^2 = 0.27$)	4.218 (Probability $> \chi^2 = 0.38$)	3.950 (Probability $> \chi^2 = 0.41$)

***/**/* -1%, 5%, 10% significance levels.

Notes: The distinction between countries with large commercial banks and, respectively, countries with small commercial banks, is based on same criteria as in Table 2.

It is interesting to note that the impact of capital markets development upon banks' capital formation appears to be extremely robust. Also, in almost all the models, the stock markets' turnover seems to reduce the banks' requirement for holding higher levels of capital. However, such substitution effect displays extremely low amplitude and it is less robust. In other words, the volume effects exercised by the capital markets on banks' capital prevail on yield effects.

With the exception of the Boone indicator, the other measures of concentration are negatively impacting the weight of non-performing loans. The size of the capital market clearly enhances the concerns of the banks for monitoring and reducing operational risks. An increase in the market size induces a reduction in the weight of non-performing loans that lies between 0.006–fold and 0.014–fold. The same applies for market turnover, yet the size of these effects is extremely low. The return on equity ratio and lending-deposit spread are supporting the reduction of the non-performing loans. Opposite, the net interest margin actually contributes to increased levels of non-performing loans.

For the pre-crisis period (Panel "B"), the outcome looks quite similar with the one for the full time span. The reverted U-shape effect of bank concentration on Z-scores is somehow clearer, while the amplitude of the effects induced by Lerner index and Boone indicator is at a certain degree lower. Once again, for the capital markets, the volume effects are more important that the yield effects. For both lending-deposit spread and net interest margin, an increase appears to inhibit the banks 'soundness as this is reflected by Z-scores. The return on equity ratio measure of efficiency plays no role in determine the regulatory capital to risk-weighted assets ratio.

The capacity of capital market development to support a better management of operational risks is fully reflected across all estimations. If bank capital to total assets ratio is involved as a proxy of soundness, it appears that there is a positive and statistical significant at 1% impact of Lerner index and Boone indicator while the effect of banks' concentration is hereinafter reverted U-shaped.

The overall picture is noticeably changed during the crisis (Panel "C"). Firstly, the squared levels of Lerner index and Boone indicator are displaying a "wrong" sign (even they are not statistically significant). Secondly, market capitalization lost its statistical significance if Z-scores and, respectively, non-performing loans are used as dependent variables. Nevertheless, it seems that market turnover is still relevant in explaining the evolutions of Z-scores and bank capital to total assets ratio soundness 'measures. Thirdly, banks are losing an important fraction of their capacity to control risks as well as to cover their risky assets through the adjustments in interest rates.

Summarizing, the banking sector's concentration supports the banks' soundness. The size and efficiency of the banks are essential in setting their levels of capital holds. The banks are also taking into account the overall availability of the financial resources. Higher levels of banks' efficiency lead to a sounder evolution, better risk management and a superior capacity to deal with moral hazard. The involved transmission channels are severely affected by the crisis.

CONCLUSION

This research book chapter is aiming to analyse the financial nexus formed by the banks' soundness, the concentration in the banking sector, the efficiency in this sector and the development of the capital markets. Based on the structure–conduct–performance and efficient-structure, as well as on the Systemic Scale Economies hypotheses, we have formulated an alternative version of a model used in the Corvoisier and Gropp (2002) and de Guevara et al (2005) studies, in which we include the development of the capital markets as an alternative explanatory variable. We use this model to provide a conceptual background and we test the conclusions emerging from this on a data sample of 63 developed and developing countries.

We find that a banking sector with large and sound banks is abler to control and transfer various types of risks and to have a balanced evolution. The relation between soundness, structural and functional characteristics of the sector is significantly influenced by the banks' performances. We employ a broad variety of robustness checks, including alternative definitions of soundness, concentration and efficiency and alternative estimation techniques to find that such relation is at a certain degree sensitive to the considered measures of the involved variables.

We also find that the development of capital markets enhances the concerns of banks for monitoring and reducing operational risks and contribute in a robust way to the banks' soundness. With the exception of the banks from the highest tail of Z-scores distribution in the developed countries, all types of banks are consistently reacting to the status of local capital markets. Although the amplitude of the effects exercised by the capital market turnover appears to be relatively small, this variable is playing a certain role, especially after the emergence and reach of a certain threshold for the integrated bank-capital markets financing system.

The outcomes of our analysis are sensitive to the tail of the banking sector. The market power influence more significant the soundness of banks in countries with large banks comparing with the ones with smaller banks. The same tail dependence is reflected by the impact of capital market development and market turnover. From the control variables, the effects of interest rates are clearly influenced by the relative importance in the entire economic system of financial intermediation taking place through banks.

These results are also heavily influenced by the differences in the overall economic development. Between the OECD and non-OECD countries from our sample there are striking distinctions in the reactions to the changes in concentration and efficiency.

The crisis induces large perturbations at the levels of the transmission mechanisms as the risks exposure is increasing and the operational efficiency is declining.

Some implications for policymaking may be derived from these findings. First of all, the content and effectiveness of prudential regulations are critical for the banking sector, as well as for the entire financial sector. However, such regulations are a complement and not a substitute of the market discipline. Secondly, there might be some advantages in supervising in a unified frame the banking sector and the capital markets. Thirdly, in designing and building prudential policies, the policymakers cannot rely on a single measure of banks soundness and efficiency.

For the interpretation of our results, several caveats should be considered. Firstly, our time span covers several business cycles with substantial changes at the level of the financial systems. For instance, we do not analyse the consequences of the current financial turmoil period which may appear as a structural breakpoint. Secondly, despite the fact that monetary policy may play a vital role in enhancing the soundness, we do not address explicitly this issue. Thirdly, we do not investigate the consequences of too big to fail systemic prudential policies, as well as the consequences of inefficient financial institutions' exit from the sector with the subsequent contagion mechanisms. Fourthly, the distinction between structural and functional consequences of banking sector concentration is only vaguely mentioned, without being fully followed. Fifthly, the transmission channels for the impact of capital markets development upon banks soundness are not explicitly described. More generally, the financial nexus should be better clarified in a more substantially developed framework to better understand the contribution of concentration, efficiency and capital markets to banks soundness.

REFERENCES

Altunbas, Y., Manganelli, S., & Marques-Ibanez, D. (2011). Bank Risk during the Financial Crisis: do Business Models Matter? European Central Bank.

Amemiya, T. (1982). Two stage least absolute deviations estimators. *Econometrica*, *50*(3), 689–711. doi:10.2307/1912608

Amemiya, T. (1985). The nonlinear tow-stage least-squares estimation. *Journal of Economics*, *2*(2), 105–110. doi:10.1016/0304-4076(74)90033-5

Antoniou, A., Guneya, Y., & Paudyala, K. (2008). The determinants of capital structure: Capital market-oriented versus bank-oriented institutions. *Journal of Financial and Quantitative Analysis*, *43*(01), 59–92. doi:10.1017/S0022109000002751

Arellano, M., & Bond, S. (1991). Some tests of specification for panel data: Monte Carlo evidence and an application to employment equations. *The Review of Economic Studies*, *58*(2), 277–297. doi:10.2307/2297968

Arellano, M., & Bover, O. (1995). Another look at the instrumental variable estimation of error-components models. *Journal of Economics*, *68*(1), 29–51. doi:10.1016/0304-4076(94)01642-D

Basel Committee on Banking Supervision. (2010). Basel III: a Global Regulatory Framework for More Resilient Banks and Banking Systems. Bank for International Settlements.

Bassett, G. Jr, & Koenker, R. (1978). Asymptotic theory of least absolute error regression. *Journal of the American Statistical Association*, *73*(363), 618–622. doi:10.1080/01621459.1978.10480065

Beck, T., Demirgüç-Kunt, A., & Levine, R. (2006). Bank concentration, competition, and crises: First results. *Journal of Banking & Finance*, *30*(5), 1581–1603. doi:10.1016/j.jbankfin.2005.05.010

Beck, T., Jakubik, P., & Piloiu, A. (2013). Non-performing Loans. What matters in addition to the economic cycle? European Central Bank.

Bengtsson, E. (2013). Shadow banking and financial stability: European money market funds in the global financial crisis. *Journal of International Money and Finance*, *32*, 579–594. doi:10.1016/j.jimonfin.2012.05.027

Berger, A. (1995). The relationship between capital and earnings in banking. *Journal of Money, Credit and Banking*, *27*(2), 432–456. doi:10.2307/2077877

Berger, A. N., & De Young, R. (1997). Problem loans and cost efficiency in commercial banks. *Journal of Banking & Finance*, *21*(6), 849–870. doi:10.1016/S0378-4266(97)00003-4

Berger, A. N., & Hannan, T. H. (1989). The Price-Concentration relationship in banking. *The Review of Economics and Statistics*, *71*(2), 291–299. doi:10.2307/1926975

Berger, A. N., & Hannan, T. H. (1998). The efficiency cost of market power in the banking industry: A test of the 'Quiet Life' and related hypotheses. *The Review of Economics and Statistics*, *80*(3), 454–465. doi:10.1162/003465398557555

Bertay, A. C., Demirgüç-Kunt, A., & Huizinga, H. (2013). Do we need big banks? Evidence on performance, strategy and market discipline. *Journal of Financial Intermediation*, *22*(4), 532–558. doi:10.1016/j.jfi.2013.02.002

Blundell, R., & Bond, S. (1998). Initial conditions and moment restrictions in dynamic panel data models. *Journal of Economics*, *87*(1), 115–143. doi:10.1016/S0304-4076(98)00009-8

Bossone, B., & Lee, J. K. (2004). In finance, size matters: The 'Systemic Scale Economies' hypothesis. *IMF Staff Papers*, *51*(1).

Boyd, J. H., & De Nicolo, G. (2005). The theory of bank risk-taking and competition revisited. *The Journal of Finance*, *60*(3), 1329–1343. doi:10.1111/j.1540-6261.2005.00763.x

Carletti, E., Hartmann, P., & Spangnolo, G. (2007). Bank mergers, competition, and liquidity. *Journal of Money, Credit and Banking*, *39*(5), 1067–1105. doi:10.1111/j.1538-4616.2007.00058.x

Casu, B., & Girardone, C. (2006). Bank competition, concentration and efficiency in the single European market. *Manchester School*, *74*(4), 441–468. doi:10.1111/j.1467-9957.2006.00503.x

Charnes, A., Cooper, W. W., & Ferguson, R. O. (1955). Optimal estimation of executive compensation by linear programming. *Management Science*, *1*(2), 138–151. doi:10.1287/mnsc.1.2.138

Chen, X. R., Bai, Z. D., Zhao, L. C., & Wu, Y. H. (1990). Asymptotic normality of minimum L1-norm estimates in linear models. *Sci. China*, *33*, 1311–1328.

Chernozhukov, V., & Hansen, C. (2005). An IV model of quantile treatment effects. *Econometrica*, *3*(1), 245–262. doi:10.1111/j.1468-0262.2005.00570.x

Chernozhukov, V., & Hansen, C. (2006). Instrumental quantile regression inference for structural and treatment effect models. *Journal of Economics*, *132*(2), 491–525. doi:10.1016/j.jeconom.2005.02.009

Chernozhukov, V., & Hansen, C. (2008). Instrumental variable quantile regression: A robust inference approach. *Journal of Economics*, *142*(1), 379–398. doi:10.1016/j.jeconom.2007.06.005

Corvoisier, S., & Gropp, R. (2002). Bank concentration and retail interest rates. *Journal of Banking & Finance*, *26*(11), 2155–2189. doi:10.1016/S0378-4266(02)00204-2

De Guevara, J. F., Maudos, J., & Perez, F. (2005). Market power in european banking sectors. *Journal of Financial Services Research*, *27*(2), 109–137. doi:10.100710693-005-6665-z

Demirgüç-Kunt, A., & Huizinga, H. (2010). Are Banks too big to fail or too big to Save? International Evidence from Equity Prices and CDS Spreads. CEPR.

Demirgüç-Kunt, A., & Martinez Peria, M. S. (2010). A Framework for Analyzing Competition in the Banking Sector: An Application to the Case of Jordan. *World Bank Policy Research Working Paper*, *WPS5499*(December).

Demsetz, H. (1973). Industry structure, market rivalry, and public policy. *The Journal of Law & Economics*, *16*(1), 1–9. doi:10.1086/466752

Demsetz, R. S., & Stahan, P. E. (1997). Diversification, size, and risk at bank holding companies. *Journal of Money, Credit and Banking*, *29*(3), 300–313. doi:10.2307/2953695

Dima, B., Dincă, M. S., & Spulbar, C. (2014). Financial nexus: Efficiency and soundness in banking and capital markets. *Journal of International Money and Finance*, *47*, 100–124. doi:10.1016/j.jimonfin.2014.05.002

Drehmann, M., & Juselius, M. (2013). Evaluating early Warning Indicators of banking Crises: Satisfying Policy Requirements. BIS.

Ferreira, C. (2012). Bank market Concentration and Efficiency in the European Union: a panel Granger Causality Approach. Technical University of Lisbon, School of Economics and Management Working Papers, 03/2012/DE/UECE.

Greene, W. H. (2008). *Econometric Analysis* (7th ed.). Prentice Hall.

Hauswald, R., & Marquez, R. (2003). Information technology and financial services competition. *Review of Financial Studies, 17*(3), 921–948. doi:10.1093/rfs/hhg017

Hauswald, R., & Marquez, R. (2006). Competition and strategic information acquisition in credit markets. *Review of Financial Studies, 19*(3), 967–1000. doi:10.1093/rfs/hhj021

Hay, D. A., & Liu, G. S. (1997). The efficiency of firms: What difference does competition make? *Economic Journal (London), 107*(442), 597–617. doi:10.1111/j.1468-0297.1997.tb00029.x

Kim, T.H. & Muller, C., (2000). Two-stage Quantile Regression. University of Nottingham.

Koenker, R., & Bassett, G. Jr. (1978). Regression quantiles. *Econometrica, 46*(1), 33–50. doi:10.2307/1913643

Konoe, S. (2010). Policy Shifts and the Changing Role of the Banks: A Comparison between Japan and Germany. *Journal of Japanese Law, 15*, 81–102.

Liu, Y., Papakirikos, E., & Yuan, M. (2004) Market Valuation and risk Assessment of Canadian Banks. Bank of Canada.

Petersen, M., & Rajan, R. (1995). The effect of credit market competition on lending relationships. *The Quarterly Journal of Economics, 110*(2), 407–443. doi:10.2307/2118445

Phillips, P. C. B. (1991). A Shortcut to LAD Estimator Asymptotics. *Econometric Theory*, 7(04), 450–463. doi:10.1017/S0266466600004709

Pollard, D. (1991). Asymptotics for least absolute deviations regression estimators. *Econometric Theory*, 7(02), 186–199. doi:10.1017/S0266466600004394

Schaeck, K., & Cihak, M. (2007). Banking Competition and Capital Ratios. International Monetary Fund. IMF.

Schaeck, K., & Cihak, M. (2008). How does Competition Affect Efficiency and Soundness in Banking? New Empirical Evidence. European Central Bank.

Schaeck, K., & Cihak, M. (2010). Competition, Efficiency, and Soundness in Banking: An Industrial Organization Perspective. European Banking Center.

Vitols, S., (2001). The Origins of Bank-based and Market-based Financial Systems: Germany, Japan, and the United States.

Vitols, S. (2002). The Transition from Banks to Markets in the German and Japanese Financial Systems. Wissenschaftszentrum Berlin für Sozialforschung (WZB). doi:10.2139srn.607581

Weiss, A. A. (1990). Least Absolute Error Estimation in the Presence of Serial Correlation. *Journal of Econometrics*, *44*(1-2), 127–158. doi:10.1016/0304-4076(90)90076-6

World Bank. (2013). World Data Bank Global Financial Development. Retrieved from http://databank.worldbank.org/data/databases.aspx?pagenumber1/45

Section 2

The Transmission Mechanism of Monetary Policy:

Dynamics and Perspectives

Chapter 5
Monetary Policy Transmission Mechanism in Romania Over the Period 2001 to 2012:
A BVAR Analysis

ABSTRACT

This chapter aims to provide additional empirical evidence on monetary policy transmission mechanism in Romania over the period 2001 to 2012 based on a BVAR analysis with a KoKo Minnesota/Litterman prior. The importance of the central bank is rising in Romania considering its main attribution to control the interest rate in accordance with its objectives. The empirical evidence provides a significant contribution to literature taking into account the characteristics of the selected emerging country, i.e. Romania, a former communist country in Central and Eastern Europe.

INTRODUCTION

Monetary policy and its effects on inflation and real economic activity have been an important subject of debate in the economic literature. Fetai and Izet (2011) consider that in contrast with conventional theory and empirical research from the developed economies, the empirical research related to the emerging countries suggests a potential weakness and instability of the conventional monetary policy instruments (i.e. interest rate, monetary base)

DOI: 10.4018/978-1-5225-9269-3.ch005

during the transition period, due to structural and institutional deficiencies from these countries (underdeveloped financial systems, high inflation rate, dollarization/eurorization of the assets and liabilities). Moreover, transition is a dynamic process. Therefore, the monetary transmission mechanism can change in time.

Darvas (2009) asserted that the monetary transmission mechanism describes the effects of monetary policy on macroeconomic and financial variables and its analysis is an important part in macroeconomic policy research and is crucial for the conduct of monetary policy. Moreover, in a monetary union it is important to have a similar business cycle and a unitary monetary mechanism transmission for all the countries. Only in such a context will a single currency have positive effects on price level and on other important macroeconomic variables.

Cogley and Sargent (2005) consider that modifications in the economy structure have an impact on the monetary policy transmission mechanism. In our opinion, in Romania, the current account liberalization, the trade deficit, the integration in the European Union, the global financial crisis are some of the processes that affected the structure of the economy. Furthermore, the new monetary policy strategy –inflation targeting- adopted in 2005 by the central bank has influenced the monetary policy mechanism. As a country that intends to join a monetary union, the analysis of the monetary policy mechanism can offer important issues regarding the euro-adoption. In these conditions, new pieces of evidence regarding the monetary transmission mechanism in emerging countries are necessary in order to assess as exactly as possible its impact on real economy.

In this study we intend to emphasize the inflation dynamics and persistence, the inflation determinants, to study the impact of a monetary shock on a set of variables, the correlations between the gross domestic product, inflation rate, interest rate, monetary aggregate M2, unemployment rate and wage index in Romania over the period 2001 to 2012. In order to achieve these objectives, we use a Bayesian Vector Autoregression (BVAR) model with a Ko Minnesota/Litterman prior distribution, as it was developed in Koop and Korobilis's paper (2009). In our opinion, the contribution of this study to the literature is important, but also original from many points of view.

First of all, from our knowledge, a BVAR model with quarterly data was rarely used to analyze Romania's monetary policy. Spulbar *et al.* (2011) used a BVAR model to analyze the monetary policy in Romania. In comparison with that paper we are using a different set of variables (i.e. real GDP, unemployment rate and wage index) and quarterly data. Secondly, the results are important for understanding the way in which the monetary policy developed. Thirdly, the time interval covered by the analysis is considerably long, comprising significant events that affected Romania's economy.

The paper is structured as follows. Section II reviews the literature on the monetary policy transmission mechanism. Section III presents the econometric methodology and the data adopted in this study. Section IV discusses the results. Finally, section V presents the conclusions.

LITERATURE ON THE MONETARY POLICY TRANSMISSION MECHANISM IN TRANSITION COUNTRIES

The use of VAR models to analyze the monetary policy transmission mechanism is widely spread in the economic literature. These models were used both for developed and emerging countries.The VAR models are considered to be the most relevant in the econometric modelling of the monetary policy transmission mechanism. Within the VAR models, the studies based on BVAR techniques have a major importance and are widely used. Furthermore, the VAR methodology was developed in the papers of Gerlach and Smets (1995), Leeper *et al.* (1996), Christiano *et al.* (1999).

The latter study offers a detailed review of various papers that use VAR models in order to analyze the monetary policy in USA. In Europe, Angeloni *et al.* (2003), Peersman and Smets (2001) studied different aspects of the monetary policy transmission mechanism in the euro area. Other studies focused on individual member states (Mojon and Peersman, 2001).

The analysis of the monetary policy transmission mechanism using VAR models was widely used for the emerging countries from Central and Eastern Europe. Hereinafter we will highlight some of the studies that focused their analysis on these countries.

Caraiani (2010) used a BVAR model to forecast the dynamics of output for the Romanian economy until Q4 2010. The results showed that the recovery will be slow and gradual. Cocriş and Nucu (2013) evaluated the effectiveness of the monetary policy transmission mechanism in Romania using a VECM model. The results indicate an efficiency improvement of the monetary policy impulses via interest rate channel.

Popescu (2013) used a VAR model to analyze the monetary policy effects on the real economic aggregates and prices in countries from Central and

Eastern Europe. The results showed a high degree of heterogeneity between the transmissions of an unexpected monetary policy shock under a different monetary policy strategy, which could create important problems in a monetary union. Birman (2012) used the VAR analysis to characterize the monetary policy transmission mechanism in Romania over the period 2000 to 2011. The results showed that the central bank was more successful in controlling the transmission mechanism after adopting an inflation targeting strategy.

Carare and Popescu (2011) analyzed the transmission of monetary policy in Hungary by applying the Bayesian estimation of VAR models. The authors stated that most of the monetary policy channels are operational despite of the high level of eurorization and despite of the fact that most of the banks are foreign-owned. Franta *et al.* (2011) investigates the evolution of the monetary policy transmission mechanism in the Czech Republic over the period 1996 to 2010 using a BVAR model. The results showed that financial shocks are less important for the aggregate economy in the environment of a stable financial system. Spulbar *et al.* (2011) used a BVAR model to analyze the monetary policy in Romania. The results reveal that the exchange rate remains an important mechanism that influences the variables of the real economy significantly and the interest rate channel is being robust in the last years.

METHODOLOGY AND DATA

Along with its introduction by Sims (1980), the VAR modelling became a standard method of evaluating the properties of macroeconomic systems. The BVAR models were introduced for the first time by Litterman (1980) as an alternative for VAR techniques. These solve the problem of the degrees of freedom common to VAR techniques, but they also offer more accurate forecast results. Also, they have some advantages in terms of objectivity and flexibility. Félix and Nunes (2002) underline, in an extensive manner, the advantages of BVAR models compared to VAR models. In this study we will investigate the monetary policy transmission mechanism in Romania using a BVAR model with a KoKo Minnesota/Litterman prior distribution. In order to illustrate the methodology, we assume the following VAR model:

$$y_t = a_0 + \sum_{l=1}^{p} A_l y_{t-l} + \varepsilon_t, \varepsilon_t \sim N\left(0, \Sigma\right) \quad (1)$$

where y_t is an $m \times 1$ vector of $t = 1,\ldots,T$ observations on m variables, a_0 is an $m \times 1$ vector of intercepts, and A_l is an $m \times m$ matrix of regression coefficients for the lth lag with the p maximum number of lags.

The VAR can be rewritten in matrix form in different ways. Koop and Korobilis (2009) proposed the following form:

$$x_t = \left[1 y_{t-1} \cdots y_{t-p}\right], X = \begin{bmatrix} x_1 \\ \vdots \\ x_T \end{bmatrix}, B = \begin{bmatrix} a_0 \\ A_1 \\ \vdots \\ A_p \end{bmatrix} \quad (2)$$

and $\beta = vec\left(B\right)$; the model (1) can be written:

$$Y_{T\times m} = X_{T\times(mp+1)} B_{(mp+1)\times m} + E_{T\times m}, E \sim N\left(0,\Sigma\right) \quad (3)$$

Using this approach, the posterior distribution can be easily produced. The choice of prior has always been a contentious issue in Bayesian analysis. In this study we will use the KoKo Minnesota prior distribution as it was developed in the study of Koop and Korobilis (2009). The simplicity of the Minnesota prior is the fact that Σ is assumed to be known. The prior for β is:

$$\beta \sim N\left(\beta_0, \underline{V}\right) \quad (4)$$

with $\beta_0 = 0$ and $\underline{V} = 0$. Koop and Korobolis specified the prior covariance matrix $\underline{V}$ as a diagonal matrix with its elements $v_{ij,l}\left(l = 1,\ldots,p\right)$, where:

$$v_{ij,l} = \begin{cases} \dfrac{a_l}{p^2} & \textit{for coefficients on own lags} \\ \dfrac{\left(a_2\sigma_i\right)}{\left(p^2\sigma_j\right)} & \textit{for coefficients on lags of variable } i \neq j \\ a_3\sigma_i & \textit{for coefficients on exogenous variables} \end{cases} \quad (5)$$

where σ_i^2 is the ith diagonal element of Σ. Koop and Korobilis (2009) provide a detailed analysis on how the conditional posteriors are derived.

In the model we have included the following variables: real gross domestic product; consumer price index; three months' short-term interest rate; unemployment rate; monetary aggregate M2 and wage index over the period 2001.Q1 to 2012.Q4. The data were extracted from the International Financial Statistics database. The data are seasonally adjusted, except for the short-term interest rate, and expressed as logarithmic first differences. The short-term interest rate is included in levels. The first three variables represent the minimum set, allowing the analysis of a small open economy (Franta et al., 2011). We have included the unemployment rate in the study in order to study the Phillips relationship between inflation and unemployment in Romania. M2 was introduced in the model to capture the relationship between monetary aggregate and real GDP and inflation. Introducing the wage index in the model will allow us to study the relationship between labour market, wage and productivity. When using BVAR models nonstationarity is not an issue, because the presence of unit roots in the data does not affect the likelihood function (Sims et al., 1990). The prior means for the coefficient on the own variable weight and relative cross-variable weight are set to 0.7, assuming a higher degree of persistence, and 0.3, respectively. The scale on the intercepts is set to 100. The results were obtained using the EViews.

RESULTS

Somewhat counterintuitive a positive inflation shock (i.e. an unexpected growth in inflation) will lead to a gross domestic product growth. This answer is not in line with economic theory. On the other hand, if we take into consideration the analyzed period, the answer can be valid. Over the period 2000 to 2008 the gross domestic product growth was achieved in a high inflationary environment, compared to other countries in Central and Eastern Europe. A positive aspect emerges from the impulse response of the gross domestic product to an unexpected growth of the short-term interest rate. Thus, a monetary policy tightening will lead to a gross domestic product decrease. This evidence comes to consolidate the monetary policy transmission channel. In line with intuition, a positive shock of the unemployment rate will lead to a lower demand, and implicitly, to a lower gross domestic product. A positive shock of the monetary aggregate M2 is associated with a GDP growth, while the wage index growth will lead to a GDP decrease. This latest answer is not in line with the economic literature, but it can be valid given the situation in which wage growth is not positively correlated with productivity.

A positive demand shock (i.e. an unexpected increase of the gross domestic product) will lead to a lower inflation rate. Even if this effect disappears in a relatively short time, it can be explained through the monetary policy reaction function, which implies an interest rate growth when the output is above the economy potential in order to reduce the inflationary pressures.

The inflation impulse response to an unexpected growth of the short-term interest rate is negative. Thus, the inflation will significantly decrease, and it will come back to its previous level after a long period due to an interest rate growth (i.e. a tighter monetary policy). An interest rate shock will lead to a higher price of money. Thus, people and business will borrow less for

Figure 1. Response of GDP

Note: horizontal axes indicate the periods (months) after the shock; vertical axes show the deviation from the baseline scenario

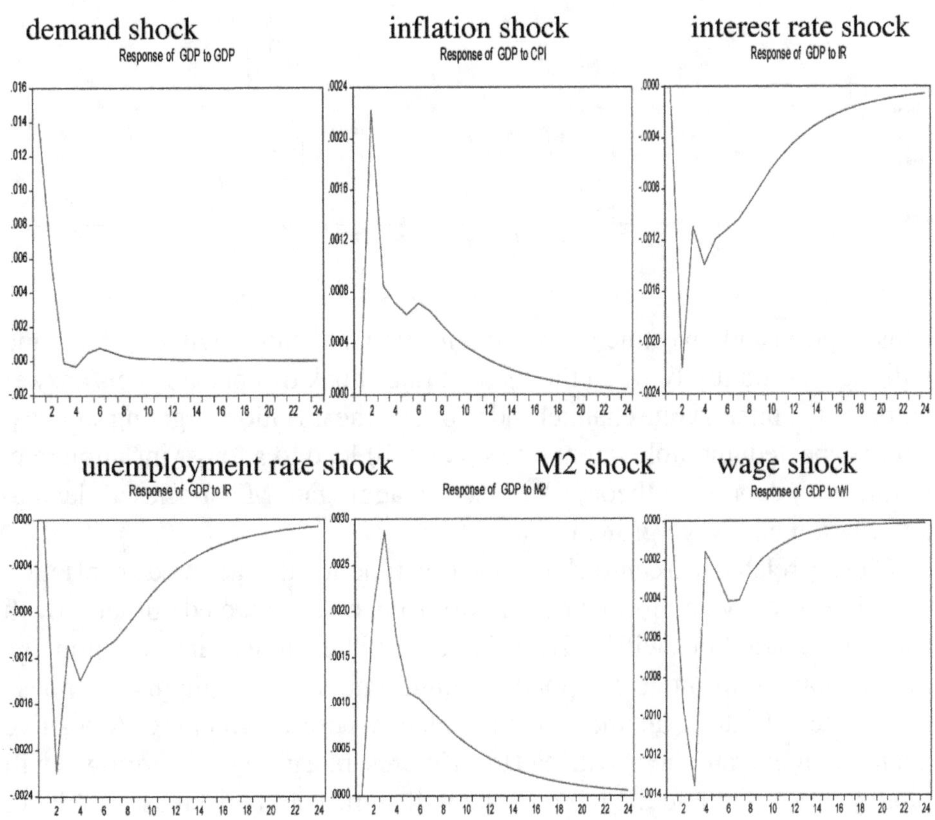

Figure 2. Response of inflation

Note: horizontal axes indicate the periods (months) after the shock; vertical axes show the deviation from the baseline scenario

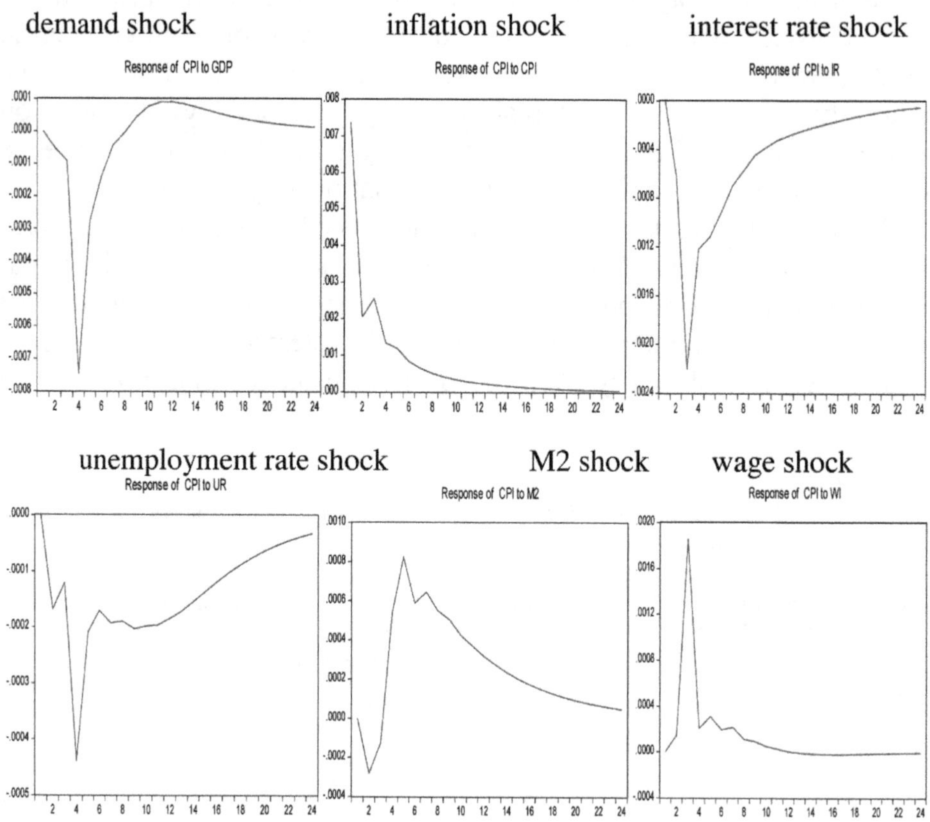

consumption and investment, so both inflation and output will decrease, and will recover gradually when the interest rate shock disappears. This answer enforces the interest rate channel and supports the inflation targeting strategy. An unexpected unemployment rate shock will lead to a lower inflation rate, in line with economic theory. A monetary aggregate M2 shock will lead to an inflation and wage growth.

Closely related to a central bank reaction function that adopted an inflation targeting strategy and following a Taylor rule, an unexpected output growth and an inflation shock will lead to an increase of the interest rate. Additionally, the gradualism in monetary policy is highlighted by the impulse response of the interest rate to an unexpected monetary policy tightening. A positive unemployment rate shock will lead to an interest rate growth. This growth will rapidly disappear, and the interest rate will significantly decrease, the latter effect being the predominant one. As a matter of fact, this response is more in line with intuition if we take into consideration the fact that central banks also pursue, within certain limits, a higher demand. A monetary aggregate M2 shock will lead, in the short term, to a lower interest rate diminution, but the effect is for the short term. A wage growth will lead to an interest rate growth, but this response will disappear relatively fast.

An unexpected growth of the gross domestic product will lead to a lower unemployment rate. Also, in accordance with the Phillips curve, an inflation rate growth will determine a lower unemployment rate. An interest rate shock will lead to a higher unemployment rate, a response in line with economic theory. A positive monetary aggregate M2 shock will result in a

Figure 3. Response of interest rate

Note: horizontal axes indicate the periods (months) after the shock; vertical axes show the deviation from the baseline scenario

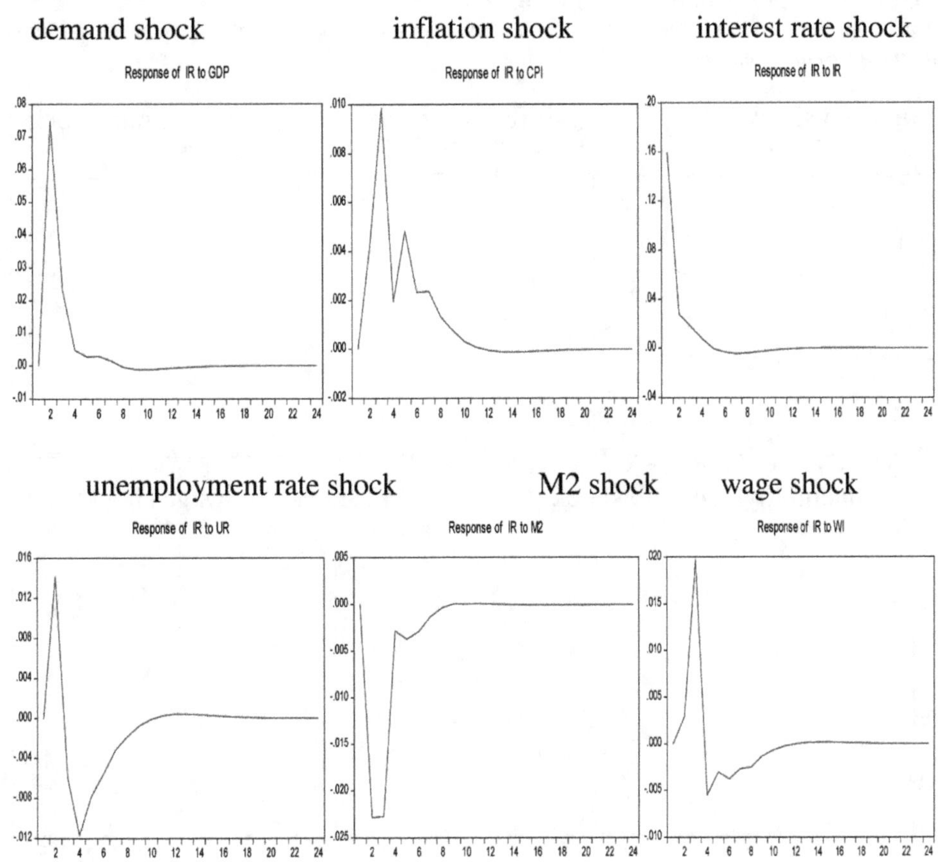

lower unemployment rate, while the unexpected positive variation of wages will lead to an unemployment rate growth.

An unexpected growth of the gross domestic product will lead to an increase in the monetary aggregate M2. The impulse response of the monetary aggregate M2 to an inflation growth will lead to a monetary mass expansion, unlike the theoretical hypothesis which indicates a lower monetary aggregate due to higher prices. However, this contradiction was also observed by Kim and Roubini (2000). In line with economic theory, the monetary aggregate M2 will decrease, following a more restrictive monetary policy. Also, an unemployment rate growth will involve a lower monetary aggregate.

A demand shock will lead to a wage growth. A similar impulse response is observed in the case of an inflation shock. This impulse response is in line with the theory, considering the negative effects of the inflation on the revenue level. A positive interest rate shock will lead to lower wages. An

Figure 4. Response of unemployment rate

Note: horizontal axes indicate the periods (months) after the shock; vertical axes show the deviation from the baseline scenario

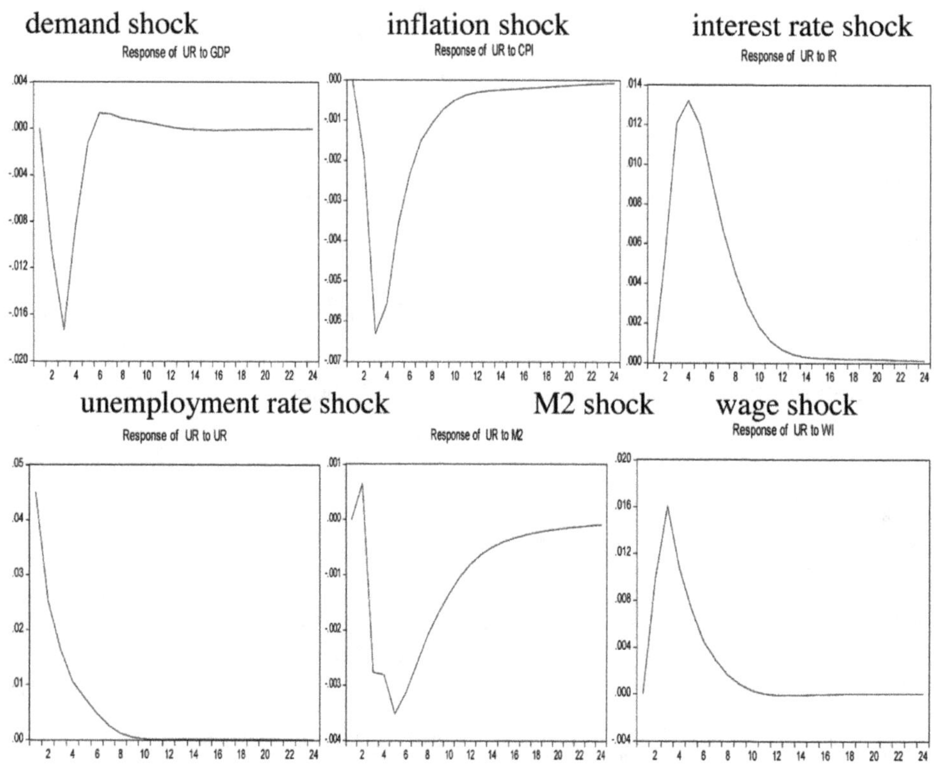

Figure 5. Response of M2
Note: horizontal axes indicate the periods (months) after the shock; vertical axes show the deviation from the baseline scenario

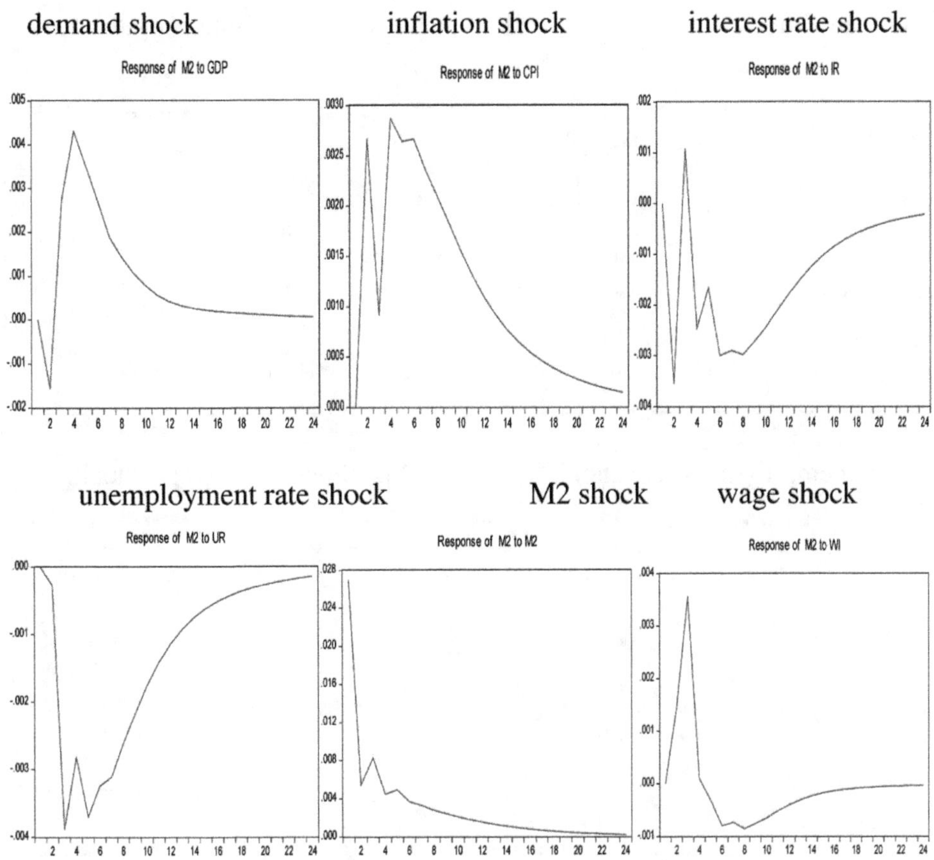

unemployment rate growth will lead to lower wages. An unexpected growth of the monetary aggregate will determine a wage growth.

CONCLUSION

In this book chapter we provided new empirical evidence on monetary policy transmission mechanisms in Romania using a BVAR model with a with a KoKo Minnesota/Litterman prior distribution. The objective was to identify the way in which some monetary and economic variables react to different shocks. Thus, in the model we have included six variables over the period 2001.Q1 to 2012.Q4.

Figure 6. Response of wages

Note: horizontal axes indicate the periods (months) after the shock; vertical axes show the deviation from the baseline scenario

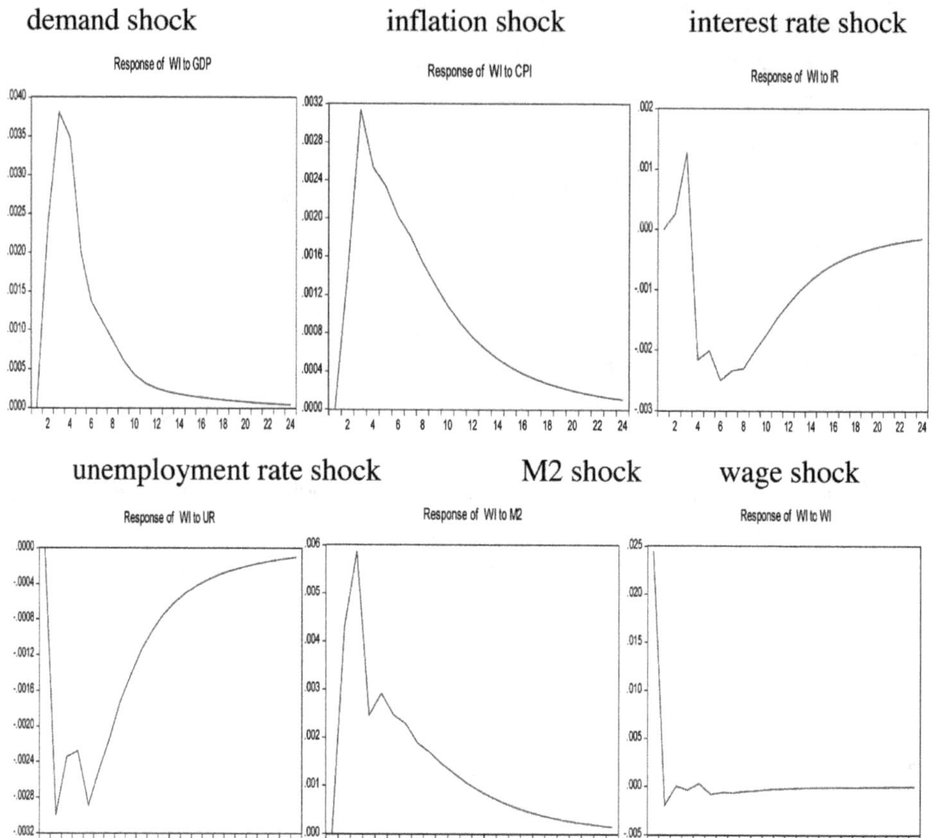

The results showed relevant conclusions. First of all, the effectiveness of the interest rate channel is to be appreciated. Most of impulse responses due to an interest rate shock are in line with theory. Thus, having in view the absence of the output puzzles (i.e. an output growth due to a tighter monetary policy) and of the price puzzle (i.e. inflation growth due to a tighter monetary policy) the interest rate channel has become more robust in the recent years. Secondly, taking into consideration these facts, we consider that the role and responsibilities of the central bank acquire an increased importance, having in view the fact that it can control the interest rate according to its objectives. Thirdly, the relation between the inflation rate and the unemployment rate in Romania is in line with the Phillips curve. In Romania the inflation has been very high in the last two decades. Therefore, the central bank's main objective was to reduce inflation. In our opinion, when the inflation is in the target range, the central bank should pay greater attention to the demand side and to the employment rate.

Admittedly, after this study new directions of research appear. In our opinion, it would be relevant to compare these results with those obtained for the countries in the Euro Area in order to compare the business cycle and the differences in the monetary policy transmission mechanism. We will leave this for future research.

REFERENCES

Angeloni, I., Kashyap, A. K., & Mojon, B. (Eds.). (2003). *Monetary policy transmission in the euro area: a study by the eurosystem monetary transmission network*. Cambridge: Cambridge University Press. doi:10.1017/CBO9780511492372

Caraiani, P. (2010). Forecasting Romanian GDP using a BVAR model. *Romanian Journal of Economic Forecasting*, *13*(4), 76–87.

Carare, A., & Popescu, A. (2011). Monetary Policy and Risk-Premium Shocks in Hungary: Results from a Large Bayesian VAR. IMF.

Christiano, L. J., Eichenbaum, M., & Evans, C. L. (1999). Monetary policy shocks: What have we learned and to what end? In Handbook of macroeconomics (Vol. 1, pp. 65–148). Elsevier.

Cocriş, V., & Nucu, A. E. (2013). Interest rate channel in Romania: Assessing the effectiveness transmission of monetary policy impulses to inflation and economic growth. *Theoretical and Applied Economics*, *18*(2), 37–50.

Cogley, T., & Sargent, T. J. (2005). Drifts and volatilities: Monetary policies and outcomes in the post WWII US. *Review of Economic Dynamics*, *8*(2), 262–302. doi:10.1016/j.red.2004.10.009

Darvas, Z. (2009). Monetary transmission in three central European economies: Evidence from time-varying coefficient vector autoregressions. *Empirica, 40(2), 363-390.*

Félix, R. M. and Nunes, L. C., (2002). Bayesian Forecasting Models for the Euro Area. *Economic Bulletin and Financial Stability Report Articles*.

Fetai, B., & Izet, Z. (2011). The impact of monetary policy and exchange rate regime on real GDP and prices in the Republic of Macedonia. *Economic and Business Review*, *12*(4), 263–284.

Franta, M., Horvath, R., & Rusnak, M. (2011). Evaluating changes in the monetary transmission mechanism in the Czech Republic. *Empirical Economics, 46(3), 827-842.*

Gerlach, S. and Smets, F., (1995) The monetary transmission mechanism: evidence from the G-7 Countries. *Centre for Economic Policy Research.*

Kim, S., & Roubini, N. (2000). Exchange Rate Anomalies in the Industrial Countries: A Solution with a Structural VAR Approach. *Journal of Monetary Economics*, *45*(3), 561–586. doi:10.1016/S0304-3932(00)00010-6

Koop, G. and Korobilis, D. (2009) Bayesian Multivariate Time Series Methods for Empirical Macroeconomics. MPRA.

Leeper, E. M., Sims, C. A., Zha, T., Hall, R. E., & Bernanke, B. S. (1996). What does monetary policy do? *Brookings Papers on Economic Activity*, (2), 1–78. doi:10.2307/2534619

Litterman, R. B. (1980). *A Bayesian procedure for forecasting with vector autoregressions, unpublished mimeo*. Cambridge: Massachusetts Institute of Technology.

Migliardo, C. (2010). Monetary Policy Transmission in Italy: A BVAR Analysis with Sign Restriction. *Czech. Economic Review*, (2), 139–167.

Mojon, B., & Peersman, G. (2001) A VAR description of the effects of monetary policy in the individual countries of the euro area. European Central Bank.

Peersman, G., & Smets, F. (2001) The Monetary Transmission Mechanism in the Euro Area: More Evidence from VAR Analysis. European Central Bank.

Popescu, V. I. (2013). The analysis of monetary policy effects with emphasis on monetary policy strategy types. A VAR approach. *Romanian Economic Journal*, *16*(47), 57–74.

Rawdanowicz, L. (2010). *The 2008-09 Crisis in Turkey: Performance, Policy Responses and Challenges for Sustaining the Recovery*. OECD Publishing.

Sims, C. A. (2012). Macroeconomics and Reality. *Econometrica*, *48*(1), 1–48. doi:10.2307/1912017

Sims, C. A., Stock, J. H., & Watson, M. W. (1990). Inference in linear time series models with some unit roots. *Econometrica*, *58*(1), 113–144. doi:10.2307/2938337

Spulbar, C., Niţoi, M. (2013). Monetary policy transmission mechanism in Romania over the period 2001 to 2012: a BVAR analysis. *Scientific Annals of the Alexandru Ioan Cuza University of Iasi*, *60*(2), 387-398.

Spulbăr, C., Niţoi, M., & Stanciu, C. (2012). Monetary policy analysis in Romania: A Bayesian VAR approach. *African Journal of Business Management*, *6*(36), 9957–9968. doi:10.5897/AJBM11.1150

Chapter 6
Analysis of the Monetary Policy Dynamics in Romania Using a Structural Vector Autoregressive Model

ABSTRACT

This chapter aims to provide an elaborate empirical analysis of the monetary policy dynamics in Romania using a structural vector autoregressive model. This chapter contributes to literature based on an empirical framework regarding the implications of exchange rate channel within the monetary policy, and the impact of the monetary aggregates channels in order to explain the evolution of the prices level in Romania.

INTRODUCTION

The efficient functioning of the enlarged future euro zone still needs some answers to a set of essential questions. One of these questions is related to the pertinence of the inflation target of 2% established by the European Central Bank (ECB). Indeed, despite of a considerable deceleration of the prices growth rhythm in the Central and Eastern Europe countries after the difficult period of transition, an inflation growth is possible after the euro adoption. According to Benassy-Quere and Lahreche-Revil (2001), this phenomenon could lead to the medium inflation growth of the euro zone of 0.25% and of

DOI: 10.4018/978-1-5225-9269-3.ch006

0.75%. In order to accomplish its mandate, ECB will be constraint to implement a restrictive monetary policy, whose deflationary incidents could compromise the real convergence process of the new members of the euro zone.

In these conditions, the exact knowledge of the monetary policy transmission mechanisms in the Central and Eastern Europe countries is extremely important for the correct application of the European Central Bank's monetary policy strategy and for limiting the disadvantages of a unique monetary policy in the countries that will adopt the single currency.

In this paper we intend to study empirically the relative importance of each monetary policy transmission channel, the prices dynamics as well as the way in which each macroeconomic variable response to the different shocks from the economy in Romania.

Our empirical study is based on the estimation of a model based on the structural vector autoregressive methodology, imposing some restrictions on short term. The auto-regressive vector is formed of the following variables: the real industrial production, the real effective exchange rate, the consumer prices index, the M2 monetary aggregate, the exchange rate between the national currency and euro and the interest rate on the interbank market. The data are monthly, being extracted from the International Monetary Fund's data base (International Financial Statistics) and from the European Central Bank data base (Statistical Data Warehouse) and they are presented in synthesis in Table 1. The period of the study comprises data from 2001 to 2009. Our Structural VAR model comes as a continuation of other similar studies from the Romanian empirical literature of specialty, such as Boţel (2002), Cozmâncă (2008), Aristide (2007). These authors' models were estimated by including different macroeconomic variables in the model and by imposing some restrictions on short term or on long term for surprising as better as possible the economy's evolutions.

Our choice of appealing to an approach based on Structural VAR model is based on the fact that these models remain, irrefutably, a reference in what concerns the shocks. These allow the illustration of the dynamics of a set of variables starting from a restraint number of hypotheses.

However, the main limit of the Structural VAR approach when it deals with the monetary shocks is the fact that these models don't take into account the unanticipated part of the monetary shock.

METHODOLOGY AND DATA

The formalization of the VAR modelling is presented in multiple sources among which we distinguish Hamilton (1994) and Enders (1995). The following approach (Favero, 2001) has for unique object the presentation of the Choleski identification, adopted in this model.

We consider the following system with n variables:

$$AX_t = C(L)X_{t-1} + Bv_t \tag{1}$$

where: A is a matrix (nxn) that describes the contemporaneous, structural relations between the variables from the system; X_t is the vector (nx1) of the macroeconomic variables, C(L) is a matrix lag polynomial; v_t is the vector of innovations, B is a matrix (nxn), which in the great majority of applications (as well as in the present one) is diagonal.

This equation can be rewritten, through pre-multiplication with A^{-1}, such as:

$$X_t = A^{-1}C(L)X_{t-1} + u_t \tag{2}$$

where: $u_t = A^{-1}Bv_t$.

The equation (1) describes the structural model, i.e. the "real" economy model. The VAR methodology, by means which will be discussed further on, can analyze the variables response from the system to the structural shocks, v_t. Unfortunately, the "real" model cannot be observed empirically. The researchers observe only some data series by means of which the coefficients of the equation (2) can be estimated, the so-called model reduced form. As it is clearly observed from the fact that $u_t = A^{-1}Bv_t$, the innovations in a reduced form, u_t, represent the linear combinations of structural innovations, v_t. For this reason, before undertaking the innovations analysis, it is necessary to solve the problem of identification, i.e. of "recovering" the structural innovations, v_t, from the information contained in the reduced form (2).

Mathematically, the structural shocks identification can be done only if some conditions concerning the number of parameters from the system are accomplished. Practically, this problem is solved, commonly, by imposing a priori some zero restrictions (i.e. the imposing of the zero values) to some coefficients of the A and B matrices. Due to the fact that in the case of the B matrix we adopt a common diagonal form in such applications the A matrix restriction remains to be solved. In order to be able to identify the structural innovations, it is necessary to impose at least n(n-1)/2 zero restrictions to the A matrix coefficients. If exactly n(n-1)/2 restrictions are imposed, then the system is exactly identified. If more restrictions are imposed, then the system is over-identified.

At this point, an important idea must be underlined. As it was specified above, the A matrix reflects the contemporaneous structural relations, that is the relations of causality or of interdependence between the variables from the model, manifested during the time unit utilized in the analysis (month, quarter etc.). Consequently, imposing zero-restrictions to the A matrix coefficients is equal to the adoption of some hypotheses on economy's interdependencies. The problem of finding the adequate zero-restrictions in order to identify the structural innovations (also named the decomposition or the orthogonalization of the innovations) was solved in the literature in many ways. The widest practice is the Choleski decomposition.

The Choleski decomposition allows the VAR identification through a perfect orthogonalization of the innovations, by imposing a triangular structure to the innovation matrix, with all the elements on the main diagonal equal to zero. Thus, implicitly a relation of recursive causality between the variables will be established. The shocks identification has as basis the Choleski decomposition, but also the introduction order of the variables in the system. The introduction order of the variables in VAR is determined. The retained criterion in order to introduce the variables for our study is the one of the decreasing exogenity of the variables. This criterion will lead to the introduction of the most exogenous variables in the beginning and of the most endogenous variables in the end. Consequently, the retained order is the following: the industrial production, the real effective exchange rate, the consumer prices index, the M2 monetary aggregate, the leu/euro exchange rate and the interbank interest rate.

In the standard Structural VAR model, X_t is a vector that comprises the following variables: the industrial production (y), the real effective exchange rate (rex), the consumer prices index (p), the M2 monetary aggregate (m), the leu/euro exchange rate (ex), the interest rate on the interbank market (r). The system response to the following structural shocks: $\varepsilon_t^{ip}, \varepsilon_t^{reer}, \varepsilon_t^{cpi}, \varepsilon_t^{m2}, \varepsilon_t^{neer}, \varepsilon_t^{ir}$, and $e_t^{ip}, e_t^{reer}, e_t^{cpi}, e_t^{m2}, e_t^{neer}, e_t^{ir}$ are the innovation terms of the system. All the data are expressed in logarithm (excepting the interest rate), and then the prime difference operator is applied. In this form, the stationarity tests (Augmented Dickey-Fuller) indicate the series stationarity with a degree of trust of over 95%. By applying the prime difference operator, we will surprise the way of answer of the variables to the growth rates. All the data are also seasonal adjusted, excepting the exchange rate and the interest rate. All the criteria indicated the Structural VAR model estimation with a lag. The Structural VAR model is stable.

Our system can be schematized as it follows $\left(C_0 = B^{-1}A_0\right)$:

$$C_0 = \begin{pmatrix} c_{11} & 0 & 0 & 0 & 0 & 0 \\ c_{21} & c_{22} & 0 & 0 & 0 & 0 \\ c_{31} & c_{32} & c_{33} & 0 & 0 & 0 \\ c_{41} & c_{42} & c_{43} & c_{44} & 0 & 0 \\ c_{51} & c_{52} & c_{53} & c_{54} & c_{55} & 0 \\ c_{61} & c_{62} & c_{63} & c_{64} & c_{65} & c_{66} \end{pmatrix}$$

The identification scheme is formed on the relation between the structural shocks and the innovation terms $\left(B\varepsilon_t = A_0 e_t\right)$:

$$\begin{bmatrix} b_{11} & 0 & 0 & 0 & 0 & 0 \\ 0 & b_{22} & 0 & 0 & 0 & 0 \\ 0 & 0 & b_{33} & 0 & 0 & 0 \\ 0 & 0 & 0 & b_{44} & 0 & 0 \\ 0 & 0 & 0 & 0 & b_{55} & 0 \\ 0 & 0 & 0 & 0 & 0 & b_{66} \end{bmatrix} \begin{bmatrix} \varepsilon_t^{ip} \\ \varepsilon_t^{reer} \\ \varepsilon_t^{cpi} \\ \varepsilon_t^{m2} \\ \varepsilon_t^{neer} \\ \varepsilon_t^{ir} \end{bmatrix} = \begin{bmatrix} 1 & 0 & 0 & 0 & 0 & 0 \\ a_{21} & 1 & 0 & 0 & 0 & 0 \\ a_{31} & a_{32} & 1 & 0 & 0 & 0 \\ a_{41} & a_{42} & a_{43} & 1 & 0 & 0 \\ a_{51} & a_{52} & a_{53} & a_{54} & 1 & 0 \\ a_{61} & a_{62} & a_{63} & a_{64} & a_{65} & 1 \end{bmatrix} \begin{bmatrix} e_t^{ip} \\ e_t^{reer} \\ e_t^{cpi} \\ e_t^{m2} \\ e_t^{neer} \\ e_t^{ir} \end{bmatrix}$$

Taking into account the empirical studies of Blanchard and Quah (1989) and Giannini (1992), our model satisfies the necessary condition of an exact identification of the system, as far as we have to estimate (n(n+1)/2) parameters. The structure of these matrices leads to 6 theoretical equations that establish a link between the innovation terms and the structural shocks.

The Choleski decomposition shows that certain coefficients of the estimated parameters are from a statistic point of view insignificant. According to Giannini *et al.* (1995) and Goux, for the amelioration of our identification, we will impose certain additional restrictions on short term on the insignificant parameters.

Making reference to the inferior triangular form of the A_0 matrix, the real effective exchange rate (the competitiveness of the national goods) should answer to an industrial production shock. However, we considered that unlike the production destined to the autochthon consumption which is immediately affected by a shock of the real offer (Blanchard and Quah, 1989), the production destined to the foreign markets isn't influenced by a production unanticipated variation. Consequently, the foreign partners' demand for autochthon goods and services and the real effective exchange rate don't response on short term to an industrial production shock. This is the hypothesis which characterizes an open small economy, such as the economy of Romania. That is why the coefficient of the a_{21} parameter is null.

Following the same approach as Goux (2003), we will suppose that an unanticipated variation of the production will affect only the prices. Consequently, the coefficients of the a_{41}, a_{51} parameters are null $\left(a_{41} = a_{51} = 0\right)$, and the real effective exchange rate shock does not affects the monetary variables on short term, so that $a_{42} = 0$.

The traditional Keynesian theories stipulate that the monetary aggregate affects uniquely only the own equation and the monetary policy equation. This approach implies the nullity of the impact on short term of an unanticipated variation of the monetary aggregate on the real production, on the real effective exchange rate, on the prices and on the exchange rate. The absence of the impact on the first three variables will result from the order of the variables, so that it will be only necessary to specify that $a_{54} = 0$.

Sims and Zha (1998) sustain that the monetary policy doesn't answer immediately to the shocks which affect the real production or the prices. The advanced argument is the absence of the statistical dates concerning the prices and the production when the monetary policy decisions are taken. This argument is translated through the nullity of the following coefficients a_{61}, a_{62}, a_{63}.

In the literature of specialty, there is a consensus concerning the absence of the monetary policy answer to the exchange rate shocks. Thus, it can express the absence of the impact on short term of the nominal exchange rate shocks imposing the nullity to the a_{65} parameter. There are also authors such as Sims (1992), Grilli and Roubini (1995), Kim and Roubini (2000) create a polemic in what concerns the relation between an exchange rate shock and the monetary policy. Indirectly, Kim and Roubini (2000) evoke a tridimensional relation between the exchange rate, the prices and the interest rate on short term. They sustain that in the small open economies the monetary authorities pay also attention to the impact of the exchange rate modifications. Consequently, they react instantaneously to the exchange rate shocks through an interest rate increase, on short term.

In these conditions we will suppose that there is an impact of the exchange rate shock on the monetary policy from Romania. As a matter of fact, the estimated coefficient of the a_{65} parameter can be accepted from a statistical point of view.

The Structural VAR identification scheme, after imposing some restrictions on short term, becomes:

$$\begin{bmatrix} b_{11} & 0 & 0 & 0 & 0 & 0 \\ 0 & b_{22} & 0 & 0 & 0 & 0 \\ 0 & 0 & b_{33} & 0 & 0 & 0 \\ 0 & 0 & 0 & b_{44} & 0 & 0 \\ 0 & 0 & 0 & 0 & b_{55} & 0 \\ 0 & 0 & 0 & 0 & 0 & b_{66} \end{bmatrix} \begin{bmatrix} \varepsilon_t^{ip} \\ \varepsilon_t^{reer} \\ \varepsilon_t^{cpi} \\ \varepsilon_t^{m2} \\ \varepsilon_t^{neer} \\ \varepsilon_t^{ir} \end{bmatrix} = \begin{bmatrix} 1 & 0 & 0 & 0 & 0 & 0 \\ 0 & 1 & 0 & 0 & 0 & 0 \\ a_{31} & 0 & 1 & 0 & 0 & 0 \\ 0 & 0 & a_{43} & 1 & 0 & 0 \\ 0 & a_{52} & a_{53} & 0 & 1 & 0 \\ 0 & 0 & 0 & a_{64} & a_{65} & 1 \end{bmatrix} \begin{bmatrix} e_t^{ip} \\ e_t^{reer} \\ e_t^{cpi} \\ e_t^{m2} \\ e_t^{neer} \\ e_t^{ir} \end{bmatrix}$$

The system is composed of the following six equations:

1. $b_{11}\varepsilon_t^{ip} = e_t^{ip}$
2. $b_{22}\varepsilon_t^{reer} = e_t^{reer}$
3. $b_{33}\varepsilon_t^{cpi} = a_{31}e_t^{ip} + e_t^{cpi}$
4. $b_{44}\varepsilon_t^{m2} = a_{43}e_t^{cpi} + e_t^{m2}$
5. $b_{55}\varepsilon_t^{neer} = a_{52}e_t^{reer} + a_{53}e_t^{cpi} + e_t^{neer}$
6. $b_{66}\varepsilon_t^{ir} = a_{64}e_t^{m2} + a_{65}e_t^{neer} + e_t^{ir}$

The first and the second equation illustrate the exogenity of the production shock and of the real exchange rate. The third equation is a function of the prices which proves that the inflation level is determined by the present real production (the principle of the aggregate offer). The variables arrangement in the system indicates the fact that there is no effect from the monetary aggregate, from the exchange rate and from the interest rate on production and on prices. This fact is in accordance with the theoretical hypothesis of the monetary shock's impact absence on the real production and on the prices (Christiano et al., 1998).

The forth equation is a monetary aggregate equation which is explained by the inflation level. The fifth equation is a form of the purchasing power parity as far as the exchange rate is influenced by the prices level and by the real effective exchange rate. The last equation is represented by the monetary authorities' reaction function. The central bank establishes the interest rate after it analyses the evolution of the monetary aggregate and of the prices level, but it doesn't take into account the mutations interfered in the sphere of production and of prices. This fact is enforced because the information concerning the last two variables is available with a lag delay.

RESULTS

A positive shock of the industrial production (Appendix 1) will lead firstly to a price increase, followed then by a period of decrease. A positive variation of production will also determine a national currency appreciation.

Conventionally, in the case of the real exchange rate shock, i.e. a national currency appreciation, we will assist to a price decrease. The national currency appreciation will grow the exports price and will reduce the imports price. The decrease of the imported products prices will also lead, in a competitive economy, to the decrease of the domestic products prices. There from the prices diminution will result. On the other hand, this response depends on the existent structure between the exports and the imports. The inflation diminution, as a consequence of a national currency appreciation will be more consistent if the imports are predominant in the national consumption. This argument seems to ply with the economy of Romania (Appendix 1) where the inflation diminished as a result of the leu's appreciation between 2004 and the end of 2007, appreciation that took place on the background of a high consumption oriented towards the imports and the low saving, increasing both the current account deficit and also the external debt.

The national currency appreciation in a period in which the current account deficit was substantial can seem ungrounded. It based preponderantly on the capital account liberalization. Along with the financial crisis outbreak, at the end of 2007 in United States, the foreign capital started to be withdrawn from Romania fact that led to significant national currency depreciation. This depreciation would have led to a significant inflation growth if it hadn't been accompanied, due to the economic crisis, by a strong contraction of the production (a negative output gap) and of a current account correction (the consumption that was directed towards imported goods significantly diminished). This mixture of events determined the maintenance of inflation on the descending trend.

The deflationist impact of a positive shock of the real effective exchange rate is reabsorbed through a diminution of the interest rate on short term. This mechanism aligns with the "exchange rate-prices-interest rate" tridimensional relation. Indeed, the unexpected national currency appreciation incites the economic agents to hold an inferior currency stock, which determines an interest rate decrease on short term.

In an economy such as the Romanian economy which adopted the inflation target strategy, the absorption and the competitiveness deterioration (a real effective exchange rate appreciation) through the usual method that is the massive intervention of the monetary authorities on the exchange market through the accumulation reserve fund, is conflictual. This intervention, if it takes place, it will generate a growth of the monetary offer and, implicitly of the inflationist pressures. In this way we can explain the central bank's non-intervention when the leu appreciated against the other currencies. Thus, the central bank will be exposed to the dilemma of practicing a new inflation target and the limitation of the national currency appreciation.

Herman (2008) states that the monetary authorities' intervention in order to absorb the national currency appreciation within the inflation target system could be profitable only in the conditions in which the economy operates under its potential (negative output gap). Thus, an expansionist monetary policy generated by the intervention on the exchange market will favor the realization of the inflation target. This situation isn't also met in Romania, because the output gap was far superior to the economy potential within the period 2004-2008.

On the other hand, the adjustment of the national currency appreciation can be realized through an interest rate growth in order to fight against the inflationist pressures generated by the monetary authorities' intervention on the exchange market and the national currency depreciation. However, the interest rate growth will cause at its turn a national currency appreciation due to the attraction of the capital waves towards the economy, capital waves attracted by the high interest differential.

Montiel and Ostry (1991) underline the fact that in the context of the free capital flow, the monetary policy task of acting against the inflation is very difficult. The offer of currency cannot be controlled very easy through a restrictive monetary policy (sterilization). As far as the economic agents can obtain foreign liquidities, the direct monetary instruments of enclosing the credit doesn't influence the money supply and thus the inflation. That is why the vocation of an inflation target strategy is one of anchoring the inflationist anticipations of the population on a level as low as possible.

The positive shock effect of the real exchange rate on the production is disputed. If we take into account the aggregate demand side the decrease of the imports prices and the decrease of the domestic goods demand, as a result of the national currency appreciation, will lead to a national production collapse. Thus, the deterioration of the competitiveness-prices of the domestic goods on international level relation will lead to the exports decrease and will generate a production decrease.

On the other hand, if we take into account the aggregate offer side, a national currency appreciation will generate a decrease of the imported intermediate goods prices included in the production factors and thus in the production cost. Consequently, it will increase the labor force demand, but also the production. In Romania (Appendix 1) the impact of the rate real appreciation on the industrial production seems to be insignificant, thus we can conclude that the effects of the aggregate offer and demand are cancelled. The positive variation of the real exchange rate will also lead to a money supply growth and to a leu's appreciation against euro.

The response of the M2 monetary aggregate to an unexpected inflation growth (Appendix 2) leads to a growth in the money supply, unlike the theoretical hypotheses according to which a prices unexpected growth indicates a money supply decrease. However, this puzzle was also observed by Kim and Roubini (2000). As an unexpected growth of the inflation leads to a depreciation of the national currency, emphasizing thus the inflationist pressures. This relation reflects the incapacity of the exchange rate of absorbing the inflationist effects of the shocks. The positive variation of the money supply (Appendix 2) will also determine an inflation growth and the national currency depreciation.

The interest rate growth at a money supply shock indicates a restrictive monetary policy, this measure being an anti-inflationist measure. A positive shock of the nominal exchange rate (Appendix 3), concretized in a leu's unexpected depreciation against euro will lead to an inflation growth and to a money supply growth.

Spulbar, Niţoi and Neţoiu (2010) suggested that a positive aspect that results from the undertaken analysis is represented by the response function of production and of inflation to a positive variation of the interest rate (Appendix 3). At the interest rate shock the inflation will decrease significantly, fact that fortifies the interest rate channel and supports the inflation target strategy. We can also observe the same response in the production case. An interest rate growth will also determine a national currency appreciation and a money supply decrease, these functions of response being in concordance with the theoretical hypotheses.

CONCLUSION

The present study represents an econometric investigation that wants to surprise the monetary policy dynamics in Romania. For this purpose, we appealed to a model based on the auto-regressive structural vector imposing some restrictions on short term. Knowing the functions of response of the main macroeconomic variables to different economic shocks represents an essential step for investigating the Romanian monetary system.

The positive aspect that results from this study is constituted by the lack of "the output puzzles" (the production growth as a result of an interest rate positive deviation) and of "the price puzzles" (the inflation growth as a result of the interest rate positive deviation). This fact can be ascribed to the inflation target strategy which was adopted by Romania.

But the conditions where the integration in the euro zone supposes apart from the prices convergence and the exchange rate convergence the interest rate convergence, the inflation target strategy adopted seems to be rather a flexible inflation target strategy. Taking into account the obtained results by this strategy, in the actual context it seems to be the optimal strategy, but a set of measures for homogenizing the monetary policy and for reducing the gaps against euro zone must be implanted. Only in such context a euro adoption will have benefic effects on the prices dynamics and on other important macroeconomic variables. We also underline the importance and the consistence of the exchange rate channel within the monetary policy, as well as the importance of the monetary aggregates channels in order to explain the evolution of the level of the prices.

REFERENCES

Aristide, O. (2007). *Impact of wages in the economy on inflation and trade deficit.* The National Bank of Romania.

Benassy-Quéré, A., & Lahreche-Revil, A. (2001). L'Elargissement de la Zone Euro. In Cepii (Ed.), L'Economie mondiale 2002, Paris, La Découverte.

Blanchard, O. J., & Et Quah, D. (1989). The Dynamic Effects of Aggregate Demand and Supply Disturbances. *The American Economic Review*, *79*(4).

Boţel, C. (2002). The Dynamic Effects of Aggregate Demand and Supply Disturbances. *The American Economic Review*, *79*(4).

Christiano, J. L., Eichenbaum, M., & Evans, C. L. (1998). Monetary Policy Shocks: What Have We Learned and to What End? National Bureau of Economic Research.

Couchrane, J. H. (1995). Identifying the Output Effects of Monetary Policy. National Bureau of Economic Research.

Cozmâncă, B. (2008). *Models for substantiating foreign exchange monetary policies*. Bucharest: Economic Publishing House.

Enders, W. (1995). *Applied econometric time series*. John Wiley & Sons, Inc.

Favero, C. A. (2001). *Applied macroeconometrics*. Oxford: Oxford University Press.

Giannini, C. (1992). *Topics in Structural VAR Econometrics, Lecture Notes in Economics and Mathematical Systems*. Springer. doi:10.1007/978-3-662-02757-8

Giannini, C., Lanzarotti, A., & Seghelini, M. (1995). A Traditional Interpretation of Macroeconomic Fluctuations: The Case of Italy. *European Journal of Political Economy*, *11*(1), 131–155. doi:10.1016/0176-2680(94)00059-S

Goux, J.F., (2003). Conditions monétaires et activité économique dans la zone euro. Groupe d'Analyse et de Théorie Économique.

Grilli, V., & Roubini, N. (1995) Liquidity and Exchange Rates: Puzzling Evidence from the G-7 Countries. Yale University.

Hamilton, J. D. (1994). *Time Series Analysis*. Princeton: Princeton University Press.

Herman, K. (2008). Is Central Bank Intervention Effective Under Inflation Targeting Regimes? The Case of Colombia. IMF.

Kim, S., & Roubini, N. (2000). Exchange Rate Anomalies in the Industrial Countries: A Solution with a Structural VAR Approach. *Journal of Monetary Economics*, *45*(3), 561–586. doi:10.1016/S0304-3932(00)00010-6

Mishkin, F. S. (2000). From Monetary Targeting to Inflation Targeting: Lessons from the Industrialized Countries. Paper presented in the conference of The Bank of Mexico.

Montiel, P., & Ostry, J. (1991). Macroeconomic Implications of Real Exchange Rate Targeting in Developing Countries. *Staff Paper*, *39*(March), 872–900. doi:10.2307/3867128

Sims, C. A., & Zha, T. (1998). Does Monetary Policy Generate Recession? Federal Reserve Bank of Atlanta.

Spulbar, C., Niţoi, M. and Neţoiu, L. (2010). The analysis of the monetary policy dynamics in Romania using a Structural Vector Autoregressive model. *Journal of Finance – Challenges of the Future, 11*, 128-140.

APPENDIX 1

Figure 1. The responses of variables to industrial production shock (Shock1) and to real effective exchange rate shock (Shock2)

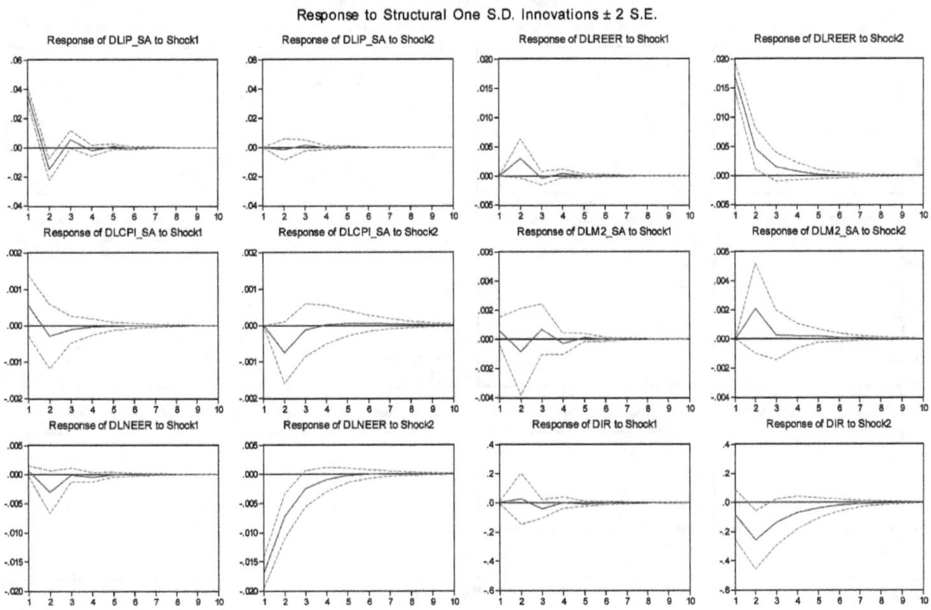

APPENDIX 2

Figure 2. The responses of variables to inflation shock (Shock3) and to aggregate monetary shock (Shock4)

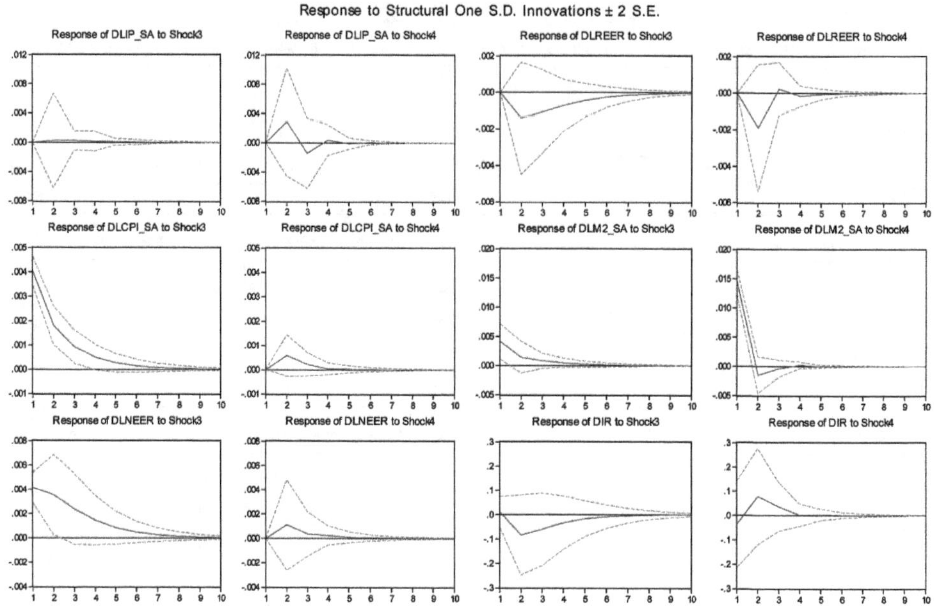

APPENDIX 3

Figure 3. The responses of variables to exchange rate shock (Shock5) and to interest rate shock (Shock6)

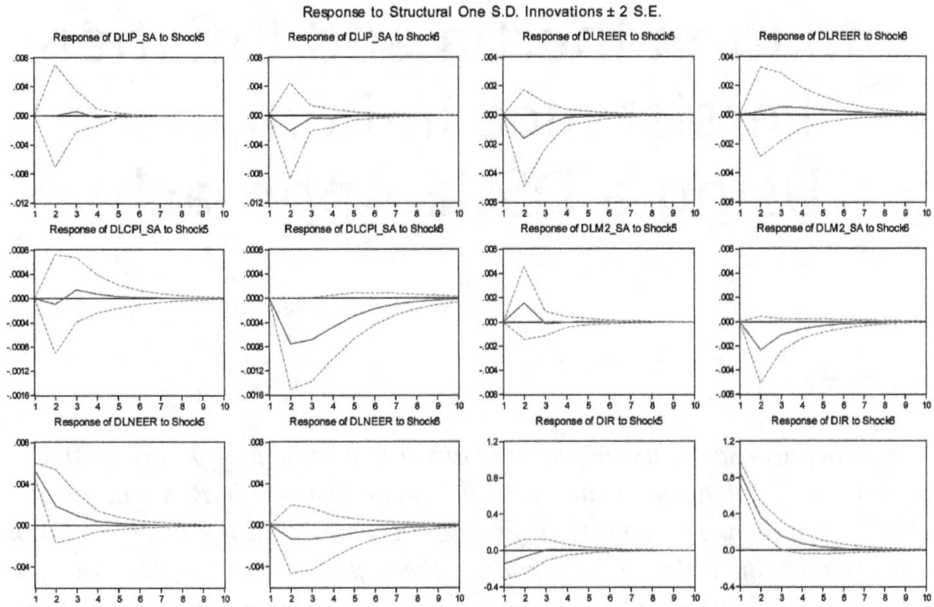

Chapter 7
Inflation Inertia and Inflation Persistence in Romania Using a DSGE Approach

ABSTRACT

The main purpose of this chapter is to investigate monetary policy dynamics, as well as the inflation inertia and inflation persistence in Romania using a DSGE approach. The empirical findings revealed that the price evolution reflects the difficulties of eliminating the inflation inertia. Moreover, in Romania, the historic inflation evolution has a significant influence in terms of inflation expectation patterns. Inflation is a negative phenomenon with dramatic consequences for Romania's economic development on long term.

INTRODUCTION

All known empirical studies are confirming the importance of knowing the monetary policy transmission mechanism and the existing literature admits that. Knowing the inflation dynamics is also crucial in the monetary analysis. A deep monetary analysis offers important information both to decision factors as well as to consumers and investors. Within this study we propose to emphasize some inflation-related aspects in Romania. More exactly, we will try to evaluate the inflation persistence and the inflation inertia. Furthermore, we will analyze the interest rate channel in Romania, and we will hold out the prospect on the central bank behavior through Taylor's rules.

DOI: 10.4018/978-1-5225-9269-3.ch007

Knowing the degree of inflation persistence (i.e. the period where inflation tends to reach its steady state level after a shock) offers to central bank vital information about how the interest rate must be adjusted in order to reach a desired target for the inflation rate. Moreover, the nature of the inflation dynamics, as well as the efficiency of monetary policy dynamics depends to a great extent on the pattern and the characteristics associated to the formation of prices. That is why it is important to determine the degree of inflation inertia and its persistence.

The inflation inertia can be defined as being the process through which the current inflation is determined by its past history, being perceived through a prices slow reaction to the disinflationary policies. The inertia can be caused by the mechanism particularities of establishing the prices or the wages, by the importance which the backward-looking component has in forming the inflationary expectations, but also by the national banks policy concerning the exchange rate (Edwards, 1998). The inflation persistence is defined as a slow dissipation of the second-round effects after the shocks. We should mention that inertia differs from persistence (Cespedes et al., 2003). Inertia is defined as the speed of reaction of inflation to the unanticipated shocks, while the persistence is measured through the period of time necessary for these shocks' effects, once transmitted, to disappear.

In order to analyze the inflation persistence and inertia, as well as the central bank's monetary policy in Romania, we will utilize two dynamic stochastic general equilibrium (DSGE) models. The recurrence to this type of analysis is motivated by two reasons. Firstly, the use of DSGE model in the case of Romania is rather reduced. Caraiani (2009a, 2009b) estimated a set of such models to detect the Romanian economic dynamics. Secondly, the DSGE models are tools that offer a coherent framework for the monetary analysis, allowing the link stability between the economy structural characteristics and the model parameters. In the last 15 years, the premises of a remarkable progress in specifying and estimating these models were created. Thus, the central banks in the developed and emergent economies are using such kind of models for analyzing the economy dynamics as well as for making forecasts.

The paper is structured as it follows. In the second section the utilized DSGE models are presented. The third section comprises references to the obtained results as well as a monetary policy evaluation concerning Romania using the parameters from Taylor's rule and using the impulse response function extracted from the DSGE analysis. In the last section the conclusions are specified.

LITERATURE REVIEW

There is a significant number of empirical studies and theoretical analyses that approach the inflation evolution and offer a perspective on the monetary policy in Romania. Scutaru and Stănică (2005) used a structural autoregressive vector to capture the output gap evolution in Romania and they evaluated the effects of the inflationist shocks to the Romanian economy. A Philips relation between unemployment and inflation is also emphasized in the study. Boţel (2010) used a univariate approach to capture CORE3 inflation inertia in Romania. Caraiani used a range of DSGE models to analyze the Romanian economy dynamics. Thus, Caraiani (2009a) tackled the problem of the inflation persistence in Romania, using a standard CIA model and an augmented CIA model.

The author concludes that although with a simple structure the standard CIA model can replicate the inflation persistence from Romania but on periods smaller than a year. Caraiani (2009b) also estimated the Romanian economy's output gap using the DSGE model. The author concludes that, in comparison with the output gap estimated with the Hodrick-Presscot filter, the results of the DSGE approach offer a better and more consistent image of the output gap with the Romanian economy dynamics.

METHODOLOGY

We will consider a simple DSGE model containing three equations: an IS curve, a Philips curve and the Taylor's rule. The IS curve is derived by maximizing the expected value of the utility function:

$$U\left(C_t, 1-N_t\right)=\frac{C_t^{1-1/\sigma}}{1-1/\sigma}-\frac{N_t^{1+\tau}}{1+\tau}.$$

To this problem of maximization, the following budgetary constraint is associated:

$$C_t + \frac{B_t}{P_t} = \left(\frac{W_t}{P_t}\right)(N_t) + (1 + i_{t-1})\left(\frac{B_{t-1}}{P_t}\right) + \Pi_t,$$

where C_t is the composite consumption good, N_t is hours worked, Π_t is real profits received from the firms, and B_t are the bonds for which a nominal interest rate is paid, i_t, for a period of time. The IS curve is:

$$y_t = (1-\delta)\,y_{t-1} + \delta E_t y_{t+1} - \sigma(i_t - \pi_{t+1}) + \varepsilon_t^y \tag{1}$$

The demand curve differs of the IS standard curve by including the expectations and the forward-looking elements. The reason for including the previous output gap is explained by Fuhrer (2000) who argues that this extension generates more persistence.

The Phillips curve has the following form:

$$\pi_t = (1-\alpha)\,\pi_{t-1} + \alpha\pi_{t+1} + \kappa y_t + \varepsilon_t^\pi \tag{2}$$

The multiple factors can constitute inflation causes. The inflation fluctuation can be determined by extrinsic factors, such as the marginal cost or the output gap and by the intrinsic factors such as dependence on the past history. An important role in forming the inflation is also held by the inflationary expectations. Each of these three factors can be associated with one of the three elements of Phillips curve where the actual inflation depends on the past inflation, on the expectations concerning the future inflation and the output gap. We should mention, that even if this equation includes a backward looking component, it`s value, $(1-\alpha)\,\pi_{t-1}$, depends on the estimated parameter of the forward looking parameter, $\alpha\pi_{t+1}$.

The model is closed by specifying a Taylor's rule of monetary policy. The Taylor's equation represents a hypothetic but representative description of the monetary policy complexity. On the other hand, Taylor (1993) pointed out that nobody would or should imagine that the monetary authorities follow these rules mechanically. The equation has the following form:

$$i_t = \rho_r i_{t-1} + (1-\rho_r)(\phi_\pi \pi_t + \phi_y y_t) + \varepsilon_t^i \tag{3}$$

Within this equation we assume that the central bank set the interest rate as a function of the interest from the previous period, ρ_r, element which will surprise the gradualism of monetary policy, inflation rate from the actual period and output gap. Taking into consideration the fact that we wish to offer a deeper perspective on the Taylor's rule we will estimate the model also with another monetary policy rule. For that purpose, we will eliminate the parameter that surprises the gradualism of monetary policy, the interest rate being established according to the inflation from the actual period and the output gap. Thc rule shape will be the following:

$$i_t = \phi_\pi \pi_t + \phi_y y_t + \varepsilon_t^i \qquad (4)$$

The models that use a neokeynesian Phillips curve were criticized due to the difficulties to reproduce the dynamics of an output gap and inflation when a certain degree of inflexibility is supposed (Gali & Gertler, 1999). The critics state that a neokeynesian Phillips curve will not succeed in generating the observed persistence of the data relative to inflation and production.

These considerations became the fundamentals in conceiving models that capture the inflation inertia. That is why through the following more complex model we will try to highlight the influence of inflation inertia on the output and prices dynamics. For that purpose, we will estimate a dynamic stochastic general equilibrium model built around some specificities that capture the inflation inertia. Our estimated model is a little bit modified in comparison with the one proposed by Gali (2008). The model has six equations. The first equation represents the aggregate demand, and r_t^n is the real natural rate of interest, defined here as being the equilibrium real rate in default of any friction. In contrast with the previous model, the inflation equation is built around a backward-looking component. The third equation is a Taylor's rule of monetary policy. The last three equations are representation of shocks that follow an AR (1) process.

$$y_t = E_t y_{t+1} - \sigma\left(i_t - \pi_{t+1} - r_t^n\right) \qquad (5)$$

$$\pi_t = \kappa y_t + \beta\left(\pi_{t+1} - \gamma\pi_t\right) + \gamma\pi_{t-1} + u_t \qquad (6)$$

$$i_t = \rho_r i_{t-1} + (1-\rho_r)(\phi_\pi \pi_t + \phi_y y_t) + e_t \tag{7}$$

$$r_t^n = \varphi_r r_{t-1}^n + \varepsilon_t^r \tag{8}$$

$$u_t = \varphi_u u_{t-1} + \varepsilon_t^u \tag{9}$$

$$e_t = \varphi_r e_{t-1} + \varepsilon_t^i \tag{10}$$

In both models, the Phillips curve combines both backward looking and forward-looking elements. Including only a backward-looking component would have made the estimation simpler and would have corresponded to the historical data. On the other hand, this specification would be vulnerable to Lucas critique and his predictive power would be weak taking into consideration the recent changes in the monetary policy. The utilization of a forward-looking component would solve the instability problem. Additionally, more credibility added by the inflation targeting behaviour - more the inflationary expectations tend to converge with the central bank target. However, such a specification raises difficulties in accurately measuring the expectations, especially when expectations-related data don't exist.

RESULTS

The data used to estimate the two models are the real gross domestic product, the consumer price index and the central bank reference interest rate. The data are quarterly, the gross domestic product being expressed in the prices of year 2000 and concerns the period between 2000.Q1 and 2010.Q3. The interest rate is calculated as a three months average of the refinancing interest rate. All the initial series were logged, seasonally adjusted and then filtered using the Hodrick Prescott filter. For estimating the two models we will use the Bayesian technique. The estimation was made using two Metropolis Hastings chains, of 500.000 iterations, the final rate of acceptance being 36,68% and 36,31%, in the case of the first model and of 33,34% and 33,36%, in the case of the second model. The rates of acceptance are situated in the widely accepted range that is 20%-40%. For both models the multivariate and especially the univariate convergence statistics indicates the convergence. The multivariate convergence diagnostics are presented in Figure 1 and Figure 2.

Estimation of the Simple Neokeynesian Model

In this section we will estimate the model given by the equations 1-3. The set of parameters which we estimate is $\{\delta, \sigma, \alpha, \kappa, \rho_r, \phi_\pi, \phi_y, \varepsilon_t^y, \varepsilon_t^\pi, \varepsilon_t^i\}$. The estimation results are presented in Table 1.

The parameter corresponding to the influence that expectations concerning the output evolution have on the gross domestic product in the actual period has a decreased value, of 0.1884. The output gap formation is influenced, significantly, by its evolution in the past. The real interest rate coefficient, equal with the difference between the nominal interest rate and the anticipated inflation rate, has an estimative value of 0.1367. The interest real rate affects

Table 1. The results of the Bayesian estimation

Parameters	Prior Mean	Posterior Mean	Confidence Interval	Confidence Interval	Prior Distribution	Standard Deviation
δ	0.400	0.1884	0.0837	0.2873	Beta	0.1000
σ	0.240	0.1367	0.0756	0.1939	Gamma	0.1000
α	0.650	0.8163	0.7236	0.9114	Beta	0.1000
κ	0.130	0.1218	0.0416	0.1997	Gamma	0.0500
ρ_r	0.500	0.4967	0.3845	0.6129	Normal	0.1000
ϕ_π	1.500	1.7504	1.4433	2.0724	Normal	0.2000
ϕ_y	0.500	0.6545	0.4196	0.9050	Normal	0.1500
ε_t^y	0.500	0.0712	0.0603	0.0814	Inverse Gamma	2.0000
ε_t^π	0.500	0.0738	0.0603	0.0844	Inverse Gamma	2.0000
ε_t^i	0.500	0.1362	0.1110	0.1610	Inverse Gamma	2.0000

the population choice between the alternatives represented by consumption and saving.

The expectations of inflation have a significant importance in forming the prices, the parameter associated to these being estimated at 0.8163. In our opinion, in Romania, the expectations of inflation are adaptive, based on learning process. They are not built around the central bank inflation target, but they are strongly influenced by the high level of prices from the past.

Inflation targeting strategy is based on stability and on an accurate value of expectations. The monetary authority is supposed to enjoy a complete credibility from population. On the other hand, the credibility is, however, a limited resource in the transition countries and, generally, in the economies with a high inflation history. The contradictory nature of the credibility demand in Romania results from the fact that it is induced by the past behavior and it is not a function of the actual behavior.

The parameters from Taylor's rule are estimated at 1.7504 for ϕ_{π}, 0.6545 for ϕ_y and 0.4967 for ρ_r. The estimation of the same model but replacing the equation 3 with 4 leads to similar results. The parameter that surprises the importance which the central bank gives to inflation has a value of 1.7516, and the output gap parameter is of 0.8685. These results indicate the fact that the Romania's central bank establishes the interest rate giving a significant weight to inflation behavior rather than to the output gap or to the interest rate from the previous period. These results are in line with the inflation targeting strategy adopted by the monetary authority.

Estimation of the Model That Captures the Inflation Inertia

Hereinafter we will estimate the model formed of equations 5-10. The set of parameters which we estimate is $\{\sigma, \kappa, \gamma, \rho_r, \phi_{\pi}, \phi_y, \varphi_r, \varphi_u, \varphi_r\}$. Before we apply the Bayesian estimation, we will adjust the β parameter at 0.99, a standard value that is widely accepted. The results of the estimation are presented in Table 2. In Phillips curve the parameter that surprises the output gap influence on the inflationist process has a value of 0.1520, a value close to the one obtained in the previous model. The estimated value for γ a parameter that captures the inflation inertia is of 0.8121. This estimation is close to the one obtained by Boţel (2010). It underlines the important role which the backward-looking component has in forming the prices. In our opinion, more the inflation will get close to values of 2%-4% a bigger weight

Table 2. The results of the Bayesian estimation

Parameters	Prior Mean	Posterior Mean	Confidence Interval	Confidence Interval	Prior Distribution	Standard Deviation
σ	0.800	0.0650	0.0473	0.0817	Normal	0.3750
κ	0.130	0.1520	0.1203	0.1841	Normal	0.0200
γ	0.800	0.8121	0.7784	0.8454	Normal	0.0200
ρ_r	0.500	0.1430	0.0261	0.2599	Normal	0.1000
ϕ_π	1.500	1.6525	1.4549	1.8491	Normal	0.1250
ϕ_y	0.500	0.5174	0.4363	0.6003	Normal	0.0500
φ_r	0.350	0.3955	0.3638	0.4272	Normal	0.0200
φ_u	0.600	0.5709	0.5384	0.6031	Normal	0.0200
φ_r	0.700	0.6592	0.6297	0.6897	Normal	0.0200

in forming the anticipation will be held by the central bank target and the high weight of inflation inertia will diminish.

The parameters form Taylor's rule that capture the importance the central bank gives to inflation and to the output gap, have values close to the previous estimated parameters. The parameter concerning the monetary policy gradualism has a lower value than the one obtained in the previous model.

The Impulse Response Functions to Shocks

Hereinafter, we propose to compare the impulse response functions and to reflect the persistence degree of the variables included in the study to an IS shock, to a cost shock and to an interest rate shock. The impulse response functions are presented in Figure 3 and Figure 4.

An IS curve shock, presented within the first model, leads to a growth of inflation and of output gap. As a response to this growth, the central bank will raise the interest rate in order to stabilize the economy.

As we notice, a cost shock leads to an inflation growth in both models. However, in the second model the persistence of inflation is more obvious, the inflation rate returns to the steady state level much more gradually, in approximately 15 quarters. In our opinion, the second estimated model is more consistent with the reality. In both models, the central bank responds to the inflation growth with an interest rate growth. A shock in the Phillips curve will lead to a contraction of the output gap. The most persistent effect on the output gap appears rapidly: after 2-3 quarters. In our opinion, one of the reasons of this rapid response is related to the to the interest rate growth. Central bank reacts to higher prices by raising interest rate, a decision consistent with the inflation targeting strategy.

It is well known that the NK standard models don't succeed in generating a hump-shaped response of inflation to a monetary shock. Within both models, an interest rate shock will lead to a decrease in inflation rate and output gap. Inflation will diminish almost instantaneously in the first model. In the second model, the outcome consists in a more delayed and gradual response of inflation due to a monetary shock, in fact the largest impact appearing after 3 quarters.

Figure 1. Multivariate convergence diagnostics for the simple neokeynesian model

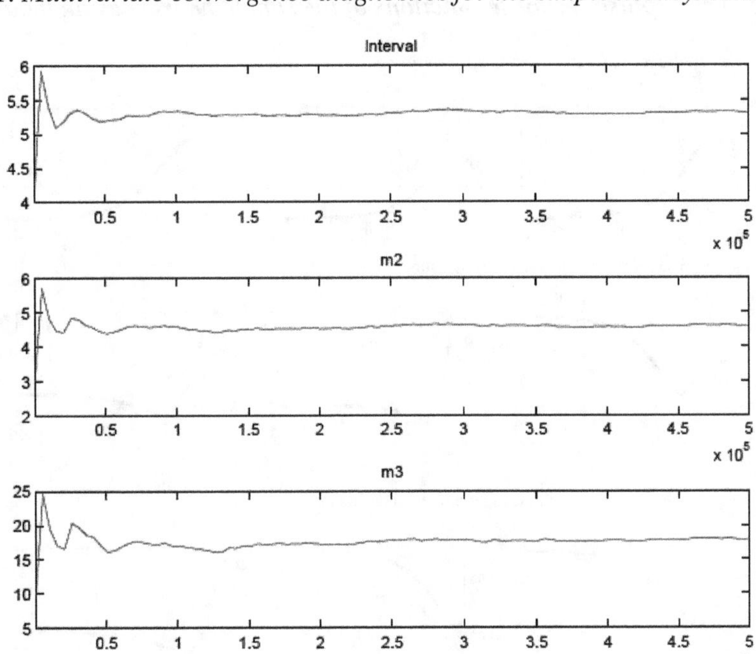

Figure 2. Multivariate convergence diagnostics the model that captures the inflation inertia

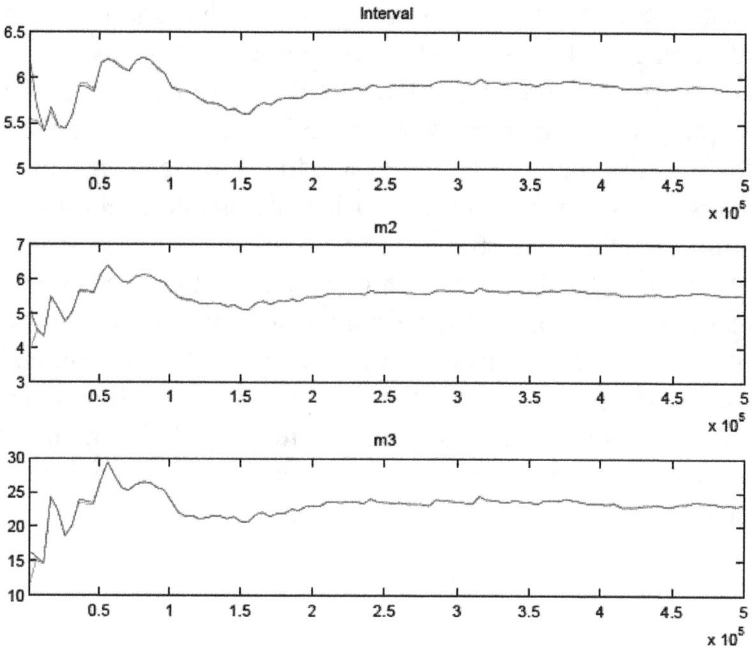

Figure 3. The impulse response functions of the simple neokeynesian model

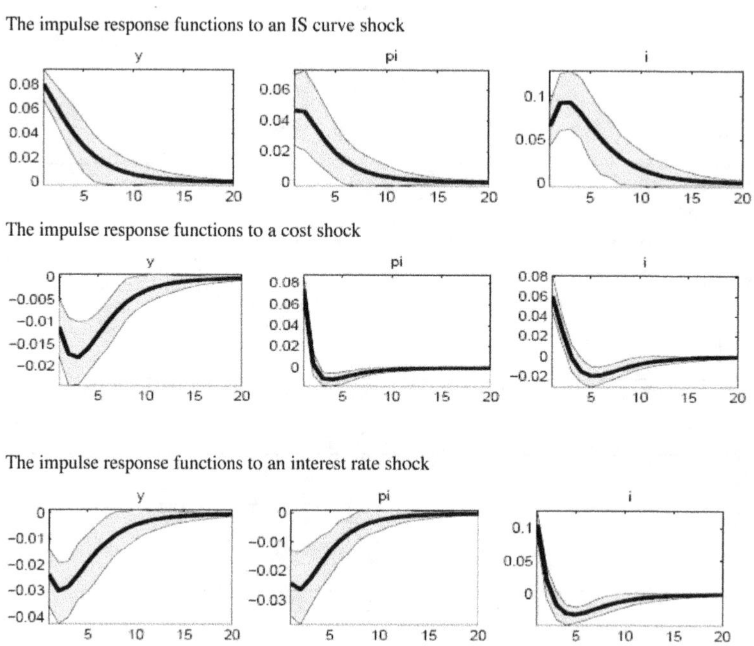

Figure 4. The impulse response functions of the model that captures the inflation inertia

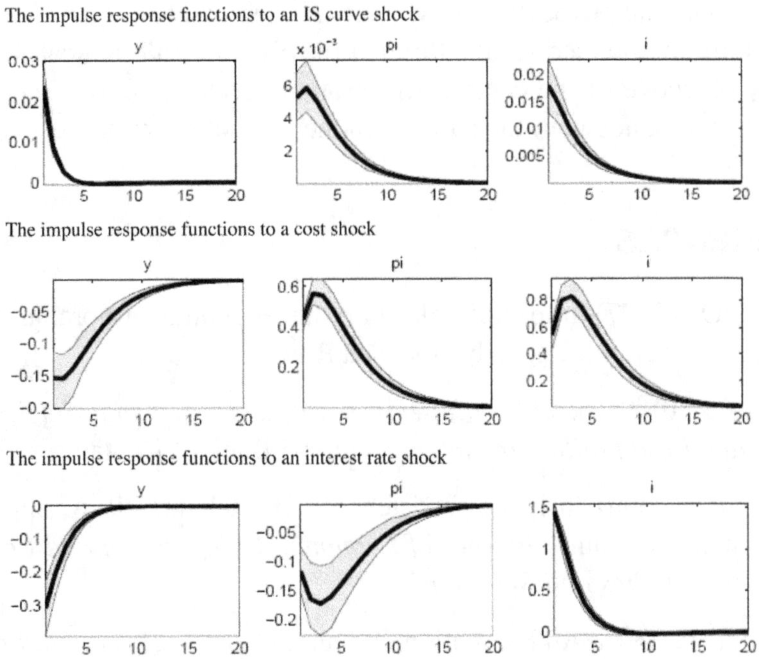

CONCLUSION

Within this study we used two DSGE models for analyzing the inflation inertia and persistence as well as the monetary policy effects in Romania. We used, firstly, a neokeynesian standard model built around a forward-looking component. Afterwards, in order to offer a more complex perspective we also estimated a DSGE model that captures the inflation inertia. In our opinion, the second model is more consistent with the reality. After estimating the two models, we noticed that the prices evolution reflects the difficulties of eliminating the inflationary inertia. In Romania, the historic inflation evolution has a major impact on the way the inflation expectations are formed. Even if the inflation decreased at a moderate level, its persistence continues for a long period of time. Factors such as inflation inertia, the domination of the backward-looking expectations contribute to this fact. In the future, more the inflation will stabilize around a diminished equilibrium value - more the backward-looking component importance will diminish in favor of the forward-looking component. This fact, since the monetary policy gradually affects the economy, will mark the transit to a forward-looking monetary policy. In such forward-looking kind of environment, the central bank forecast, and the inflationary expectations will have higher influence on inflation. The analysis of the obtained results through the Taylor's rule indicates that the primary objective of the central bank was the price stability - such a goal being in accordance with the adopted monetary policy strategy.

REFERENCES

Aristide, O. (2007) Impactul salariilor din economie asupra inflaţiei şi deficitului comercial. Banca Naţională a României.

Boţel, C. (2010). *Persistenţa inflaţiei şi cauzele acesteia. Colocviul Provocări actuale la adresa politicii monetare*. National Bank of Romania.

Caraiani, P., (2009a). Inflation persistence and DSGE models. An application on Romanian economy. *Journal of Economic Computation and Economic Cybernetics Studies and Research*, 3.

Caraiani, P. (2009b). An Estimation Of Output Gap. In *Romanian Economy Using The DSGE Approach. Prague Economic Papers* (Vol. 4, pp. 366–379). Prague: University of Economics.

Cespedes, L., Kumhof, M., & Parrado, E. 2003. Pricing Policies and Inflation Inertia. IMF.

Chauvet, M., & Kim, I. (2010). *Microfoundations of Ination Persistence in the New Keynesian Phillips Curve*. MPRA.

Edwards, S. (1998). Two crises: Inflationary Inertia and Credibility. *Economic Journal, 108*, 680–702.

Evans, G. W., & Honkapohja, S. (2001). *Learning and Expectations in Macroeconomics*. Princeton University Press. doi:10.1515/9781400824267

Fuhrer, J. C. (2000). Habit Formation in Consumption and Its Implications for Monetary Policy Models. *The American Economic Review, 90*(3), 367–390. doi:10.1257/aer.90.3.367

Gali, J. (2007). *Monetary Policy, Inflation, and the Business Cycle An Introduction to the New Keynesian Framework*. Princeton University Press.

Gali, J., & Gertler, M. (1999). Inflation Dynamics: A Structural Econometric Analysis. *Journal of Monetary Economics*, *44*(2), 195–222. doi:10.1016/S0304-3932(99)00023-9

Lendvai, J. (2004). *Inflation inertia and monetary policy shocks, Discussion Papers 2004/17*. Institute of Economics Hungarian Academy of Sciences.

Lucas, R. (1976). Economic policy evaluation: a critique. In K. Brunner and A.M. Meltzer (Eds.), The Phillips Curve and labour markets.

Milani, F. (2006). A Bayesian DSGE Model with Infinite-Horizon Learning: Do "Mechanical" Sources of Persistence Become Superfluous? *International Journal of Central Banking*, *2*(3), 87–106.

Scutaru, C., & Stanica, C. (2005). Determining the output gap and the dynamics of inflationary shocks. The case of Romania. Institute for Economic Forecasting.

Spulbar, C., Niţoi, M., & Stanciu, C. (2012). Inflation inertia and inflation persistence in Romania using a DSGE approach. *Annals of the Alexandru Ioan Cuza University-Economics*, *59*(1), 115–124. doi:10.2478/v10316-012-0008-7

Taylor, J. B. (1993). Discretion versus Policy Rules in Practice. *Carnegie-Rochester Conference Series on Public Policy*, *39*, 195–214. doi:10.1016/0167-2231(93)90009-L

Section 3

Understanding Financial Market Behavior:

Empirical Case Studies

Chapter 8
Testing Weak-Form Efficiency and Long-Term Causality of the Emerging Capital Markets in Romania, India, Poland, and Hungary

ABSTRACT

The main purpose of this chapter is testing weak-form efficiency and long-term causality of the emerging capital markets in Romania, India, Poland and Hungary. According to Spulbar and Birau, the empirical analysis is focused on BET index (Romania), WIG 20 index (Poland), BSE index (India) and BUX index (Hungary) from January 2000 to July 2018. The empirical results revealed that there is no long-term causality between the selected emerging stock markets analyzed during the period of January 2000 to July 2018. The book chapter provides additional empirical evidence of emerging capital markets behavior since the empirical analysis revealed that ADF t statistics rejected the null hypotheses of a unit root, so the selected financial data series are stationary in all selected cases. Moreover, the empirical results have revealed that the efficient market hypothesis has not been validated and there is no long-term causality between the selected emerging stock markets during the sample period from January 2000 to July 2018.

DOI: 10.4018/978-1-5225-9269-3.ch008

INTRODUCTION

In terms of justifying the selection of the international portfolio, we will highlight in the paragraphs below both the similarities and the differences between the markets in Romania, Poland, Hungary and India. Romania, Poland and Hungary are member states of the European Union but reveals different levels of socio-economic development. Moreover, Romania, Poland and Hungary, are all former communist countries in Central and Eastern Europe. Hungary and Romania are neighbors and share a common past in certain key aspects. Nevertheless, Hungary and Poland joined the European Union (EU) in 2004 and Romania became a member in 2007. Moreover, all three countries are full members of NATO. All the three selected European countries are democratic.

According to FTSE Country Classifications, data provided on March 2018, there is the following classification of countries: developed, advanced emerging, secondary emerging and frontier. Hungary is included in the category of advanced emerging markets, while Romania is included in the category of frontier markets, but on the Watch List for a possible reclassification from frontier to secondary emerging. On the other hand, Poland is also included in the category of advanced emerging markets, but it will be promoted to developed market status, effective from September 2018.

India is included in the category of secondary emerging and also member of the BRICS group which includes Brazil, Russia, India, China and South Africa. As can be easily noticed, India is perceived as an alternative in case of a Black Swan[1] event based on international portfolio diversification. The Indian stock market is seemingly uncorrelated with the capital markets in Europe and this aspect can lead to significant long-term diversification benefits. Stock market interdependencies are very important in the context of a diversified international portfolio.

This book subchapter provides a comprehensive investigation of the efficient market hypothesis in terms of emerging capital markets as an extension of previous research studies of the authors. One of the essential assumptions of classical finances implies that investors are rational, and they are concerned to select an efficient portfolio a combination of asset classes chosen as to achieve the greatest possible returns over the long term, but under the conditions of a tolerable level of risk. The efficient market hypothesis is based on the "random walk" theory.

This approach leads to the quintessence of efficient market theory, which is based on the idea that an efficient market "fully reflect" available information. The efficient market hypothesis focuses on three main pillars, i.e.: investor rationality, uncorrelated errors, and the idea that there are no limits to arbitrage. Technically, arbitrage is defined as "the simultaneous purchase and sale of the same, or essentially similar, security in two different markets for advantageously different prices" (Sharpe & Alexander, 1990). A market is efficient with respect to a set of information if it is impossible to obtain economic profits by trading on the basis of this information set (Ross, 1987).

Fama (1965) stated that: "an efficient market is defined as a market where there are large numbers of rational, profit-maximizers actively competing, with each trying to predict future market values of individual securities, and where important current information is almost freely available to all participants." On the other hand, Peters (1994) suggested that: "If all information had the same impact on all investors, there would be no liquidity. When they received information, all investors would be executing the same trade, trying to get the same price."

Korajczyk (1995) suggested that "the measure of market segmentation tends to be much larger for emerging markets than for developed markets, which is consistent with larger barriers to capital flows into or out of the emerging markets". However, emerging capital markets are characterized by a number of inefficiencies such as: mispricings (Korajczyk, 1995), financial frictions, misallocation of financial resources (capital), irrational investment decision making, the impact of informational asymmetry and return anomalies.

The central idea of efficient market hypothesis suggests the fact that stock market security prices always incorporate and reflect all relevant information. According to Fama (1970) the ideal financial market would be guided by the principle that prices provide accurate signals for resource allocation. In other words, the concept of market efficiency implies that security prices at any moment of time "fully reflect" all available information.

Fama (1998), also known as the father of efficient market hypothesis argued that: "Consistent with the market efficiency hypothesis that the anomalies are chance results, apparent overreaction to information is about as common as underreaction, and post event continuation of pre-event abnormal returns is about as frequent as post-event reversal."

Efficient market hypothesis argued that market provides correct pricing and current prices of securities are close to their fundamental values. Thus, in an efficient market the arbitrage opportunities are rather insignificant. Moreover, the paradigm focuses on the premise that it's not possible to outperform the market over the long-term.

An alternative theoretical approach is fractal market hypothesis which is based on chaos theory. Short-term price changes have a predisposition to be more volatile than long-term price trends. Peters (1994) suggested that based on fractal market hypothesis, we can understand why self-similar statistical structures exist, as well as how risk is shared distributed among investors. According to Mandelbrot (2008), in finance, a fractal is not a rootless abstraction but a theoretical reformulation of a down-to-earth bit of market folklore - namely, that movements of a capital or currency all look alike when a market chart is enlarged or reduced so that it fits the same time and price scale.

On the other hand, Barberis and Thaler (2002) suggested that behavioral finance is focused on two fundamental parts, i.e. limits to arbitrage and psychology. Behavioral finance is a psychology-based paradigm which disapproves the rationality of market participants and suggests that emotional biases, irrational human behaviors or cognitive deviations significantly affects the investment process.

LITERATURE REVIEW

The main objective of the literature review is to provide a comprehensive framework of the available literature in the chosen research area. In this respect, we will highlight a series of convergent and divergent theoretical opinions based on heterogeneous empirical studies.

Birau (2012) examined in a comparative manner the weak-form efficiency in the case of two neighboring emerging capital markets, i.e. Bucharest Stock Exchange (Romania) and Budapest Stock Exchange (Hungary), in the context of global financial crisis. Patel (2016) investigated co-movement based on a diversified international portfolio among certain stock markets such as "BSE" - India, "Hangseng" - China, "MXX" - Mexico, "RTS" - Russia, "BVSP" - Brazil, "FTSE-100" – U.K., "Nikkei" – Japan and "NASDAQ" – U.S.A.

Palamalai, Kalaivani and Devakumar (2013) have conducted a research study on stock market integration among major stock markets of emerging Asia-Pacific economies, viz. India, Malaysia, Hong Kong, Singapore, South

Korea, Taiwan, Japan, China, and Indonesia. The empirical results have highlighted the existence of stock market interdependencies and dynamic interactions among the selected stock markets which generates short-term investment opportunities based on international portfolio diversification.

Tripathi and Shruti (2012) have provided additional empirical findings on inter-linkages of Indian stock market (CNX S&P NIFTY 50 stock index) with advanced emerging markets, ie Brazil (BOVESPA stock index), Hungary (BUX stock index), Taiwan (TAIEX stock index), Mexico (INMEX stock index), Poland (WIG stock index) and South Africa (JSE FTSE stock index) over the period ranging from 1 January 1992 to 31 December 2009 based on Johansen co-integration test and Granger's causality test.

Grambovas (2003) have performed an empirical analysis on the long-run and short-run dynamics between exchange rate fluctuations and equity prices in three European emerging financial markets, Greece, the Czech Republic, and Hungary. The author concluded that the Hungarian and Greek authorities should consider the strong link between foreign exchange and capital markets before taking any policy measures. Chen and Chen (2012) investigated the non-linear causal nexus between stock prices and exchange rates in 12 OECD countries. The author concluded based on the empirical results that a long-run level equilibrium relationship among the exchange rates and stock prices exists in only seven out of twelve countries.

Singh and Sharma (2012) have conducted an empirical research study on international inter-linkages between stock markets of Brazil, Russia, India, and China, ie BRIC nations. The empirical results have revealed certain international interactions and the authors concluded that Russian, Indian and Brazilian stock exchanges affect each other and get affected by their own return but none of these affect Chinese stock exchange whether they all get affected by Chinese stock exchange.

FINANCIAL DATA SERIES AND APPLIED METHODOLOGY

The continuously-compounded daily returns are calculated using the log-difference of stock markets selected indices as follows:

$$r_t = \ln\left(\frac{p_t}{p_{t-1}}\right) = \ln\left(p_t\right) - \ln\left(p_{t-1}\right)$$

where p is the daily closing price.

According to Spulbar and Birau (2018), the applied financial econometrics approach includes various research tools such as descriptive statistics, Unit Root Test, Hodrick-Prescott (HP) filter, Augmented Dickey-Fuller stationary test, BDS test and Granger causality test.

The empirical analysis is focused on BET index (Romania), WIG 20 (Poland), BSE (India) and BUX index (Hungary). Financial data series consists of the daily closing prices for each selected index from January 2000 to July 2018 with the exception of legal holidays or other events when stock markets haven't performed any financial transactions.

The basic statistical characteristics of BET index (Romania), WIG 20 (Poland), BSE (India) and BUX index (Hungary) stock indices are represented by the following: Jarque-Bera test's statistic which allows to eliminate the normality of distribution hypothesis, parameter of asymmetry of distribution or Skewness and Kurtosis parameter which measures the peakedness or flatness of the distribution, ie leptokurtic distribution.

The fundamental characteristics of selected indices are represented by the following issues: Jarque-Bera test's statistic which allows to eliminate the normality of distribution hypothesis, parameter of asymmetry distribution or Skewness and Kurtosis parameter which measures the peakedness or flatness of the distribution (leptokurtic distribution). The test Jarque-Bera is based on the following mathematical expressions:

$$JB = n\left[\frac{s^2}{6} + \frac{(k-3)^2}{24}\right] = \frac{n}{6}\cdot\left(s^2 + \frac{(k-3)^2}{4}\right), \text{ considering:}$$

$$s = \frac{\hat{\mu}_3}{\hat{\sigma}^3} = \frac{\frac{1}{n}\sum_{i=1}^{n}\left(x_i - \bar{x}\right)^3}{\left[\frac{1}{n}\sum_{i=1}^{n}\left(x_i - \bar{x}\right)^2\right]^{\frac{3}{2}}}$$

$$k = \frac{\hat{\mu}_4}{\hat{\sigma}^4} = \frac{\frac{1}{n}\sum_{i=1}^{n}(x_i - \bar{x})^4}{\left[\frac{1}{n}\sum_{i=1}^{n}\left(x_i - \bar{x}\right)^2\right]^2}$$

Augmented Dickey-Fuller (ADF) test is used in order to determine the non-stationarity or the integration order of a financial time series. A series noted y_t is integrated of order one, i.e. $y_t \sim I(1)$ and contains a unit root if y_t is non-stationary, but on the other hand Δy_t is stationary, i.e. $\Delta y_t = y_t - y_{t-1}$. Moreover, extrapolating the previous expression, a series y_t is integrated of order d, i.e. $y_t \sim I(d)$ if y_t is non-stationary, but $\Delta^d y_t$ is stationary. Practically, ADF diagnostic test investigates the potential presence of unit roots divided into the following categories: unit root with a constant and a trend, unit root with a constant, but without a time trend, and finally unit root without constant and temporal trend. Theoretically, ADF test is focused on the following regression model:

$$\Delta y_t = c + \beta \cdot t + \delta \cdot y_{t-1} + \sum_{i=1}^{p} \gamma_i \Delta y_{t-i} + \varepsilon_t$$

where p represents the number of lags for which it was investigated whether fulfilling the condition that residuals are white noise, c is a constant, t is the indicator for time trend and Δ is the symbol for differencing. In addition, it is important to emphasize the essence of a stochastic trend that can not be predicted due to the time dependence of residual's variance. Strictly related to the ADF test, if the coefficients to be estimated β and δ have the null value then the analyzed financial time series is characterized by a stochastic trend. The null hypothesis, i.e. the time series has a unit root is rejected if t-statistics is lower than the critical value.

Augmented Dickey-Fuller test was applied in order to determine the stationarity of the selected financial time series. The null hypothesis is that the selected financial time series contains a unit root and it is implicitly non-stationary. Empirical analysis based on the log-returns of the selected indices reflects the fact that $t_{test-}ADF < t_{critic}$ (1%, 5%, 10%) so the null hypothesis H_0 is rejected and the analyzed time series is stationary. Simultaneous, obtains the following result: Prob (0%) < test levels (1%, 5%, 10%) so the null hypothesis H_0 is rejected and the selected financial time series is stationary.

The BDS test was used in order to determine whether the residuals are independent and identically distributed. BDS test is a two-tailed test and is based on the following hypothesis:

H_0: sample observations are independently and identically distributed (I.I.D.)

H$_1$: sample observations are not I.I.D., aspect involving that the time series is non-linearly dependent if first differences of the natural logarithm have been calculated.

The BDS methodology involves a time series x_t for t=1, 2, 3…T based on its m-history $x_t^m = \left(x_t, x_{t-1}, \ldots, x_{t-m+1}\right)$ where m is the called embedding dimension. Implicitly, the *correlation integral* (a measure of time patterns frequency) is estimated as follows:

$$C_{m,\varepsilon} = \frac{2}{T_m\left(T_m - 1\right)} \sum_{m \leq s} \sum_{< t \leq T} I\left(x_t^m, x_s^m, \varepsilon\right)$$

and $C_m\left(\varepsilon\right) = \lim_{n \to \infty} C_{m,n}\left(\varepsilon\right)$

where T_m = T-m+1 and $I\left(x_t^m, x_s^m, \varepsilon\right)$ represents a binary function, which has the following values for i=0, 1, 2…m-1:

$$I\left(x_t^m, x_s^m, \varepsilon\right) = \begin{cases} 1 & if \left|x_{t-i} - x_{s-i}\right| < \varepsilon \\ 0 & otherwise \end{cases}$$

Brock, Dechert, Scheinkman, LeBaron (1996) argued that the BDS statistics is calculated as follows:

$$V_{m,\varepsilon} = \sqrt{T} \frac{C_{m,\varepsilon} - C_{1,\varepsilon}^m}{S_{m,\varepsilon}}$$

where $S_{m,\varepsilon}$ is defined as the standard deviation of $\sqrt{T\left(C_{m,\varepsilon} - C_{1,\varepsilon}^m\right)}$. In addition, the BDS statistics converges in distribution to N(0,1) thus the null hypothesis of independent and identically distributed is rejected based on a result such as $\left|V_{m,\varepsilon}\right| > 1{,}96$ in terms of a 5% significance level.

The null hypothesis was rejected in all sample cases based on selected stock indices. The following outputs highlight the value of the standardised BDS statistics and the corresponding two-sided probabilities. The BDS test was used in order to determine whether the residuals are independent and identically distributed. The BDS statistics converges in distribution to N(0,1) thus the null hypothesis of independent and identically distributed is rejected based on a result such as in terms of a 5% significance level.

The empirical analysis includes the use of Hodrick-Prescott (HP) filter which is a specialized filter for trend and business cycle estimation. Hodrick-Prescott filter has a wide applicability in economics. The basic idea suggests that in the center of the sample financial time series the filter is symmetric and towards the end of the series is becoming increasingly asymmetric. On the other hand, Hodrick-Prescott filter involves the decomposition of the sample financial time series into a trend component and a residual component, which may or may not include a cyclical component.

Granger (1969) argued that if some other time series Yt contains information regarding the past periods which are useful in the prediction of Xt so this informations are included in no other series used in the predictor, then this implies that Yt caused Xt. In addition, Granger argued that if X_t and Y_t are two different stationary time series variables with zero means, then the canonical causal model has the following form:

$$X_t = \sum_{j=1}^{m} a_j X_{t-j} + \sum_{j=1}^{m} b_j Y_{t-j} + \varepsilon_t$$

$$Y_t = \sum_{j=1}^{m} c_j X_{t-j} + \sum_{j=1}^{m} d_j Y_{t-j} + \eta_t$$

where ε_t and η_t play the role of two uncorrelated white-noise series, namely $E\left[\varepsilon_t \varepsilon_s\right] = 0 = E\left[\eta_t \eta_s\right]$ for $s \neq t$ and on the other hand $E\left[\varepsilon_t \varepsilon_s\right] = 0$ for $\forall t, s$. Practically, the basic concept of causality requires that in the case when Y_t is causing X_t some b_j is different from zero and vice versa, ie in the case when X_t is causing Y_t some c_j is different from zero. A different situation implies that causality is valid simultaneously in both directions or simply a so-called "feedback relationship between X_t and Y_t". The F-distribution test is used to test the Granger causality hypotheses based on the following formula:

$$F = \frac{\left(RSS_R - RSS_{UR}\right) / m}{RSS_{UR} / \left(n - k\right)}$$

where RSS_R is the residual sum of squares, RSS_{UR} is the unrestricted residual sum of squares, m is the number of lagged X_t variables, K is the number of parameters in the restricted regression. The null hypothesis Ho implies that lagged X_t terms do not belong in the regression. The null hypothesis is rejected if the F-value exceeds the critical F value at the selected level of significance (5%) or if the P-value is lower than the α level of significance.

EMPIRICAL RESULTS

According to Spulbar and Birau (2018), the empirical analysis is focused on BET index (Romania), WIG 20 index (Poland), BSE index (India) and BUX index (Hungary) from January 2000 to July 2018. The analyzed period is a very long interval that incorporates daily closing price of selected stock indices. The individual trend of selected indices mentioned above was very fluctuating, even strongly decreasing in all four cases in correlation with the impact of the global financial crisis (see Figure 1).

Financial time series exhibit time variation in mean and variance, so exhibit a non-stationary behavior, requiring to be transformed to stationary series. The financial time series adapted to econometric requirements are based on continuously compounded returns. The continuously compounded returns calculated for selected stock indices, respectively BET index (Romania), WIG 20 index (Poland), BSE index (India) and BUX index (Hungary) is graphically represented in the Figures 2 (joint graphics) and 3 (individual graphics) included in Appendices.

A basic characteristic feature of emerging capital markets is that the distribution of continuously compounded returns deviates from the normal distribution or Gaussian distribution. The histograms of the analyzed stock market indices have been included in Appendices (see Figure 6). The empirical analysis also focuses on Skewness and Kurtosis based on data distribution. Statistically, skewness is a measure of asymmetry of the distribution of a financial data series around its means, but the skewness of a symmetric distribution is zero.

Taking into account the financial implications of efficient markets hypothesis it is obvious that in the case of normal distribution, the skewness is null. Positive skewness highlights that the distribution has a long right tail, while negative skewness implies that the distribution has a long left tail. Kurtosis measures the peakedness or flatness of the distribution of a return financial data series. The kurtosis of a normal distribution is 3, but if the kurtosis exceeds 3, the distribution is peaked (Leptokurtic) relative to the normal. Moreover, if the kurtosis is less than 3, the distribution is flat (Platykurtic) relative to normal. The empirical results revealed that in all four cases, respectively for BET index (Romania) is -0,433526, for WIG 20 index (Poland) is -0,138691, for BSE index (India) is -0,164621 and for BUX index (Hungary) is -0,040782 indicate the existence of negative skewness which implies that the distribution has a long left tail. The kurtosis exceeds 3 in all four cases, respectively for BET index (Romania) is 10,57696, for WIG 20 index (Poland) is 5,624807, for BSE index (India) is 11,41479 and for BUX index (Hungary) is 9,003293 so that the distribution is peaked (Leptokurtic) relative to the normal.

The Augmented Dickey-Fuller test was applied in order to determine the stationarity of selected financial time series. The empirical results obtained based on continuously compounded returns indicate that the null hypothesis H_0 is rejected in all four cases because $t_{test-}ADF < t_{critic}$ (1%, 5%, 10%) which implies that all the analyzed time series are stationary. We also can use the formula Prob (0%) < test levels (1%, 5%, 10%) which leads to the same conclusion that all the analyzed time series are stationary (see Table 1).

The BDS test was performed in order to determine whether the residuals are independent and identically distributed. The null hypothesis is rejected if the BDS test statistic is greater than or less than the critical values. The level of significance, respectively, an a of 5% (if a = 0.05, the critical value = ±1.96) is considered in this hypothesis testing. In the case of continuously compounded returns, the null hypothesis was rejected in all four cases (see Table 2).

Applying Granger causality test, the null hypothesis is rejected if the F-value exceeds the critical F value at the selected level of significance (5%) or if the P value is lower than the α level of significance. The financial data series of BET index (Romania), WIG 20 index (Poland), BSE index (India) and BUX index (Hungary) from January 2000 to July 2018 based on continuously compounded returns indicate that there is no causality between the following pairs of emerging stock markets, in the sample period, ie: Romania and India, Hungary and India, Poland and India, Romania and Hungary, Poland and Hungary respectively Poland and Romania (see Table 3).

Figure 1. The trend of R.I.P.H stock indices - individual graphics
Source: Author's own computations based on selected financial data series

Figure 2. The log-returns of R.I.P.H stock indices - joint graphics
Source: Author's own computations based on selected financial data series

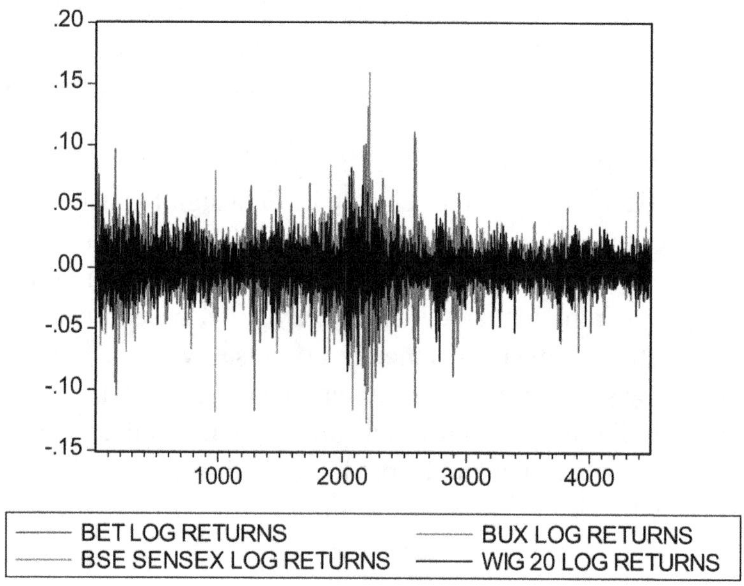

Figure 3. Log returns series of R.I.P.H stock indices - individual graphics
Source: Author's own computations based on selected financial data series

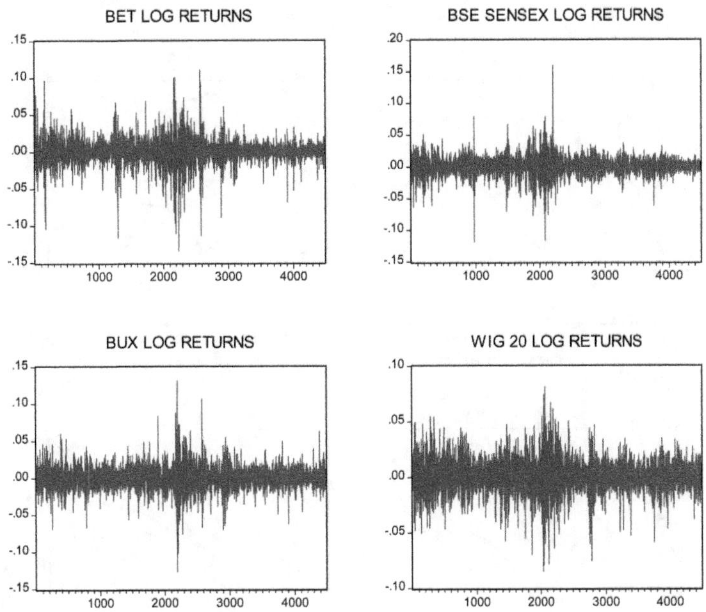

Figure 4. Matrix of all pairs of selected stock market indices
Source: Own computations based on selected financial data series

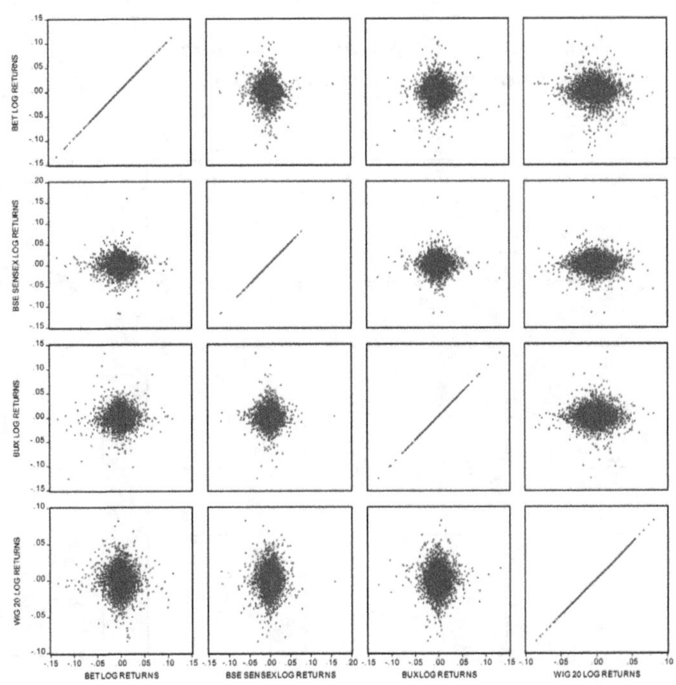

Figure 5. Theoretical quantile-quantile plots (extreme values)
Source: Own computations based on selected financial data series

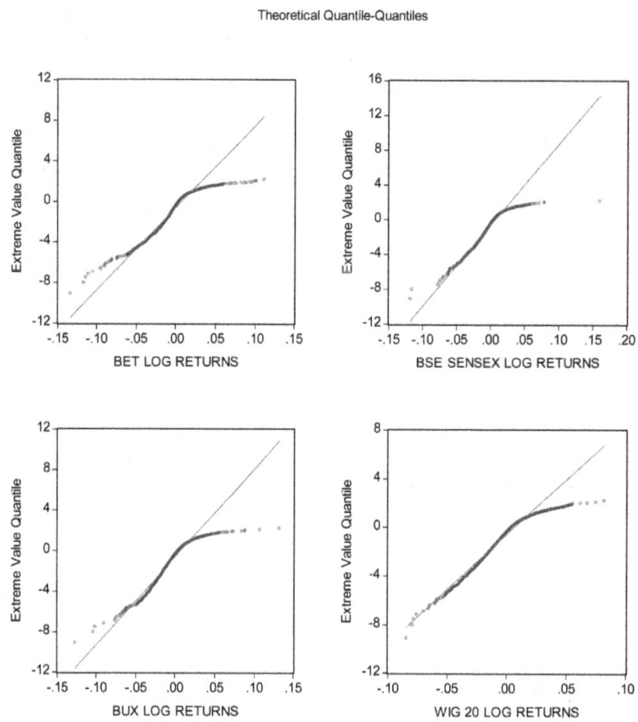

Figure 6. Distribution graphics CDF - survivor – quantile
Source: Own computations based on selected financial data series

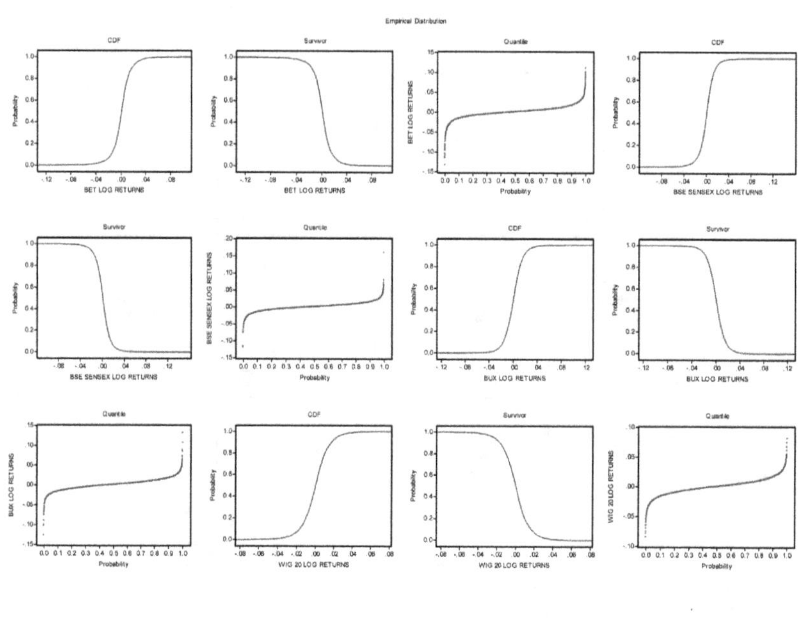

Figure 7. Basic statistical characteristics of R.I.P.H stock indices
Source: Own computations based on selected financial data series

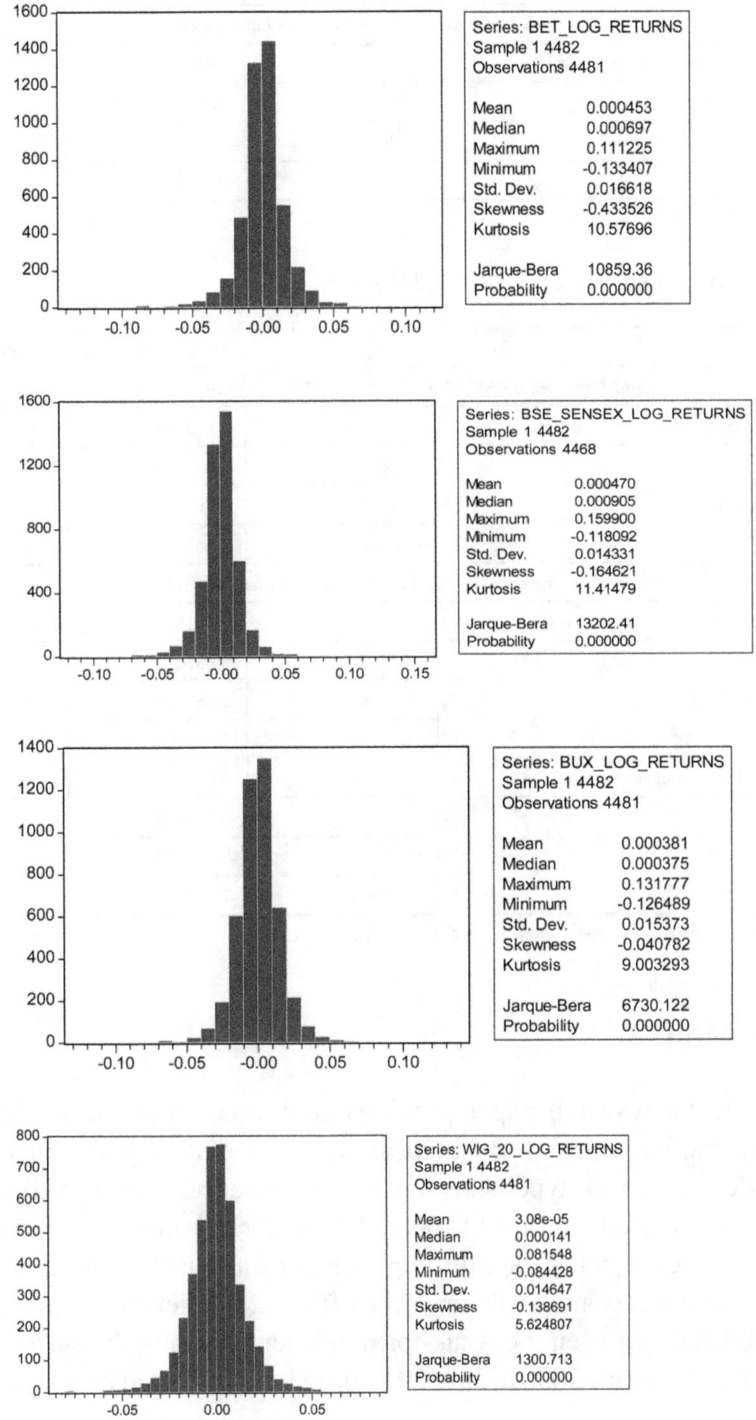

Table 1. Augmented Dickey-Fuller (ADF) test

		t-Statistic	Prob.*
Null Hypothesis: BET_LOG_RETURNS has a unit root			
Augmented Dickey-Fuller test statistic		-59.97641	0.0001
Test critical values:	1% level	-3.431626	
	5% level	-2.861989	
	10% level	-2.567052	

Table 2. Augmented Dickey-Fuller (ADF) test

		t-Statistic	Prob.*
Null Hypothesis: BSE_SENSEX_LOG_RETURNS has a unit root			
Augmented Dickey-Fuller test statistic		-47.62223	0.0001
Test critical values:	1% level	-3.431628	
	5% level	-2.861990	
	10% level	-2.567052	
Null Hypothesis: BUX_LOG_RETURNS has a unit root			
Augmented Dickey-Fuller test statistic		-32.81521	0.0000
Test critical values:	1% level	-3.431627	
	5% level	-2.861989	
	10% level	-2.567052	
Augmented Dickey-Fuller test statistic		-63.93847	0.0001
Test critical values:	1% level	-3.431626	
	5% level	-2.861989	
	10% level	-2.567052	

Source: Own computations based on selected financial data series

CONCLUSION

This particular research paper provides additional empirical evidence of emerging capital markets behaviorin order to diversify the investment risk. Efficient market hypothesis has as quintessence random walks which implies the requirement of unit roots. The empirical analysis revealed that ADF t statistics rejected the null hypotheses of a unit root, so the selected financial data series are stationary. The efficient market hypothesis has not been validated, not even the weak-form efficiency during the selected time interval from January 2000 to July 2018 based on continuously compounded

Table 3. BDS test

Dimension	BDS Statistic	Std. Error	z-Statistic	Prob.
BDS Test for BET_LOG_RETURNS				
2	0.039934	0.001498	26.65707	0.0000
3	0.075117	0.002377	31.60700	0.0000
4	0.099804	0.002826	35.31842	0.0000
5	0.113540	0.002941	38.60188	0.0000
6	0.119716	0.002833	42.25958	0.0000
BDS Test for BSE_SENSEX_LOG_RETURNS				
2	0.025242	0.001389	18.16931	0.0000
3	0.050943	0.002204	23.11541	0.0000
4	0.069495	0.002620	26.52455	0.0000
5	0.080448	0.002726	29.50674	0.0000
6	0.085304	0.002625	32.49391	0.0000
BDS Test for BUX_LOG_RETURNS				
2	0.015466	0.001263	12.24557	0.0000
3	0.031003	0.002003	15.48164	0.0000
4	0.042230	0.002379	17.74926	0.0000
5	0.049011	0.002474	19.80900	0.0000
6	0.051446	0.002381	21.61042	0.0000
BDS Test for WIG_20_log_returns				
2	0.010641	0.001296	8.210468	0.0000
3	0.023092	0.002054	11.24055	0.0000
4	0.034389	0.002440	14.09313	0.0000
5	0.042110	0.002537	16.59927	0.0000
6	0.046230	0.002440	18.94404	0.0000

Source: Own computations based on selected financial data series

returns. Moreover, empirical results also revealed that there is no long-term causality between the selected emerging stock markets, ie Romania, India, Poland and Hungary during the period of January 2000 to July 2018. A further extension of this research paper will focus on investigating co-movements and inter-linkage between developed and emerging capital markets based on international portfolio diversification.

Birau (2012) reached similar conclusions, i.e. that efficient market hypothesis is not accomplished, not even the weak-form efficiency, during the period of January 2007 to November 2011, both for Bucharest Stock

Figure 8. Hodrick – Prescott filter
Source: Own computations based on selected financial data series

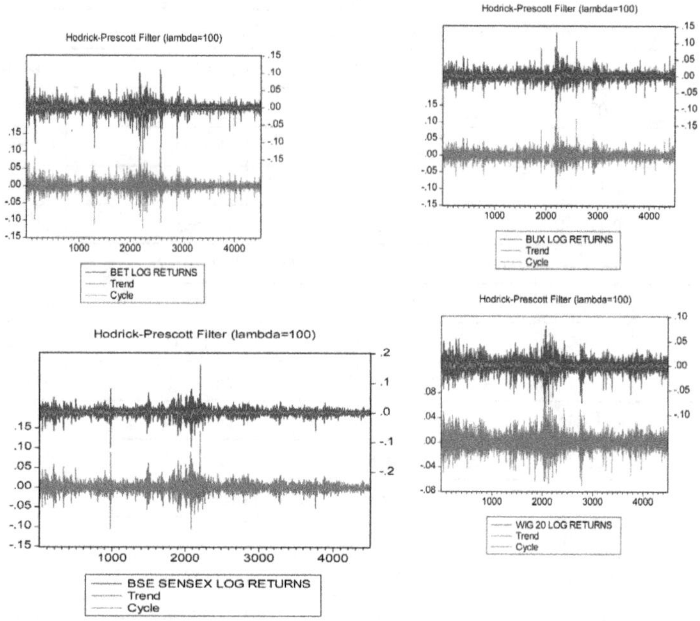

Figure 9. Impulse response analysis to Cholesky One S.D. innovations
Source: Own computations based on selected financial data series

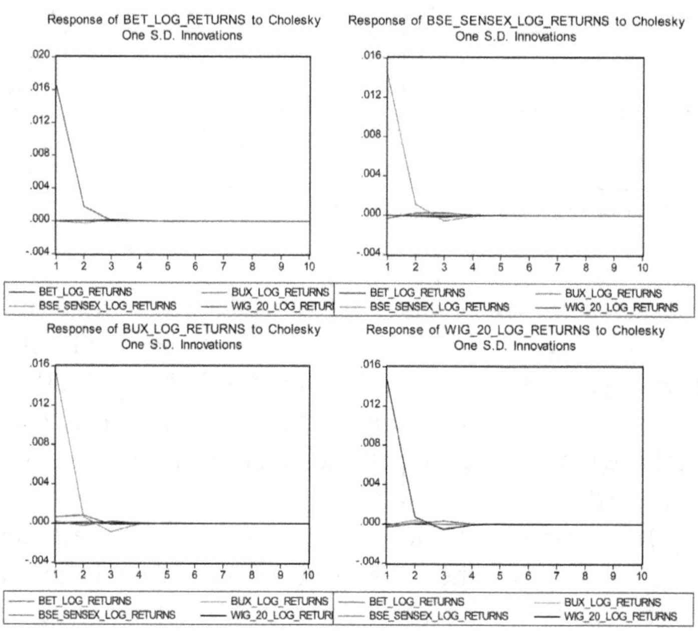

Table 4. Granger Causality tests

Pairwise Granger Causality Tests			
Null Hypothesis	**Obs**	**F-Statistic**	**Probability**
BSE_SENSEX_LOG_RETURNS does not Granger Cause BET_LOG_RETURNS	4478	0.54388	0.65227
BET_LOG_RETURNS does not Granger Cause BSE_SENSEX_LOG_RETURNS		0.65625	0.57897
BUX_LOG_RETURNS does not Granger Cause BET_LOG_RETURNS	4478	0.87271	0.45440
BET_LOG_RETURNS does not Granger Cause BUX_LOG_RETURNS		4.43097	0.00408
WIG_20_LOG_RETURNS does not Granger Cause BET_LOG_RETURNS	4478	0.09808	0.96111
BET_LOG_RETURNS does not Granger Cause WIG_20_LOG_RETURNS		0.94982	0.41552
BUX_LOG_RETURNS does not Granger Cause BSE_SENSEX_LOG_RETURNS	4478	2.63009	0.04847
BSE_SENSEX_LOG_RETURNS does not Granger Cause BUX_LOG_RETURNS		0.88113	0.45002
WIG_20_LOG_RETURNS does not Granger Cause BSE_SENSEX_LOG_RETURNS	4478	1.41259	0.23706
BSE_SENSEX_LOG_RETURNS does not Granger Cause WIG_20_LOG_RETURNS		0.78400	0.50270
WIG_20_LOG_RETURNS does not Granger Cause BUX_LOG_RETURNS	4478	1.91021	0.12564
BUX_LOG_RETURNS does not Granger Cause WIG_20_LOG_RETURNS		3.45349	0.01582

Source: Own computations based on selected financial data series

Exchange and Budapest Stock Exchange. According to Tripathi and Shruti (2012), the empirical results based on Granger causality test results revealed unidirectional relationship of precedence in most cases, i.e. the Indian stock market was found to be positively and significantly correlated with all the advanced emerging markets for total time period (from 1 January 1992 to 31 December 2009). Patel (2016) suggested that RTS (Russia) has dependency on the FTSE-100 (UK) and Hangseng (China), while RTS depend on FTSE 100, and meanwhile FTSE 100 is affected by BVSP, MXX and NASDAQ, whereas Hangseng is affected by BSE, BVSP, FTSE 100, MXX and NASDAQ, but concurrently Granger causality test indicates that the BSE is Granger caused by BVSP, FTSE 100, MXX, NASDAQ and the RTS stock market.

REFERENCES

Barberis, N., & Thaler, R. (2003). A survey of behavioral finance. In *Handbook of the Economics of Finance*. Elsevier.

Birau, F. R. (2012). *Emerging capital market efficiency: a comparative analysis of weak-form efficiency in Romania and Hungary in the context of the global financial crisis*. AI & SOCIETY Journal of Knowledge, Culture and Communication.

Chen, S. W., & Chen, T. C. (2012). Untangling the non-linear causal nexus between exchange rates and stock prices: New evidence from the OECD countries. *Journal of Economic Studies*, *39*(2), 231–259. doi:10.1108/01443581211222671

Fama, E. (1965). Random Walks in Stock Market Prices. *Financial Analysts Journal*, *21*(5), 55–59. doi:10.2469/faj.v21.n5.55

Fama, E. (1970). Efficient Capital Markets: A review of theory and empirical work. *The Journal of Finance*, *25*(2), 383–417. doi:10.2307/2325486

Fama, E. (1998). Market efficiency, long-term returns, and behavioral finance. *Journal of Financial Economics*, *49*, 283–306. doi:10.1016/S0304-405X(98)00026-9

Grambovas, C. A. (2003). Exchange Rate Volatility and Equity Markets: Evidence from the Czech Republic, Greece, and Hungary. *Eastern European Economics*, *41*(5), 24-48. Retrieved from https://www.jstor.org/stable/438035

Korajczyk, R. (1995). A Measure of Stock Market Integration for Developed and Emerging Markets. The World Bank. doi:10.1596/1813-9450-1482

Mandelbrot, B. (2008). How Fractals Can Explain What's Wrong with Wall Street. The geometry that describes the shape of coastlines and the patterns of galaxies also elucidates how capital prices soar and plummet. *Scientific American*.

Palamalai, S., Kalaivani, M., & Devakumar, C. (2013). Stock Market Linkages in Emerging Asia-Pacific Markets. doi:10.1177/2158244013514060

Patel, R. (2016). An Empirical Study of Co-movement in Selected Stock Exchanges. *Asia-Pacific Journal of Management Research and Innovation*, *12*(1), 23–30. doi:10.1177/2319510X16647293

Peters, E. (1994). *Fractal Market Analysis: Applying Chaos Theory to Investment and Economics*. New York: John Wiley & Sons.

Ross, S. (1987). The Interrelations of Finance and Economics: Theoretical Perspectives. *The American Economic Review*, *77*(2), 29–34.

Scutaru, C., & Stanica, C. (2005). *Determinarea output-gap şi a dinamicii şocurilor inflaţioniste*. Institute for Economic Forecasting.

Sharpe, W., & Alexander, G. (1990). Investments (4th ed.). Englewood Cliffs, NJ: Prentice Hall.

Singh, S., & Sharma, G. D. (2012) Inter-linkages between stock exchanges: A study of BRIC nations, *International Journal of Marketing, Financial Services & Management Research*, *1*(3). Retrieved from http://indianresearchjournals.com/pdf/IJMFSMR/2012/March/1.pdf

Spulbar, C., & Birau, R. (2018). Testing weak-form efficiency and long-term causality of the R.I.P.H emerging capital markets. *International Journal of Business Quantitative Economics and Applied Management Research*, *5*(2), 1–19.

Tripathi, V., & Shruti, S. (2012). Inter Linkages of Indian Stock Market with Advanced Emerging Markets. *Asia-Pacific Finance and Accounting Review*, *1*(1), 34–51.

ENDNOTE

1 A Black Swan event is extremely rare, unpredictable, unexpected, highly improbable but generates catastrophic effects. The appearance of extreme events can generate major financial losses but it can also lead to abnormal stock market returns.

Chapter 9
Modeling and Estimating Long-Term Volatility of Stock Markets in Romania, Poland, Greece, and USA

ABSTRACT

The main purpose of this chapter is to examine long-term volatility of stock markets in Romania, Poland, Greece, and USA using asymmetric GARCH class models. The selected financial databases include daily log-returns of sample stock market major indices during the period from January 2000 until January 2014. The empirical results provide an additional contribution to existing literature regarding volatility estimations and international portfolio investment strategies. Moreover, this book chapter provides a useful empirical approach for a better understanding of volatility behavioral patterns, similar reaction to external shocks, international contagion, the impact of new information on the market and risk management optimal strategies, investor risk aversion and international portfolio diversification benefits.

DOI: 10.4018/978-1-5225-9269-3.ch009

INTRODUCTION

The main aim of this subchapter is to investigate long-term volatility of stock markets in Romania, Poland, Greece and USA stock markets using asymmetric GARCH class models. According to Birau, Siminica and Trivedi (2014), in recent past, international stock markets have become connected among each other in terms of financial liberalization and globalization. Consequently, international dynamic linkages between emerging and developed stock markets emphasize the global impact of causal transmission patterns due to financial shocks propagation. The empirical framework provides additional evidence regarding volatility patterns, similar reaction to external shocks, international contagion, the impact of new information on the market and risk management optimal strategies, investor risk aversion and international portfolio diversification benefits.

Further analysis suggests that volatility does not diverge to infinity and seems to react significantly different considering the case of high positive or high negative stock returns. Moreover, this research paper attempts to provide a better understanding of the relationship between the R.P.G.U stock markets in order to facilitate global diversification investing perspective for international investors. The sample financial data series are based on daily returns of selected stock markets major indices during the period from January 2000 until January 2014.

Moreover, the role of this subchapter is to emphasize that stock market volatility estimation is a topic of great interest and a major challenge not only for investors and academics, but also reach global perspectives in terms of modern finance. Globalization, financial liberalization, information technology, deregulation processes, the rise in trading volume of securities, financial penetration border investment policy harmonization led to intensification of integration between developed and emerging stock markets in different economies worldwide. Stock price movements exhibit certain stylized facts such as the following: volatility clustering (Mandelbrot, 1963), financial leverage effects (Black, 1976), heavy tailed empirical distribution, asymmetric volatility effects, unconditional time-varying moments, conditional heteroskedasticity, leptokurtosis and other deviations from normality.

R.P.G.U stands as the acronym for Romania, Poland, Greece and USA. This selection is based on economic, historical, political, social, ethnical, demographic and cultural criteria. According to the most recent official report of FTSE Country Classification issued on September 2013 the main criteria for country classification includes the following subcategories: developed, advanced emerging, secondary emerging and frontier. The main category of developed countries includes among others USA. Romania is included in the frontier market category, while Greece is on the watch list for possible demotion from developed to advanced emerging market. On the other hand, Poland is included in the category of advanced emerging countries. R.P.G.U stock markets represent a rather atypical and complex conglomerate, but financial benefits provided by international portfolio diversification are very attractive especially in terms of globalization.

APPROACHES TO LITERATURE

Financial literature on capital market volatility is extremely vast. The empirical results of each research have provided certain directions for investors, decision makers and financial researchers. As additional empirical contribution, each research study regarding this issue gives equal chance to learn and understand the unforeseeable behavior of stock markets. According to Engle (1982) traditional econometric models assume a constant one-period forecast variance and therefore in order to generalize this implausible assumption, it was implemented a new class of stochastic processes called autoregressive conditional heteroscedastic (ARCH) processes.

Bollerslev (1986) has generalized ARCH model by including lagged valued of the conditional variance. The GARCH models are much more permissive considering a wider range of behavior patterns for more persistent volatility. The most general form of the model is GARCH (1, 1) where GARCH stands for Generalized Autoregressive Conditional Heteroscedasticity. Moreover, a GARCH model or basically or Generalized ARCH model represents an extension of the ARCH model which otherwise is very similar to an ARMA model. According to Brooks (1996) such a generalization of the ARCH model, i.e. the GARCH model can be viewed as an infinite order ARCH model. Moreover, Brooks (1996) suggested that it is highly unlikely that a GARCH model of order greater than one in the autoregressive and moving average components would be required, since by definition, a GARCH (1,1) model implies an infinitely long memory with respect to past innovations.

Schwert (1989) investigated the relation of stock volatility with real and nominal macroeconomic volatility, economic activity, financial leverage, and stock trading activity using monthly data during the sample from 1857 to 1987. Antoniou and Holmes (1995) have estimated intraday relationship between returns and volatility returns. Their study has covered Indian stock index by using Bi-Variate GARCH models to estimate volatility. They conclude that there is strong volatility impact in spot and future stock returns. On the other hand, Choudhry (1996) have conducted a research study on volatility on the basis of risk premia and persistence of volatility in six emerging stock markets AMIMTZ, Argentina, Greece, India, Mexico, Thailand and Zimbabwe using monthly data series between January of 1976 and August of 1994. The empirical analysis was based on GARCH in the mean model or GARCH-M and the final results suggested changes in the ARCH parameter, risk premia and persistence of volatility before and after the 1987 financial crash.

Kim and Singal (1997) studied the behavior of stock prices in order to examine potential benefits of opening stock markets to foreign investors. The authors concluded that stock returns increase immediately after market opening without a concomitant increase in volatility. The result reveals that there is no systematic effect of liberalization on stock market volatility. Moreover, Gregory and Michael (1996) investigated the manner in which volatility of S&P 500 index futures affects the S&P 500 index volatility given that heteroscedasticity implies non constant volatility. In this research paper volatility was estimated using E-GARCH model and the authors concluded that the impact of bad news increases the volatility significantly more than the good news considering that the asymmetry is much higher on futures markets. Mecagni and Sourial (1999) conducted efficiency test and volatility effects on Egyptian stock market by using GARCH (P, Q) model. They concluded that the ESE stock returns are characterized by severe deviations from efficient market hypothesis, volatility clustering and positive linkage between risk and stock asset returns. Furthermore, Ezzat (2012) expand the research study using GARCH, EGARCH and TGARCH in order to examine the temporal volatility dynamics of each specific industry based on Egyptian Exchange sector indices. The author concludes the existence of volatility clustering, long memory volatility and the leverage effect.

Engle and Rangel (2004) have introduced a new model to measure unconditional volatility namely Spline-GARCH. They have implemented model to equity markets of 50 countries by using 50 years of daily indices. The result has revealed that macroeconomic determinants of unconditional volatility. They also conclude that volatility is higher for emerging stock markets and for markets which has small number of listing but exist in large economies.

Rao, Kanagaraj and Tripathy (2008) have focused on modeling asymmetric volatility on Indian stock market. They have used two different nonlinear asymmetric models, i.e. EGARCH and TGARCH models in order to estimate volatility of BSE 500 stock returns. The authors revealed that series exhibit leverage effect and also other stylized facts such as volatility clustering and leptokurtosis. Emenike (2010) investigated the behavior of stock return volatility of the Nigerian Stock Exchange returns using GARCH (1,1) and the GJR-GARCH (1,1) models considering the assumption of Generalized Error Distribution (GED). Final results indicate the existence of volatility clustering, leverage effects and leptokurtic returns distribution.

Angabini and Wasiuzzaman (2011) studied the change in volatility of the Malaysian stock market, in terms of the global financial crisis using both symmetric and asymmetric Generalized Autoregressive conditional heteroscedasticity (GARCH) models. The final conclusions of the research study highlight that AR (4) is the most suitable in modelling the conditional mean and GARCH (1, 1), EGARCH (1, 1), GJR-GARCH (1, 1) for conditional variance. The authors have concluded that there was a significant increase in volatility and leverage effect with just a minor decrease in persistency due to the global financial crisis effects.

Ahmed and Zakaria (2011) developed a research study using Generalized Autoregressive Conditional Heteroscedastic models in order to estimate volatility, i.e. conditional variance in the daily stock returns of the Khartoum Stock Exchange (KSE) of Sudan, over the sample time period from January 2006 to November 2010. The empirical analysis results and revealed the fact that the conditional variance process is highly persistent and even more than that it was identified the existence of risk premium for the selected stock market. The authors confirm the accuracy of asymmetric models based on the presence of leverage effect and high volatility.

Goudarzi and Ramanarayanan, (2011) investigated the impact of good and bad news effects on volatility in the Indian stock markets using asymmetric ARCH models, i.e. EGARCH and TGARCH models during the recent global financial crisis. The final conclusions suggested that the impact of bad news (innovations) in the Indian stock market increases volatility more than good news due to asymmetric volatility and leverage effect. The empirical analysis investigated the behavior of both emerging (Poland, Romania, Brazil, Russia, India, China – BRIC countries) and developed stock markets (Japan, U.K). This research studies provide additional empirical evidence regarding investment opportunities and risk management based on international portfolio diversification.

The phenomenon of international financial contagion is very intense in terms of globalization. According to Siminică and Birau (2014), in recent past, the global phenomenon of increasing co-integration, co-movement and financial contagion between developed and emerging stock markets have significantly influenced foreign investment behavior. Trivedi (2014) has developed a research study on modeling volatility using symmetric and asymmetric models, i.e. GARCH (1, 1), Exponential GARCH and GJR-GARCH based on the case study of Athex Composite Index stock exchange (Greece) during the sample period from January 2000 to January 2014. The empirical results revealed that conditional variances are unstable in Athex Composite Index stock return series. Moreover, Trivedi and Birau (2014) applied asymmetric GARCH models on developed capital markets, such as French stock exchange. The authors employed asymmetric GARCH models such as Exponential GARCH a (EGARCH) and GJR GARCH models and the final empirical results highlighted the presence of leverage effect in financial series stock returns.

DATA AND APPLIED METHODOLOGY

According to Birau, Siminica and Trivedi (2014) in this research study it was implemented Generalized autoregressive conditional heteroskedasticity model, well known as GARCH model which proved to be most used and successful to estimate volatility. This paper focuses on estimating volatility of emerging markets of Romania and Polonia while markets of Greece and USA and developed markets. The complexity of the econometric analysis derives from the originality of the financial series selection.

In other words, the empirical analysis involves focusing on the major stock indices in each selected stock market i.e. BET-C Index (Romania), WIG 20 Index (Poland), Athex Composite Index Composite Index (Greece) and DJIA Index (USA). Data time lag is from first transaction day of January 2000 to January 2014. We use GARCH (1, 1) model to estimating emerging stock market volatility by Bollerslev and Taylor (1986). We employ GARCH model with lag (1) and Order (1) under normal distribution errors. We provide following detail description about GARCH (1, 1) model and how it used.

The sample data series consists of the daily closing prices for each sample selected stock index during the period between January 2000 and January 2014 with the exception of legal holidays or other events when stock markets haven't performed transactions. The continuously-compounded daily returns are calculated using the log-difference of the closing prices of stock markets selected indices, i.e. BET-C Index (Romania), WIG 20 Index (Poland), Athex Composite Index Composite Index (Greece) and DJIA Index (USA) as follows:

$$R_t = \ln\left(\frac{P_t}{P_{t-1}}\right) = \ln(P_t) - \ln(P_{t-1})$$

where R_t represents daily returns of indices and P_t stands for daily closing prices of indices. GARCH (1, 1) model was developed by Bollerslev and Taylor (1986). This model allows conditional variance of all variables to be dependent upon previous legs and it reflects on entire series. However, the first leg of squared residual will be from mean equation and this presents idea about volatility from the previous time periods. General most used model for formulate GARCH (1, 1) is based on the following mathematical expression:

$$h_t = \omega + \alpha_1 u_{t-1}^{\ 2} + \beta_1\, h_{t-1}$$

In order to to apply the model it is important to follow the hypothesis of covariance stationary as unconditional variance and if it is exist to use it processed by the following equations:

$$\sigma^2 = \mathrm{Var}(u_t) = E(u_t^2) = E(\omega + \alpha_1 u_{t-1}^{\ 2} + \beta_1\, h_{t-1})$$

$$= \omega + \alpha_1\, E(u_{t-1}^{\ 2}) + \beta\, E(h_{t-1}) = \omega + \alpha_1\, \sigma^2 + \beta_1 \sigma^2$$

And it executes the following expression:

$$\sigma^2 = \omega\alpha\beta$$

Furthermore, it is applied GARCH (1, 1) model conditional variance equation $\mathrm{Var}(u_t \mid h_{t-1}) = E(u_t^2 \mid h_{t-1}) = h_{t,}$ which can be expressed in simplified form as: $h_t = \omega + \alpha_1 u_{t-1}^{\ 2} + \beta_1\, h_{t-1}$.

If there is presence of unconditional variance, it can be case where we employ the process to find $\alpha_1 + \beta_1 < 1$ and for converting it into generates positive result, we require that $\alpha_0 > 0$. Positive result will indicate good news (inovation) for stock market. For the constant, conditional mean we followed $E(y_t|\Omega_{t-1})$, where $E= c + \phi\, y_{t-1} + 0$, and y_{t-1} is included in $|\Omega_{t-1.}$ We would be able to conclude our result by $h_t = \omega + \alpha_1 u_{t-1}^2 + \beta_1 h_{t-1.}$ Where, $\alpha_1 u_{t-1}^2$ represents ARCH component and $\beta_1 h_{t-1}$ constitutes the GARCH component. Moreover, the basic formulation of GARCH (1,1) is based on $h_t = \omega + \alpha_1 u_{t-1}^2 + \beta_1 h_{t-1.}$

EMPIRICAL ANALYSIS

An important aspect of empirical analysis is the wide difference between min index and max index which has produced high standard deviation in regards of number of observation (3530). Nevertheless, the actual difference between Min and Max reveals high degree of volatility in R.P.G.U stock markets for open ended stocks. Log transformation has reduced degree with unchanged results. In following Table 1 we can see that the mean is close to zero and positive for time series returns. It also indicates the presence of negative Skewness, [for all selected stock indices, i.e. BET-C Index (Romania), WIG 20 Index (Poland), Athex Composite Index Composite Index (Greece) and DJIA Index (USA)] which represents an asymmetric tail which exceeds towards negative values rather than positive. This negative tail also indicates that all indices are non-symmetric returns and are leptokurtic as well since its large kurtosis (see Table 1).

The results included in the previous table indicate basic statistics for proxy financial series of sample emerging and developed stock markets. Data indicates large difference between Min to Max which exceeds more than 5 times for all emerging markets. Furthermore, statistics represents high degree

Table 1. Descriptive statistics

Variance	Romania - BET-C index	Poland WIG 20 index	Greece – Athex Composite index	USA - DJIA index
Basic Statistics				
Mean	0.00052	6.80551e-005	0.00046	0.00010
Median	0.000666	0.0002595	0.00000	0.00040
Min	-0.121184	-0.0844276	-0.13431	-0.08200
Max	0.108906	0.0815484	0.10214	0.10508
Std.Dev	0.0150688	0.0160881	0.01788	0.01224
Skewness	-0.632785	-0.134681	-0.02674	-0.05239
Kurtosis	8.25079	2.23999	4.36376	7.77982
Unit Root Test (tested at 1%, 5% and 10%), data significant at all levels using 6 lags.				

Source: Author's own computations based on selected financial data series

of standard deviation for the stock market of Greece followed by Poland and Romania. However, lowest degree of standard deviation it characterizes the developed stock market of USA. These large differences represent the degree of volatility in developed and emerging markets. That is also an opportunity for investors and decision makers. Nevertheless, Standard deviation presents degree of risks which found higher in Athex Composite Index, WIG 20 index and BET-C index (see Table 1).

The fundamental characteristics of selected indices are represented by the following issues: Jarque-Bera test's statistic which allows to eliminate the normality of distribution hypothesis, parameter of asymmetry distribution or Skewness and Kurtosis parameter which measures the peakedness or flatness of the distribution (leptokurtic distribution). Skewness provides evidence of high Kurtosis, and force indices towards more negative trend instead of positive as indicated by its tail. However, it also reveals that stock markets fall down more frequently than ups, but investments at such time creates volatility of stock returns. This also remarks that upper side of index is not stronger than lower side and otherwise. We tested long tail impact on graphs which is not furnished in this paper but available on request. Furthermore, Table 1 indicates that Kurtosis exceeds normal value of 3 and thus it creates fat tails for proxy financial markets log returns. The last-mentioned line in Table 1 provides us final tested result of Augment Dickey-Fuller test (ADF test) which represents unit root problems under hypothesis Ho = p_0 and p_1.

Generally, all-time series has unit root problems and it must be filtered and allowed for ARCH processes. For this purpose we have allowed trend for all indices by adding intercept to the model y_t (or Δy_t) on 1, y_{t-1}, $\Delta y_{t-1}, \ldots, \Delta y_{t-p+1}$, computing the t-statistic which can resulted in $\tau_t = \frac{\hat{\rho}-1}{se(\hat{\rho})}$ this process comparing its value to percentiles of DF τ_μ distribution. It has produced higher negative value than its critical value at 1%, 5% and 10% level which allows series for ARCH and proves no unit root problems. This is well enough to process for GARCH (1, 1) model to estimate volatility of emerging and developed markets (see Table 2).

The detailed observations for Figure 1 provide significant information regarding the relevance of stock market financial transmission patterns for BET-C Index, WIG 20 Index and DJIA Index. Stock market movements for Athex Composite Index have been identified and perceived to be much different and independent compared to behavior of other develop and emerging markets. Second, Romanian and Poland stock markets were on an upward

Figure 1. The trend of R.P.G.U stock indices - individual graphics
Source: Author's own computations based on selected financial data series

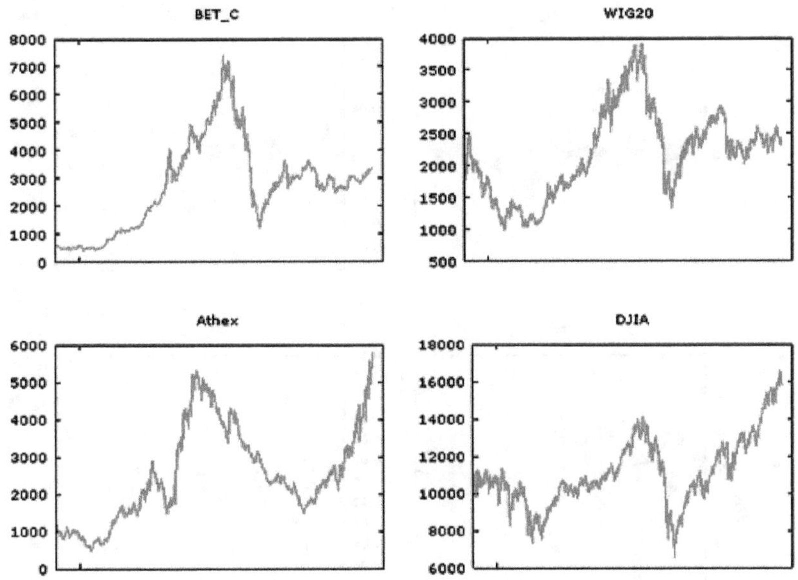

trend before the dramatic commencement of the global financial crisis and yet to reach that level again. The positioning for developed market is improvised and seemed to be recovered from the negative impact of the global financial crisis and about to make their new high picks. These indices graph also represents index level at beginning and ups and down during study periods.

It requires stationary data series to employ GARCH (1, 1) model and hence the data converted to logs and tested stationary with ADF test. The final outcome of ADF test result is mentioned (see Table 1). All financial series represents stationary data series (see Figure 2) and financial shocks clearly visible with long scratches. The focused observation on stationary graph represents volatility effects on all financial markets. We can see that financial behaviors of all four study markets are individual and independent. The comparative study of both emerging market, Romanian market (BET-C) and Poland market (WIG20) represents huge differences for volatility shocks. WIG20 market has more abnormal shocks compared to BET-C. The least number of shocks is observed in DJIA, USA market. It is surprising to see market moments of Greece with proxy Athex Composite Index financial market. International financial crisis is not visible in the series returns. An independent study on Athex Composite Index market will bring more interesting results.

Figure 2. Log returns series of R.P.G.U stock indices - individual graphics
Source: Author's own computations based on selected financial data series

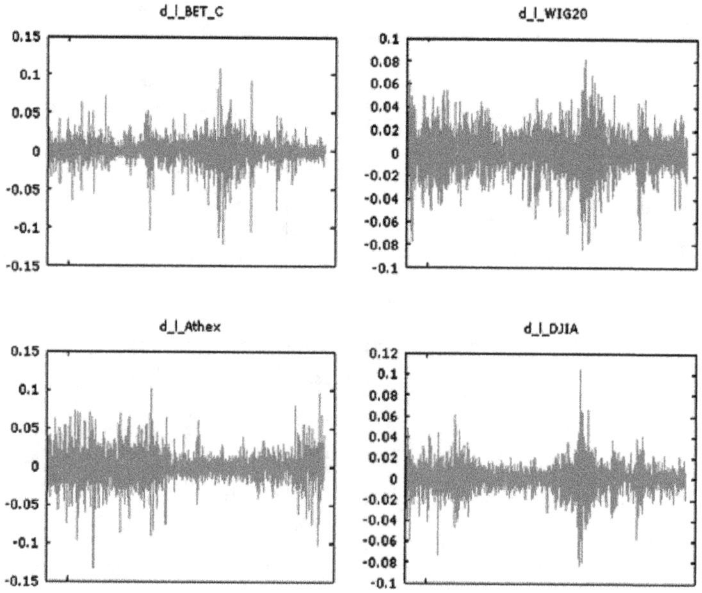

The empirical analysis was based on large financial data series with 3530 observations for all selected stock markets. The above figure represents entire log series return of the period and thus it seems not very easy for all readers, Long sketches represents degree of ups and down volatility shocks. The above series also represents stationarity of data to employ econometric model. The overall correspondence of all data series suggests that all financial markets have larger number of negative shocks than positive shocks. Romanian stock market index BET-C, Athex Composite Index of Greece and WIG 20 index of Poland stock market have provided higher number of volatility shocks compared to USA stock market index - DJIA. In GARCH outcome, conditional variance should not exceed 1, positively and thus $\alpha_1 + \beta_1 < 1$ proved successfully.

For Romania – BET-C index:

$$= 0.204804\ (\alpha_1 u_{t-1}^2) + 0.788196\ (h_{t-1}) = 0.993000 < 1$$

For Poland – WIG 20 index:

$$= 0.0581371\ (\alpha_1 u_{t-1}^2) + 0.933892\ (h_{t-1}) = 0.9920291 < 1$$

For Greece - AthexComposite Index:

$= 0.0845264\ (\alpha_1 u_{t-1}^2) + 0.915284\ (h_{t-1})\ 0.999810 < 1$

For USA – DJIA index:

$= 0.0928464\ (\alpha_1 u_{t-1}^2) + 0.896330\ (h_{t-1}) = 0.9891764 < 1$

The previous volatility estimation suggests that Athex Composite Index Greece market had the highest total among other study markets. That indicates highest volatility ratio and that represents a greater number of ups and downs. It is important to take note that Greece stock market is developed market and we can consider above case as rare where such volatility proved in developed financial markets. The Romanian stock market index BET-C represents the second rank for high ups and down and may be that can be priors first an emerging market investment option. Further that is followed by WIG 20 index of Poland stock market and lastly DJIA index which is representative for USA stock market.

DJIA index behavior indicates least volatility, or stable investment with lowest degree of standard deviation. This would be best investment option for long term investors, particularly for safe investment. Poland stock market (WIG 20 index) is the second-best alternative option to invest in terms of selected emerging stock markets. Nevertheless, the GARCH (1, 1) model estimated Romania stock market (BET-C index) as the first (frontier) stock market investment option, but overall with consideration of basic statistics with GARCH results, that is headed by WIG 20 index. The skewness is higher in Romanian market compared to Poland market. Thus, we rank WIG 20 index as first option to invest in emerging markets.

GARCH (1, 1) model is combination of ARCH (1) and GARCH (1) term which is denoted by $\alpha_1 + \beta_1$ which shows positively results for study markets. The final for all financial markets is sum up here:

1. Romania - BET-C index: $\alpha_1 + \beta_1 = 0.993000$
2. Poland WIG 20 index: $\alpha_1 + \beta_1 = 0.9920291$
3. Greece - Athex Composite Index: $\alpha_1 + \beta_1 = 0.999810$
4. USA - DJIA index: $\alpha_1 + \beta_1 = 0.9891764$.

All respective results represent value less than 1, it proves that GARCH (1, 1) model fitted to all financial data series perfectly. Romanian market (BET-C index) has proved with highest volatility compared with other emerging market but with high degree of skewness. Thus, that rank allotted to Poland market (WIG20) for an investment option among study of emerging markets. Greece stock market which is one of (still) developed market in study, has come up with very interesting outcomes. We can see highest total near to 1, that generally happens with emerging markets (see above equations). USA market (DJIA index) has proved as stable and safe investment options among developed market. We have represented entire outcomes of GARCH (1, 1) which represents constants, omega, alpha and beta. These outcomes represented in Table 2 mentioned below. Investors and readers can go for more predictions and estimations using following calculated data.

The previous GARCH (1, 1) model (see Table 2) estimation value of mean covariance π provides all positive results for emerging and developed market indices. It is outcome of processed data that is called stationary data. First, we converted original data series into logs, and considered first difference to make data stationary, justified with ADF test. Table 2 suggests that there are larger effects of negative shocks on listed stocks among study markets.

Table 2. The GARCH (1, 1) model estimations

Variable		Coefficient	p-value
Romania – BET-C index	π	0.000898	0.0000
	ω	5.55174e-06	0.027
	α	0.204804	0.0000
	β	0.788196	0.0000
Poland – WIG 20 index	π	0.000428602	0.049
	ω	1.96150e-06	0.0000
	α	0.0588371	0.0000
	β	0.933892	0.0000
Greece - Athex Composite Index	π	0.000422534	0.0777*
	ω	1.66174e-06	0.0489
	α	0.0845264	0.0000
	β	0.915284	0.0000
USA – DJIA index	π	0.000505877	0.0000
	ω	1.51072e-06	0.0000
	α	0.0928464	0.0000
	β	0.896330	0.0000

Source: Author's own computations based on selected financial data series

Hence it was necessary to convert data into logs to make data stationary, original data provided for all years in Figure 1. The research study suggests that volatility in emerging markets is higher than in the case of selected developed stock markets. We found that Athex Composite Index of Greece developed stock market emphasizes a higher volatility ratio than selected indices of emerging markets.

CONCLUSION

The major objective of this research paper is to investigate long-term volatility of R.P.G.U (Romania, Poland, Greece and USA) stock markets using asymmetric GARCH class models. The final conclusions can be divided into two subcategories, i.e. those regarding developed stock markets (Greece and USA) and others who are considering emerging stock markets (Romania and Poland). First of all, the empirical analysis revealed a very interesting volatility behaviors based on the movements of Athex Composite Index (Greece) that has proved to attract additional investor interest considering its independent dynamics. It also has lower kurtosis than other developed market. This can be perceived as a great option for international investors strategies by considering the degree of standard deviations.

On the other hand, DJIA index (USA) proved to be the most safe and effective investment option primarily for investors who believe in low risk operandi. Nevertheless, DJIA index is strong while considering the movements of developed stock markets and generated returns for investors. Lower degree of standard deviations and skewness are indicators of good stock returns in last five years. An independent study can bring out degree of best ever returns from investment in developed financial market and may be than might be higher than stock returns exhibited by emerging markets.

Secondly, the empirical results based on GARCH (1, 1) model suggested that Romanian stock market (BET-C index) can generate early investment returns for investors compared to Poland stock market (WIG 20 index). It has higher degree of market volatility, but standard statistics suggests higher degree of skewness and kurtosis compared to other emerging market. That can be a plus for Poland stock market where skewness and kurtosis is lower than Romanian market. Investors are advised to consider the basic statistics with GARCH (1, 1) volatility estimations.

REFERENCES

Ahmed, A. E. M., & Zakaria, S. (2011). Modeling stock market volatility using GARCH models evidence from Sudan. *International Journal of Business and Social Science*, *2*(23), 114–128.

Angabini, A., & Wasiuzzaman, S. (2011). GARCH Models and the Financial Crisis-A Study of the Malaysian Stock Market. *International Journal of Applied Economics and Finance*, *5*(3), 226–236. doi:10.3923/ijaef.2011.226.236

Antoniou, A., & Holmes, P. (1995). Futures Trading, Information and Spot Price Volatility: Evidence For the FTSE 100 Stock Index and Futures Contract Using GARCH. *Journal of Banking & Finance*, *19*(1), 117–129. doi:10.1016/0378-4266(94)00059-C

Awartani, B. M. A., & Corradi, V. (2005). Predicting the volatility of the S&P-500 stock index via GARCH models: The role of asymmetries. *International Journal of Forecasting*, *21*(1), 167–183. doi:10.1016/j.ijforecast.2004.08.003

Barucci, E., & Reno, R. (2002). On measuring volatility and the GARCH forecasting performance. *Journal of International Financial Markets, Institutions and Money*, *12*(3), 183–200. doi:10.1016/S1042-4431(02)00002-1

Birau, R., Siminica, M., & Trivedi, J. (2014). Modeling and Estimating Long-Term Volatility of R.P.G.U Stock Markets. In Recent Advances in Energy, Environment and Financial Planning (pp. 272-280).

Birau, R., & Trivedi, J. (2013a). Investigating Long-Term Volatility of Warsaw Stock Exchange Based on Garch Family Models. *International Journal of Scientific Research*, *2*(9), 239–241.

Birau, R. & Trivedi, J. (2013b). Modeling Juri Stock Market Volatility: An Asymmetric Garch Models Approach. *PARIPEX - Indian Journal of Research*, 2(9), 44-46.

Birau, R., & Trivedi, J. (2013c). Estimating Emerging Stock Market Volatility Using Garch Family Models. *Indian Journal of Applied Research*, *3*(9), 331–333.

Birau, R., & Trivedi, J. (2013d). Modeling return volatility of BRIC emerging stock markets using GARCH family models. *Indian Journal of Applied Research*, *3*(11), 119–121.

Black, F. (1976). Studies of stock market volatility changes. In *Proceedings of the American Statistical Association, Business and Economic Statistics Section* (pp. 177-181).

Bollerslev, T. (1986). Generalized autoregressive conditional heteroskedasticity. *Journal of Economics*, *31*(3), 307–327. doi:10.1016/0304-4076(86)90063-1

Brailsford, T. J., & Faff, R. W. (1996). An evaluation of volatility forecasting techniques. *Journal of Banking & Finance*, *20*(3), 419–438. doi:10.1016/0378-4266(95)00015-1

Brooks, C. (1996). Testing for Non-Linearity in Daily Sterling Exchange Rates. *Applied Financial Economics*, *6*(4), 307–317. doi:10.1080/096031096334105

Choudhry, T. (1996). Stock Market Volatility and the Crash of 1987: Evidence from Six Emerging Markets. *Journal of International Money and Finance*, *15*(6), 969–981. doi:10.1016/S0261-5606(96)00036-8

Dickey, D. A., & Fuller, W. A. (1979). Distribution of the estimators for autoregressive time series with a unit root. *Journal of the American Statistical Association*, *74*, 427–431.

Emenike, K. O. (2010). Modelling Stock Returns Volatility In Nigeria Using GARCH Models. In *Proceeding of International Conference on Management and Enterprise Development*, University of Port Harcourt, Nigeria (pp. 5-11).

Engle, R. F. (1982). Autoregressive Conditional Heteroscedasticity with Estimates of the Variance of UK Inflation. *Econometrica*, *50*(4), 987–1008. doi:10.2307/1912773

Engle, R. F., & Rangel, J. G. (2004). The Sp-line GARCH Model for Unconditional Volatility and Its Global Macro-Economic Causes. *Review of Financial Studies*, *21*(3), 1187–1222. doi:10.1093/rfs/hhn004

Ezzat, H. (2012). The Application of GARCH Methods in Modeling Volatility Using Sector Indices from the Egyptian Exchange, *Journal of Money. Investment and Banking*, *27*, 68–85.

Goudarzi, H., & Ramanarayanan, C. S. (2011). Modeling Asymmetric volatility in the Indian stock market. *International Journal of Business and Management*, *6*(3), 221–231. doi:10.5539/ijbm.v6n3p221

Gregory, K., & Michael, T. (1996). Temporal Relationships and Dynamic Interactions between Spot and Futures Markets. *Journal of Futures Markets*, *16*(1), 55–69. doi:10.1002/(SICI)1096-9934(199602)16:1<55::AID-FUT3>3.0.CO;2-G

Kim, E.H. & Singal, V. (1997). Opening up of Stock Markets: Lessons from Emerging Economies, *The Journal of Business, 73*(1), 25-66.

Mandelbrot, B. (1963). The variation of certain speculative prices. *The Journal of Business*, *36*(4), 394–419. doi:10.1086/294632

Mecagni, M., & Sourial, M. S. (1999). The Egyptian stock market: Efficiency tests and volatility effects. International Monetary Fund.

Rao, R., & Kanagaraj, S. V. A. (2008). Tripathy, N., Does Individual Stock Futures Affect Stock Market Volatility in India? *Journal of the Indian Institute of Economics*, *50*(1), 125–135.

Schwert, G. W. (1989). Why Does Stock Market Volatility Change Over Time? *The Journal of Finance*, *44*(5), 1115–1153. doi:10.1111/j.1540-6261.1989.tb02647.x

Siminică, M., & Birau, R. (2014). Investigating International Causal Linkages Between Latin European Stock Markets In Terms Of Global Financial Crisis: A Case Study For Romania, Spain And Italy, *International Journal of Business Quantitative Economics and Applied Management Research,* 1(1), 12-36.

Trivedi, J. (2014). Modeling volatility and financial market behavior using symmetric and asymmetric models: The case study of Athex Composite Index stock exchange, *International Journal of Business Quantitative Economics and Applied Management Research, 1*(1).

Trivedi, J., & Birau, G. (2014). Applying asymmetric GARCH models on developed capital markets: An empirical case study on French stock exchange. *International Journal of Business Quantitative Economics and Applied Management Research, 1*(1).

Chapter 10
Analyzing Long-Term Dynamic Causal Linkages and Financial Integration Between the Capital Markets in Romania and Hungary

ABSTRACT

This chapter aims to investigate long-term dynamic causal linkages between stock markets in Hungary and Romania in order to obtain additional benefits based on international portfolio diversification, especially in terms of globalization. Emerging stock markets are generally considered to be more attractive for both institutional and individual financial investors due to certain stylized facts. The volatility transmission patterns, financial contagion effects, international interdependence and long-run causal linkages between international stock markets highlight the importance of a functional and stable financial environment. Technically, the structure of this subchapter includes both theoretical developments and additional empirical results. Moreover, the empirical analysis provides a quantitative perspective on global interdependencies between Romania and Hungary.

DOI: 10.4018/978-1-5225-9269-3.ch010

INTRODUCTION

As an element of originality, this subchapter includes two distinct empirical analyzes, which is differentiated by both financial series as well as through selected stock market indices. According to Birau and Antonescu (2014), the econometric analysis is based on daily returns of selected stock markets major indices during the sample period between January 2000 and January 2014. The financial econometrics framework includes descriptive statistics, Unit Root Test, Augmented Dickey-Fuller stationary test, BDS test and Granger causality test. The final results of this empirical study are highly relevant in order to understand investment decision making process and stock market stability.

The bilateral relationship between Romania and Hungary has proved to be very complex and somewhat unstable based on the disputes concerning institutional, cultural and territorial autonomy. Romania's national minorities comprise a fairly heterogeneous structure, which have potentially significant direct impact on the economic and financial field. According to the National Institute of Statistics (INSSE) based on the final results of the Population and Housing Census conducted in 2011, the Hungarian minority of Romania is represented by a significant number of 1.259.914 people and consisting in a proportion of about 6,26148% of the total population (20.121.641). Moreover, ethnic Hungarians constitute the largest ethnic minority in Romania. Nevertheless, from peaceful coexistence to recurrent bilateral tensions is more than a political issue. One of the most significant aspect is the fact that the fundamental practice of bilateral agreements based on good relations between neighboring countries is considerable influencing the economic environment. Nevertheless, the foreign relations between Romania and Hungary have deep historical roots, with profound economic implications, especially in terms of globalization.

Romania and Hungary are two member states of the European Union but reveals different levels of socio-economic development. Hungary and Romania are neighbors and have a common history in some respects. On the other hand, Hungary joined the European Union (EU) in 2004 and Romania became a member in 2007. The Hungarian community in Romania is particularly significant in some counties in Transylvania such as Harghita and Covasna. Moreover, according to the official statistics of World Bank on Romania provided in April 2017, the share of Romanians at risk of poverty after social transfers increased from 22.9% in 2012 to 25.4% in 2015, while the share of the population at risk of poverty and social exclusion decreased from 43.2% in 2012 to 37.4% in 2015.

Certainly, Hungary has more attractive economic prospects. However, in recent years, political tensions and austerity measures have caused a negative influence in terms of investor confidence, especially in Romania. Consequently, the economic context is more favorable for Hungary considering a wide range of influential factors. In recent past, the Hungarian economy managed to achieve much higher levels of development even better than expected. The influence of the real economy is reflected in the field of financial investments. Furthermore, economic growth and financial stability are mutually reinforcing especially in terms of international integration.

According to FTSE Country Classifications, data provided on March 2017, Hungary is included in the category of advanced emerging markets, while Romania is included in the category of frontier markets. Moreover, the main categories provided by FTSE Country Classifications are the following: developed, advanced emerging, secondary emerging and frontier. Concretely, Bucharest Stock Exchange (Romania) is a frontier market and Budapest Stock Exchange is an advanced emerging market (Hungary). In recent decades, there has been an important structural reform of international stock markets based on cross-border transactions, exchange control, investment policy non-restrictions, derivatives, international portfolio diversification, liberalization of financial operations (Birau & Trivedi, 2013). Moreover, emerging capital markets are less efficient than the developed markets considering their long-term structural imbalances, periodic cycles of significant contractions and expansions, asymmetric volatility effects, informational frictions, along with severe functional disturbances.

LITERATURE REVIEW

According to Siminica and Birau (2014), the liberalization and integration process of financial markets emphasizes various opportunities based on reduction of capital transaction cost and foreign capital inflows. Furthermore, international investors are focused on the potential correlation among returns of different national stock markets in order to diversify the investment risk based on international diversification of portfolios. Moreover, the authors suggested that the multidimensional implications of financial integration generate the possibility of identifying investment strategies in order to optimize the structure of risk management.

Eun and Shim (1989) empirically analyzed the interdependence structure of major national stock markets. Moreover, the authors suggested that innovations in U.S. market are suddenly transmitted to other stock markets despite the fact that none of these markets can adequately justify its movements. They investigated the existence of international transmission of stock market movements among several mature markets, such as: Australia, Japan, Hong Kong, U.K, Switzerland, France, Germany, Canada and U.S.A. Moreover, Abimanyu et al. (2008) investigated the international linkages of the Indonesian capital market using cointegration tests to examine the long-run equilibrium relationship between the stock markets of Indonesia with China, France, Germany, Hong Kong, Japan, Korea, Malaysia, Netherlands, Philippine, Singapore, Thailand, Taiwan, the United Kingdom and the United States.

According to Birau (2014c) the investment process can be significantly affected by irrational decisions generated by emotional biases or cognitive deviations considering that financial investors have a certain limit regarding the processing and assimilating of new information as a maximum level (human emotions, psychological deviations and cognitive biases broadly affect the financial market behavior.).

Balios and Xanthakis (2003) investigated international interdependence and dynamic linkages between developed stock markets, namely U.K, Germany, France, Italy, Spain, U.S. and Japan. They concluded that U.S. stock market is the leading stock market in the world and U.K stock market is the leading stock market in Europe. On the other hand, Singh (2010) investigated Chinese and Indian stock market linkages with several developed stock markets, such as U.S., U.K., Japan and Hong Kong. The empirical results revealed that both Chinese and Indian market are correlated with all the selected developed markets based on the analysis of Granger causality. Pretorious (2002) suggested that it is very important for international investors to understand the forces behind the interdependence of emerging stock markets in order to be informed about the potential occurrence of systemic risks and their global implications.

Phylaktisa and Ravazzolob (2005) analyzed the stock market linkages in emerging markets considering the implications for international portfolio diversification over the period 1980–1998. The empirical results for the 1980s revealed that the relaxation of foreign ownership restrictions was not sufficient to attract foreign investors' attention and that other factors must have affected the portfolio diversification decision. On the other hand, the final empirical results of the 1990s suggested that the relaxation of the restrictions might have strengthened international market interrelations.

Khan (2011) investigated cointegration of international stock markets based on a complex perspective regarding diversification opportunities and suggested that an increasing number of investors are interested to invest in developing countries. Moreover, the author investigated the existence of cointegration between stock markets of US and 22 other major economies.

Birau and Trivedi (2013a) empirically analyzed the existence of cointegration and international linkage between Bucharest stock exchange and certain European developed stock markets, i.e. France, Germany and Greece. The empirical research covered the sample period from January 2003 until December 2012 which were divided into two sub-periods in order to examine both pre-crisis and post-crisis effects. Regarding the first period of analysis, i.e. January 2003 – December 2007, it appears that there is no particular causality between Greek and Romanian, German and Romanian, respectively French and Romanian stock markets. The second period of analysis, i.e. January 2008 – December 2012 suggested that Granger causality runs one way, from Greece to Romania, but not the other way and there is no particular causality between German and Romanian, respectively French and Romanian stock markets.

Birau (2014b) investigated the existence of dynamic causal linkages between international developed stock markets of Spain and Canada. According to the previous author, the empirical results of Granger causality tests among developed stock markets of Spain and Canada highlighted significant investment opportunities based on international portfolio diversification and risk management strategies. Granger causality runs simultaneously in both directions for Spain and Canada based on a feedback relationship.

Siminica and Birau (2014) investigated international causal linkages between Latin European stock markets in terms of global financial crisis based on a complex case study for Romania, Spain and Italy. The empirical analysis revealed that there is no particular causality between Italy and Spain, Romania and Italy and not even between Romania and Spain in the sample period, i.e. the period between January 2007 and April 2013.

APPLIED METHODOLOGY AND EMPIRICAL RESULTS

The continuously-compounded daily returns are calculated using the log-difference of stock markets selected indices as follows: $r_t = \ln\left(\frac{p_t}{p_{t-1}}\right) = \ln(p_t) - \ln(p_{t-1})$ where p is the daily closing price.

The applied financial econometrics research methodology includes in both cases: descriptive statistics, Unit Root Test, Augmented Dickey-Fuller stationary test, BDS test and Granger causality test.

According to Birau (2017), the influential factors are varied and highlight very important issues. In the following figure is provided a comparative analysis between Romania and Hungary based on GDP per capita, PPP (current international $) during 1990 – 2016 (see Figure 1).

Technically, official statistics suggest that Romania has one of the most significant poverty rates in the European Union considering that for the previous year 2016 the GDP in current US$ billion had the value 187.0 and the GDP per capita, i.e. the gross domestic product converted to international dollars using purchasing power parity rates, in current US$ had the value 9,528.

Moreover, in the following is provided a Comparative analysis between Romania and Hungary based on poverty headcount ratio at national poverty lines (% of population) during 2004 – 2014.

Figure 1. Comparative analysis between Romania and Hungary based on GDP per capita, PPP (current international $) during 1990 - 2016
Source: World Bank, International Comparison Program database

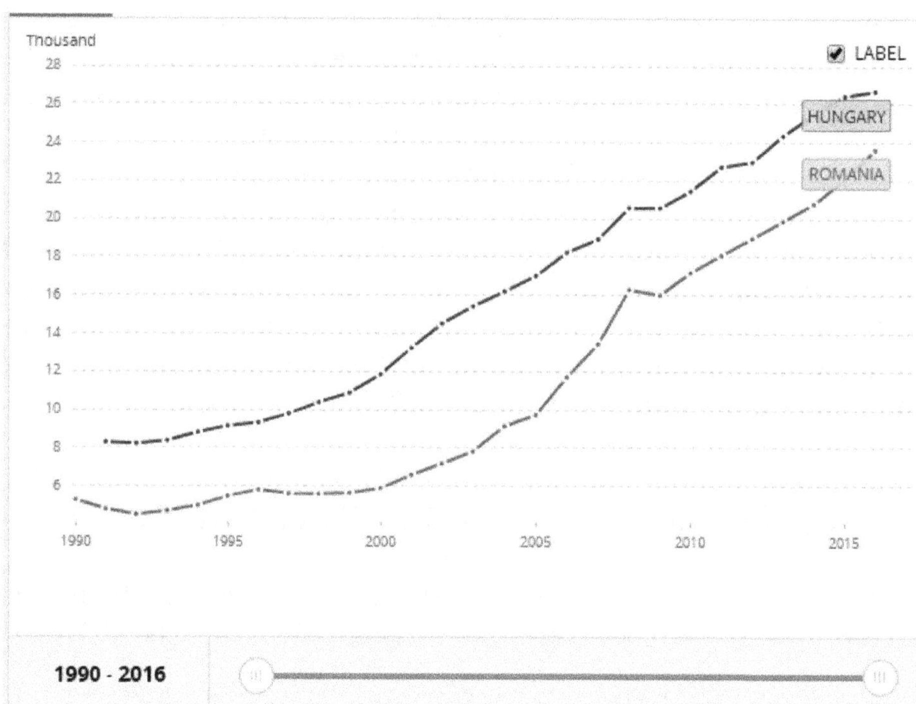

Figure 2. Comparative analysis between Romania and Hungary based on poverty headcount ratio at national poverty lines (% of population) during 2004 - 2014
Source: World Bank, Global Poverty Working Group

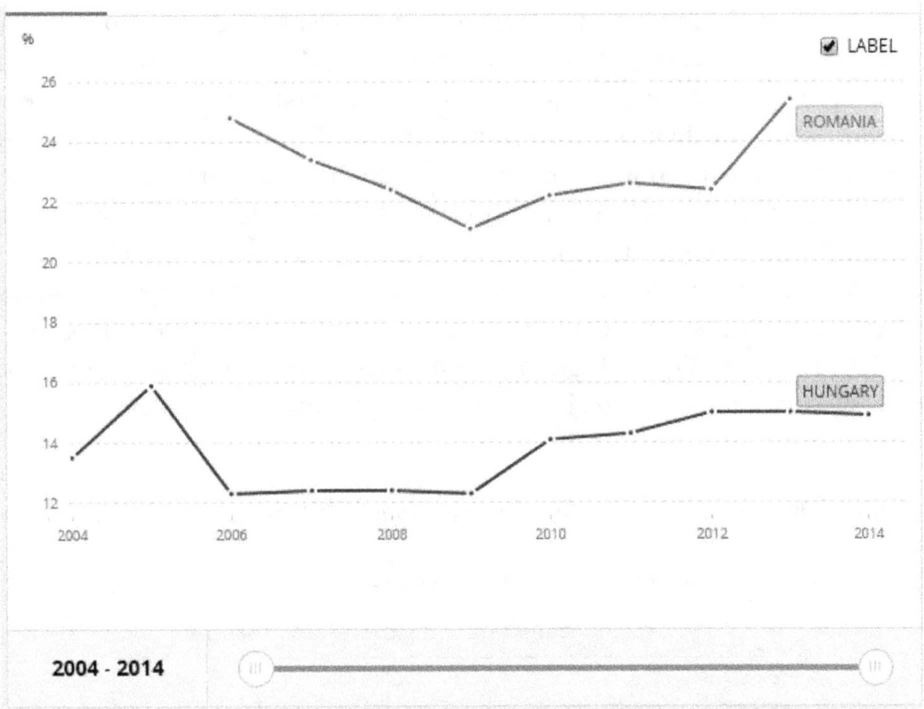

The empirical analysis is based on the daily returns of the major stock indices during the sample period between January 2000 and January 2014. The continuously-compounded daily returns are calculated using the log-difference of the closing prices of stock markets selected indices, ie BET-C Index (Romania) and BUX Index (Hungary). Data series consists of the daily closing prices for each sample stock index during the period between January 2000 and January 2014 with the exception of legal holidays or other events when stock markets haven't performed any financial transactions.

The BET-C index is the composite index of Bucharest stock exchange (BSE). It is a market capitalization weighted index and reflects the price movement of all the companies listed on the BSE regulated market, i.e. 1st and 2nd category, excepting the SIFs. The BUX index of Budapest Stock Exchange Index is a capitalization-weighted index adjusted for free float. Moreover, BUX index is the official benchmark index of blue-chip shares listed on the

Budapest Stock Exchange (BSE) which is also is one of the most liquid and transparent stock markets in Central and Eastern Europe.

The empirical results of Granger causality tests highlight the importance of a functional and stable financial environment considering certain influential factors such as: economic, political, intercultural, historical, ethnical and geographical. Regarding the sample period of analysis, ie the period between January 2000 and January 2014, it appears that Granger causality runs one way, from Hungary to Romania, but not the other way considering the fact that null hypothesis of no Granger causality is rejected. Therefore, based on unidirectional return causalities, long-term dynamic causal linkages between Hungarian and Romanian stock markets are very important in the investment process and risk management strategies. Nevertheless, this result leads to the possibility of obtaining significant benefits based on international diversification of portfolios in a globalized investment context.

Figure 3. The trend of BET-C Index (Romania) and BUX Index (Hungary) - individual graphics
Source: Own computations based on selected financial data series

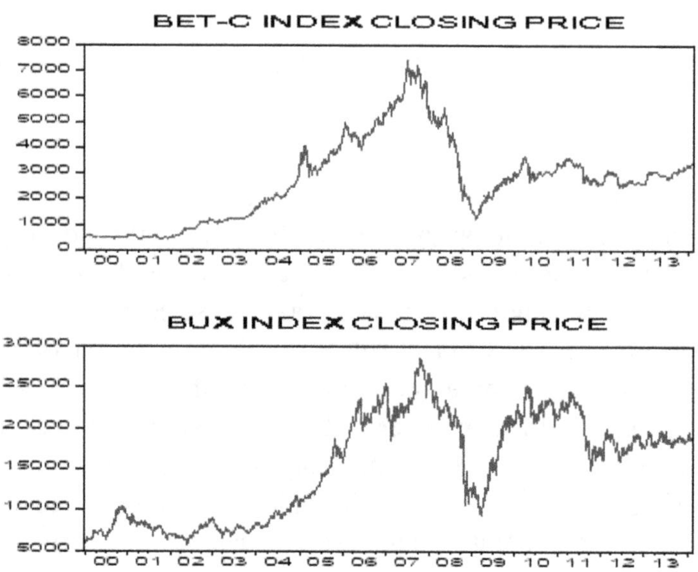

Figure 4. The log-returns of BET-C Index (Romania) and BUX Index (Hungary) - joint graphics
Source: Own computations based on selected financial data series

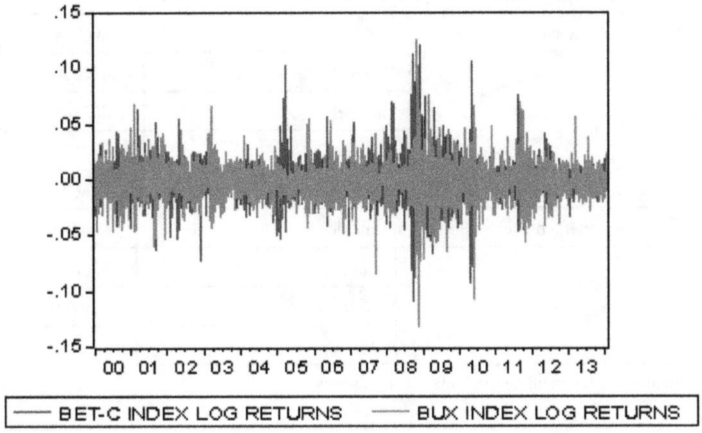

**For a more accurate representation see the electronic version.*

Figure 5. The log-returns of BET-C Index (Romania) and BUX Index (Hungary) - individual graphics
Source: Own computations based on selected financial data series

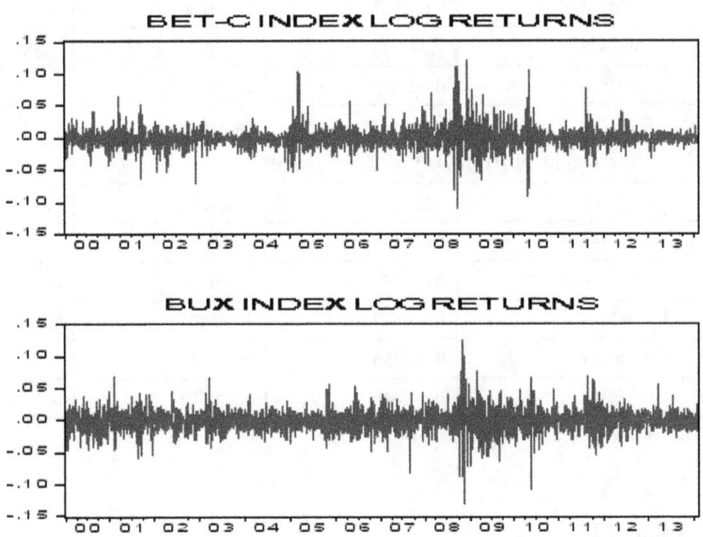

Table 1. Augmented Dickey-Fuller (ADF) Test

		t-Statistic	Prob.*
Null Hypothesis: BUX_INDEX_LOG_RETURNS has a unit root			
Augmented Dickey-Fuller test statistic		-9.866224	0.0000
Test critical values:	1% level	-3.432030	
	5% level	-2.862168	
	10% level	-2.567148	
Null Hypothesis: BET_C_INDEX_LOG_RETURNS has a unit root			
Augmented Dickey-Fuller test statistic		-9.020085	0.0000
Test critical values:	1% level	-3.432031	
	5% level	-2.862168	
	10% level	-2.567148	

Source: Own computations based on selected financial data series

Table 2. BDS Test

Dimension	BDS Statistic	Std. Error	z-Statistic	Prob.
BDS Test for BET_C_INDEX_LOG_RETURNS				
2	0.038806	0.001681	23.08696	0.0000
3	0.070744	0.002667	26.52236	0.0000
4	0.092472	0.003172	29.14897	0.0000
5	0.104536	0.003303	31.64976	0.0000
6	0.109240	0.003182	34.33097	0.0000
BDS Test for BUX_INDEX_LOG_RETURNS				
Dimension	BDS Statistic	Std. Error	z-Statistic	Prob.
2	0.014396	0.001410	10.20725	0.0000
3	0.028829	0.002234	12.90227	0.0000
4	0.039668	0.002652	14.95577	0.0000
5	0.046164	0.002756	16.75135	0.0000
6	0.048497	0.002649	18.30612	0.0000

Source: Own computations based on selected financial data series

CONCLUSION

The main aim of this book chapter is to investigate the potential existence of international causal linkages between certain European emerging stock markets, such as Bucharest stock exchange (Romania) and Budapest Stock

Figure 6. Theoretical Quantile-Quantile Plots (Extreme values)
Source: Own computations based on selected financial data series

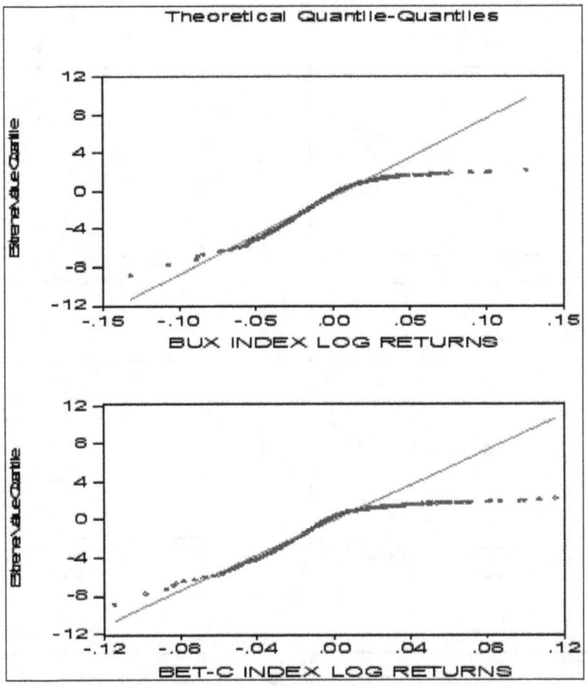

**For a more accurate representation see the electronic version.*

Exchange (Hungary) in order to obtain additional benefits based on international portfolio diversification, especially in terms of globalization. Nevertheless, it also provides a general framework with regard to the quantitative financial dimension of a controversial issue of relatively high current interest, such as the existence of international interdependence and dynamic causal linkages between stock markets. The integrated approach of this book chapter provides additional empirical evidence regarding emerging capital markets behavior. It is important to emphasize the fact that this particular category of stock markets is generally considered to be more attractive for both institutional and individual financial investors based on particular stylized facts.

The behavior of emerging capital market, and even more so in the case of frontier market is characterized by certain stylized facts such as: volatility clustering, non-stationarity of price levels, leverage effect, heteroskedastic log returns, time variation, unpredictability, fat-tailed distribution, chaos, deviations from normal distribution, high risk, high profit opportunities, atypical movements. Practically, frontier capital markets are much less liquid, considerably more volatile and highlighting lower market capitalization than

Figure 7. Distribution graphics CDF - SURVIVOR – QUANTILE
Source: Own computations based on selected financial data series

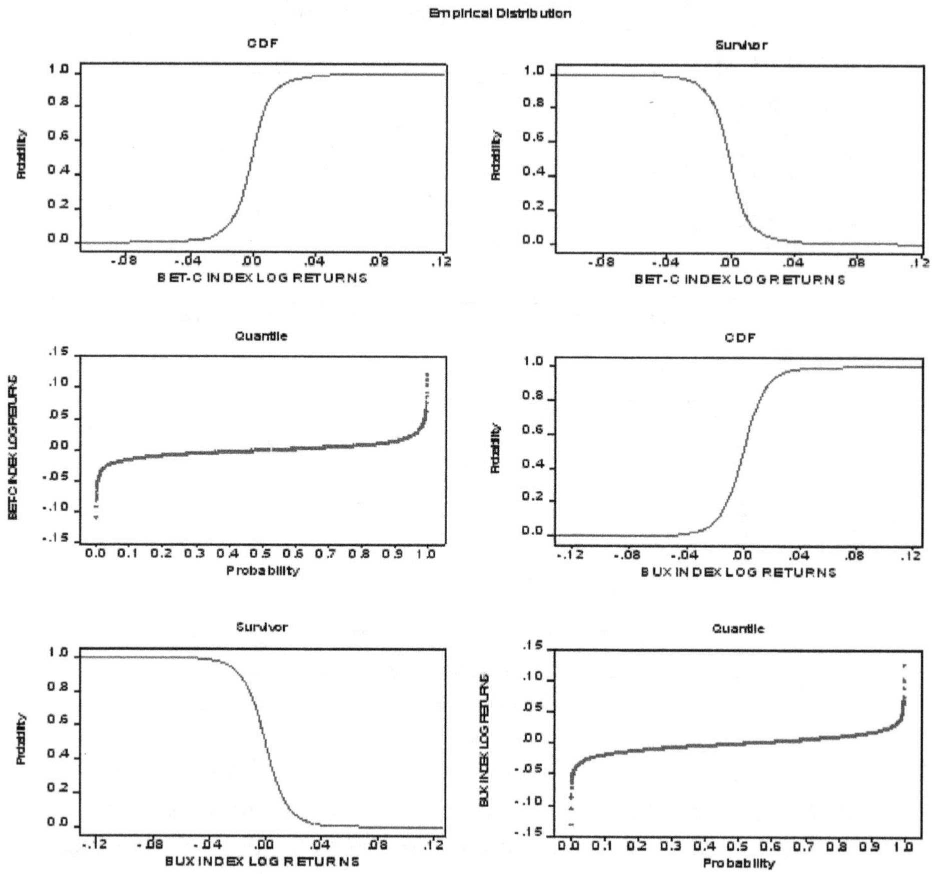

Table 3. Granger Causality tests

Null Hypothesis	Obs	F-Statistic	Probability
Pairwise Granger Causality Tests			
BET_C_INDEX_LOG_RETURNS does not Granger Cause BUX_INDEX_LOG_RETURNS	3527	0.45123	0.63688
BUX_INDEX_LOG_RETURNS does not Granger Cause BET_C_INDEX_LOG_RETURNS		5.53061	0.00400

Source: Own computations based on selected financial data series

emerging (advanced or secondary) or developed capital markets. Thereby it is also obvious the difference of socio-economic progress between Romania and Hungary. Hungary's nominal GDP per capita is also significantly higher than in the case of Romania. The empirical results and final conclusions based on the two case studies also lead to the possibility of obtaining significant benefits based on international diversification of portfolios in a globalized investment context.

REFERENCES

Abimanyu, Y. (2008). *International Linkages to the Indonesian Capital Market: Cointegration Test*. Capital Market and Financial Institution Supervisory Agency, Ministry of Finance of Indonesia.

Balios, D., & Xanthakis, M. (2003). International interdependence and dynamic linkages between developed stock markets. *South Eastern Europe Journal of Economics*, *1*(1), 105–130.

Birau, R. (2017). Approaching the concept of national identity based on a case study regarding long - term causality and financial integration between the capital markets in Romania and Hungary. *Journal of the "Constantin Brâncuşi" University of Târgu-Jiu, Horizons For Sustainability*, (2), 5-17.

Birau, R., & Antonescu, M. (2014). Investigating Long-term Dynamic Causal Linkages between Hungarian and Romanian Stock Markets. *Procedia Economics and Finance*, *16*, 669–679. doi:10.1016/S2212-5671(14)00855-7

Birau, R., & Trivedi, J. (2013). Analyzing cointegration and international linkage between Bucharest stock exchange and European developed stock markets. *NAUN International Journal of Economics and Statistics*, *4*(1), 237–246.

Birau, R., & Trivedi, J. (2015). Investigating Causal Linkages between International Stock Markets in Hungary and Austria in Terms of Economic Globalization. *Annual Research Journal of Symbiosis Centre for Management Studies*, *3*, 78–88.

Birau, R., Trivedi, J., & Antonescu, M. (2014). Modeling S&P Bombay Stock Exchange BANKEX Index Volatility Patterns Using GARCH Model. *Procedia Economics and Finance*, *32*, 520–525. doi:10.1016/S2212-5671(15)01427-6

Birau, R., Trivedi, J., & Siminica, M. (2014). Modeling and Estimating Long-Term Volatility of R.P.G.U Stock Markets. In *Recent Advances in Energy, Environment and Financial Planning*, Florence, Italy (pp. 272-280).

Brock, W.A., Dechert, W.D. & Scheinkman, J.A. (1987). A Test for Independence Based on the Correlation Dimension.

Dickey, D. A., & Fuller, W. A. (1981). Likelihood Ratio Statistics for Autoregressive Time Series with a Unit Root. *Econometrica, 49*(4), 1057–1072. doi:10.2307/1912517

Engle, R. F., & Granger, C. W. J. (1987). Cointegration and Error Correction: Representation, Estimation and Testing. *Econometrica, 55*(2), 251–276. doi:10.2307/1913236

Eun, C. S., & Shim, S. (1989). International Transmission of Stock Market Movements. *Journal of Financial and Quantitative Analysis, 24*(2), 241–256. doi:10.2307/2330774

Granger, C. W. J. (1969). Investigating Causal Relations by Econometric Models and Cross-spectral Methods. *Econometrica, 37*(3), 424–438. doi:10.2307/1912791

Khan, T. A. (2011). Cointegration of International Stock Markets: An Investigation of Diversification Opportunities. *Undergraduate Economic Review, 8*(1).

Phylaktisa, K., & Ravazzolob, F. (2005). Stock market linkages in emerging markets: Implications for international portfolio diversification. *Int. Fin. Markets. Inst. and Money, 15*(2), 91–106. doi:10.1016/j.intfin.2004.03.001

Siminică, M., & Birau, R. (2014). Investigating International Causal Linkages Between Latin European Stock Markets In Terms Of Global Financial Crisis: A Case Study For Romania, Spain And Italy. *International Journal of Business Quantitative Economics and Applied Management Research, 1*(1), 12–36.

Singh, G. S. P. (2010). Chinese and Indian stock market linkages with developed stock markets. *Asian Journal of Finance & Accounting, 2*(2), E2.

Chapter 11
Estimating Long-Term Volatility on National Stock Exchange of India

ABSTRACT

The main objective of this chapter is to provide an elaborate framework on the long-term volatility of the National Stock Exchange of India based on Generalized Autoregressive Conditional Heteroskedasticity (GARCH) models. The CNX-100 index is one of the most diversified Indian stock indices which includes over 38 sectors of the economy. This stock index represents about 81.57% of the free-floating market capitalization of stocks listed on the National Stock Exchange (NSE) of India from March 2014. Moreover, this book chapter empirically tested volatility clusters of CNX100 index using a large sample database from October 2007 to July 2014.

INTRODUCTION

The National Stock Exchange (NSE) of India is perceived as one of the most representative stock exchanges in the world based on the criterion regarding the volume of transactions and market-capitalization. This stock market is a benchmark for the Indian investment system considering the extremely wide geographical area coverage. Most of all, NSE is the result of a complex reform process which includes various aspects such as microstructure, trading volumes, infrastructure, financial innovations, electronic market technology,

DOI: 10.4018/978-1-5225-9269-3.ch011

market practices and policies, sophisticated financial services. Moreover, considering that India is an emerging country with an impressive investment potential, the National Stock Exchange represents a pioneering direction in terms of financial trading and risk management strategies.

ECONOMETRIC METHODOLOGY

The main purpose of this subchapter is to investigate the estimation process of long-term volatility impact in National Stock Exchange of India using CNX 100 index. The econometric analysis includes applying Generalized Autoregressive Conditional Heteroskedistity which is also known as GARCH models (Bollerslev 1986). In this this subchapter, the econometric framework includes GARCH (1, 1) model, that is a combination of one ARCH term and one GARCH term. The GARCH (1, 1) model is capable to estimate volatility more particularly and measures the impact of shocks on financial market. GARCH (1, 1) model developed by Bollerslev and Taylor (1986) and which in detail mentioned below. The financial series stationarity is tested using Augmented Dickey Fuller test (ADF) and Kwiatkowski–Phillips–Schmidt–Shin test (KPSS). The empirical results are significant at level of 10%, 5% and 1% where 5% significant level considered for the further modeling process.

The financial time series consists of daily closing prices for sample stock index during the period between October 2007 to July 2014 with the exception of legal holidays or other events when stock markets haven't performed transactions. In addition, the sample data series includes a total number of 1698 of daily observations. The continuously-compounded daily returns are calculated using the log-difference of the closing prices of stock market selected index, i.e. CNX 100 index as follows:

$$r_t = \ln\left(\frac{p_t}{p_{t-1}}\right) = \ln\left(p_t\right) - \ln\left(p_{t-1}\right)$$

where p is the daily closing price.

The GARCH (1, 1) model was developed by Bollerslev and Taylor (1986). This model allows conditional variance of all variables to be dependent upon previous logs and it reflects on the entire financial time series. However, the first log of squared residual will be obtained from the mean equation and this presents idea about volatility from the previous time periods. The most widely used GARCH (1, 1) model is based on the following mathematical expression:

$$h_t = \omega + \alpha_1 u_{t-1}^2 + \beta_1 h_{t-1}$$

The empirical analysis is necessary to follow the hypothesis of stationary covariance as unconditional variance and to exist that it processed based on the following expressions:

$$h_t = \omega + \alpha_1 u_{t-1}^2 + \beta_1 h_{t-1}$$

The empirical analysis is necessary to follow the hypothesis of covariance stationary as unconditional variance and to exist that it processed based on the following expressions:

$$\sigma^2 = Var\left(u_t\right) = E\left(u_t^2\right) = E\left(\omega + \alpha_1 u_{t-1}^2 + \beta_1 h_{t-1}\right)$$

$$\sigma^2 = \omega + \alpha_1 E\left(u_{t-1}^2\right) + \beta E(h_{t-1}) = \omega + \alpha_1 \sigma^2 + \beta_1 \sigma^2$$

The research includes implementation of GARCH (1, 1) model conditional variance equation:

$$Var\left(u_t \middle| h_{t-1}\right) = E\left(u_t^2 \middle| h_{t-1}\right) = h_t$$

and thus, it can simply take the following form, i.e.:

$$h_t = \omega + \alpha_1 u_{t-1}^2 + \beta_1 h_{t-1}.$$

Basically, the final formulation includes the expression $h_t = \omega + \alpha_1 u_{t-1}^2 + \beta_1 h_{t-1}$ based on both ARCH term and GARCH term, where, $\alpha_1 u_{t-1}^2$ represents ARCH component and $\beta_1 h_{t-1}$ GARCH component.

Model specifications is based on the following econometric framework. In case of a detected presence of unconditional variance, the situation requires to employ the financial modeling process that basically involves calculating the following mathematical expression: $\alpha_1 + \beta_1 < 1$ and for converting it into generates positive result, it is required the clear validation of the condition: $\alpha_0 > 0$.

Positive results will indicate good news for market. For the constant, conditional mean we applied the formula: $E\left(y_t \middle| O_{t-1}\right)$ where $E = c + \varphi y_{t-1} + o$ and y_{t-1} is included in $|O_{t-1}$

The previous frame will facilitate the final empirical result using $h_t = \omega + \alpha_1 u_{t-1}^2 + \beta_1 h_{t-1}$.

EMPIRICAL RESULTS

The CNX 100 index daily data series from October 2007 to July 2014 filtered from summary of basic statistics which suggest risk levels and abnormal returns. The financial series from the data period has not out from the financial global crisis. Though the large number of volatility shocks recorded in study period. Highest number of shocks at upper side exceeds 14% of the degree level recorded during mid-2009. Similarly, highest degree of lower level shocks recorded during global financial crisis which recorded over 7%. Mean and Median value almost near to zero. Further, basis statistics suggests that the close difference from Min value to Max value exceeds 120% percentages of changes within the period of 7 years.

The CNX100 index series return from October 2007 to July 2014 provides investment patterns in National Stock Exchange and ups and down scales. The global financial crisis has impacted CNX100 strongly where the index falls from over 6200 to 2500 about less than 5 months. The index downfall

Table 1. Descriptive statistics

Variance	CNX100
Mean	0.000236159
Median	0.000104560
Min	-0.130142
Max	0.163343
Std.Dev	0.0166160
Skewness	0.162120
Kurtosis	9.72878

Source: Author's own computations based on selected financial data series

Figure 1. The trend of CNX 100 index (individual chart)
Source: Author's own computations based on selected financial data series

Figure 2. Log returns series of CNX 100 index
Source: Author's own computations based on selected financial data series

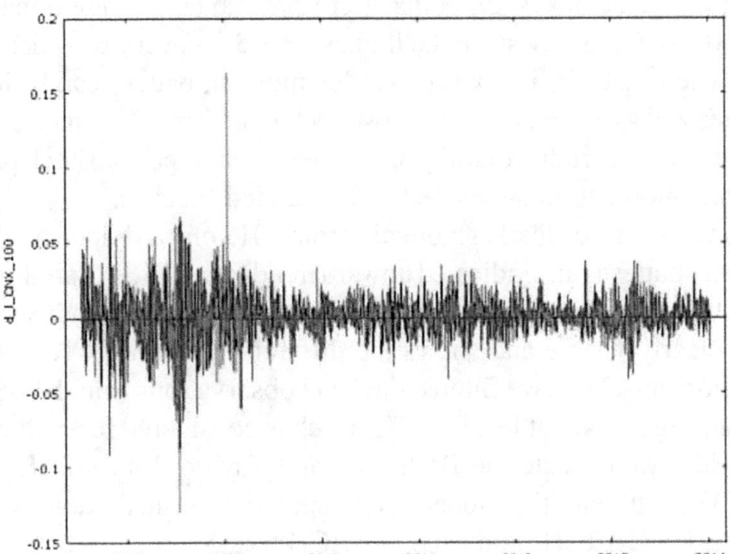

Figure 3. The Q-Q plot for CNX 100 index
Source: Author's own computations based on selected financial data series

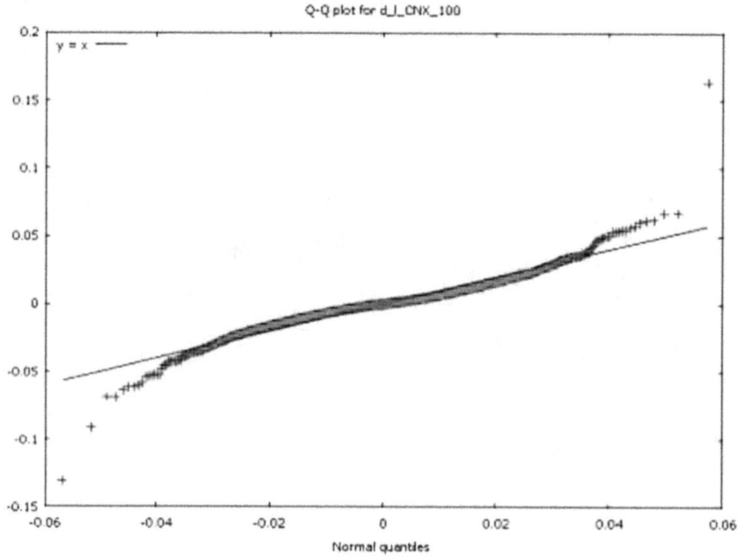

creates more than 150% changes in total returns. That can be averaged 30% (approx..) per month which gives the highest volatile moments through study period. Immediate next six months after financial crisis were remarkable in CNX 100 index journey since the highest speed recovery recorded in series returns. The CNX 100 index series index moment pattern can be identified and cauterized as a category from post 2009 to before 2013 since entire time period runs with certain volatility shocks level. No type 'B' shock presented, and market moment remains lined and predicted specific.

However, the stock market moments from 2013 onwards indicated changes in volatility patterns and indicated upward trend after 2013. That can be tallied from the serried return graph shown in Figure 1. A straight indicated upside jump is clearly visible and shows the different pattern of CNX 100 index market moments. We have filtered the 1697 observations from KPSS test and found data significant at level of 5%, which is considered for autoregressive model. Here we execute the Bollerslev and Taylor (1986) GARCH (1, 1) model. We formulate the model which specified in methodology part and represents (1) GARCH term and (1) ARCH term.

Table 2. GARCH (1, 1) model estimations

Variable		Coefficient	p-Value
GARCH (1, 1)	π	0.000693756	0.0186
	ω	1.68283e-06	0.0866*
	α	0.0747679	0.0000
	β	0.920068	0.0000

Source: Author's own computations based on selected financial data series

The stationary data series is used to compute GARCH (1, 1) to estimate the volatility for CNX100 National Stock Exchange index and the model fitted well on financial series. The final result of computation is described in Table 2 while the model executions is mentioned in the following paragraphs:

The final expression for GARCH (1, 1) model based on CNX 100 index data series is:

$$= 0.0747679\ (\alpha_1 u_{t-1}^{2}) + 0.920068\ (h_{t-1})\ 0.9948359 = < 1$$

Estimated volatility in CNX100 (National Stock Exchange index) in GARCH (1, 1) model fitted perfectly and resulted 0.9948359 that is <1 and very close to 1. It indicates that series have strong volatility presence and have strong impact on listed stocks. The GARCH model formulations are based on 1 arch term and 1 garch term. The results indicate that long term investments in any of 38 listed economic sectors in CNX100 index would be profitable and may generate high degree of returns. The short-term volatility found steady and long-term volatility absorbs abnormal patterns of sketches.

CONCLUSION

The initial idea to investigate CNX 100 index stock market volatility from October 2007 to July 2014 is focused on estimating the normal and abnormal market patterns, which includes before and after financial crisis. The summary of statistics suggests degree of risks 0.01661, while mean and medium returns are near to zero. The CNX100 market study found positive skewness (non-negative) in run for 7-year daily market observations using 1697 observations. However, the degree of kurtosis exceeds the level of normal kurtosis more than twice i.e. 9.72.

Bollerslev and Tylor (1986) GARCH (1, 1) model fitted well on financial series and market volatility pattern recorded changed after 2013 and onwards. The market pattern for CNX 100 index found normal volatility from post 2009 to early 2013 period. High degree of kurtosis, positive skewness and considering the lower degree of standard deviations has allowed investors for maximum returns on investments. National Stock Exchange (NSE) index CNX100 can be positive alternate for investors which allows the group of 38 economic sectors and holding free market capital flow from 75% to 82%.

REFERENCES

Birau, R., & Trivedi, J. (2014). Estimating Long-term Volatility on National Stock Exchange of India. *Procedia - Economics and Finance*, *32*, 574-579, doi:10.1016/S2212-5671(15)01434-3

Bollerslev, T. (1986). Generalized autoregressive conditional heteroskedasticity. *Journal of Economics*, *31*(3), 307–327. doi:10.1016/0304-4076(86)90063-1

Brailsford, T. J., & Faff, R. W. (1996). An evaluation of volatility forecasting techniques. *Journal of Banking & Finance*, *20*(3), 419–438. doi:10.1016/0378-4266(95)00015-1

Brooks, C. (1996). Testing for Non-Linearity in Daily Sterling Exchange Rates. *Applied Financial Economics*, *6*(4), 307–317. doi:10.1080/096031096334105

Choudhry, T. (1996). Stock Market Volatility and the Crash of 1987: Evidence from Six Emerging Markets. *Journal of International Money and Finance*, *15*(6), 969–981. doi:10.1016/S0261-5606(96)00036-8

Dickey, D. A., & Fuller, W. A. (1981). Likelihood Ratio Statistics for Autoregressive Time Series with a Unit Root. *Econometrica*, *49*(4), 1057–1072. doi:10.2307/1912517

Engle, R. F. (1982). Autoregressive Conditional Heteroscedasticity with Estimates of the Variance of UK Inflation. *Econometrica*, *50*(4), 987–1008. doi:10.2307/1912773

Engle, R. F., & Granger, C. W. J. (1987). Cointegration and Error Correction: Representation, Estimation and Testing. *Econometrica*, *55*(2), 251–276. doi:10.2307/1913236

Engle, R. F., & Rangel, J. G. (2004). The Sp-line GARCH Model for Unconditional Volatility and Its Global Macro-Economic Causes. *Review of Financial Studies*, *21*(3), 1187–1222. doi:10.1093/rfs/hhn004

Chapter 12
Investigating International Causal Linkages Between Latin European Stock Markets in Terms of Global Financial Crisis:
A Case Study for Romania, Spain, and Italy

ABSTRACT

The main objective of this chapter is to investigate international causal linkages between selected Latin European stock markets, such as Romania, Spain, and Italy, in terms of global financial crises. Moreover, the structure of this book chapter includes both theoretical developments and new empirical findings. In recent past, the global phenomenon of increasing cointegration, co-movements and financial contagion patterns between developed and emerging stock markets have significantly influenced foreign investment

DOI: 10.4018/978-1-5225-9269-3.ch012

behavior. The global financial crisis has seriously affected the international financial architecture and global economic stability due to unprecedented dynamic financial contractions. In addition, as strictly economic approach, Romanian labor migration is very high level in Italy and Spain. On the other hand, financial integration and the international causal linkages suggest a certain behavioral pattern between receiving societies. The financial econometrics approach includes various tools such as Unit Root Test, Hodrick-Prescott (HP) filter, Augmented Dickey-Fuller stationary test, BDS test and Granger causality test. The final results provide a comprehensive framework regarding international portfolio diversification, risk management and strategic investment decision making process.

INTRODUCTION

Causality and international linkage between emerging and developed stock markets highlight the significant influence of dynamic transmission patterns focused on financial shocks propagation. Beyond the effects of globalization, financial markets are influenced by certain issues such as: cross-border transactions, investment policy reforms and liberalization of financial operations. The liberalization and integration process of financial markets emphasizes various opportunities based on reduction of capital transaction cost and foreign capital inflows.

According to Siminică and Birau (2014) international investors are focused on the potential correlation among returns of different national stock markets in order to diversify the investment risk based on international diversification of portfolios. The multidimensional implications of financial integration generate the possibility of identifying investment strategies in order to optimize the structure of risk management. Technically, financial time series, such as daily stock market returns are defined on the basis of certain stylized facts, namely: volatility clustering, high-frequency, non-stationarity of price levels, leverage effect, heteroskedastic log returns, extreme variations in time, deterministic chaos, fat-tailed distribution (leptokurtosis), nonlinearity, asymmetry.

The formal regulatory regarding the latest official assessment report of FTSE Country Classification issued on September 2013 provides the following classification of countries: developed, advanced emerging, secondary emerging and frontier. According to the previous classification, Romania is included in the frontier market category on the basis of significant selection criteria. Moreover, it is characterized by negative features such as: illiquidity, insufficient transparency, financial regulation issues, underdeveloped trading mechanisms. Thus, Bucharest Stock Exchange is assimilated as a relatively young, fragmented and not very stable stock market. However, the condition of frontier market can be very attractive considering the fact that it generates rapid growth and various opportunities for international investors. On the other hand, Spain and Italy are included in the category developed countries. In other words, Milan Stock Exchange (Milano Italia Borsa) and Madrid Stock Exchange (Bolsa de Madrid) represent more stable and efficient stock markets.

LITERATURE REVIEW

The global financial crisis that erupted in mid-2007 in U.S.A. triggered dramatic consequences for most of stock markets across the world. An extreme financial phenomenon does not follow a historical pattern so it is very difficult to predict with high accuracy. According to Birau (2014a) various stock crashes followed by severe financial crisis occurred rather frequently in the last century and sometimes reaching global magnitude, such as: the Great Depression between the years 1929-1933, Latin American financial debt crisis of the 1980s, Black Monday (Black Monday) in 1987, the Asian financial crisis of 1997 – 1998, Russian financial crisis or Ruble crisis in 1998, DOTCOM bubble during 2000 and 2002 and the Subprime crisis that erupted in August 2007 in U.S.A.

Eun and Shim (1989) empirically analyzed the interdependence structure of major national stock markets. Moreover, the authors suggested that innovations in U.S. market are suddenly transmitted to other stock markets despite the fact that none of these markets can adequately justify its movements. They investigated the existence of international transmission of stock market movements among several mature markets, such as: Australia, Japan, Hong Kong, U.K, Switzerland, France, Germany, Canada and U.S.A. Moreover, Abimanyu et. all (2008) investigated the international linkages of the Indonesian capital market using cointegration tests to examine the long-run equilibrium relationship between the stock markets of Indonesia with China, France, Germany, Hong Kong, Japan, Korea, Malaysia, Netherlands, Philippine, Singapore, Thailand, Taiwan, the United Kingdom and the United States.

Balios and Xanthakis (2003) investigated international interdependence and dynamic linkages between developed stock markets, namely U.K, Germany, France, Italy, Spain, U.S. and Japan. They concluded that U.S. stock market is the leading stock market in the world and U.K stock market is the leading stock market in Europe. On the other hand, Singh (2010) investigated Chinese and Indian stock market linkages with several developed stock markets, such as U.S., U.K., Japan and Hong Kong. The empirical results revealed that both Chinese and Indian market are correlated with all the selected developed markets based on the analysis of Granger causality. Pretorious (2002) suggested that it is very important for international investors to understand the forces behind the interdependence of emerging stock markets in order to be informed about the potential occurrence of systemic risks and their global implications.

According to Khan (2011), an increasing number of investors are interested to invest in developing countries, so it is very important to answer the following rhetorical question "Does sensitivity to the world economy explain country performance over the great recession?" The author investigated the existence of cointegration between stock markets of US and 22 other major economies.

Birau and Trivedi (2013) empirically analyzed the existence of cointegration and international linkage between Bucharest stock exchange and certain European developed stock markets, i.e., France, Germany and Greece. The empirical research covered the sample period from January 2003 until December 2012 which were divided into two sub-periods in order to examine both pre-crisis and post-crisis effects. Regarding the first period of analysis, i.e., January 2003 – December 2007, it appears that there is no particular causality between Greek and Romanian, German and Romanian, respectively French and Romanian stock markets.

The second period of analysis, i.e., January 2008 – December 2012, suggested that Granger causality runs one way, from Greece to Romania, but not the other way and there is no particular causality between German and Romanian, respectively French and Romanian stock markets. Birau (2014b) investigated the existence of dynamic causal linkages between international developed stock markets of Spain and Canada. The empirical results of Granger causality tests among developed stock markets of Spain and Canada highlighted significant investment opportunities based on international portfolio diversification and risk management strategies. Granger causality runs simultaneously in both directions for Spain and Canada based on a feedback relationship.

A MACROECONOMIC APPROACH BASED ON STATISTICAL SURVEYS

Basically, this research paper provides additional empirical evidence and a consistent theoretical approach. Currently, Romania (2007), Spain (1986) and Italy (1952) are member states in the European Union (EU28) but are characterized by rather different development levels. Beyond the common Latin roots, the national languages of Romania, Spain and Italy are closely related to each other based on linguistic similarities. Moreover, Romanian labor migration revealed a very high level in Italy and Spain as main destination countries.

The World Bank provides a wide range of information on GNI per capita, i.e. formerly GNP per capita, which is basically the gross national income converted to the U.S. dollar, based on the Atlas method, divided by the mid-year population. According to the official presentation based on World Bank national accounts data and OECD National Accounts data files, GNI represents the sum of value added by all resident producers including any product taxes (less subsidies) not included in the valuation of output plus net receipts of primary income (compensation of employees and property income) from abroad.

Considering the world development indicators highlighted by the World Bank, Italy is a high-income country with a total population of 59.54 million (2012) and a Gross Domestic Product (GDP) (current US$) of $2.013 trillion (2012). However, The GDP growth in Italy was negative, i.e., -2.5% per 2012 and the inflation was 1.2% per 2013. Moreover, Spain is also a high-income country with a total population of 46.76 million (2012) and a GDP (current US$) of $1.322 trillion (2012).

In addition, the GDP growth in Spain was negative, i.e. -1.6% per 2012 and the inflation was 1.4% per 2013. On the other hand, Romania is an upper middle-income country with a total population of 20.08 million (2012) and a relatively low GDP (current US$) of $169.4 billion (2012). Nevertheless, the GDP growth in Romania was positive, i.e. 0.4% in 2012 and the inflation was 4.0% in 2013.

Figure 1. GNI per capita based on World Bank Atlas method of conversion (U.S. dollars)

Source: The World Bank – computation based on World Bank national accounts data and OECD National Accounts data files

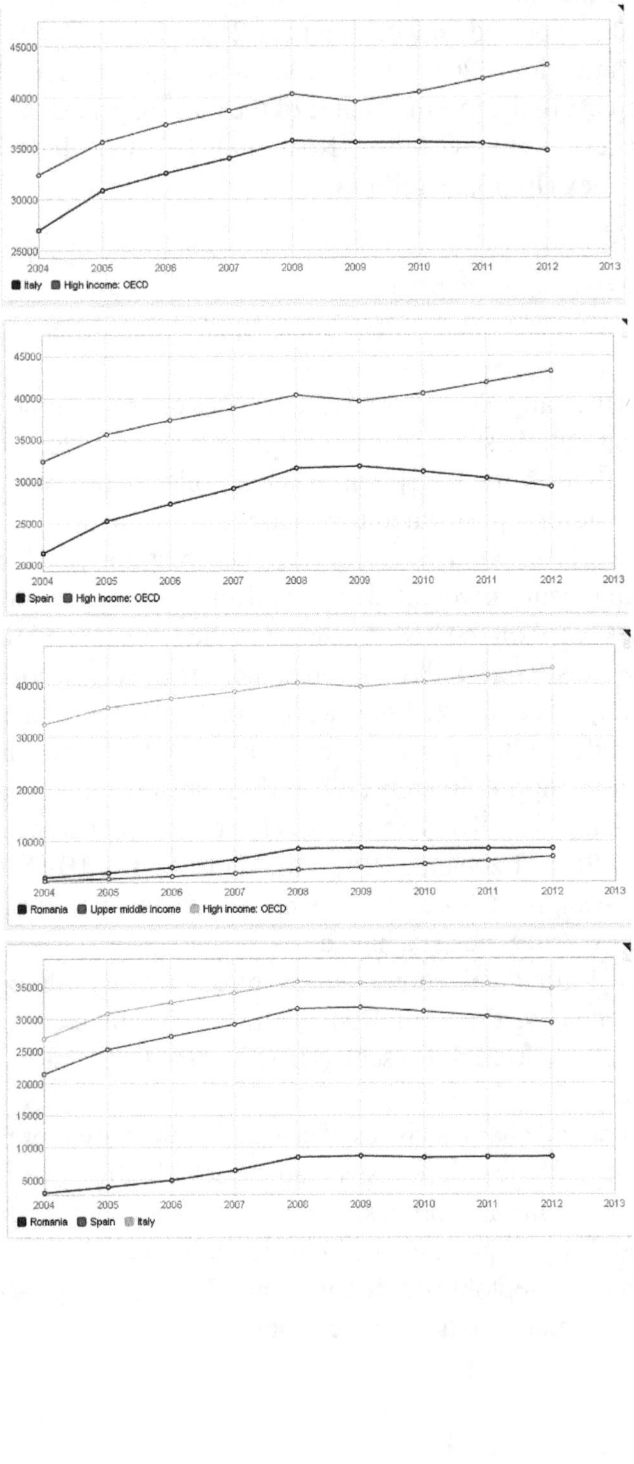

METHODOLOGICAL APPROACH AND EMPIRICAL RESULTS

The empirical analysis is based on the daily returns of the major stock indices during the sample period between January 2007 and April 2013. According to Siminică and Birau (2014) the continuously-compounded daily returns are calculated using the log-difference of the closing prices of stock markets selected indices, ie BET-C Index (Romania), IBEX 35 Index (Spain) and FTSE MIB Index (Italy), as follows:

$$r_t = \ln\left(\frac{p_t}{p_{t-1}}\right) = \ln\left(p_t\right) - \ln\left(p_{t-1}\right)$$

where p is the daily closing price. Data series consists of the daily closing prices for each sample stock index during the period between January 2007 and April 2013 with the exception of legal holidays or other events when stock markets haven't performed transactions.

BET-C index is the composite index of Bucharest stock exchange (BSE). It is a market capitalization weighted index and reflects the price movement of all the companies listed on the BSE regulated market, i.e. Ist and IInd Category, excepting the SIFs. The FTSE MIB index measures the performance of 40 of the most liquid and capitalized stocks listed on the Borsa Italiana. Moreover, FTSE MIB index is the primary benchmark index for the Italian equity markets capturing approximately 80% of the domestic market capitalization. On the other hand, The IBEX 35 index is the benchmark stock market index of the Madrid Stock Exchange (Bolsa de Madrid). The IBEX 35 index is a capitalization-weighted index comprising the 35 most liquid Spanish stocks traded in the Madrid Stock Exchange.

The applied financial econometrics research methodology includes: descriptive statistics, the Unit Root Test, the Augmented Dickey-Fuller stationary test, the sHodrick-Prescott (HP) filter, the BDS test and the Granger causality test.

The fundamental characteristics of selected indices are represented by the following issues: Jarque-Bera test's statistic which allows to eliminate the normality of distribution hypothesis, parameter of asymmetry distribution or Skewness and Kurtosis parameter which measures the peakedness or flatness of the distribution (leptokurtic distribution). The test Jarque-Bera is based on the following mathematical expressions:

Figure 2. The trend of BET-C Index (Romania), IBEX 35 Index (Spain) and FTSE MIB Index (Italy) - individual graphics
Source: Author's own computations based on selected financial data series

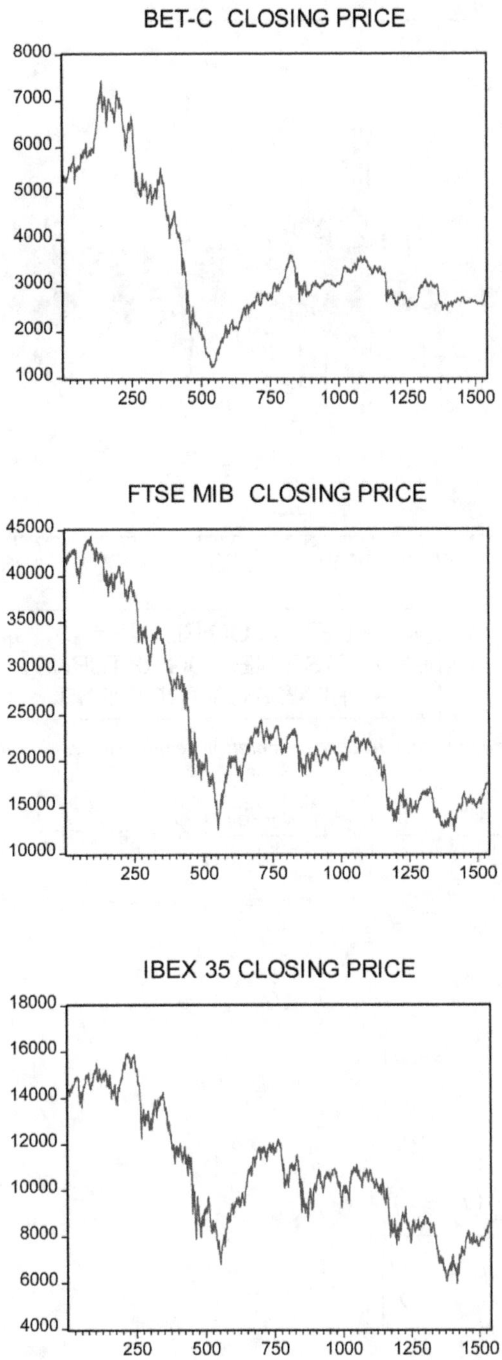

Figure 3. The log-returns of BET-C Index (Romania), IBEX 35 Index (Spain) and FTSE MIB Index (Italy) - joint graphic
Source: Author's own computations based on selected financial data series

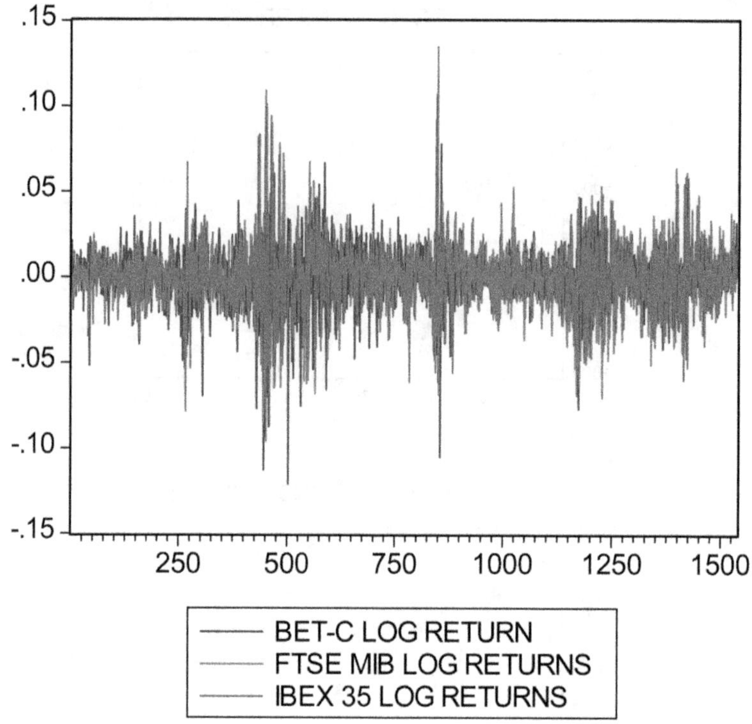

**For a more accurate representation see the electronic version.*

$$JB = n\left[\frac{s^2}{6} + \frac{(k-3)^2}{24}\right] = \frac{n}{6}\cdot\left(s^2 + \frac{(k-3)^2}{4}\right)$$, considering:

$$s = \frac{\hat{\mu}_3}{\hat{\sigma}^3} = \frac{\frac{1}{n}\sum_{i=1}^{n}(x_i - \overline{x})^3}{\left[\frac{1}{n}\sum_{i=1}^{n}(x_i - \overline{x})^2\right]^{\frac{3}{2}}}$$

$$k = \frac{\hat{\mu}_4}{\hat{\sigma}^4} = \frac{\frac{1}{n}\sum_{i=1}^{n}(x_i - \overline{x})^4}{\left[\frac{1}{n}\sum_{i=1}^{n}\left(x_i - \overline{x}\right)^2\right]^2}$$

Figure 4. The log-returns of BET-C Index (Romania), IBEX 35 Index (Spain) and FTSE MIB Index (Italy) - individual graphics
Source: Author's own computations based on selected financial data series

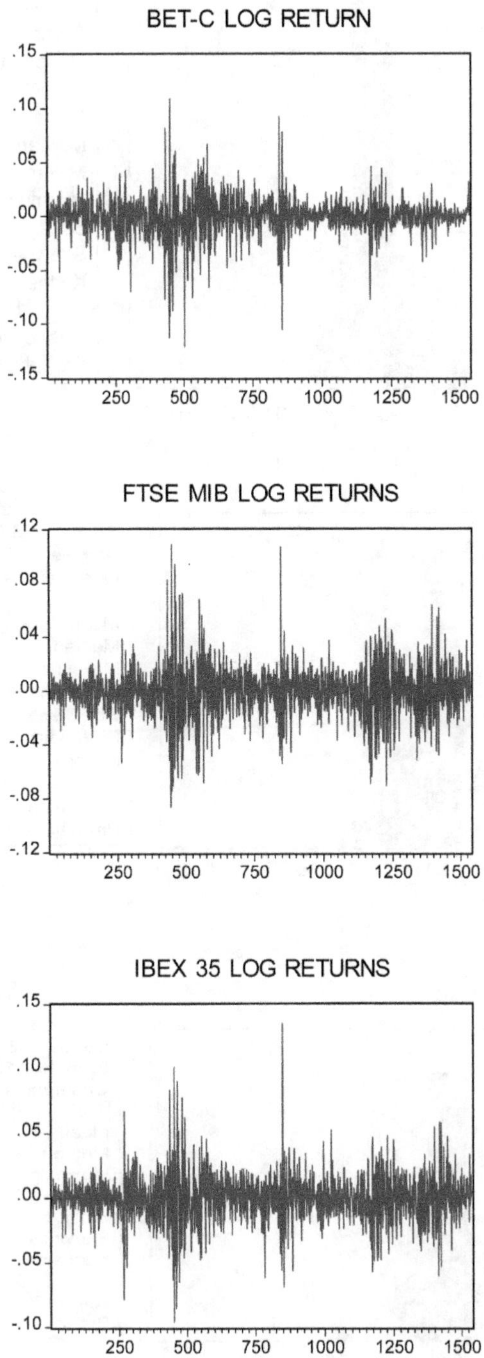

Figure 5. Basic statistical characteristics of selected stock indices
Source: Own computations based on selected financial data series

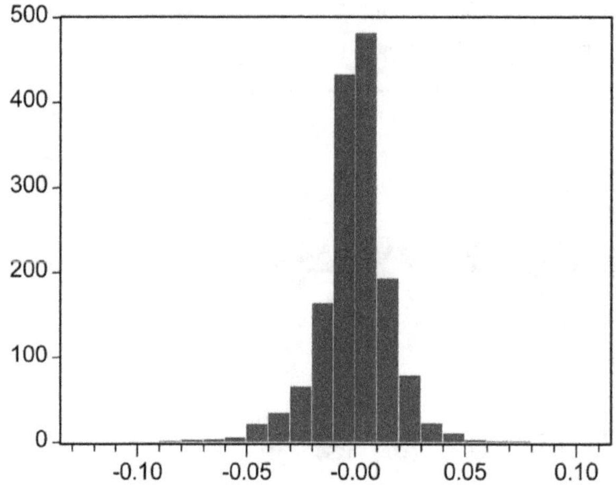

Series: BET_C_LOG_RETURN
Sample 1 1538
Observations 1537

Mean	-0.000393
Median	0.000197
Maximum	0.108906
Minimum	-0.121184
Std. Dev.	0.017836
Skewness	-0.685424
Kurtosis	10.16679
Jarque-Bera	3409.716
Probability	0.000000

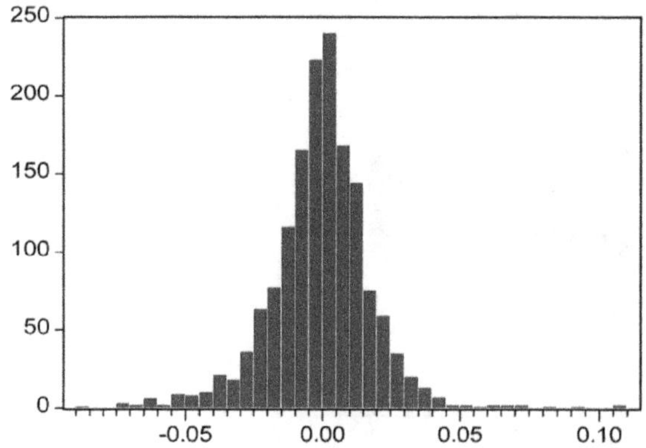

Series: FTSE_MIB_LOG_RETURNS
Sample 1 1538
Observations 1536

Mean	-0.000565
Median	0.000230
Maximum	0.108742
Minimum	-0.085991
Std. Dev.	0.018504
Skewness	0.030021
Kurtosis	6.767386
Jarque-Bera	908.5954
Probability	0.000000

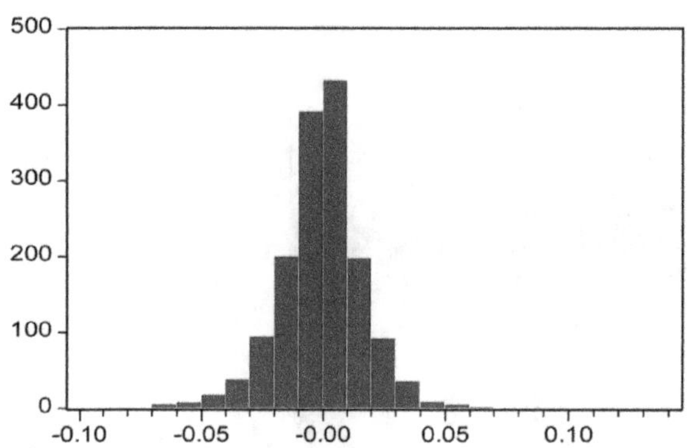

Series: IBEX_35_LOG_RETURNS
Sample 1 1538
Observations 1536

Mean	-0.000329
Median	0.000154
Maximum	0.134836
Minimum	-0.095859
Std. Dev.	0.018043
Skewness	0.204707
Kurtosis	8.038991
Jarque-Bera	1635.779
Probability	0.000000

Augmented Dickey-Fuller (ADF) test is used in order to determine the non-stationarity or the integration order of a financial time series. A series noted y_t is integrated of order one, ie $y_t \sim I(1)$ and contains a unit root if y_t is non-stationary, but on the other hand Δy_t is stationary, ie $\Delta y_t = y_t - y_{t-1}$. Moreover, extrapolating the previous expression, a series y_t is integrated of order d, ie $y_t \sim I(d)$ if y_t is non-stationary, but $\Delta^d y_t$ is stationary. Practically, ADF diagnostic test investigates the potential presence of unit roots divided into the following categories: unit root with a constant and a trend, unit root with a constant, but without a time trend, and finally unit root without constant and temporal trend. Theoretically, ADF test is focused on the following regression model:

$$\Delta y_t = c + \beta \cdot t + \delta \cdot y_{t-1} + \sum_{i=1}^{p} \gamma_i \Delta y_{t-i} + \varepsilon_t$$

where p represents the number of lags for which it was investigated whether fulfilling the condition that residuals are white noise, c is a constant, t is the indicator for time trend and Δ is the symbol for differencing. In addition, it is important to emphasize the essence of a stochastic trend that cannot be predicted due to the time dependence of residual's variance. Strictly related to the ADF test, if the coefficients to be estimated β and δ have the null value then the analyzed financial time series is characterized by a stochastic trend. The null hypothesis, i.e. the time series has a unit root is rejected if t-statistics is lower than the critical value.

The BDS test was used in order to determine whether the residuals are independent and identically distributed. BDS test is a two-tailed test and is based on the following hypothesis:

H_0: sample observations are independently and identically distributed (I.I.D.)
H_1: sample observations are not I.I.D., aspect involving that the time series is non-linearly dependent if first differences of the natural logarithm have been calculated.

The BDS methodology involves a time series x_t for t = 1, 2, 3…T based on its m-history $x_t^m = (x_t, x_{t-1}, \ldots, x_{t-m+1})$ where m is the called embedding dimension. Implicitly, the correlation integral (a measure of time patterns frequency) is estimated as follows:

Table 1. Augmented Dickey-Fuller (ADF) Test

		t-Statistic	Prob.*
Null Hypothesis: BET_C_LOG_RETURN has a unit root			
Augmented Dickey-Fuller test statistic		-6.649379	0.0000
Test critical values:	1% level	-3.434459	
	5% level	-2.863242	
	10% level	-2.567724	
Null Hypothesis: FTSE_MIB_LOG_RETURNS has a unit root			
Augmented Dickey-Fuller test statistic		-19.12321	0.0000
Test critical values:	1% level	-3.434415	
	5% level	-2.863222	
	10% level	-2.567714	
Null Hypothesis: IBEX_35_LOG_RETURNS has a unit root			
Augmented Dickey-Fuller test statistic		-19.70668	0.0000
Test critical values:	1% level	-3.434415	
	5% level	-2.863222	
	10% level	-2.567714	

Source: Own computations based on selected financial data series

$$C_{m,\varepsilon} = \frac{2}{T_m\left(T_m - 1\right)} \sum_{m \le s} \sum_{< t \le T} I\left(x_t^m, x_s^m, \varepsilon\right)$$

And $C_m\left(\varepsilon\right) = \lim_{n \to \infty} C_{m,n}\left(\varepsilon\right)$

where T_m = T-m+1 and $I\left(x_t^m, x_s^m, \varepsilon\right)$ represents a binary function, which has the following values for i = 0, 1, 2, …, m-1:

$$I\left(x_t^m, x_s^m, \varepsilon\right) = \begin{cases} 1 & if \left|x_{t-i} - x_{s-i}\right| < \varepsilon \\ 0 & otherwise \end{cases}$$

According to Brock, Dechert, Scheinkman, LeBaron (1996), the BDS statistics is calculated as follows:

Table 2. BDS Test

Dimension	BDS Statistic	Std. Error	z-Statistic	Prob.
BDS Test for BET_C_LOG_RETURN				
2	0.037404	0.002553	14.65042	0.0000
3	0.069451	0.004061	17.10348	0.0000
4	0.093462	0.004840	19.30854	0.0000
5	0.109259	0.005051	21.63141	0.0000
6	0.115585	0.004877	23.69986	0.0000
BDS Test for FTSE_MIB_LOG_RETURNS				
2	0.014375	0.002304	6.239415	0.0000
3	0.035941	0.003656	9.830998	0.0000
4	0.052971	0.004347	12.18478	0.0000
5	0.064634	0.004525	14.28432	0.0000
6	0.071673	0.004358	16.44745	0.0000
2	0.013962	0.002266	6.162988	0.0000
3	0.030358	0.003602	8.428382	0.0000
4	0.041428	0.004291	9.654089	0.0000
5	0.051520	0.004475	11.51306	0.0000
6	0.057228	0.004318	13.25392	0.0000

Source: Own computations based on selected financial data series

$$V_{m,\varepsilon} = \sqrt{T}\,\frac{C_{m,\varepsilon} - C_{1,\varepsilon}^{m}}{S_{m,\varepsilon}}$$

where $S_{m,\varepsilon}$ is defined as the standard deviation of $\sqrt{T\left(C_{m,\varepsilon} - C_{1,\varepsilon}^{m}\right)}$. In addition, the BDS statistics converges in distribution to N(0,1) thus the null hypothesis of independent and identically distributed is rejected based on a result such as $\left|V_{m,\varepsilon}\right| > 1,96$ in terms of a 5% significance level.

The null hypothesis was rejected in all three sample cases based on selected stock indices. The following outputs highlight the value of the standardised BDS statistics and the corresponding two-sided probabilities.

The empirical analysis includes the use of Hodrick-Prescott (HP) filter which is a specialized filter for trend and business cycle estimation. Hodrick-Prescott filter has a wide applicability in economics. The basic idea suggests that in the center of the sample financial time series the filter is symmetric and towards the end of the series is becoming increasingly asymmetric. On the other hand, Hodrick-Prescott filter involves the decomposition of the sample financial time series into a trend component and a residual component, which may or may not include a cyclical component.

Figures 6-9 highlight the use of Hodrick – Prescott Filter in the case selected stock returns.

Granger (1969) argued that if some other time series Yt contains information regarding the past periods which are useful in the prediction Xt and in addition this information are included in no other series used in the predictor, then this implies that Yt caused Xt.

In addition, Granger suggested that if X_t and Y_t are two different stationary time series variables with zero means, then the canonical causal model has the following form:

$$X_t = \sum_{j=1}^{m} a_j X_{t-j} + \sum_{j=1}^{m} b_j Y_{t-j} + \varepsilon_t$$

$$Y_t = \sum_{j=1}^{m} c_j X_{t-j} + \sum_{j=1}^{m} d_j Y_{t-j} + \eta_t$$

where ε_t and η_t play the role of two uncorrelated white-noise series, namely $E\left[\varepsilon_t \varepsilon_s\right] = 0 = E\left[\eta_t \eta_s\right]$ for $s \neq t$ and on the other hand the following expression is obtained $E\left[\varepsilon_t \varepsilon_s\right] = 0$ for $\forall t, s$.

The concept of causality requires that in the case when Y_t is causing X_t some b_j is different from zero and vice versa, i.e., in the case when X_t is causing Y_t some c_j is different from zero.

A different context implies that causality is valid simultaneously in both directions or simply a so-called "feedback relationship between X_t and Y_t". The F-distribution test is used to test the Granger causality hypotheses based on the following formula:

$$F = \frac{\left(RSS_R - RSS_{UR}\right) / m}{RSS_{UR} / \left(n - k\right)}$$

where RSS_R is the residual sum of squares, RSS_{UR} is the unrestricted residual sum of squares, m is the number of lagged X_t variables, K is the number of parameters in the restricted regression.

Figure 6. Hodrick – Prescott Filter
Source: Author's own computations based on selected financial data series

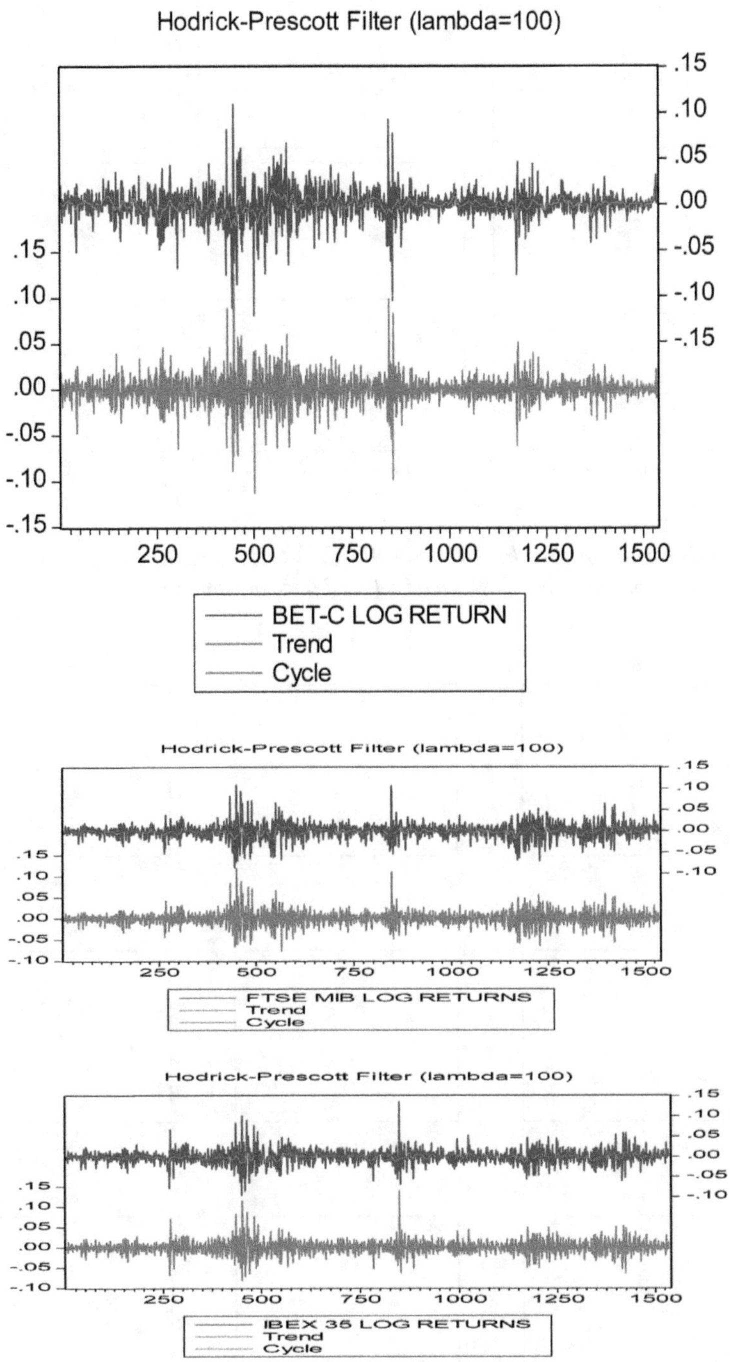

**For a more accurate representation see the electronic version.*

Figure 7. Matrix of all pairs of selected stock market indices
Source: Author's own computations based on selected financial data series

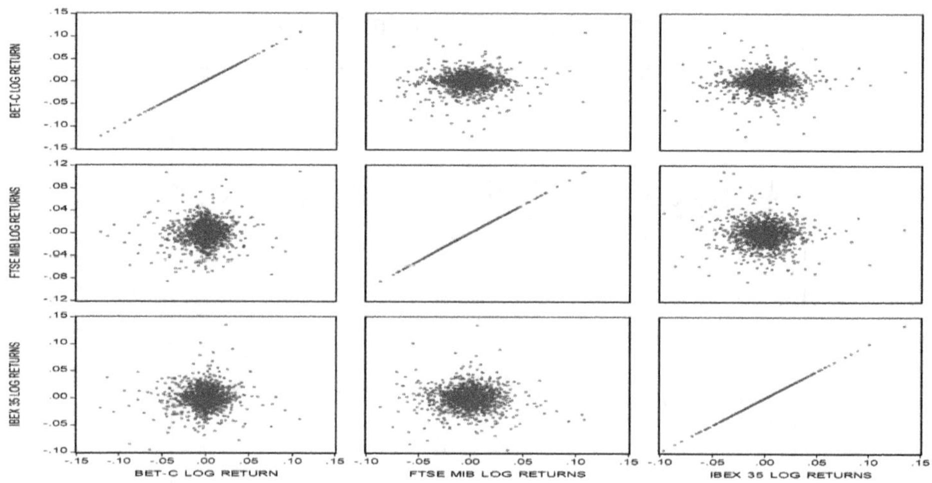

Figure 8. Distribution graphics CDF - SURVIVOR – QUANTILE
Source: Author's own computations based on selected financial data series

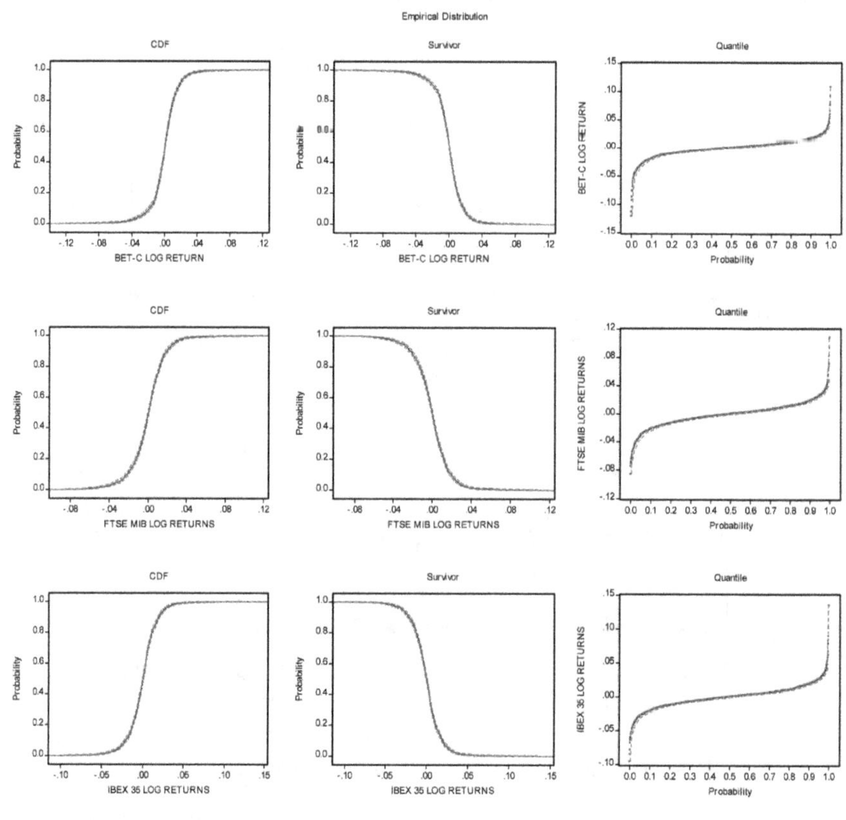

Figure 9. Theoretical quantile-quantile plots (extreme values)
Source: Author's own computations based on selected financial data series

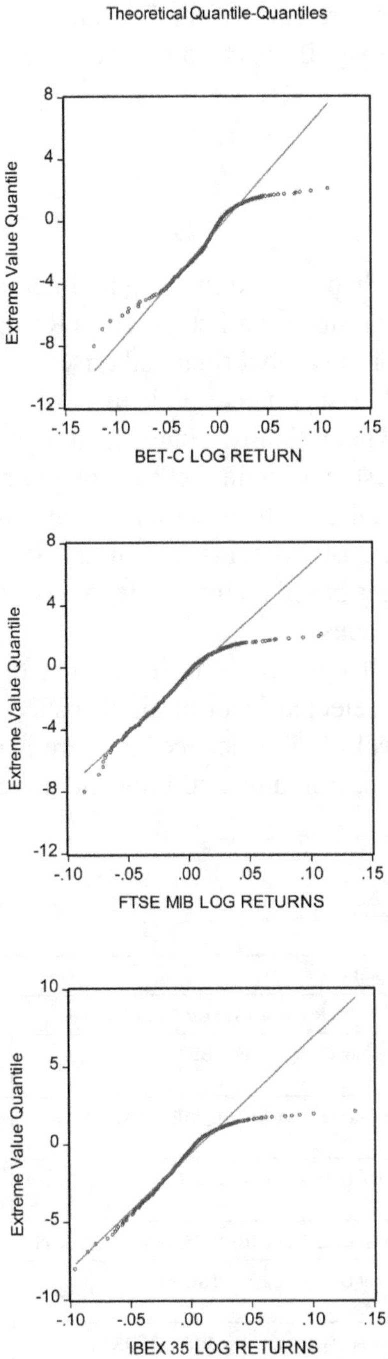

**For a more accurate representation see the electronic version.*

Aneconometric interpretation suggested that the null hypothesis Ho implies that lagged X_t terms do not belong in the regression.

The null hypothesis is rejected if the F-value exceeds the critical F value at the selected level of significance (5%) or if the P-value is lower than the α level of significance.

CONCLUSION

The main aim of this chapter is to investigate international causal linkages between Latin European stock markets, such as Romania, Spain and Italy in the turbulent context of the global financial crises. In recent past, the impact of the global financial crisis on economic migration was extremely high as global implications. Theoretically, financial integration and international causal linkages suggest a certain behavioral pattern between receiving societies. The empirical results of Granger causality tests among Latin European stock markets of Romania, Spain and Italy highlight significant investment opportunities based on international portfolio diversification and risk management strategies.

Technically, the null hypothesis is rejected if the F-value exceeds the critical F value at the selected level of significance (5%) or if the P-value is lower than the α level of significance, so there is no particular causality between Italy and Spain, Romania and Italy and not even between Romania

Table 3. Granger Causality tests

Null Hypothesis	Obs	F-Statistic	Probability
Pairwise Granger Causality Tests			
FTSE_MIB_LOG_RETURNS does not Granger Cause BET_C_LOG_RETURN	1534	0.63020	0.53262
BET_C_LOG_RETURN does not Granger Cause FTSE_MIB_LOG_RETURNS		0.90168	0.40610
IBEX_35_LOG_RETURNS does not Granger Cause BET_C_LOG_RETURN	1534	1.26421	0.28276
BET_C_LOG_RETURN does not Granger Cause IBEX_35_LOG_RETURNS		1.01013	0.36441
IBEX_35_LOG_RETURNS does not Granger Cause FTSE_MIB_LOG_RETURNS	1534	0.13020	0.87793
FTSE_MIB_LOG_RETURNS does not Granger Cause IBEX_35_LOG_RETURNS		1.02881	0.35768

Source: Own computations based on selected financial data series

and Spain in the sample period, i.e., the period between January 2007 and April 2013. Consequently, it appears that the null hypothesis of no Granger causality is not rejected, so there is no causal relationship between analyzed stock markets. International portfolio diversification benefits in globalized stock markets highlight the opportunity of investing in various categories of financial assets across national (local) stock markets with lower correlations in order to achieve high returns.

REFERENCES

Abimanyu, Y. (2008). *International Linkages to the Indonesian Capital Market: Cointegration Test*. Capital Market and Financial Institution Supervisory Agency, Ministry of Finance of Indonesia.

Balios, D., & Xanthakis, M. (2003). International interdependence and dynamic linkages between developed stock markets. South Eastern Europe Journal of Economics, 1(1), 105-130.

Birau, R. (2014a). Investigating Long-Term Behavior of Milan Stock Exchange: An Empirical Analysis. *Journal of Management and Social Science, 1*(2), 29-37.

Birau, R. (2014b). Analyzing Dynamic Causal Linkages Between Developed Stock Markets Of Spain And Canada, *International Journal Of Core Engineering & Management, 1*(2), 1-9.

Birau, R., & Trivedi, J. (2013). Analyzing cointegration and international linkage between Bucharest stock exchange and European developed stock markets. *NAUN International Journal of Economics and Statistics*, *4*(1), 237–246.

Brock, W.A., Dechert, W.D. & Scheinkman, J.A. (1987) A Test for Independence Based on the Correlation Dimension. University of Chicago.

Dickey, D. A., & Fuller, W. A. (1981). Likelihood Ratio Statistics for Autoregressive Time Series with a Unit Root. *Econometrica*, *49*(4), 1057–1072. doi:10.2307/1912517

Engle, R. F., & Granger, C. W. J. (1987). Cointegration and Error Correction: Representation, Estimation and Testing. *Econometrica*, *55*(2), 251–276. doi:10.2307/1913236

Eun, C. S., & Shim, S. (1989). International Transmission of Stock Market Movements. *Journal of Financial and Quantitative Analysis*, *24*(2), 241–256. doi:10.2307/2330774

Granger, C., & Morgenstern, O. (1970). *Predictability of stock market prices, MA*. Lexington: Heath Lexington Books.

Granger, C. W. J. (1969). Investigating Causal Relations by Econometric Models and Cross-spectral Methods. *Econometrica*, *37*(3), 424–438. doi:10.2307/1912791

Granger, C. W. J. (1986). Developments in the Study of Cointegrated Economic Variables. *Oxford Bulletin of Economics and Statistics*, 48.

Khan, T. A. (2011). Cointegration of International Stock Markets: An Investigation of Diversification Opportunities, *Undergraduate. Economic Review (Kansas City, Mo.)*, *8*(1).

Siminică, M., & Birau, R. (2014) Investigating International Causal Linkages Between Latin European Stock Markets in Terms of Global Financial Crisis: A Case Study for Romania, Spain And Italy. *International Journal of Business Quantitative Economics and Applied Management Research*

Singh, G. S. P. (2010). Chinese and Indian Stock Market Linkages with Developed Stock Markets. *Asian Journal of Finance & Accounting*, *2*(2), E2.

Singh, S., & Sharma, G. D. (2012). Inter-linkages between stock exchanges: A study of BRIC nations. *International Journal of Marketing, Financial Services & Management Research*, *1*(3).

Chapter 13
Modeling S&P Bombay Stock Exchange BANKEX Index Volatility Patterns Using GARCH Model

ABSTRACT

The main objective of this chapter is to estimate volatility patterns in the case of S&P Bombay Stock Exchange (BSE) BANKEX index in India. In recent past, the Indian banking sector was one of the fastest-growing industries and all major banks have been included in S&P BANKEX index as index benchmark constituent companies. The financial econometric framework is based on asymmetric GARCH (1, 1) model which is performed in order to capture asymmetric volatility clustering and leptokurtosis. Data time lag is considered from the first transaction day of January 2002 to last transaction day of June 2014. The empirical results revealed the existence of volatility shocks in the selected time series and also volatility clustering. The volatility impact has generated highly positive clockwise and impacted actual stocks. Moreover, the empirical findings reveal that the BANKEX index grown over 17 times in 12 years and volatility returns have been found present in listed stocks.

DOI: 10.4018/978-1-5225-9269-3.ch013

INTRODUCTION

In recent past, stock market volatility modeling and estimation have established certain issues of great interest not only for investors, financial practitioners and academics, especially in terms of modern finance perspectives. Moreover, one of the main aims of investment process is to reduce the high exposure to risk considering the fact that international portfolio diversification provides superior risk-adjusted returns. In this sense, globalization and financial liberalization have significantly contributed to the accuracy of the investment process. However, on a deeper level, certain global factors such as economic, historical, political, social, demographic and cultural have a critical influence on the investment framework.

Financial modeling highlights the fact that stock price movements exhibit certain stylized facts such as volatility clustering (Mandelbrot, 1963), financial leverage effects (Black, 1976), leptokurtosis, heavy tailed distribution, conditional heteroskedasticity, asymmetric volatility effects, unconditional time-varying moments and severe deviations from normality in the context of extreme events.

According to the official report of FTSE Country Classification issued on September 2013, following subcategories are included, i. e. developed, advanced emerging, secondary emerging and frontier. India is included in the category of secondary emerging countries. The financial benefits and investment opportunities provided by international portfolio diversification strategies are very attractive in terms of Bombay Stock Exchange.

LITERATURE REVIEW

Bollerslev (1986) has generalized ARCH model by including lagged valued of the conditional variance. The GARCH model allows a wider range of behavior and patterns especially in the case of more persistent volatility. The most general form of the model is GARCH (1,1) where GARCH stands for Generalized Autoregressive Conditional Heteroscedasticity. Moreover, a GARCH model or basically or Generalized ARCH model represents an extension of the ARCH model which otherwise is very similar to an ARMA model.

According to Brooks (1996) such a generalization of ARCH model, namely GARCH model can be perceived as an infinite order ARCH model. Engle (1982) argued that traditional econometric models assume a constant one period forecast variance and therefore in order to generalize this implausible assumption, it was implemented a new class of stochastic processes called autoregressive conditional heteroscedastic (ARCH) processes. On the other hand, Brooks (1996) suggested that it is highly unlikely that a GARCH model of order greater than one in the autoregressive and moving average components would be required, since by definition, a GARCH (1,1) model implies an infinitely long memory with respect to past news, i.e. innovations.

Prasanna and Menon (2013) suggested that the global process of financial integration between Indian stock market and international stock markets caused the absorption domestic and global news into the asset prices and stock indices. Trivedi (2013) argued that generally the banking sector in India was distinguished by accuracy and high confidence even in dramatic periods caused by extreme events such as the global financial crisis.

Nateson et al. (2013) investigated spillover effect of volatility in Indian BSE Sensex on BSE sectoral indices based on GARCH (1,1) model. The authors emphasized the importance of financial integration due to volatility transmission patterns especially in terms of risk management strategies and portfolio diversification for all investment sectors in India. Moreover, Basabi, Roy and Niyogi (2009) examined conditional volatility patterns of the BSE BANKEX index based on symmetric and asymmetric GARCH models. The authors revealed the existence of leverage effect considering the response to positive and negative news (innovations).

METHODOLOGICAL APPROACH

According to Birau, Trivedi and Antonescu (2014) the financial data series consist of daily closing asset prices for the selected stock index during the period between January 2002 and June 2014 with the exception of legal holidays or other events when stock markets haven't performed transactions. The continuously-compounded daily returns are calculated using the log difference of the closing prices of stock market selected index, i.e. S&P Bombay Stock Exchange (BSE) BANKEX index as follows:

$$r_t = \ln\left(\frac{p_t}{p_{t-1}}\right) = \ln\left(p_t\right) - \ln\left(p_{t-1}\right)$$

where p is the daily closing price.

Generalized autoregressive modeling known as GARCH has become one of the popular methods to estimate financial market volatility. GARCH (1, 1) model which developed by Bollerslev and Taylor (1986). This model allows conditional variance of all variables to be dependent upon previous legs and it reflects on entire series. However, the first leg of squared residual will be from mean equation and this presents idea about volatility from the previous time periods.

General most used model for formulate GARCH (1, 1) is as follows:

$$h_t = \omega + \alpha_1 u_{t-1}{}^2 + \beta_1 h_{t-1}$$

We need to follow hypothesis of covariance stationary as unconditional variance and to exist that it processed by following:

$$\sigma^2 = Var(u_t) = E(u_t^2) = E(\omega + \alpha_1 u_{t-1}{}^2 + \beta_1 h_{t-1})$$

$$\sigma^2 = \omega\alpha\beta$$

We implement GARCH (1, 1) conditional variance equation $Var(u_t | h_{t-1}) = E(u_t^2 | h_{t-1}) = h_t$, and thus it can simply follow the form $h_t = \omega + \alpha_1 u_{t-1}{}^2 + \beta_1 h_{t-1}$.

Hence, the final formulation will take form of $_{ht} = \omega + \alpha_1 u_{t-1}{}^2 + \beta_1 h_{t-1}$ and the Arch term and GARCH term.

The implementation of GARCH model limits the stationarity of the data and presence of ARCH effect in time series of BANKEX index. However, we test the results by using ADF test also called as Augment Dickey-Fuller test which represents an econometric tool for unit root problems under hypothesis Ho=p0, & p1. Generally, all-time series has unit root problems and it must be filtered and allowed for ARCH processes. Inorder to achieve this objective we have allowed trend for all indices by adding intercept to the model y_t (or Δy_t) on 1, y_{t-1}, $\Delta y_{t-1}, \ldots, \Delta y_{t-p+1}$, computing the t-statistic which can resulted in $\tau_t = \frac{\hat{\rho} - 1}{se(\hat{\rho})}$ this process comparing its value to percentiles of DF τ_μ distribution.

EMPIRICAL RESULTS

Applying econometric methodology, it has produced higher negative value than its critical value at 1%, 5% and 10% level which allows series for ARCH and proves no unit root problems. According to Birau, Trivedi and Antonescu (2014), this is well enough to process for GARCH (1, 1) model to estimate volatility of BANKEX index. The first step in the empirical analysis process is to evaluate the basic statistics data series, such as following features: Mean: 000.0918151, Median: 0.00123011, Min: -0.144804, Max:0.175483, Std. Dev.: 0.0201306, Skewness: -0.0579478 and Ex. Kurtosis: 5.67762. This basic statistic represents a summary of statistics of BANKEX index from January 2002 to June 2014 as it can be distinguished in Figure 1.

The S&P BSE BANKEX index represents banking stock moments listed on Bombay Stock Exchange and the Fig1represents the historical graph of BANKEX moments from year 2002 to 2014 (see Figure 1). The mean value near to zero followed by median, a large difference is visible from Min value to Max value of the BANKEX index through all these years. The standard deviations figures are comparatively important since that explores the degree of risks and returns which represents 0.0201 (of the log first difference values) and negative skewness and exceeding value of Kurtosis by 2.67 (5.67). The S&P BSE BANKEX index reveals upper-side strong moment of stocks from January 2002 to June 2014 with visible downfall between the years 2008-

Figure 1. Descriptive statistics and the trend of S&P BSE BANKEX index (individual chart)
Source: Author's own computations based on selected financial data series

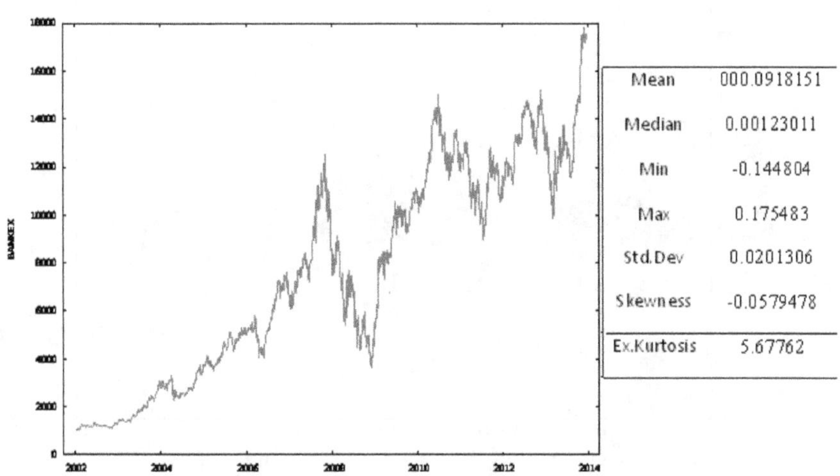

2009 and strong recovery of banking sector after global financial crisis. The stock index journey started with base point, i.e. 1000 points on January 01, 2002 and reached to 17475 at last day of trading in covered study period. It shows the journey growth of 17 times of the base index in 12 years including financial recession.

This fundamental math suggests strong banking fundamentals in India which includes major public sector banks. The original financial data series has been converted to log returns for all years. We used 3122 daily observations as data from January 2002 to June 2014. The first log difference is considered and ADF test (KPSS) test has been tested. The ADF test statistics results are significant at degree of 1%, 5% and 10% level. Moreover Figure 2 represents the stationary data outcome and ADF test statistics results.

The long sketches are visible (see Figure 2) clearly in year 2004, 2007, 2008 and 2009. These long sketches moments are not casual and represents abnormal market behavior. Nevertheless, the international global financial crisis is clearly visible in the market history. Negative skewness and higher kurtosis creates a leptokurtosis impact which makes the long tail (see Figure 3). The banking sector index of Bombay Stock exchange suggests lowest pick level in year 2004 and measurable highest up level sketches in year 2009.

The other small and medium size sketches resulted from standard volatility of BANKEX. Augment Dickey-Fuller test (ADFtest) provides significance

Figure 2. Log returns series of S&P BSE BANKEX index (individual chart)
Source: Author's own computations based on selected financial data series

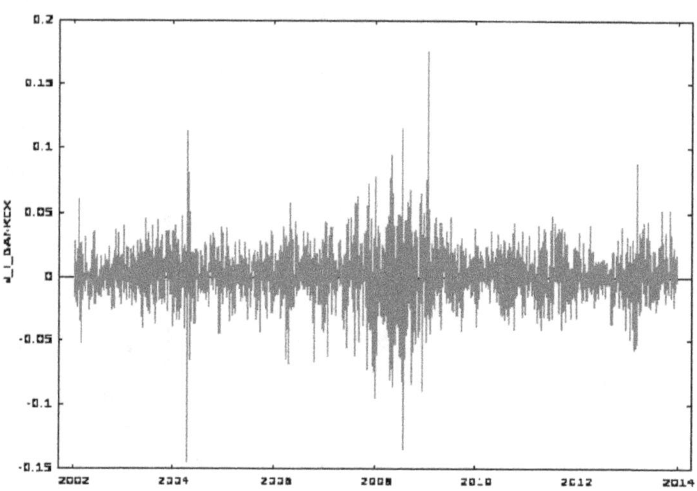

Test statistic = 0.148101 10% 5% 1% 0.347 0.461 0.743

Figure 3. The Q-Q plot, Residual ACF and Residual PACF for of S&P BSE BANKEX index

Source: Author's own computations based on selected financial data series

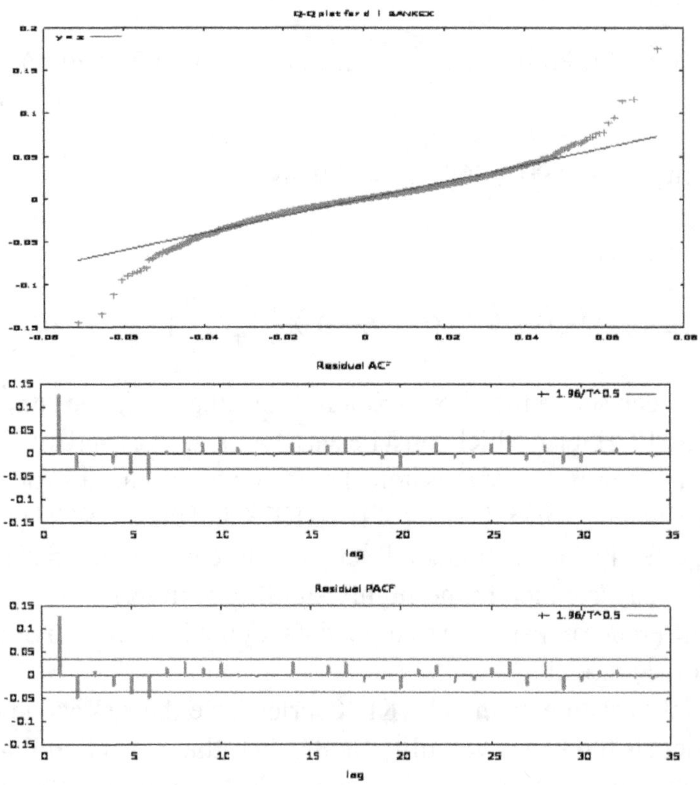

of BANKEX index at level of 1%, 5% and 10%. We consider significance at level of5%. Furthermore, the negative skewness and higher kurtosis created long tail (see Figure 3) which mentioned by Q-Qploting of BANKEX index. The degree of negative skewness and higher kurtosis has lasted the tail from level of -0.15 degree to over +0.15 degree visible in Figure 3.

We can see the ACF and PACF pattern which represents mild negative autocorrelations in BANKEX timeseries. These patterns are collected from GARCH model output which represents strong positive autocorrelations (see Figure 3). The ACF and PACF patters also represent strong stationary series and presence of AR term in financial series of BANKEX. Generalized autoregressive modeling can be now proceeded to estimate the volatility in the series. We employ here GARCH model with (1) GARCH term and (1) ARCH term, also known as the GARCH (1, 1) model.

The GARCH (1, 1) model can be formulated in the following estimation:

$$h_t = \omega + \alpha_1 u_{t-1}^2 + \beta_1 h_{t-1}$$

We can form the entire outcome in the above equations and can be explore as follows:

$$0.0825931\alpha_1 u_{t-1}^2 + 0.901536\beta_1 h_{t-1} = 0.9841291<1$$

It also results that:

$$(\alpha_1) + (\beta_1) = 0.0825931 + 0.901536= 0.9841291<1$$

What we can see in the above explored formulation is the sum of ARCH term and GARCH term which must be less than 1 (i.e <1) and this hypothesis is proved in the previous expression. This issue highlights a strong presence of volatility in the financial series of BANKEX and the GARCH (1, 1) model is fitted perfectly in the financial series. The calculative answers do not disclosed in paper which found highly significant in terms of final answer. First log difference considered as input data for the formulation of Bollerslev GARCH (1, 1) model.

Financial investments in BANKEX series have the risk value of 0.2013 degree whereas the series volatility 0.9841291, that is very similar to 1 and proves high degree of changes at upper side (positive shocks) and lower side (negative shocks). The return ratios and the index growth i.e. 1000 to over 17000 represent the great investor interest in the BANKEX stocks. Nevertheless, the stock is capable to recover from great negative shocks or even from global financial crisis as that has evident to fast recovery.

CONCLUSION

The major objective of this research paper is to investigate the behavior of S&P Bombay Stock Exchange (BSE) BANKEX Index volatility patterns using GARCH model. A S&P BSE BANKEX index moment of last12 years represents also the great attractions of investors and the high volume of turnovers. Bollerslev GARCH(1, 1) model fitted well on BANKEX financial series. Nevertheless, the actual difference between Min and Max reveals high degree of volatility in Bombay Stock Exchange for open ended stocks. We considered data ranging from 1st January 2002 to last day of June 2014. Basic statistics shows the mean and risk value in the BANKEX index (0.2013). The returns are over 17 times higher during the analysis period of 12 years and BANKEX index have absorbed the global financial crisis rather well. The stock fluctuations are abnormal and highly volatile since the evidence presence in year 2004 for down effect shocks and 2009 for positive shocks. ACF and PACF shows less degree of negative patterns and more positive patterns and presence of AR effect in series.

REFERENCES

Basabi, B., Roy, S., & Niyogi, T. (2009). Volatility and Forecasting of BSE BANKEX, Journal of Quantitative Economics. *New Series*, *7*(1), 1–26.

Birau, R., Trivedi, J., & Antonescu, M. (2014). Modeling S&P Bombay Stock Exchange BANKEX Index Volatility Patterns Using GARCH Model. *Procedia Economics and Finance*, *32*, 520-525. doi:10.1016/S2212-5671(15)01427-6

Black, F. (1976). Studies of stock market volatility changes. In *Proceedings of the American Statistical Association, Business and Economic Statistics Section* (pp. 177–181).

Bollerslev, T. (1986). Generalized autoregressive conditional heteroskedasticity. *Journal of Economics*, *31*(3), 307–327. doi:10.1016/0304-4076(86)90063-1

Brooks, C. (1996). Testing for Non-Linearity in Daily Sterling Exchange Rates. *Applied Financial Economics*, *6*(4), 307–317. doi:10.1080/096031096334105

Engle, R. F. (1982). Autoregressive Conditional Heteroscedasticity with Estimates of the Variance of UK Inflation. *Econometrica*, *50*(4), 987–1008. doi:10.2307/1912773

Mandelbrot, B. (1963). The variation of certain speculative prices. *The Journal of Business*, *36*(4), 394–419. doi:10.1086/294632

Nateson, C., Palanisamy, R., Renukadevi, P., & Suganya, D. (2013). Spillover Effect of Volatility in BSE Sensex on BSE Sectoral Indices. *International Journal of Management & Business Studies*, 3(1), 92-95.

Prasanna, P. K., & Menon, A. S. (2013). Speed of information adjustment in Indian stock indices. *IIMB Management Review*, *25*(3), 150–159. doi:10.1016/j.iimb.2013.05.003

Trivedi, J. (2013). Performance Analysis of Bankex Banks Through CAMEL Model. *Management Dynamics*, *13*(2), 1–13.

Chapter 14
Investigating Causal Linkages Between International Stock Markets in Hungary and Austria in Terms of Economic Globalization

ABSTRACT

The main aim of this chapter is to examine causal linkages between selected stock markets of Hungary and Austria in terms of economic globalization. The sample databases cover a long time period from January 2000 to December 2013. The selected ATX stock index represents Austria index, while BUX represents the main stock index of Hungary. The empirical findings highlighted that stock market in Hungary is significantly more volatile and provides comparatively higher investing opportunities for financial asset returns. There are strong evidences of no casual linkages between selected markets of Austria and Hungary. The econometric analysis includes BDS and Granger causality tests. The results are classified in a comparative manner. This book chapter will support decision makings on escalation ratios depending on the international financial market transmitting patterns.

DOI: 10.4018/978-1-5225-9269-3.ch014

INTRODUCTION

Financial market volatility has been the subject of greater interest for international investors, researchers and academicians. It has delivered plenty of research in the areas of stock market volatility, transmitting pattern, risk evaluations, investment opportunity, international linkages and so on. This paper focuses particularly on the casual linkages between the stock market of Hungary (BUX) and Austria (ATX). According to FTSE Country Classification as at September 2014 which is the most recent official report, Austria is included in the category of developed countries and Hungary is included in the category of advanced emerging countries. Austria financial market follows comparative more stable investment opportunity for the international investors all over the world. The risk ratios and volatility patterns are less escalated with international financial market moments. The Hungary market (BUX) classified as the advance emerging markets which represents higher escalation rates at upper side and lower side with market volatility.

The advance emerging markets provides greener opportunities for risk taker investors. It is investigated from previous studies that not only developed countries but also financial markets of developed and developing countries become interrelated (Aktar, 2009). Eun and Shim (1989) have provided interesting results regarding the international transmission of stock market movements among several mature markets, such as: Australia, Japan, Hong Kong, U.K, Switzerland, France, Germany, Canada and U.S.A., considering the fact that a series of multilateral interconnections were identified. Panton, Lessig, and Joy (1976) investigated co-movements of international equity markets in the light of investment opportunities arising from portfolio diversifications.

There are vast number of research papers on financial market volatile linkages and provided the greater support to investors in decision makings. This paper basically emphasized on the international financial market volatility linkages on advance emerging market and developed market. This paper will support decision makings on escalation ratios depending on the international financial market transmitting patterns. For instance, Tokyo and New York major stock indices, namely NIKKEI 225 and S&P500. Kasa (1992) investigated common stochastic trends in international stock markets. Trivedi and Birau (2013) investigated the distinguishing characteristic are stability of developed capital market and stable emerging market.

According to Antonescu and Birau (2014), beyond inherent advantages, global liberalization and international integration provide a conducive environment for obtaining reprehensible illegal benefits based on complex activities related to cybercrimes, especially in terms of emerging countries. The authors suggested that cybercrime includes a wide range of illegal activities such as: cyber bullying, cyber terrorism, identity theft, cyber stalking, virtual pornography (via the Internet), cyber espionage (illegally obtaining confidential data), computer hacking, computer fraud, online harassment, phishing, online piracy, blackmailing proceeding, cyber extortion, spam attacks, copyright infringement, computer virus programs (installing malicious software programs such as Trojan horse viruses).

Those groups of capital market stay in the particular bracket have spreading impact of volatility (bullish and bearish) reflected from stable and developed capital market. The impact spreads through inter-linkage between developed and emerging markets. These findings can be idle to bridging the pattern gap and impact on volatility.

METHODOLOGICAL APPROACH

The empirical analysis is based on the daily returns of the major stock indices during the sample period between January 2000 and December 2013. The continuously-compounded daily returns are calculated using the log-difference of the closing prices of stock markets selected indices, ie ATX Index (Austria) and BUX Index (Hungary), as follows:

$$r_t = \ln\left(\frac{p_t}{p_{t-1}}\right) = \ln\left(p_t\right) - \ln\left(p_{t-1}\right)$$

In the above formula, p represents the daily closing price. Data series consists of the daily closing prices for each sample stock index during the period between January 2000 and December 2013 with the exception of legal holidays or other events when stock markets have not performed any financial transactions. Augmented Dickey-Fuller (ADF) test is used in order to determine the non-stationarity or the integration order of a financial time series. A series noted y_t is integrated of order one, i.e. $y_t \sim I(1)$ and contains a unit root if y_t is non-stationary, but on the other hand Δy_t is stationary, i.e. $\Delta y_t = y_t - y_{t-1}$.

Moreover, extrapolating the previous expression, a series y_t is integrated of order d, i.e. $y_t \sim I(d)$ if y_t is non-stationary, but $\Delta^d y_t$ is stationary.

The ADF diagnostic test investigates the potential presence of unit roots divided into the following categories: unit root with a constant and a trend, unit root with a constant, but without a time trend, and finally unit root without constant and temporal trend. The ADF test is based on the following regression model:

$$\Delta y_t = c + \beta \cdot t + \delta \cdot y_{t-1} + \sum_{i=1}^{p} \gamma_i \Delta y_{t-i} + \varepsilon_t$$

where p represents the number of lags for which it was investigated whether fulfilling the condition that residuals are white noise, c is a constant, t is the indicator for time trend and Δ is the symbol for differencing. In addition, it is important to emphasize the essence of a stochastic trend that cannot be predicted due to the time dependence of residual's variance. Strictly related to the ADF test, if the coefficients to be estimated β and δ have the null value then the analyzed financial time series is characterized by a stochastic trend.

The null hypothesis, namely if the time series has a unit root, is rejected if t-statistics is lower than the critical value. We followed basic statistical characteristics of selected indices are represented by the following issues: Jarque-Bera test's statistic which allows to eliminate the normality of distribution hypothesis, parameter of asymmetry distribution or Skewness and Kurtosis parameter which measures the peakness or flatness of the distribution, i.e. leptokurtic distribution.

The BDS test was used in order to determine whether the residuals are independent and identically distributed. BDS test is a two-tailed test and is based on the following hypothesis:

H_0: sample observations are independently and identically distributed (I.I.D.)
H_1: sample observations are not I.I.D.

This includes aspect involving that the time series is non-linearly dependent if first differences of the natural logarithm have been calculated. The BDS statistics converges in distribution to N(0,1) thus the null hypothesis of independent and identically distributed is rejected based on a result such as

$\left|V_{m,\varepsilon}\right| > 1{,}96$ in terms of a 5% significance level. The null hypothesis was rejected in both cases based on selected stock indices.

Granger (1969) suggested that, if some other time series Y_t contains information regarding the past periods which are useful in the prediction of Xt and in addition this information is included in no other series used in the predictor, then this implies that Y_t caused X_t. Moreover, Granger suggested that if Xtand $Y_t$are two different stationary time series variables with zero means, then the canonical causal model has the following form:

$$X_t = \sum_{j=1}^{m} a_j X_{t-j} + \sum_{j=1}^{m} b_j Y_{t-j} + \varepsilon_t$$

$$Y_t = \sum_{j=1}^{m} c_j X_{t-j} + \sum_{j=1}^{m} d_j Y_{t-j} + \eta_t$$

where ε_t and η_t play the role of two uncorrelated white-noise series, namely: $E\left[\varepsilon_t \varepsilon_s\right] = 0 = E\left[\eta_t \eta_s\right]$ for $s \neq t$ and simultaneously: $E\left[\varepsilon_t \varepsilon_s\right] = 0$ for $\forall t, s$. Practically, the very idea of causality requires that in the case when Y_t is causing X_t some b_j is different from zero and vice versa, ie in the case when X_t is causing Y_t some c_j is different from zero.

A different situation implies that causality is valid simultaneously in both directions or simply a so-called "feedback relationship between X_t and Y_t." The F-distribution test is used to test the Granger causality hypotheses based on the following formula:

$$F = \frac{\left(RSS_R - RSS_{UR}\right) / m}{RSS_{UR} / \left(n - k\right)}$$

where RSS_R is the residual sum of squares, RSS_{UR} represents the unrestricted residual sum of squares, m is the number of lagged X_t variables, K is the number of parameters in the restricted regression. According to representation theorem, the null hypothesis H_0 implies that lagged X_t terms do not belong in the regression. The null hypothesis is rejected if the F-value exceeds the critical F value at the selected level of significance (5%) or if the P-value is lower than the α level of significance.

EMPIRICAL RESULTS

According to Trivedi and Birau (2015) the historical financial data series represent financial indices, i.e. ATX and BUX stock index from January 2000 to December 2013. The empirical analysis has highlighted the fact that from the beginning of the selected study period there are comparatively more ups and downs sketches in the advance emerging market compared to the developed market. The analysis results provided by stationary graph highlights a more detailed overview. (See Figure 2).

The Austria's stock market is a developed market while Hungary's stock market is included in the category of advance emerging markets. The Austria stock market is represented in this empirical analysis by ATX stock index returns and Hungary stock market is represented by BUX stock index returns.

Emerging capital markets, including advance emerging markets are always more volatile compared to developed capital markets. The transmitting pattern changes are clearly visible with higher escalation rates and with observation we can find that advance emerging markets follows the developed market with higher degree of escalation rates for both sides. It also increases the risk factor for the investors and offers exciting opportunities for the investors and researchers in daily based stock trading.

According to Trivedi and Birau (2015), the basic stock statistics includes 3524 observations for Austria stock market and Hungary stock market. The log returns and histogram chats suggests higher degree of volatility and changes of stock prices at higher sides in advance emerging market during the comparative study (See Figure 3). It also increases the degree of standard deviations and min to max rates. We can see that Skewness is higher in ATX log returns whereas Kurtosis is lower in BUX log returns. It means that stock moments are making more stronger impact on stock prices compared to the developed market of Austria stock market based on ATX index.

The Augmented Dickey-fuller test results are significant for Austria (ATX) and Hungary (BUX) (See Table 1).

The BDS tests results suggests independent and identifiable distributions of Austria stock market and Hungary stock market. It represents that time series is non-linearly dependent in case of the first differences of the natural logarithm been calculated. In Table 2 (See Table 2) it rejects the distributions of n(0,1) and thus the null hypotheses of independent and identically distribution is rejected for Austria (AUX) market and Hungary (BUX) market returns. It means that the statistical distribution of BDS tests arrives to result such as

Figure 1. The trend of ATX Index (Austria) and BUX Index (Hungary) individual graphics
Source: Author's computation using financial series of ATX and BUX stock indices.

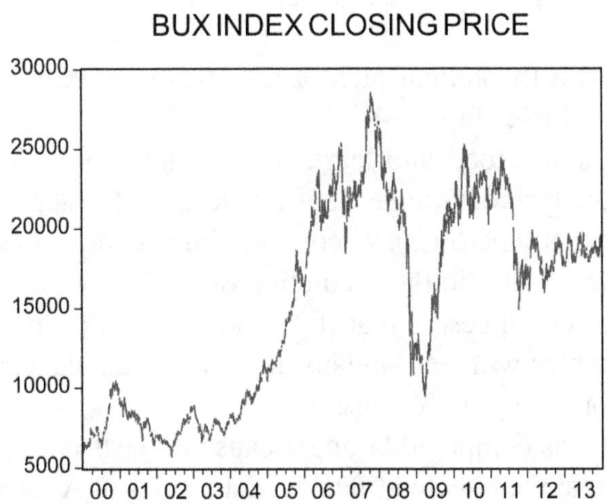

$\left|V_{m,\varepsilon}\right| > 1,96$ in terms of a 5% significance level. The null hypothesis was rejected in both cases based on selected stock indices of AUX and BUX from January 2000 to December 2013.

BDS test results has identified and verified that there are no independent and identifiable relationship between the develop market and advance emerging market. However, the transmitting pattern seems similar because of international transmitting pattern linkage and no evidence found for

Figure 2. The log-returns of ATX Index (Austria) and BUX Index (Hungary)
Source: Author's computation using financial series of ATX and BUX stock indices.

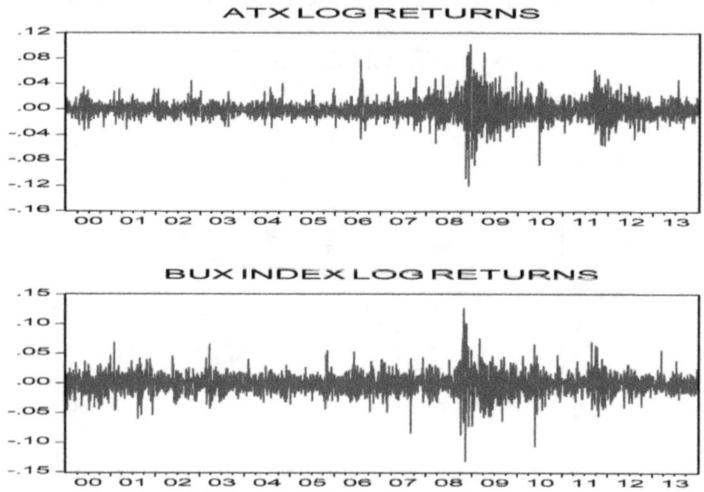

independent casual linkage. We now follow Granger causality tests to check on result 1.

We disclosed the theoretical quantile test results for AUX and BUX market visible in Figure 4 (See Figure 4).

As we have understood and learned in methodology chapter about the evaluation and analysis of Granger causality tests, this tests strongly identifies the casual linkages where (if) Y_t contains information regarding the past periods which are useful in the prediction of Xt, in such case Y_t caused X_t. Moreover, Granger suggested that if X_t and Y_t are two different stationary time series variables with zero means, then the canonical causal model has the following form only if Yt caused Xt.

In Table 3 it was computed Granger causality tests and it was arrived to the conclusion that the selected financial data series of AUX and BUX stock markets indices are not being followed by the above-mentioned form. The financial time series follows the feedback distribution forms since the F value exceeds the critical F value at the selected level of significance ie. 5% and in alternate if the P value is lower than the a level of significance. It proves that there is no casual linkage or significance between the developed stock market of Austria (AUX index) and emerging stock market of Hungary (BUX index).

Figure 3. ATX and BUX stock indices log returns histograms
Source: Author's computation using financial series of ATX and BUX stock indices

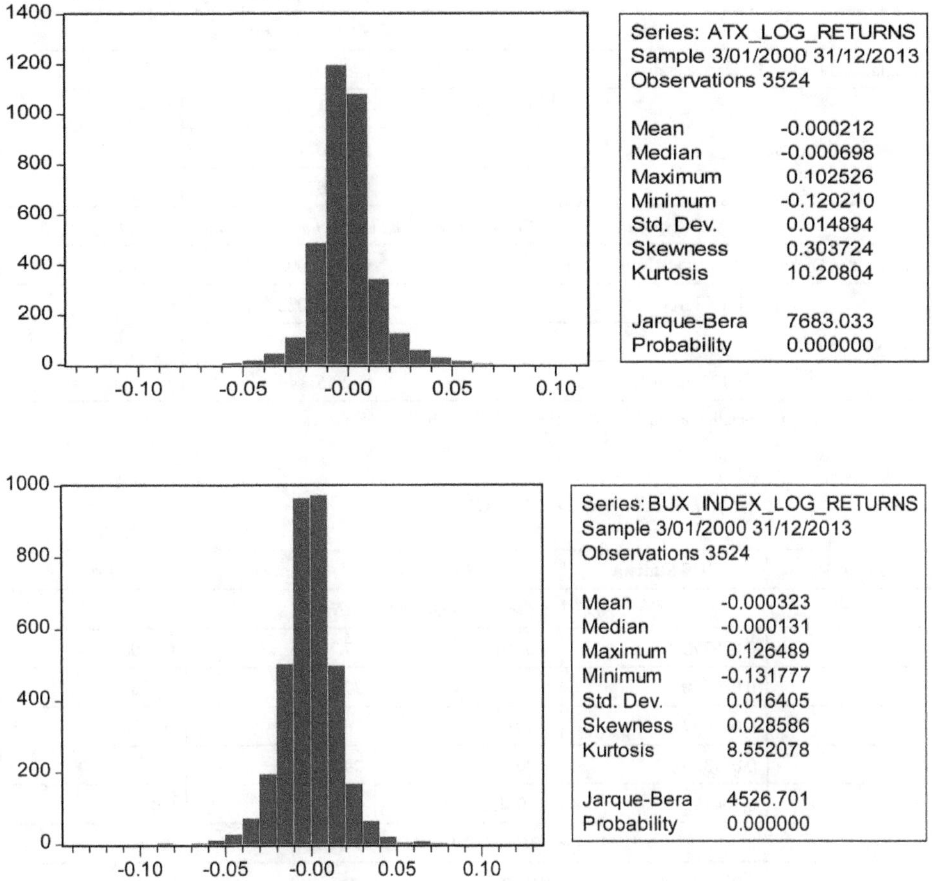

CONCLUSION

This subchapter covers the empirical study based on casual linkages between developed specimen stock market (AUX) and emerging specimen stock market (BUX). Economic globalization can be defined as a dynamic process of growth and dependency links between national states with complex long-term implications. Austria and Hungary are neighboring countries with a significant common history and both are European Union member states. However, the empirical results of Granger causality tests between international stock markets in Hungary and Austria suggests the absence of a causal relationship.

Table 1. Augmented Dickey-Fuller (ADF) Test

		t-Statistic	Prob.*
Null Hypothesis: ATX_LOG_RETURNS has a unit root			
Augmented Dickey-Fuller test statistic		-10.07775	0.0000
Test critical values:	1% level	-3.432033	
	5% level	-2.862169	
	10% level	-2.567148	
Null Hypothesis: BUX_INDEX_LOG_RETURNS has a unit root			
Augmented Dickey-Fuller test statistic		-23.56008	0.0000
Test critical values:	1% level	-3.432022	
	5% level	-2.862164	
	10% level	-2.567146	

Source: Author's computation using financial series of ATX and BUX stock indices

Table 2. BDS Test for ATX and BUX indices

Dimension	BDS Statistic	Std. Error	z-Statistic	Prob.
BDS Test for ATX_LOG_RETURNS				
2	0.029273	0.001645	17.79286	0.0000
3	0.059810	0.002619	22.83755	0.0000
4	0.082977	0.003124	26.55777	0.0000
5	0.097385	0.003263	29.84695	0.0000
6	0.104193	0.003153	33.04710	0.0000
BDS Test for BUX_INDEX_LOG_RETURNS				
2	0.014479	0.001412	10.25199	0.0000
3	0.028827	0.002238	12.88295	0.0000
4	0.039747	0.002656	14.96375	0.0000
5	0.046320	0.002760	16.78362	0.0000
6	0.048644	0.002653	18.33404	0.0000

Source: Author's computation using financial series of ATX and BUX stock indices

Figure 4. Theoretical quantile tests for AUX and BUX stock indices (Extreme values)
Source: Author's computation using financial series of ATX and BUX stock indices

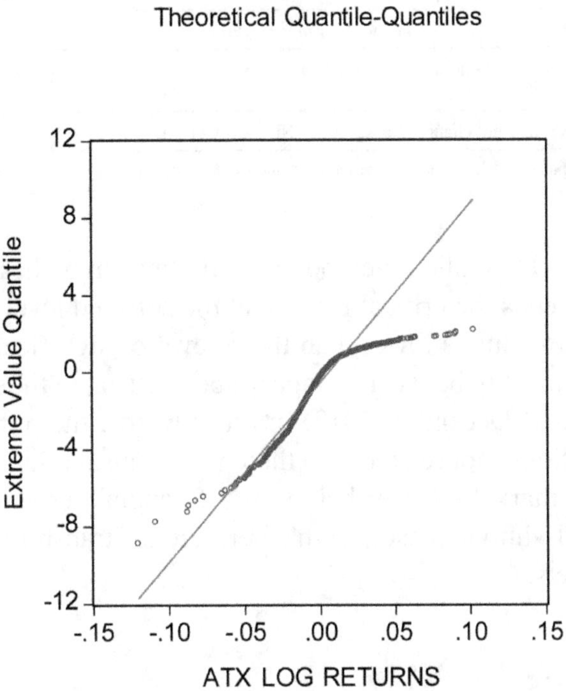

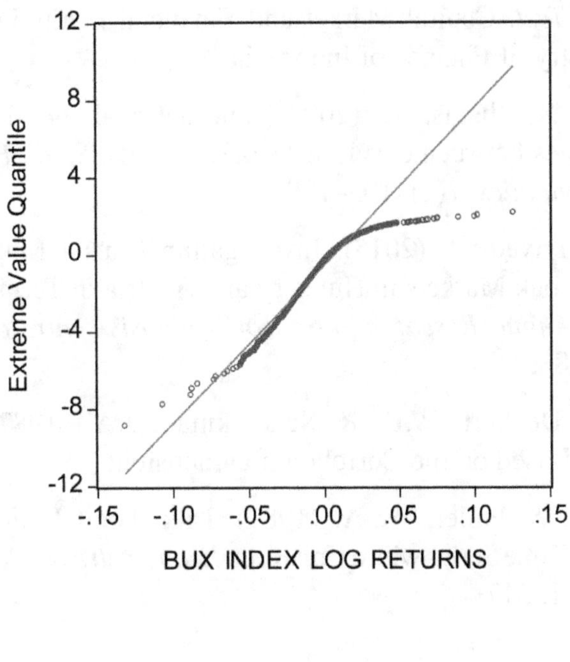

Table 3. Granger Causality tests

Null Hypothesis	Obs	F-Statistic	Probability
Pairwise Granger Causality Tests			
BUX_INDEX_LOG_RETURNS does not Granger Cause ATX_LOG_RETURNS	3522	0.01525	0.98487
ATX_LOG_RETURNS does not Granger Cause BUX_INDEX_LOG_RETURNS		0.36763	0.69240

Source: Author's computation using financial series of ATX and BUX stock indices

Considering the applied methodology, the null hypothesis is rejected if the F-value exceeds the critical F value at the selected level of significance (5%) or if the P-value is lower than the α level of significance, so there is no particular causality between Hungary and Austria, in the period between January 2000 and December 2013. In other words, the null hypothesis of Granger causality is not rejected, so there is no causal relationship between selected stock markets. Nevertheless, the financial series patterns seems to relevant and similar reason with international transmitting patterns of financial markets.

REFERENCES

Abimanyu, Y. (2008). *International Linkages to the Indonesian Capital Market: Cointegration Test.* Capital Market and Financial Institution Supervisory Agency, Ministry of Finance of Indonesia.

Balios, D., & Xanthakis, M. (2003). International interdependence and dynamic linkages between developed stock markets. *South Eastern Europe Journal of Economics*, *1*(1), 105–130.

Birau, R., & Trivedi, J. (2015). Investigating Causal Linkages between International Stock Markets in Hungary and Austria in Terms of Economic Globalization. *Annual Research Journal of Symbiosis Centre for Management Studies*, *3*, 78–88.

Brock, W.A., Dechert, W.D. & Scheinkman, J.A. (1987). A Test for Independence Based on the Correlation Dimension.

Dickey, D. A., & Fuller, W. A. (1981). Likelihood Ratio Statistics for Autoregressive Time Series with a Unit Root. *Econometrica*, *49*(4), 1057–1072. doi:10.2307/1912517

Engle, R. F., & Granger, C. W. J. (1987). Cointegration and Error Correction: Representation, Estimation and Testing. *Econometrica*, *55*(2), 251–276. doi:10.2307/1913236

Eun, C. S., & Shim, S. (1989). International Transmission of Stock Market Movements. *Journal of Financial and Quantitative Analysis*, *24*(2), 241–256. doi:10.2307/2330774

Granger, C. W. J. (1969). Investigating Causal Relations by Econometric Models and Cross-spectral Methods. *Econometrica*, *37*(3), 424–438. doi:10.2307/1912791

Khan, T.A. (2011). Cointegration of International Stock Markets: An Investigation of Diversification Opportunities. *Undergraduate Economic Review*, *8*(1).

Phylaktisa, K., & Ravazzolob, F. (2005). Stock market linkages in emerging markets: Implications for international portfolio diversification. *Journal of International Financial Markets, Institutions and Money*, *15*(2), 91–106. doi:10.1016/j.intfin.2004.03.001

Trivedi, J., & Birau, R. (2013). Investigating international transmitting pattern of stock price volatility. *Advances in Accounting, Auditing and Risk Management*, 126–131.

Chapter 15
Analyzing Dynamic Causal Linkages Between Developed Stock Markets of Spain and Canada

ABSTRACT

The main objective of this chapter involves analyzing dynamic causal linkages between developed stock markets of Spain and Canada. The long-run dynamic causal linkages between international stock markets highlight the importance of a functional and stable financial environment. As an explanation based on chaos theory, seemingly insignificant structural imbalances can easily generate dramatic consequences in the context of a globalized and integrated worldwide financial structure. The empirical analysis is based on daily log-returns of selected developed stock markets major indices during the sample period between June 1993 and December 2013. The financial econometrics empirical research includes the Unit Root Test, the Augmented Dickey-Fuller stationary test, the BDS test and the Granger causality test. The empirical results provide a useful framework on international portfolio diversification and risk management.

DOI: 10.4018/978-1-5225-9269-3.ch015

INTRODUCTION

This book subchapter focuses on analyzing dynamic causal linkages between developed stock markets of Spain and Canada. The long-run dynamic causal linkages between international stock markets highlight the importance of a functional and stable financial environment. Seemingly insignificant structural imbalances can easily generate dramatic consequences in the context of a globalized and integrated worldwide perspective.

According to Birau (2014) the empirical analysis is based on daily returns of selected developed stock markets major indices during the period between June 1993 and December 2013. The financial econometrics empirical research is based on descriptive statistics, Unit Root Test, Augmented Dickey-Fuller stationary test, BDS test and Granger causality test. The final results provide a comprehensive perspective on international portfolio diversification and risk management.

In the context of globalization, the long-run dynamic causal linkages between international stock markets, such as Spain and Canada functional and stable financial environment emphasize the major relevance of a functional and stable financial environment. Moreover, according to FTSE Country Classification issued on September 2013 based on the latest official report, Spain and Canada are included in the first most important category of countries, i.e. developed. Generally, there are the following four fundamental categories of countries: developed, advanced emerging, secondary emerging and frontier. If ranked by total land area, Canada is the largest country in North America and the second largest country in the world. Canada have also the longest coastlines in the world with the Pacific, Arctic and Atlantic Oceans.

On the other hand, Spain is the second largest country in Western Europe and have both Atlantic and Mediterranean coastlines. According to the Embassy of Canada to Spain: "Canada and Spain enjoy a close relationship of active cooperation and the bilateral relations between the two countries are increasingly dynamic, notably in the areas of education and business". It is also highlighted the importance of dynamic regional relationships between Canada and Spain.

METHODOLOGICAL APPROACH AND EMPIRICAL RESULTS

The empirical analysis is based on daily stock returns of selected developed stock markets major indices during the period between June 1993 and December 2013. The IBEX 35 index is a market capitalization weighted index and it is also the benchmark stock market index of the Bolsa de Madrid (Madrid Stock Exchange), i.e. the main stock exchange in Spain. The S&P TSX Composite Index is a capitalization-weighted index designed in order to measure market activity of the largest companies listed on the Toronto Stock Exchange.

The applied financial econometrics research methodology includes: Unit Root Test, Augmented Dickey-Fuller stationary test, BDS test and Granger causality test. The continuously-compounded daily returns are calculated using the log-difference of the closing prices of stock markets selected indices, ie IBEX 35 Index (Spain) and S&P TSX Composite Index (Canada), as follows:

$$r_t = \ln\left(\frac{p_t}{p_{t-1}}\right) = \ln\left(p_t\right) - \ln\left(p_{t-1}\right)$$

where p is the daily closing price. Data series consists of the daily closing prices for each sample stock index during the period between June 1993 and December 2013. with the exception of legal holidays or other events when stock markets haven't performed transactions.

The basic statistical characteristics of selected indices, i.e. IBEX 35 Index (Spain) and S&P TSX Composite Index (Canada) are analyzed based on the following: Jarque-Bera test's statistic whose importance derives from the fact that it allows to eliminate the normality of distribution hypothesis, parameter of asymmetry of distribution or Skewness and Kurtosis parameter which measures the peakedness or flatness of the distribution or leptokurtic distribution.

The empirical analysis also includes the use of Hodrick-Prescott (HP) filter which is a specialized filter for trend and business cycle estimation decomposing the series into a trend component and a residual component, which may or may not include a cyclical component.

Figure 1. The trend of IBEX 35 Index (Spain) and S&P TSX Composite Index (Canada)
Source: Author's computation using financial series of ATX and BUX stock indices

**For a more accurate representation see the electronic version.*

The Augmented Dickey-Fuller (ADF) test was applied for the sample period in order to determine the stationarity of the analyzed time series. The null hypothesis suggests that the analyzed time series contains a unit root and consequently it is non-stationary. Empirical analysis based on the log-returns of the selected indices reflects the fact that ttest_ADF<t_{critic} (1%, 5%, 10%) so the null hypothesis H_0 is rejected and the analyzed time series is stationary. Simultaneous, it is obtain the following result: Prob (0%) < test levels (1%, 5%, 10%) so the null hypothesis H_0 is rejected and the analyzed time series is stationary.

The *BDS test* was used in order to determine whether the residuals are independent and identically distributed. The BDS statistics converges in distribution to N(0,1) thus the null hypothesis of independent and identically distributed is rejected based on a result such as $\left|V_{m,\varepsilon}\right| > 1,96$ in terms of a 5% significance level. BDS test is a two-tailed test and is based on the following hypothesis:

H_0: sample observations are independently and identically distributed (I.I.D.)
H_1: sample observations are not I.I.D., ie the financial time series is non-linearly dependent if first differences of the natural logarithm have been calculated. The null hypothesis was rejected in both sample cases.

Figure 2. The trend of IBEX 35 Index (Spain) and S&P TSX Composite Index (Canada)
Source: Author's computation using financial series of ATX and BUX stock indices

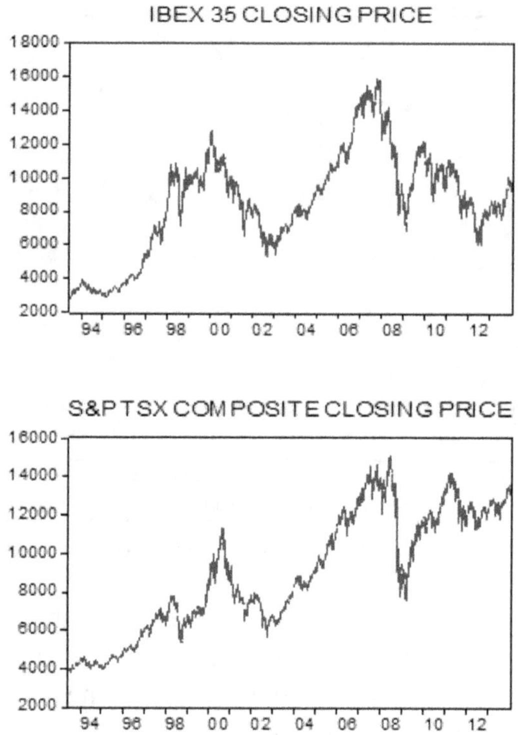

Figure 3. The log-returns of IBEX 35 Index (Spain) and S&P TSX Composite Index (Canada): Joint graphic
Source: Author's computation using financial series of ATX and BUX stock indices

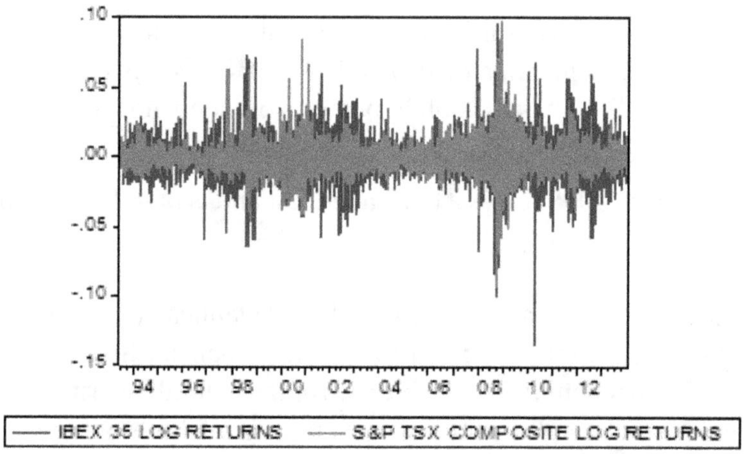

**For a more accurate representation see the electronic version.*

Figure 4. The log-returns of IBEX 35 Index (Spain) and S&P TSX Composite Index (Canada): Individual graphics
Source: Author's computation using financial series of ATX and BUX stock indices

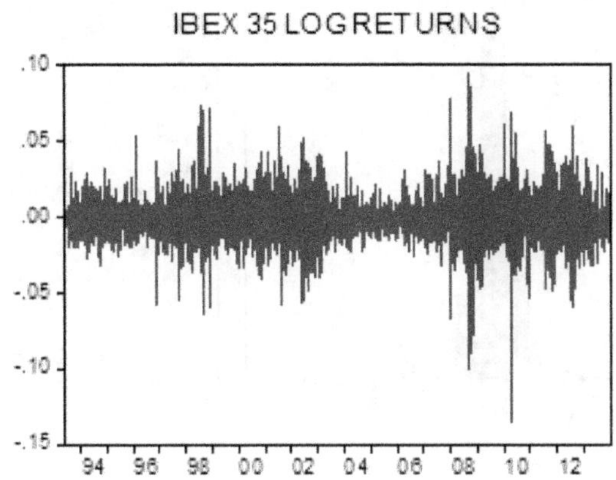

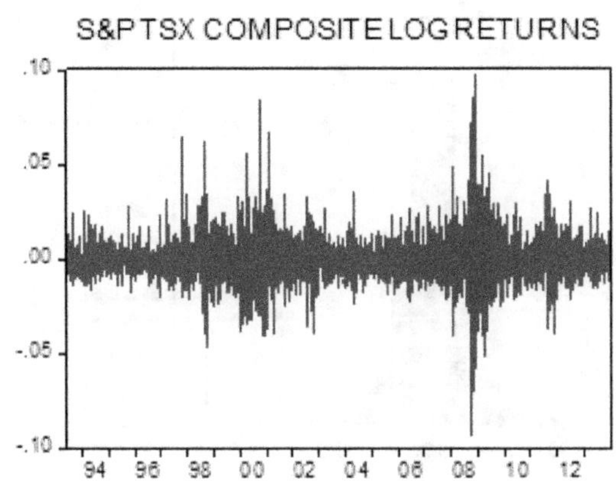

According to Granger (1969), if some other time series Y_t contains informations regarding the past periods which are useful in the prediction X_t and in addition this informations are included in no other series used in the predictor, then this implies that Y_t caused X_t. Granger suggested that if X_t and Y_t are two different stationary time series variables with zero means, then the canonical causal model has the following form:

$$X_t = \sum_{j=1}^{m} a_j X_{t-j} + \sum_{j=1}^{m} b_j Y_{t-j} + \varepsilon_t$$

Figure 5. Basic statistical characteristics of selected indices
Source: Author's computation using financial series of ATX and BUX stock indices

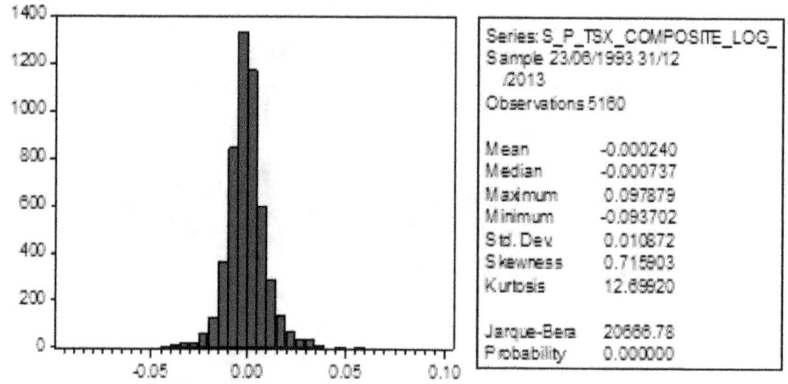

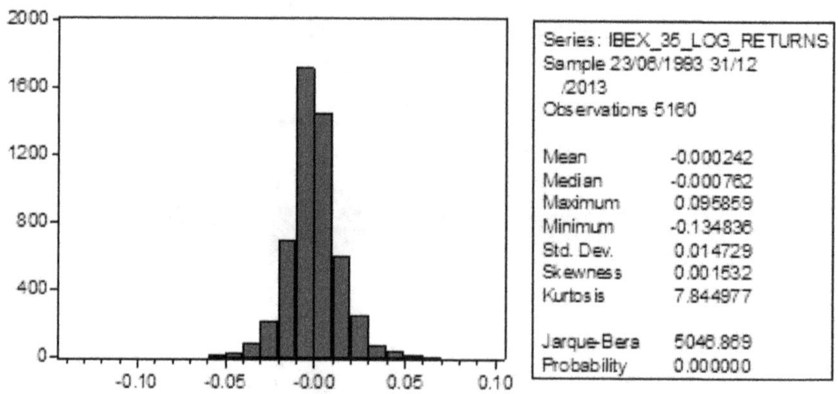

$$Y_t = \sum_{j=1}^{m} c_j X_{t-j} + \sum_{j=1}^{m} d_j Y_{t-j} + \eta_t$$

where ε_t and η_t play the role of two uncorrelated white-noise series, namely $E\left[\varepsilon_t \varepsilon_s\right] = 0 = E\left[\eta_t \eta_s\right]$ for $s \neq t$ and on the other hand $E\left[\varepsilon_t \varepsilon_s\right] = 0$ for $\forall t, s$. The assumption of causality requires that in the case when Y_t is causing X_t some b_j is different from zero and vice versa, ie in the case when X_t is causing Y_t some c_j is different from zero. A different situation implies that causality is valid simultaneously in both directions or "feedback relationship between X_t and Y_t".

Figure 6. Hodrick – Prescott Filter
Source: Author's computation using financial series of ATX and BUX stock indices

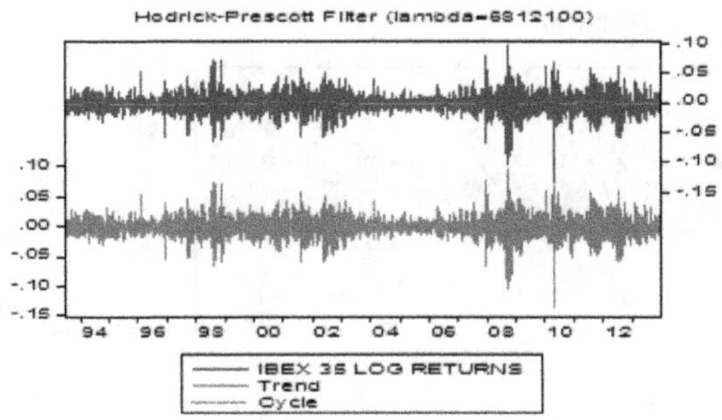

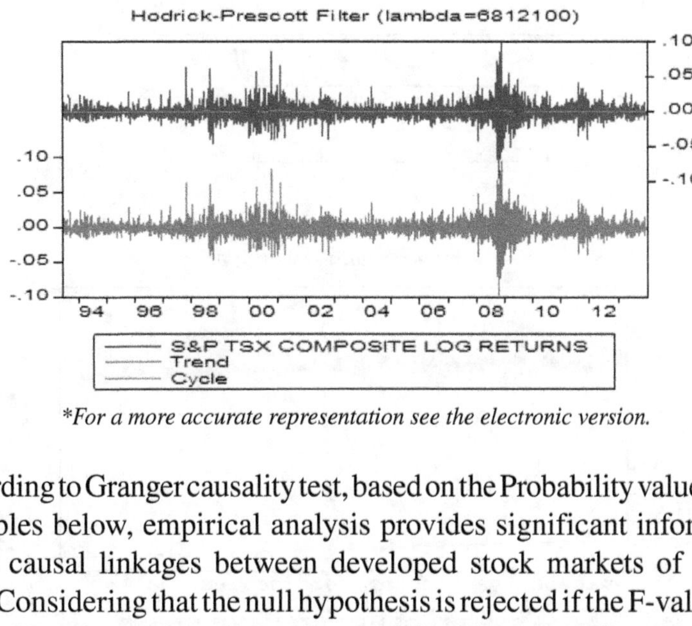

**For a more accurate representation see the electronic version.*

According to Granger causality test, based on the Probability values included in the tables below, empirical analysis provides significant information on dynamic causal linkages between developed stock markets of Spain and Canada. Considering that the null hypothesis is rejected if the F-value exceeds the critical F value at the selected level of significance (5%) or if the P-value is lower than the α level of significance, financial crisis impact is even more significant.

CONCLUSION

This particular book subchapter provides additional empirical evidence regarding dynamic causal linkages between international developed stock markets such as Spain and Canada. The results of Granger causality tests among developed stock markets of Spain and Canada highlights significant

Figure 7. Asymmetric time-varying filter
Source: Author's computation using financial series of ATX and BUX stock indices

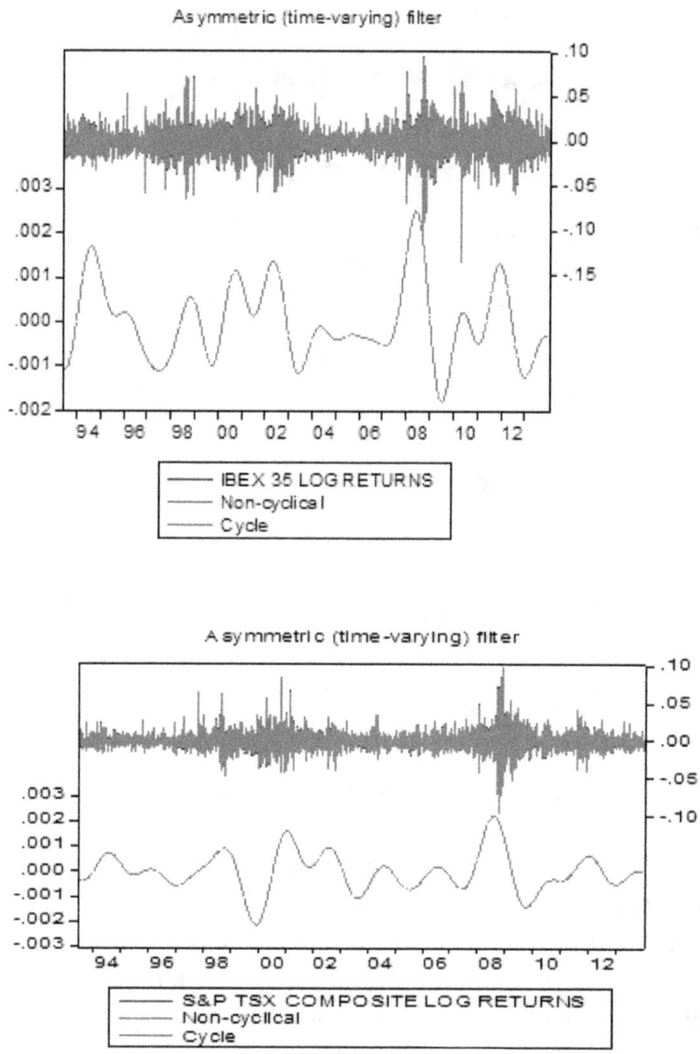

**For a more accurate representation see the electronic version.*

investment opportunities based on international portfolio diversification and risk management. Granger causality runs simultaneously in both directions for Spain and Canada (feedback relationship). Empirical analysis included the calculation for both lags = 1 and lags = 2, so the results are quite different considering the behavior of causal relationships. The impulse response under the sample period of time is very relevant in the context of globalization.

Figure 8. Theoretical quantile-quantile plots (extreme values)
Source: Author's computation using financial series of ATX and BUX stock indices

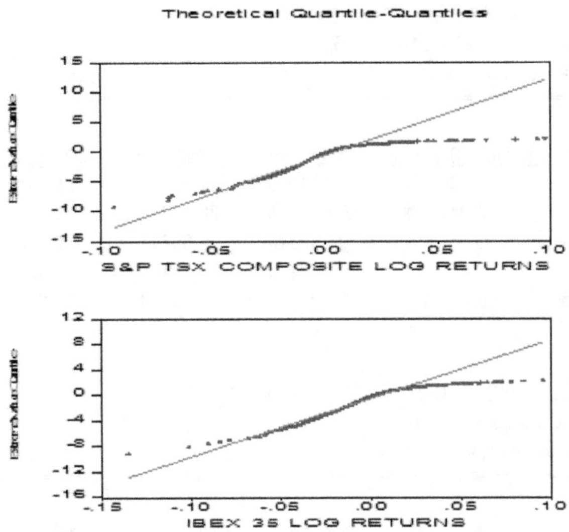

**For a more accurate representation see the electronic version.*

Table 1. Augmented Dickey-Fuller Test

Null Hypothesis: IBEX_35_LOG_RETURNS has a unit root

		t-Statistic	Prob.*
Augmented Dickey-Fuller test statistic		-15.88440	0.0000
Test critical values:	1% level	-3.431440	
	5% level	-2.861907	
	10% level	-2.567008	

Null Hypothesis: S_P_TSX_COMPOSITE_LOG_RE has a unit root
Exogenous: Constant
Lag Length: 28 (Automatic based on Modified HQ, MAXLAG=32)

		t-Statistic	Prob.*
Augmented Dickey-Fuller test statistic		-11.86166	0.0000
Test critical values:	1% level	-3.431443	
	5% level	-2.861908	
	10% level	-2.567008	

Null Hypothesis: S_P_TSX_COMPOSITE_LOG_RE has a unit root
Exogenous: Constant
Lag Length: 28 (Automatic based on Modified HQ, MAXLAG=32)

		t-Statistic	Prob.*
Augmented Dickey-Fuller test statistic		-11.86166	0.0000
Test critical values:	1% level	-3.431443	
	5% level	-2.861908	
	10% level	-2.567008	

Table 2. BDS test

BDS Test for IBEX_35_LOG_RETURNS
Sample: 23/06/1993 31/12/2013
Included observations: 5161

Dimension	BDS Statistic	Std. Error	z-Statistic	Prob.
2	0.017540	0.001233	14.22686	0.0000
3	0.040075	0.001955	20.49507	0.0000
4	0.058114	0.002324	25.00711	0.0000
5	0.070682	0.002418	29.23761	0.0000
6	0.077025	0.002327	33.10128	0.0000

BDS Test for S_P_TSX_COMPOSITE_LOG_RE
Sample: 23/06/1993 31/12/2013
Included observations: 5161

Dimension	BDS Statistic	Std. Error	z-Statistic	Prob.
2	0.023252	0.001328	17.50768	0.0000
3	0.049417	0.002108	23.44760	0.0000
4	0.069399	0.002506	27.68813	0.0000
5	0.082330	0.002609	31.55291	0.0000
6	0.088476	0.002513	35.20169	0.0000

Source: Author's own computations based on selected financial data series

Table 3. Granger Causality tests

Pairwise Granger Causality Tests
Lags: 2

Null Hypothesis:	Obs	F-Statistic	Probability
IBEX_35_LOG_RETURNS does not Granger Cause S_P_TSX_COMPOSITE_LOG_RE	5158	6.33709	0.00178
S_P_TSX_COMPOSITE_LOG_RE does not Granger Cause IBEX_35_LOG_RETURNS		4.79032	0.00835

Pairwise Granger Causality Tests
Lags: 1

Null Hypothesis:	Obs	F-Statistic	Probability
IBEX_35_LOG_RETURNS does not Granger Cause S_P_TSX_COMPOSITE_LOG_RE	5159	5.86835	0.01545
S_P_TSX_COMPOSITE_LOG_RE does not Granger Cause IBEX_35_LOG_RETURNS		10.1684	0.00144

Source: Own computations based on selected financial data series

REFERENCES

Birau, R. (2014). Analyzing Dynamic Causal Linkages between Developed Stock Markets of Spain and Canada. *International Journal of Core Engineering & Management*, *1*(2), 1-9.

Granger, C., & Morgenstern, O. (1970). *Predictability of stock market prices*. Lexington, MA: Heath Lexington Books.

Granger, C. W. J. (1969). Investigating Causal Relations by Econometric Models and Cross-spectral Methods. *Econometrica*, *37*(3), 424–438. doi:10.2307/1912791

Granger, C. W. J. (1986). Developments in the Study of Cointegrated Economic Variables. *Oxford Bulletin of Economics and Statistics*, 48.

Gujarati, D. N. (2003). Basic Econometrics (4th ed.). West Point: McGraw-Hill Higher Education.

Harris, R., & Sollis, R. (2003). *Applied Time Series Modelling and Forecasting*. John Wiley & Sons, Inc.

Chapter 16
The Global Implications of Financial Contagion in Developed Capital Markets:
Evidence for USA, France, UK, and Germany

ABSTRACT

The main aim of this chapter is to provide an econometric analysis focused on investigating the consequences of financial contagion between certain developed capital markets, such as USA, France, UK, and Germany in terms of global financial crisis. In the recent past, the impact of international transmission mechanisms significantly affected the investment behavior due to the propagation of financial shocks. More specifically, the risk of financial contagion highlights the vulnerability of traditional assumptions based on efficiency and rationality considering the global implications of resource allocation performance and international portfolio diversification.

DOI: 10.4018/978-1-5225-9269-3.ch016

INTRODUCTION

The financial time series exhibits several stylized facts, such as: high-frequency, volatility clustering, leverage effect, chaotic behavior, heteroskedastic log returns, deviations from the assumption of normality, non-stationarity of price levels, fat-tailed distribution. The risk management strategies highlight the vulnerability of investment process based on behavioral patterns. According to FTSE Country Classification as at September 2014 which is the most recent official report, USA, France, UK and Germany are included in the category of developed countries. Moreover, developed capital markets are more stable and liquid than emerging capital markets. However, causal transmission patterns provide an atypical investment insight especially in conditions of extreme events such as the global financial crisis. On the other hand, the impact of globalization generates the propagation of financial shocks.

METHODOLOGICAL APPROACH

The methodological approach is based on applying Unit Root Test, Augmented Dickey-Fuller stationary test, BDS test and Granger causality test.

According to Birau (2015) the continuously-compounded daily returns are calculated using the log-difference of the closing prices of sample capital markets major indices, ie DJIA Index (USA), CAC 40 Index (France), FTSE 100 Index (UK) and DAX Index (Germany) for the selected period from January 2007 to March 2013 with the exception of legal holidays or other events when selected capital markets haven't performed financial transactions, as follows:

$$r_t = \ln\left(\frac{p_t}{p_{t-1}}\right) = \ln\left(p_t\right) - \ln\left(p_{t-1}\right)$$

where R_t represents daily returns of indices and P_t stands for daily closing prices of indices.

DATA SERIES AND EMPIRICAL ANALYSIS

The empirical analysis is based on daily stock returns of selected stock markets major indices for the period January 2007 until March 2013 with the exception of legal holidays or other events when selected capital markets haven't performed financial transactions.

The Augmented Dickey-Fuller (ADF) test is used in order to determine the non-stationarity or the integration order of a financial time series. Practically, the ADF diagnostic test investigates the existence of unit roots and includes the following categories: unit root with a constant and a trend, unit root with a constant, but without a time trend, and finally unit root without constant and temporal trend, based on the following regression model:

$$\Delta y_t = c + \beta \cdot t + \delta \cdot y_{t-1} + \sum_{i=1}^{p} \gamma_i \Delta y_{t-i} + \varepsilon_t$$

where p represents the number of lags for which it was investigated whether fulfilling the condition that residuals are white noise, c is a constant, t is the indicator for time trend and Δ is the symbol for differencing. The stochastic trend cannot be predicted due to the time dependence of residual's variance. Moreover, in case that the coefficients to be estimated β and δ have the null value then the analyzed financial time series is characterized by a stochastic trend. The null hypothesis, i.e. the time series has a unit root is rejected if t-statistics is lower than the critical value.

The BDS test (Brock, Dechert and Scheinkman, 1987) was computed in order to determine whether the residuals are independent and identically distributed, especially in the case of a nonlinear system. In this respect BDS test is an econometric tool for detecting serial dependence in financial time series. Technically, the BDS diagnostic test is based on the null hypothesis of independent and identically distributed (i.i.d) time series.

The Granger causality test is mainly considering the possible relationships between two or more time series. Basically, it is a statistical hypothesis test that highlights the possible influence of a time series data in forecasting another series. Primary, causality highlights a relationship between cause and effect.

According to Granger (1969), if some other time series Y_t contains information regarding the past periods which are useful in the prediction X_t and in addition this information are included in no other series used in the predictor, then this implies that Y_t caused X_t. Granger suggested that if X_t

and Y_t are two different stationary time series variables with zero means, then the canonical causal model has the following form:

$$X_t = \sum_{j=1}^{m} a_j X_{t-j} + \sum_{j=1}^{m} b_j Y_{t-j} + \varepsilon_t$$

Figure 1. The trend of DJIA, FTSE 100, CAC40 and DAX stock indices: Individual graphs

Source: Own computations based on selected financial data series

Figure 2. The log-returns of DJIA, FTSE 100, CAC40 and DAX indices (joint graphs)

Source: Own computations based on selected financial data series

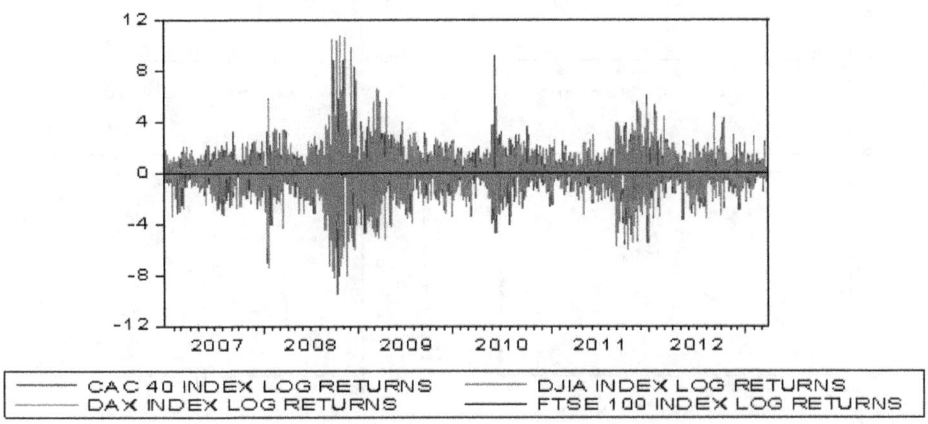

**For a more accurate representation see the electronic version.*

Figure 3. The log-returns of DJIA, FTSE 100, CAC40 and DAX stock indices: Individual graphs
Source: Own computations based on selected financial data series

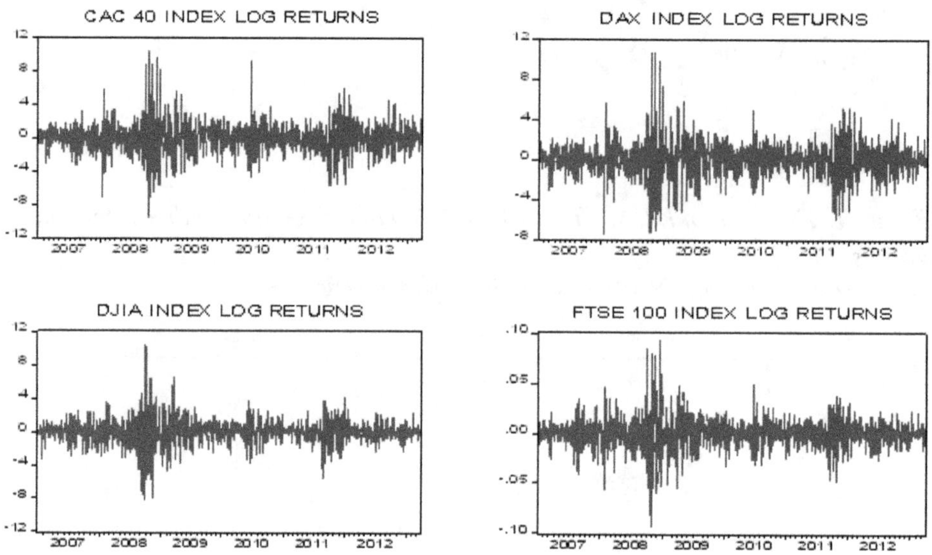

Figure 4. Theoretical quantile: Quantiles (extreme values)
Source: Own computations based on selected financial data series

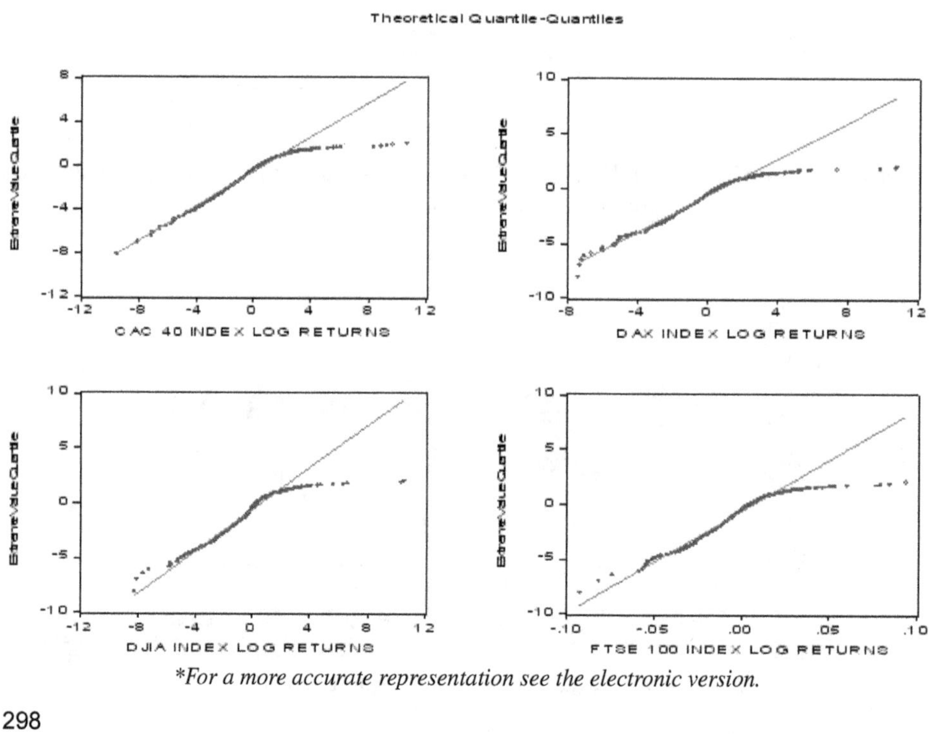

*For a more accurate representation see the electronic version.

Table 1. Basic statistical characteristics of selected indices

	CAC_40_INDEX_LOG_RETURNS	DAX_INDEX_LOG_RETURNS	DJIA_INDEX_LOG_RETURNS	FTSE_100_INDEX_LOG_RETURNS
Mean	-0.026828	0.010033	0.006142	5.87E-06
Median	0.002707	0.062552	0.043051	0.000155
Maximum	10.59459	10.79747	10.50835	0.093843
Minimum	-9.471537	-7.433464	-8.200513	-0.092656
Std. Dev.	1.709085	1.624498	1.418498	0.014491
Skewness	0.119975	0.102899	-0.036764	-0.106514
Kurtosis	8.118876	8.548801	10.90187	9.234873
Jarque-Bera	1680.670	1973.219	3996.475	2490.817
Probability	0.000000	0.000000	0.000000	0.000000
Sum	-41.20790	15.41007	9.434077	0.009010
Sum Sq. Dev.	4483.694	4050.856	3088.628	0.322328
Observations	1536	1536	1536	1536

Source: Own computations based on selected financial data series

Figure 5. Matrix of all pairs of selected stock market indices
Source: Own computations based on selected financial data series

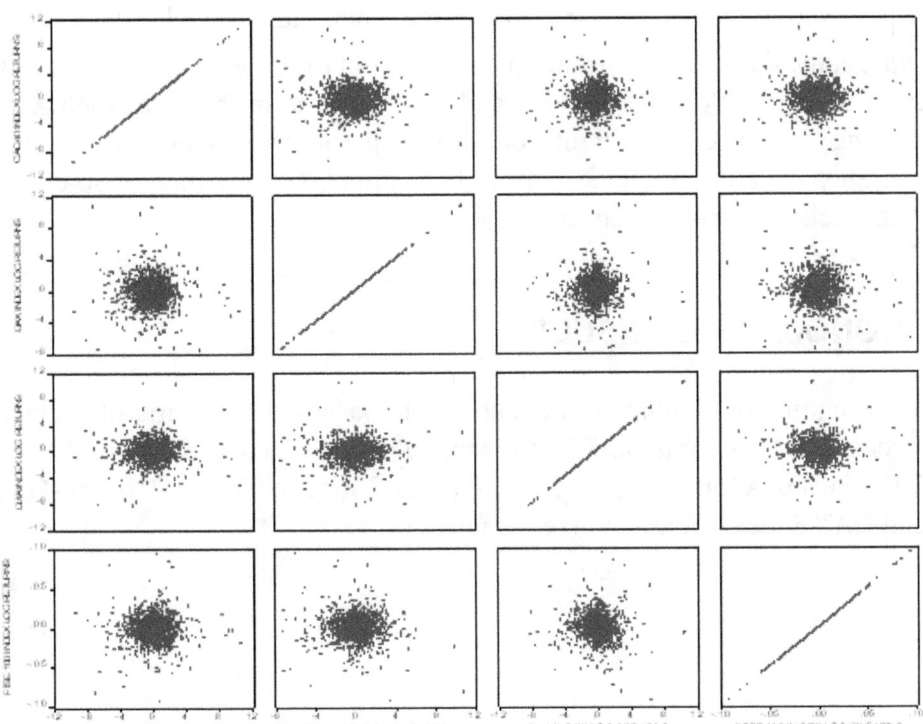

Table 2. Augmented Dickey-Fuller Test

Null Hypothesis: CAC_40_INDEX_LOG_RETURNS has a unit root				
			t-Statistic	Prob.*
Augmented Dickey-Fuller test statistic			-19.44818	0.0000
Test critical values:	1% level		-3.434415	
	5% level		-2.863222	
	10% level		-2.567714	
Null Hypothesis: DAX_INDEX_LOG_RETURNS has a unit root				
			t-Statistic	Prob.*
Augmented Dickey-Fuller test statistic			-18.72169	0.0000
Test critical values:	1% level		-3.434415	
	5% level		-2.863222	
	10% level		-2.567714	

Source: Own computations based on selected financial data series

$$Y_t = \sum_{j=1}^{m} c_j X_{t-j} + \sum_{j=1}^{m} d_j Y_{t-j} + \eta_t$$

where ε_t and η_t play the role of two uncorrelated white-noise series, namely $E\left[\varepsilon_t \varepsilon_s\right] = 0 = E\left[\eta_t \eta_s\right]$ for $s \neq t$ and on the other hand $E\left[\varepsilon_t \varepsilon_s\right] = 0$ for $\forall t, s$. Practically, the idea of causality requires that in the case when Y_t is causing X_t some b_j is different from zero and vice versa, ie in the case when X_t is causing Y_t some c_j is different from zero. A particular situation implies that causality is valid simultaneously in both directions or simply a so-called "feedback relationship between X_t and Y_t."

ECONOMETRIC RESULTS

The econometric results were obtained on the basis of daily returns of selected stock markets major indices for the sample period January 2007 until March 2013, i.e. DJIA Index (USA), CAC 40 Index (France), FTSE 100 Index (UK) and DAX Index (Germany) (see Figure 1).

Table 3. BDS Test

BDS Test for CAC_40_INDEX_LOG_RETURNS				
Sample: 2/01/2007 25/03/2013				
Dimension	BDS Statistic	Std. Error	z-Statistic	Prob.
2	0.010935	0.002285	4.785428	0.0000
3	0.030107	0.003631	8.291204	0.0000
4	0.043587	0.004324	10.08027	0.0000
5	0.053483	0.004507	11.86697	0.0000
6	0.058866	0.004347	13.54314	0.0000
BDS Test for DAX_INDEX_LOG_RETURNS				
Dimension	BDS Statistic	Std. Error	z-Statistic	Prob.
2	0.013388	0.002402	5.572800	0.0000
3	0.033586	0.003821	8.789096	0.0000
4	0.050009	0.004555	10.97846	0.0000
5	0.059636	0.004753	12.54684	0.0000
6	0.065182	0.004589	14.20379	0.0000
BDS Test for DJIA_INDEX_LOG_RETURNS				
Dimension	BDS Statistic	Std. Error	z-Statistic	Prob.
2	0.019598	0.002659	7.370212	0.0000
3	0.044742	0.004236	10.56245	0.0000
4	0.065486	0.005058	12.94714	0.0000
5	0.079289	0.005287	14.99722	0.0000
6	0.087095	0.005114	17.03169	0.0000
BDS Test for FTSE_100_INDEX_LOG_RETUR				
Dimension	BDS Statistic	Std. Error	z-Statistic	Prob.
2	0.020100	0.002389	8.414650	0.0000
3	0.041002	0.003790	10.81837	0.0000
4	0.057128	0.004506	12.67678	0.0000
5	0.066987	0.004690	14.28185	0.0000
6	0.072041	0.004517	15.94889	0.0000

Source: Own computations based on selected financial data series

CONCLUSION

The econometric approach in this article highlights the global implications of financial contagion in developed capital markets. The empirical results of Granger causality tests among selected developed capital markets, i.e. USA, France, UK, and Germany revealed the significant impact of the global financial crisis. Considering the fact that the null hypothesis is rejected if the F-value exceeds the critical F value at the selected level of significance (5%) or if the P-value is lower than the α level of significance, the final results are very

Table 4. Granger Causality tests

Pairwise Granger Causality Tests			
Null Hypothesis:	Obs	F-Statistic	Probability
DAX_INDEX_LOG_RETURNS does not Granger Cause CAC_40_INDEX_LOG_RETURNS	1533	7.02609	0.00311
CAC_40_INDEX_LOG_RETURNS does not Granger Cause DAX_INDEX_LOG_RETURNS		0.97496	0.37744
DJIA_INDEX_LOG_RETURNS does not Granger Cause CAC_40_INDEX_LOG_RETURNS	1533	1.84644	0.13679
CAC_40_INDEX_LOG_RETURNS does not Granger Cause DJIA_INDEX_LOG_RETURNS		1.07960	0.35659
FTSE_100_INDEX_LOG_RETUR does not Granger Cause CAC_40_INDEX_LOG_RETURNS	1533	0.72010	0.53997
CAC_40_INDEX_LOG_RETURNS does not Granger Cause FTSE_100_INDEX_LOG_RETUR		6.20600	0.00034
DJIA_INDEX_LOG_RETURNS does not Granger Cause DAX_INDEX_LOG_RETURNS	1533	0.23893	0.86924
DAX_INDEX_LOG_RETURNS does not Granger Cause DJIA_INDEX_LOG_RETURNS		0.55561	0.64442
FTSE_100_INDEX_LOG_RETUR does not Granger Cause DAX_INDEX_LOG_RETURNS	1533	2.16510	0.09031
DAX_INDEX_LOG_RETURNS does not Granger Cause FTSE_100_INDEX_LOG_RETUR		0.89386	0.44362
FTSE_100_INDEX_LOG_RETUR does not Granger Cause DJIA_INDEX_LOG_RETURNS	1533	0.90570	0.43759
DJIA_INDEX_LOG_RETURNS does not Granger Cause FTSE_100_INDEX_LOG_RETUR		4.59761	0.00329

Source: Own computations based on selected financial data series

interesting in terms of international diversification of portfolios. Concretely, there is no particular causality between USA and France, USA and Germany, respectively UK and Germany (although the result is quite close). However, the empirical analysis based on unidirectional return causalities suggested that Granger causality runs one way in several cases, ie from Germany to France, from USA to UK and from France to UK, but not the other way in any of these cases.

REFERENCES

Birau, R. (2015). The Global Implications of Financial Contagion in Developed Capital Markets. In *WSEAS 9th International Conference on Business Administration (ICBA '15) - Advances in Business and Economic Development*, Dubai, United Arab Emirates (pp. 122-126).

Black, F. (1976) Studies of stock market volatility changes. In *Proceedings of the American Statistical Association, Business and Economic Statistics Section* (pp. 177-181).

Bollerslev, T. (1986). Generalized autoregressive conditional heteroskedasticity. *Journal of Economics*, *31*(3), 307–327. doi:10.1016/0304-4076(86)90063-1

Brock, W.A., Dechert, W.D. & Scheinkman, J.A. (1987). A Test for Independence Based on the Correlation Dimension.

Brooks, C. (1996). Testing for Non-Linearity in Daily Sterling Exchange Rates. *Applied Financial Economics*, *6*(4), 307–317. doi:10.1080/096031096334105

Dickey, D. A., & Fuller, W. A. (1981). Likelihood Ratio Statistics for Autoregressive Time Series with a Unit Root. *Econometrica*, *49*(4), 1057–1072. doi:10.2307/1912517

Engle, R. F., & Granger, C. W. J. (1987). Cointegration and Error Correction: Representation, Estimation and Testing. *Econometrica*, *55*(2), 251–276. doi:10.2307/1913236

Granger, C., & Morgenstern, O. (1970). *Predictability of stock market prices*. Lexington, MA: Heath Lexington Books.

Granger, C. W. J. (1969). Investigating Causal Relations by Econometric Models and Cross-spectral Methods. *Econometrica*, *37*(3), 424–438. doi:10.2307/1912791

Granger, C. W. J. (1986). Developments in the Study of Cointegrated Economic Variables. *Oxford Bulletin of Economics and Statistics*, 48.

Chapter 17
Investigating Long-Term Behavior of Milan Stock Exchange (Italy)

ABSTRACT

The main purpose of this chapter is to highlight the long-term behavior of Milan Stock Exchange (Italy) based on the FTSE MIB major stock market index. The empirical analysis covers a long period of time from January 1999 to December 2013 and describes the daily stock price movements in order to identify both financial expansion and contraction cycles. However, Milan Stock Exchange is a developed stock market that exhibits a more stable behavior than emerging stock markets, even stylized facts are much lower in this case. The econometric analysis provides an exhaustive perspective, because selected stock market behavior has changed completely due to the negative influence of the global financial crisis.

INTRODUCTION

Stock markets are characterized by certain features, such as: high volatility, systemic instabilities, underdeveloped trading mechanisms, financial regulation issues, illiquidity, insufficient transparency, difficult access to all available information, exiguous volume trading, diversification opportunities, various risk categories and high uncertainty. These particular characteristics generate an environment for triggering extreme financial events, even just as propagation effects.

DOI: 10.4018/978-1-5225-9269-3.ch017

Financial econometrics is the area that captures the impact of extreme events which are relatively rare and unpredictable but have significant consequences. By their very nature, these extreme events cannot be anticipated because didn't follow a historical pattern. In this context, the black swan metaphor synthesizes in a meaningful manner the global dimension of the opposition between appearance and essence in financial practice. The dilemma is how to model available observations so to observe the presence of extreme phenomena thereby to minimize their negative consequences. The econometric approach of the issue achieves a wide perspective in the context of long-term modeling.

In another train of thoughts, the paper aims to highlight the behavior of the tails of the analyzed financial time series. Consequently, the objective is to investigate asymptotic dependence and to estimate the degree of extreme tail dependence using statistical tools. Another aim of this research project is to emphasize the resonance in the current financial practice of the normal distribution assumption, especially in emerging stock markets analysis.

The normal distribution is a symmetrical distribution which follows a bell-shaped curve. This particular curve is characterized the highest frequency in the center and decreases on either side. Apparently, there is a insignificant probability that extreme events to occur compared to some other distributions. However, this theory is severely contradicted by financial practice. An indisputable argument in this regard is the current global financial crisis.

APPLIED METHODOLOGY

Birau (2014a) argued that the results of the empirical analysis enable access to subsequent advance stock market performance based on the case of Milan Stock Exchange (Italy). This study empirically established the relationship between the long-term behavior of Milan stock exchange and the recent financial crisis.

The global financial crisis that erupted in mid-2007 in U.S.A. triggered severe consequences on various stock markets all over across the world. Dramatically, such an extreme event is relatively rare and highly unpredictable, while being almost impossible to predict because does not follow a historical pattern. Therefore, beyond the arguments that support the validity of normal distribution assumption, dramatic financial events followed by significant stock market disturbances or crashes occurred quite frequently in recent past.

Birau, R. (2014d) suggested that the influence of economic, monetary, financial and technical factors holds a massive weight in terms of investment phenomenon dimensions considering that the significant benefits of internalization derived from international linkages and global economic interdependencies. In this regard, the impact of technical factors is determined by the widespread use of high-performance computers, high-frequency trading, increasingly sophisticated software and communications systems, in addition with the increasing volume of financial transactions, especially speculative trades.

Moreover, stock crashes followed by severe financial crisis occurred quite frequently in the last century, sometimes reaching global dimensions, such as: the Great Depression between the years 1929-1933, Latin American financial debt crisis of the 1980s, Black Monday (Black Monday) in 1987, the Asian financial crisis of 1997 – 1998, Russian financial crisis or Ruble crisis in 1998, DOTCOM bubble during 2000 and 2002 and the Subprime crisis that erupted in August 2007 in U.S.A.

Financial time series, such as daily stock market returns are characterized by high-frequency and excessive volatility, respectively the stylized facts called "volatility clustering". The continuously-compounded daily returns are calculated using the log-difference of stock markets selected indices, as follows:

$$r_t = \ln\left(\frac{p_t}{p_{t-1}}\right) = \ln(p_t) - \ln(p_{t-1})$$

where p is the daily closing price.

The empirical analysis methodology is based on Unit Root Test, Augmented Dickey-Fuller stationary test, diagnostic tests for detecting heteroscedasticity and BDS test. The final results have significant implications for financial stability, international portfolio optimization, risk management and assessment of potential financing options. The statistic characteristics of selected stock indices are represented by the following specifications: Jarque-Bera test's statistic which allows to eliminate the normality of distribution hypothesis, parameter of asymmetry of distribution or Skewness and Kurtosis parameter which measures the peakness or flatness of the distribution, i.e. leptokurtic distribution.

Effectively, the empirical analysis is based on the daily closing prices of the following major stock market index: FTSE MIB (Italy), for the sample period January 1999 until December 2013 (financial time series). Another relevant issue of empirical analysis is the concept of stationarity, which implies that the mean and autocovariances of the financial time series do not depend on time.

EMPIRICAL RESULTS

Birau (2014a) stated that selected financial data series consists of the daily closing prices for each selected index, ie FTSE MIB (Italy), for the period January 1999 to December 2013 with the exception of legal holidays or other events when stock markets haven't performed transactions.

In the analyzed period, the behavior of the selected stock indices reflected very accurately the impact of the recent global financial crisis, as it can be seen in Figure 1.

The continuously compounded returns which are calculated using the log-difference of the daily closing price of the selected stock indices for the sample period are illustrated in Figure 2.

Augmented Dickey-Fuller test was applied in order to determine the stationarity of the sample financial time series. The null hypothesis concerns that the data series has a unit root and therefore it is non-stationary. Empirical analysis based on the FTSE MIB index log-returns established that $t_{test-}ADF<t_{critic}$ (1%, 5%, 10%) so the null hypothesis H_0 is rejected and the analyzed time series is stationary. Simultaneous, it is obtaining the following

Figure 1. The trend of FTSE MIB index
Source: Own computations based on selected financial data series

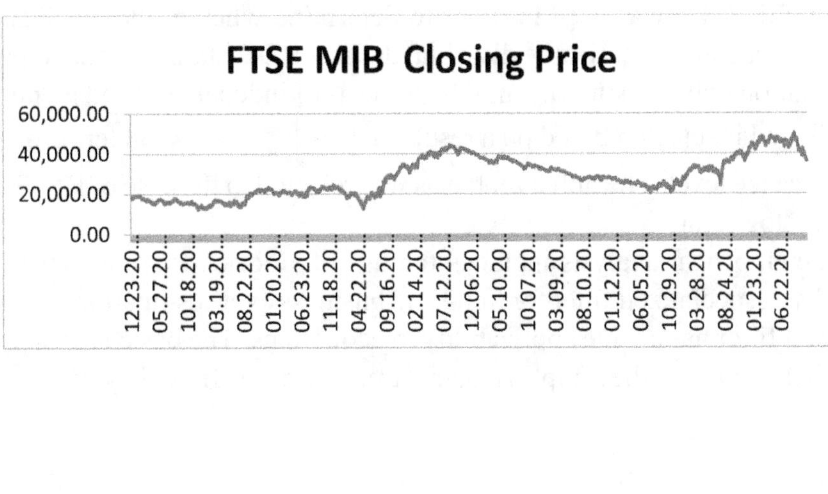

Figure 2. The log-returns of FTSE MIB index
Source: Own computations based on selected financial data series

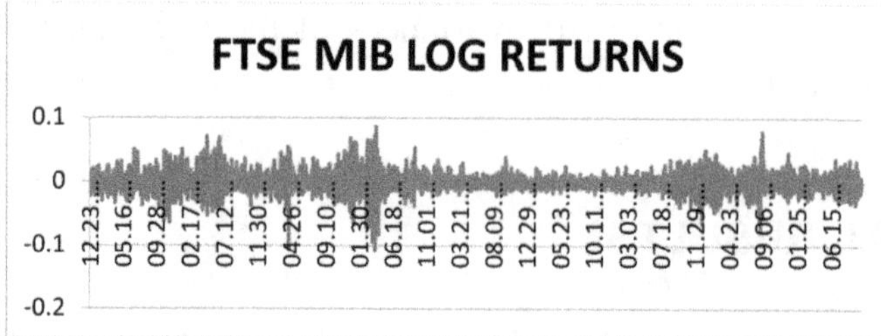

Figure 3. Basic statistical characteristics of FTSE MIB index: Log returns
Source: Own computations based on selected financial data series

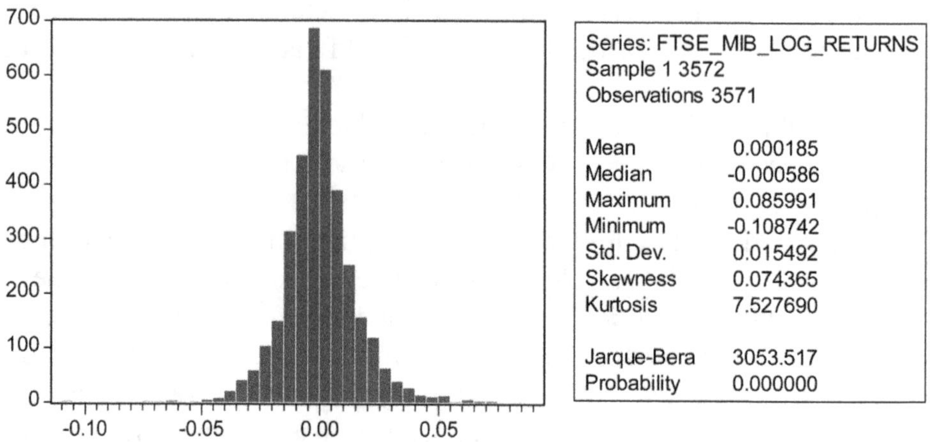

result: Prob (0%) < test levels (1%, 5%, 10%) so the null hypothesis H_0 is rejected and the sample financial time series is stationary.

The BDS test was used in order to determine whether the residuals are independent and identically distributed. The BDS statistics converges in distribution to N(0,1) thus the null hypothesis of independent and identically distributed is rejected based on a result such as $\left|V_{m,\varepsilon}\right| > 1,96$ in terms of a 5% significance level. The null hypothesis was rejected in the case of FTSE MIB index – log return.

The empirical analysis includes the use of Hodrick-Prescott (HP) filter which is a specialized filter for trend and business cycle estimation. Hodrick-Prescott filter has a wide applicability in economics. The basic idea suggests that in the center of the sample financial time series the filter is symmetric and

Figure 4. Theoretical Quantile: Quantile Plots of FTSE MIB index – log return
Source: Own computations based on selected financial data series

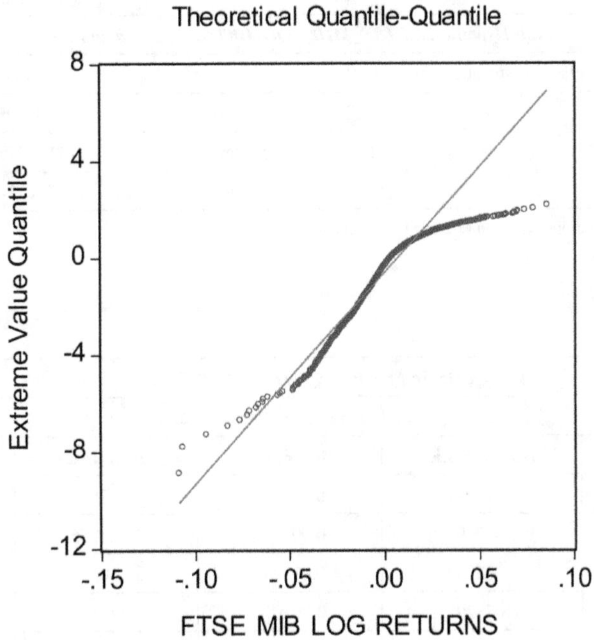

Figure 5. Kernel Density Estimation
Source: Own computations based on selected financial data series

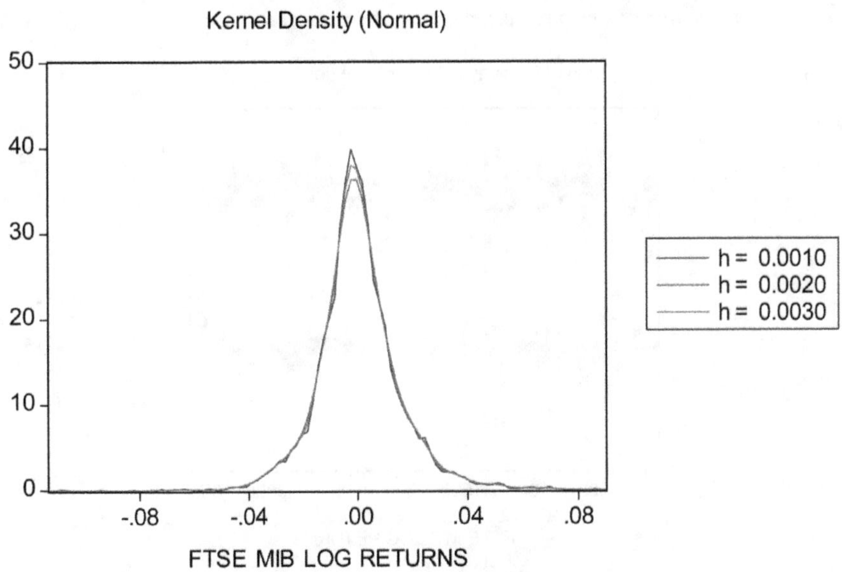

**For a more accurate representation see the electronic version.*

Table 1. Augmented Dickey-Fuller Test

		t-Statistic	Prob.*
Null Hypothesis: FTSE_MIB_LOG_RETURNS has a unit root			
Augmented Dickey-Fuller test statistic		-27.93046	0.0000
Test critical values:	1% level	-3.431997	
	5% level	-2.862153	
	10% level	-2.567140	

Source: Own computations based on selected financial data series

Table 2. BDS test

BDS Test for FTSE_MIB_LOG_RETURNS				
Included observations: 3572				
Dimension	**BDS Statistic**	**Std. Error**	**z-Statistic**	**Prob.**
2	0.017944	0.001550	11.57885	0.0000
3	0.042296	0.002466	17.14955	0.0000
4	0.063253	0.002941	21.50519	0.0000
5	0.078291	0.003070	25.49800	0.0000
6	0.087336	0.002966	29.44721	0.0000

Source: Own computations based on selected financial data series

Figure 6. Hodrick – Prescott Filter
Source: Own computations based on selected financial data series

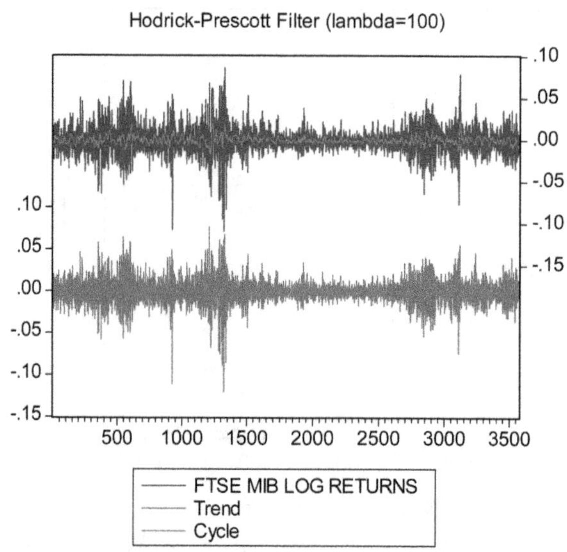

For a more accurate representation see the electronic version.

towards the end of the series is becoming increasingly asymmetric. On the other hand, Hodrick-Prescott filter involves the decomposition of the sample financial time series into a trend component and a residual component, which may or may not include a cyclical component.

Figure 6 highlights the use of Hodrick – Prescott Filter in the case of FTSE MIB index log-returns.

CONCLUSION

The main aim of this subchapter is to highlight the impact of global financial crisis on the behavior of Milan stock market. The intrinsic motivation to accomplish this research study derives from the necessity to determine the probability of extreme events and international contagion effects on stock markets in the turbulent context of the global financial crisis. This situation leads to the possibility of obtaining significant benefits based on international diversification of financial portfolios.

REFERENCES

Birau, R. (2014). Investigating Long-Term Behavior of Milan Stock Exchange: An Empirical Analysis. *Journal of Management and Social Science*, *1*(2), 29-37.

Franke, J., Härdle, W. K., & Hafner, C. M. (2011). *Statistics of Financial Markets, An Introduction* (3rd ed.). Springer. doi:10.1007/978-3-642-16521-4

Gajda, J. A., & Wyłomańska, A. (2012) Geometric Brownian motion with tempered stable waiting times, *Journal of Statistical Physics*, *148*(2), 296-305.

Gujarati, D. N. (2003). Basic Econometrics (4th ed.). West Point: McGraw-Hill Higher Education.

Njegic, J., Savin, M., & Zivkov, Z. (2012). Stock Market Volatility After the Financial Crisis: Evidence from Eastern Europe and Balkan Region. In *Advances in Finance and Accounting - Proceedings of the 1st WSEAS International Conference on Finance, Accounting and Auditing (FAA '12)* (pp. 343-348).

Phylaktis, K., & Ravazzolo, F. (2005). Stock market linkages in emerging markets: Implications for international portfolio diversification. *Journal of International Financial Markets, Institutions and Money, 15*(2), 91–106. doi:10.1016/j.intfin.2004.03.001

Conclusion

The banks solidity and effective activity present a special importance for the economic growth, the credit allocation, the financial stability, as well as for the firm's development and competitiveness. The credit institutions, due to their significant dimension, play an essential role in the economy through the asset's transformation, the risk management facilitation, the commerce financing and the technological innovations stimulation. European Commission (2005) has mentioned that the banks accomplish two important functions that contribute to the resource's effective assignment: the monitoring function for investors and the consulting function for companies.

Regarding the first function, we underline that the financial system is characterized by the information asymmetry between those who want to benefit of credits at the lowest costs and those who want to invest in the conditions of obtaining some higher profits. This kind of asymmetry generates risks for the investor, because the credit beneficiary can't be totally transparent from the solvability point of view. Verifying the degree of solvability of each credit beneficiary is an expensive process, which can be feasible only in the case of important investors who have material possibilities necessary for carrying out an analysis regarding the situation of the own credit, while the small investors don't dispose of the resources necessary to accomplish such an analysis. In these conditions, the bank is the one that assumes the role of monitoring the credit qualities on the small investors' account, assuring thus the highest possible level of financing for the respective investments.

On the other hand, considering the second function, we mention that, in default of an intermediate who assures monitoring, the investors display the tendency to assign an average value to all the investment opportunities, which can imply ample investments in projects with a diminished quality and reduced investments in projects with an increased quality. Through their capacity of categorizing the investment opportunities according to their quality, the banks guarantee the canalization of the resources towards projects with the highest rate of return (adjusted according to the risk), assuring thus the obtainment of the best productivity from the investment.

This important function suggests the positive correlation between the stability and efficiency of the banking sector and the economic evolution. On the other hand, the lack of these functions means an inefficient banking system and represents a basis for the appearance of a significant macroeconomic unbalance.

So far as the banks represent a central element of the financial system, the economy condition and the banking system structure are closely related to assuring the banks efficiency and solidity. The implications which the concentration and competition from the banking sector can have on the banking system are relevant for their assuring. Even if there isn't an obvious correlation from the theoretical point of view, the practical studies indicate the fact that a higher concentration and a lower level of competition have a positive influence. However, so far as the competition seems to have intensified- despite the process of banking consolidation, such a correlation can't be defenseless applied to the European banking systems.

The importance of the previously mentioned aspects has been the basis of the analysis of the cost's efficiency and banking systems productivity. Also, the identification of the efficiency determining factors, but also the relation between the risk and efficiency will allow us to easily understand the mechanisms that are the basis of the banks stable and solid performance.

The channels of monetary policy transmission and the efficiency in its accomplishing depend, fundamentally, on the implementing way. The direct control on the credit and the interest rate can cause a significant inefficiency of the monetary policy and can promote deleveraging, with effects on the macro objectives. The pass from direct instruments to indirect ones represents a complex process that includes simultaneously reforms in organizing and functions the central banks as well as the entire banking system. At present, the main ways of influencing the quantities of central currency to which the central banks appeals are the open market operations, the modifications in the compulsory minimum reserve level and the modifications in the reference interest.

The academic discussions from the latest decades have revealed a significant number of challenges with which the strategies of monetary policy confront. The older discussion of choosing between "rules of guiding the monetary policy or a discretionary monetary policy" has extended, regarding the more detailed aspects of the monetary rules optimization. Habitually, it is wanted the optimization of a losing function, taking into consideration more assumptions, models or circumstances. Starting with 1990, the dynamic stochastic general equilibrium models (DSGE) have formed the basis of this research. Contrary to these formulations, often very technical and sophisticated, the enunciation of Taylor's rule (Taylor, 1993) has offered an alternative in the form of a simple and pragmatic rule. An important problem is the way in which the monetary policy manages the incertitude. The incertitude derives, for example, from inaccurate or delayed data regarding the evolution of the macroeconomic indicators, the incertitude concerning the most appropriate economic model (in a certain country and in certain circumstances), and the incertitude concerning the transmission of monetary policy measures in the real economy. One of the conclusions of the literature is that the monetary policy should be conceived in a sound way: instead of opting for an optimum which could be achieved only in certain conditions, the monetary authorities should avoid the major mistakes which could appear in different circumstances. Another possible effect of the uncertainty is that the central banks act prudently in modifying the interest rate; this "gradualism" (Bernanke, 2004) has become a standard in what concerns the empirical estimations regarding the central bank behavior when it establishes the interest rate.

The monetary policy of the National Bank of Romania is oriented towards maintaining a low inflation. Targeting the inflation is flexible, and it is given importance to the variability of the inflation and of the production. The administration council establishes the reference interest rate. NBR analyses, besides the prices evolution, the financial institutions situation for identifying the evolution which could diminish the financial system. The motivations are the following: i) the monetary policy must give enough attention to the possible risks for the financial stability; ii) in establishing the measures of monetary policy all the available information that could influence in the future the inflation and production must be taken into consideration. The interest rate policy must be evaluated taking into consideration the evolutions of the accommodations prices and of the credit. Big fluctuations of these variables could constitute sources of instability of the demand and productivity on a longer term; iii) empirical and structural information referring to important factors for analyzing the financial stability, such as the financial market, the assets price, the financial institutions and the capacity of the population and of the debt repayment companies, offer further data on the Romanian economy evolution.

Financial market efficiency seems to be a myth of current economic reality, although it has been a major theoretical pillar of classical finance. The degree of informational efficiency includes the following categories:

weak form efficiency, semi-strong form efficiency and strong form efficiency. Globalization is an undisputed answer to classical finance theory that advocated all available information is incorporated in financial asset prices. Financial markets are often characterized by a chaotic and unpredictable behavior especially in the context of extreme events such as the global financial crisis. The global financial crisis that debuted in 2008 has seriously affected international financial architecture and global economic stability due to unprecedented dynamics degenerate in chaotic and unpredictable behavior of financial markets contraction.

International investors focus on potential correlation between stock returns of different national capital markets in order to diversify portfolio risks by allocating financial asset investments. The multidimensional implications of financial integration generate the possibility of identifying investment strategies in order to optimize the risk management structure. From a technical point of view, the financial time series, such as stock market daily log returns, are defined on the basis of characteristic features, so-called stylized facts, namely: volatility clusters, heteroskedasticity of log returns, high diversification opportunities, non-linearity, volatility, high-frequency, non-stationarity of price levels, leverage effect, heteroskedastic log returns, extreme variations in time, existence of bubbles, deterministic chaos, financial frictions, fat-tailed distribution (leptokurtosis), non-normal distributions, misallocation of resources (capital), asymmetry and residual risk.

The international causality and interdependence between emerging and developed stock markets highlights the significant influence of dynamic transmission models centered on the spread of financial shocks. Enhancing transparency is a sine qua non condition to ensure the efficiency of capital markets, especially in the case of emerging capital markets. Causality, financial integration and global interdependence between emerging and developed stock markets reveal major implications of dynamic transmission models centered on the spread of financial shocks. Financial markets are influenced by certain factors such as banking regulations, investment policy reforms, economic and financial globalization through the expansion of cross-border transactions, instability of macroeconomic policies and liberalization of financial instrument operations. Financial cointegration reflects the fact that the analyzed financial time series exhibit a long-term balance.

REFERENCES

Bernanke, B. S. (2004). *Gradualism.* Remarks at an Economics Luncheon Co-Sponsored by the Federal Reserve Bank of San Francisco (Seattle Branch) and the University of Washington, Seattle, WA.

European Commission. (2005). *European banking integration, The EU Economy 2005 Review*. Author.

Taylor, J. B. (1993). Discretion versus policy rules in practice. In Carnegie-Rochester conference series on public policy (vol. 39, pp. 195-214). North-Holland. doi:10.1016/0167-2231(93)90009-L

About the Authors

Cristi Spulbar is the Executive Director of the Banking and Financial Research Center (CEBAFI) at the University of Craiova, Romania, and Professor Ph.D, Habilitated Doctor at the Faculty of Economics and Business Administration, University of Craiova. Moreover, Dr. Cristi Spulbar is a Doctoral Advisor in the field of Finance at the Doctoral School of Economic Sciences, University of Craiova, Romania and was appointed Regional Director for Romania by Eurasian Doctoral Summer Academy (EDSA), Bulgaria (Varna). His habilitation thesis, "Research on Efficiency of Banking Systems and Monetary Policy," was publicly defended in 2016, and after that he became a member of the University of Craiova's Doctoral School of Economic Sciences, where he has supervised the awarding of Ph.D. degrees in the financial field. In 2018, he received the Doctor Honoris Causa award, field Economics and Finance, from British American University, Florida, USA. Dr. Spulbar has published more than 200 research papers in journals and conference proceedings and has authored/co-authored more than 20 books. He became a Doctor of Economics in 1999 at the University of Craiova, with a Ph.D. thesis titled, "Optimization of Banking Management in Terms of Market Economy." His current research interests include banking management, quantitative finance, financial markets, economics, international monetary economy, money and credit, and corporate finance. . In addition, he is the Scientific Director of both the International Journal of Business Quantitative Economics and Applied Management Research (IJBEMR) and the International Journal of Core Engineering and Management (iJCEM), India. Building his academic profile since 1995, he has also gained broad experience as a practical practitioner in the financial field. Through continuous training and study, he has achieved a benchmark level of additional professional qualifications, enabling him to serve as an investment consultant, economic and financial evaluator, securities agent, and commercial agent (including being a broker and dealer).

Ramona Birau is a Lecturer on the Faculty of Education Science, Law and Public Administration at the Constantin Brancusi University of Targu Jiu, Romania. Dr. Birau has more than 10 years experience as Superior Financial Inspector at the Regional Public Finances General Directorate of Craiova, Romania. In addition, she is the Editor in Chief of both the International Journal of Business Quantitative Economics and Applied Management Research (IJBEMR) and the International Journal of Core Engineering and Management (iJCEM), India. Dr. Ramona Birau was appointed as Registrar of the British American University (BAU), Florida, USA starting February 2019. In 2018 she joined the Academic Council of Adarsh Institute of Management and Information Technology, Bangalore, India and the International Advisory Board (IAB) of CT University, India. Dr. Ramona Birau has published more than 100 research papers in journals and conference proceedings and has authored/co-authored 6 books. She became a Doctor of Cybernetics and Statistics in 2013 at the University of Craiova, Faculty of Economics and Business Administration with a Ph.D. thesis titled, "Modeling and prediction of emerging capital markets." Currently, she is following her second doctorate (PhD) in the field of Sociology at the University of Craiova, Faculty of Social Sciences. Her current research interests include financial markets, economics, cybernetics and statistics, quantitative finance, financial econometrics, behavioral psychology, economic sociology, management. Dr. Birau has also served as a teaching assistant during 2010-2012 and 2014-2015 at the University of Craiova, Faculty of Economics and Business Administration. Apart from that she is also a member of the Romanian Body of Chartered and Certified Accountants since 2012. She has a Master's degree in Finance, specialization Analysis and Financial Evaluation of Organizations and another one in the field of Administrative Sciences, specialization European Public Administration.

Index

T

U

V

Z

www.ingramcontent.com/pod-product-compliance
Lightning Source LLC
LaVergne TN
LVHW061550290926
849162LV00004B/964